France
Independen

RAC

WEST ONE PUBLISHING
LONDON

Published by West One Publishing Ltd,
Portland House, 4 Great Portland Street,
London W1N 5AA.

© West One (Trade) Publishing Ltd. 1998.

Publisher	Alan Wakeford
Managing Editor	Stan Dover
Production Manager	Ted Timberlake
Production Team	Martina Kritikou
	John Jones
	Sandra De Sousa
	Graeme Kay
Editorial	Richard Knight
	Sarah Jenkin
Advertising	
Sales Director	Marcia Smythe
Sales Executives	Virginie Bellivier
	Sandra de Sousa

Finance and Administration Team

Sarah Browne
Freddie Brexendorff
Katya Staff
Emma Keans
Zehra Arabadji

Chief Executive Officer   Martin Coleman

ISBN 1 900327 07 4

Printed and bound by Artes Gráficas ELKAR S. Coop., 48012 Bilbao

Acknowledgments

Pictures reproduced with the kind permission of: Alsace Tourist Board (p.155); Auvergne Tourist Board (p.202); Aquitaine Tourist Board (pp.234–235, 237 and 238); Blakes Holidays (p.13 (Rowan Harris-Bates); Burgundy Tourist Board (pp.177 (Nicole Lejeune), 178 (E Spiegelhalter) and 180 (A Doire)); Calais Tourist Board (pp.64–65 (P Nones) and 68); Champagne Tourist Board (pp.24 and 139); Chantilly Tourist Office (p. 67 (Didier Cry); Fireworks (title page, pp.2 and 118); Franche-Comté Tourist Board (pp.193 and 194); Languedoc-Roussillon Tourist Board (pp.20 and 270 (F Orel, C Bertrand)); Limousin Tourist Board (p.203); Lorraine Tourist Board (pp.151 (A Nancy), 153 and 154 (DM Hughes)); Midi-Pyrénées Tourist Board pp.14, 253, 254 and 255 (D Viet) and 251); Normandy Tourist Board (pp.45, 48 (G Rigoulet), 49 and 115); Paris Tourist Board (pp.18, 109, 111, 112, 113, 114, 115, 116, 117 and 119); Picardy Tourist Board (p.69 (Robin Frangois)); Poitou-Charentes Tourist Board (pp.165, 167 and 168); Robert Harding (cover, pp. 12, 23, 152 and 268 (John Miller), 25, 46, 279 and 282 (Roy Rainford), 26, 27, 175, 190–191, 193, 198–199 and 283 (David Hughes), 32 (Phillip Craven), 148–149, 201 (C Bowman), 265 (Adam Woolfit), 267 (Jennifer Fry)); Rhône-Alpes Tourist Board (pp.18, 214 and 216 (Aline Perier), 210–211, 213 (F Da Costa), 215 and 217 (Jean Luc Rigaux)); Val de Loire Tourist Board (pp.87 (C Lang) and 88); Zefa (pp.7, 29, 31, 43, 47, 83, 86, 136–137, 140, 269, 281 and 284)

Contents

About the Guide

Welcome to France for the Independent Traveller! The guide for those who prefer to plan their own journeys and who enjoy the freedom to choose their own accommodation.

Each region in the guide has its own introduction with a regional map, practical information and an overview of the things to do and to see in the area. This is followed in each case by the accommodation directory, in which the hotels of that region are grouped according to their town, city or resort. The full addresses of the hotels, together with the map references, will give an indication of their exact locations, but precise directions to your chosen establishment should be requested when booking.

The establishment descriptions give an idea of the style of the accommodation and should not be taken as being comprehensive. They generally indicate facilities and local attractions. The number of

bedrooms is also given, followed by the details of ensuite facilities. The hotels have been inspected by the French Tourist Board. We hope that you find the information easy to use and helpful, but remember that details may change throughout the year, so it is always wise to phone or fax ahead to confirm facilities and prices.

Booking

As a general rule, it is advisable to book your hotel break, even out of peak season. Chance callers seeking a night's accommodation may well find a vacancy, but this may prove difficult at weekends, during the peak holiday times and in the popular areas.

A deposit is usually payable in advance, which will be deducted from the total bill, and you should confirm when and how payment should be made. Always confirm your booking in writing.

Cancellations

Should you, for any reason, cancel, fail to take up the accommodation or leave earlier than planned, your deposit may be forfeited and an additional payment may be demanded, if the accommodation cannot be re-let for the booked period.

Prices

Prices are shown, if applicable, for a room for two people (**DB**), for half board per person (**HB**), for bed and breakfast per person (**B**) and with a range of restaurant prices for a set meal (**✗**).

If an establishment only indicates one price, this should be taken as the minimum price per person. If a range of prices appears, it denotes the minimum and maximum price per person, unless otherwise stated. These are based on low and high season, single and sharing, and the quality of the accommodation. If an hotel accepts credit cards as payment for accommodation and meals, the appropriate cards are listed.

The prices quoted here are forecasts by the owners of what they expect to charge this season. As they are set well in advance, there may be changes and it is advisable to check the price when booking.

We have asked each hotel if they would give discounts to our readers and those marked with an **RAC** symbol will provide a discount. Please make sure that you agree the discount when you check in or reserve your room and be prepared to show a copy of this book.

Prices are all in French francs and so will fluctuate with exchange rates.

Complaints

Should you have any cause for complaint at an hotel featured in this guide, speak to the owners as soon as the problem arises. This gives them the opportunity to put it right and you the chance to enjoy your stay.

Symbols and abbreviations

♿	facilities for the disabled
P	parking
🐕	dogs permitted
CC	credit cards
MC	MasterCard/Access
Visa	Visa card
Amex	American Express
🎾	tennis
🧖	sauna
🏌	golf course at the hotel
⚑	golf course near the hotel
🎣	fishing
🏋	gymnasium
🏇	riding
🏊	indoor swimming pool
🏊	outdoor swimming pool
✗	meal information
♨	conference facilities and number of delegates

Guide to the Regions
with regional map page numbers

Distance Chart
in kilometres

HOLIDAY FRANCE & SPAIN
DIRECT

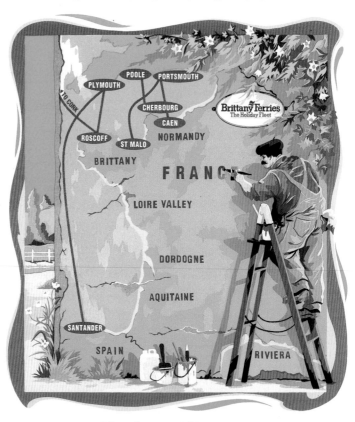

LUXURY CRUISE-FERRIES

AWARD-WINNING SERVICE

EXCELLENT RESTAURANTS

DIRECT TO BRITTANY, NORMANDY & SPAIN

IDEAL FOR ALL OF HOLIDAY FRANCE & SPAIN

HUGE CHOICE OF HOLIDAYS

Sailing with your car to Holiday France?
Why drive the long way round when you can sail with us, direct to Brittany, Normandy and Spain?
Our luxury cruise-ferries, with their award-winning service
and value, land you closer to where you'd like to be, saving you wasted fuel and effort.
And our huge range of self-catering and self-drive holidays and breaks
offer you all the finest pleasures of Holiday France and Spain.

Getting There…

Crossing the English Channel has never been easier. Fierce competition between air, ferry, coach and rail operators has led to better services at cheaper prices. Travellers can now choose between well-priced flights, luxurious ferry crossings or the new and easy-to-use Channel Tunnel.

How you get to France will depend on where you want to go and how you plan to travel once you get there.

Le Shuttle delivers drivers to France very quickly. If you plan to drive south or east, it might be better to take a ferry to a more southerly port such as Le Havre, St-Malo or Roscoff.

It is worth remembering that motoring in France is a real pleasure; it is certainly possible to make the journey a part of the holiday.

Foot passengers can get from London Waterloo to Paris Gare du Nord in an impressive three hours. For most destinations, however, flying is still the fastest method.

Below: London Waterloo Eurostar Terminal

By air

ROUTES

Aberdeen
- to Nice British Midland
- to Paris British Airways

Belfast
- to Nice British Midland
- to Paris British Airways

Birmingham
- to Nice British Airways
- to Paris Air France

Bristol
- to Paris Brit Air (see Air France), British Airways

Cardiff
- to Paris British Airways

Channel Islands
- to Cherbourg Aurigny Air Services
- to Dinard Aurigny Air Services
- to Paris British Airways

Edinburgh
- to Nice British Airways, British Midland
- to Paris Air France, British Airways

Gatwick
- to Bordeaux British Airways
- to Brest Brit Air (see Air France)
- to Caen Brit Air (see Air France)
- to Le Havre Brit Air (see Air France)
- to Lyons British Airways
- to Quimper Brit Air (see Air France)
- to Marseille British Airways
- to Montpellier British Airways
- to Nantes Brit Air (see Air France)
- to Nice British Airways
- to Paris British Airways
- to Perpignan British Airways
- to Rouen Brit Air (see Air France)
- to Deauville Brit Air (see Air France)
- to Rennes Brit Air (see Air France)

Glasgow
- to Paris British Airways

Heathrow
- to Bordeaux Air France,
- to Lyon Air France, British Airways
- to Marseille Air France
- to Nice British Airways
- to Paris Air France, British Airways
- to Strasbourg Air France
- to Toulouse Air France

Inverness
- to Paris British Airways

Leeds
- to Nice British Midland
- to Paris British Midland

London City
- to Paris Air Jet

London Luton
- to Nice Easyjet

London Stansted
- to Dijon Proteus (see Air France)
- to Lille Proteus (see Air France)
- to Marseille Air France
- to Paris Air UK

Manchester
- to Lyon Air Littoral (see Air France)
- to Montpellier Air Littoral (see Air France)
- to Nice British Airways
- to Paris Air France, British Airways

Newcastle
- to Paris British Airways

Newquay
- to Paris British Airways

Plymouth
- to Paris British Airways

Southampton
- to Paris British Airways

Teeside
- to Nice British Midland
- to Paris British Midland

AIRLINES

Air France (Air Littoral, Brit Air, Proteus Air)
Colet Court, 100 Hammersmith Road,
London W6 7JP
☎ 0181 742 6600
Air Jet
London City Airport, Royal Docks, London
E16 2PX
☎ 0171 476 6000
Air UK
Stansted Airport, Stansted, Essex CM24 1AE
☎ 0990 074074
Aurigny Air Services
States Airport, La Planque Lane Forest,
Guernsey JI9 3AG
☎ 01481 822886
British Airways
156 Regent Street, London W1R 5TA
☎ 0345 222111
British Midland Airways
Donington Hall, Castle Donington, Derby
DE74 2SB
☎ 0345 554554
Easyjet
Easyland, London Luton Airport LU2 9LS
☎ 01582 445566

By boat

ROUTES

Channel Islands–St Malo
- 1 hr 10 mins
  Operator: Condor Jersey

Dover–Calais
- 1 hr 15 mins or 45 mins on Superferry
  35 mins by hovercraft
  Operators: Hoverspeed, P&O
  European Ferries, Sea France Ltd,
  Stena Line

Folkestone–Boulogne
- 55 mins by hovercraft
  Operator: Hoverspeed

Newhaven–Dieppe
- 4 hrs or 2 hrs 15 mins on Superferry
  Operator: Stena Line

Plymouth–Roscoff
- 6 hrs
  Operator: Brittany Ferries

Poole–Cherbourg
- 4 hrs 30 mins
  Operator: Brittany Ferries

Poole–St-Malo
- 8 hrs
  Operator: Brittany Ferries

Portsmouth–Caen
- 6 hrs
  Operator: Brittany Ferries

Portsmouth–Cherbourg
- 5 hrs
  Operator: P&O European Ferries

Portsmouth–Le Havre
- 5 hrs 30 mins
  Operator: P&O European Ferries

Portsmouth–St-Malo
- 9 hrs
  Operator: Brittany Ferries

Southampton–Cherbourg
- 8 hrs or 5 hrs on Superferry
  Operator: Stena Line

FERRY COMPANIES

Brittany Ferries
The Brittany Centre, Wharf Road,
Portsmouth PO2 8RU
☎ 0990 360 360

Condor Jersey
Elizabeth Terminal, St Hellier, Jersey (JE2 3NW)
☎ 01534 601000

Hoverspeed
Western Docks, Dover CT17 9TG
☎ 01304 240241

P&O European Ferries
Channel House, Channel View Road, Dover CT17 9TJ
☎ 0990 980980

Sally Ferries
York Street, Ramsgate, Kent CT11 9DS
☎ 0990 595522

Sea France Ltd
Eastern Dock, Dover CT16 1JA
☎ 0990 711711

Stena Line
Charter House, Park Street, Ashford, Kent TN24 8EX
☎ 0990 707070

By car or coach

Motorists can take their cars to France on-board either a ferry (see above) or Le Shuttle (see below).
Travelling by coach is often the cheapest option. Coach services to France are operated by:

Eurolines
52 Grosvenor Gardens, London SW1 0AU
☎ 01582 404511

By rail

Two rail services run to France through the Channel Tunnel: Eurostar and Le Shuttle. Eurostar is a passenger-only service from London Waterloo to Paris Gare du Nord. It takes just three hours to travel between the two capitals.
Le Shuttle is a 35-minute passenger- and car-carrying service from Folkestone to Calais.

Eurostar
Kent House, Station Road, Ashford, Kent TN23 1PP
☎ 0345 303030

Le Shuttle
PO Box 300, Folkestone, Kent CT19 4QW
☎ 0990 353535

Getting Around...

France has well-developed road and rail networks which help to make life easy for the independent traveller. If that's just a bit too easy, cycling and boating are popular alternatives (see pages 13–14).

By air

Air Inter Europe, part of the Air France group, offers the most comprehensive network of internal flights in France. For bookings, contact:
Air France (Air Littoral, Brit Air, Proteus Air)
Colet Court, 100 Hammersmith Road, London W6 7JP
☎ 0181 742 6600

By bus

Long-distance coach travel in France is difficult. Strangely, French Railways is the only national coach operator. For information, contact:
French Railways
179 Piccadilly, London W1V 0BA
☎ 0171 203 7000
Local services are better, but information is only held locally at bus stations and tourist offices.

By car

Once you've mastered driving on the right, motoring in France is fairly hassle-free.
However, there are certain rules and conventions with which one should be familiar:

*   Speed limits are:
    toll motorways – 130 km/h (110 km/h when wet, 50 km/h in fog)
    dual carriageways and non-toll motoways – 110 km/h (50 km/h in fog)
    other roads – 90 km/h (80 km/h when wet)
    urban areas – 50 km/h
*   Headlight beams need to be adjusted, or deflectors used, to point to the right.

FRENCH ROAD SIGNS

Most conform to the standard international pattern. Others include the following:

Allumez vos phares – Switch on headlights
Attention au feu – Fire hazard
Attention travaux – Road works ahead
Chaussée deformée – Uneven road surface
Fin d'interdiction de stationner – End of restricted parking
Gravillons – Loose chippings
Haute tension – Electrified lines
Interdit aux piétons – No pedestrians
Nids de poules – Pot-holes
Priorité à droite – Give way to traffic from the right (see above)
Passage protégé – You have right of way
Rappel – Remember (displayed on speed limit signs)
Route barrée – Road closed

- The minimum age for driving is 18.
- It is not permitted to drive in France on a provisional UK licence.
- Do not cross single white lines.
- Seatbelts must be worn in the front and back.
- If a driver flashes his headlights at you, it probably means wait rather than proceed as is the custom in Britain.
- The French traffic light sequence is similar to that of Britain, except there is no red-and-amber light after the red.
- There is no longer a legal obligation for headlights to emit a yellow beam.

Classification of roads

E – European motorway
A – national motorway (*autoroute*)
N – major road (*routes nationales*)
C – minor roads (*routes communales*)

Roads that are marked with the Crafty Bison (*Bison Fute*) sign (below) are shortcuts which avoid the busiest roads. Crafty Bison maps are available from Crafty Bison information centres, which are scattered along most major routes, or from tourist boards.

Priority

Priorité à droite – which means give way to vehicles from the right – is no longer applied to all roads.
Generally, the major road now has priority. Where two major roads cross, *priorité à droite* resumes.
A sign with *Passage protégé* means that you have the right of way. In the absence of signs, you should give way to the right.

Traffic already on a roundabout has priority. Triangular signs with red borders which display the roundabout symbol and the words *vous n'avez pas la priorité* are usually found at the approach to roundabouts and indicate this. Occasionally, however, the old ruling still applies. Approach with care if there is no such sign present.

Toll motorways

Most motorways in France are toll roads or *autoroutes a péage*. Prices vary, but expect to pay around 400 FF per 1,000 km. Although most major credit cards are accepted at toll stations (*péage*), it is useful to keep some cash handy because the amounts are so small.

Petrol

4-star – *super*; unleaded – *sans plomb*; super unleaded – *super sans plomb*; diesel – *gas-oil* or *gaz-oil*

Penalties and fines

French roads are carefully policed. Speeding or dangerous driving can result in heavy on-the-spot fines.
Don't drink and drive! The legal limit for alcohol in the blood-stream is 0.5 g/litre of blood. Random tests are common.

Motor insurance

Ask your insurer for a green card. These give comprehensive motor insurance for driving in France.

Breakdown assistance

Each section of French motorway has its own official breakdown operator. Drivers are not permitted to call other breakdown operators. There is a government-set charge for this service. The RAC ☎ 0800 550 055 offers breakdown assistance in France.

Driving in winter

Snow chains can be hired or bought from garages or hypermarkets.
Studded tyres are allowed on vehicles weighing under 3.5 tons between early November and late March.
Drivers using studded tyres are obliged to keep their speed below 90 km/h and to attach a '90' sticker to the rear of their vehicle.

Car hire

For insurance reasons, it is often more straightforward to pick up a hire-car once you arrive in France than to take one across the Channel from Britain – although that is usually possible.

The minimum age limit for hire-car drivers is 21. Some companies will penalise under-25-year-old drivers with heavy surcharges.

Prices vary enormously, depending on the time of year and whether you opt for the budget hatchback or the soft-top sports car. Over the summer months, air-conditioning is almost essential in the South of France.

The following international hire-car companies have offices across France:

Avis Rent-a-Car
Trident House, Station Road, Hayes, Middlesex UB3 4DJ
☎ 0990 900500

Budget Leisure Cars
Dalton House, The Green, Letchmore Heath, Herts ED2 8ER
☎ 01923 855080

Eurodollar Rent-a-Car Ltd
Beasley Court, 3 Warwick Place, Uxbridge UB8 1PE
☎ 0990 365365

Europcar Interrent
Interrent House, Aldenham Road, Watford, WD2 2LX
☎ 0345 222525

Hertz Rent-a-Car
Radnor House, 1272 London Road, Norbury, London SW16 4XW
☎ 0990 996699

By rail

After Britain, where delays can be frequent and the prices high, France is train heaven. Ultra-high-speed *Trains a Grande Vitesse* (TGVs) race from city to city at terrific speeds and are invariably clean and reasonably-priced.

Over 2,000 destinations are linked to the French rail network, which also operates a Motorail service (i.e. carrying cars and passengers overnight).

Watch out for *Autorrain* services, which stop at every opportunity.

If you intend to use the trains a lot, consider buying a Eurodomino Rover Ticket.

These tickets offer unlimited travel for 3, 5 or 10 days.

It might also be worth investigating the Travel *a la Carte* system, which offers reduced-priced accommodation to frequent rail users.

These and other tickets can be bought from:
French Railways
179 Piccadilly, London W1V 0BA
☎ 0171 203 7000

By taxi

If you are hoping to travel some short distances by taxi, remember that taxis will only pick up from taxi ranks (*stations de taxi*).

Agree a price in advance for out-of-town journeys or airport transfers.

Below: TGV Train

The waterways of France

Above: A Blakes cruise along the Moselle
Below: Josselin in Brittany

There are few more relaxing ways to see
France than from a boat, and it is no
surprise that river- and canal-cruising have
become popular holiday options.
Companies now offer boats for hire on most
of the great rivers of France from the Seine
to the Saône.
The independent traveller will enjoy the
freedom of boating. Once you have picked
up your craft, you're on your own!
For information and bookings, you can
contact the following firms.

Blakes Holidays
Wroxham, Norwich NR12 8DH
☎ 01603 784131

Crown Blue Line
8 Ber Street, Norwich NR1 1EJ
☎ 01603 630513

Headwater Holidays
164 London Road, Northwich CW9 5HH
☎ 01606 42220

Hoseasons Holidays Abroad
Sunway House, Raglan Road, Lowestoft,
Suffolk NR32 2LW
☎ 01502 500555

Cycling in France

France is a wonderful country in which to cycle. There are several well-established cycling holiday specialists which will organise such trips for you.
Try the following:

Action Vacances
30 Brackley Road, Stockport SK4 2RE
☎ 0161 442 6130
Alternative Travel
69-71 Banbury Road, Oxford OX2 6PE
☎ 01865 513333
Belle France
Bayham Abbey, Lamberhurst TN3 8BG
☎ 01892 890885
Bike Tours
PO Box 75, Bath BA1 1BX
☎ 01225 480130
Cycling for Softies
2/4 Birch Polygon, Rusholme, Manchester M14 5HX
☎ 0161 248 8282
Exodus Travel
9 Weir Road, London SW12 0LT
☎ 0181 675 5550
Headwater Holidays
146 London Road, Northwich CW9 5HH
Sherpa Expeditions
131 Heston Road, Hounslow TW5 0RD
☎ 0181 5772717
Tall Stories
67a High Street, Walton-on-Thames, Surrey KT12 1DJ
☎ 01932 252002
VFB Holidays
Normandy House, High Street, Cheltenham GL50 3FB
☎ 01242 240340

Practical

Information

Essentials

Communications
Post offices are called either *Bureau de Poste* or *PTT*. Opening times are usually: 8am–12pm, 2.30pm–7pm Mon–Fri and 8am–12pm Sat. Stamps (*timbres*) can also be bought from *tabacs*. International calls can be made from any telephone box or from metered units in post offices. Most phones will only take phonecards (*télécartes*) which start at 40 FF. The international code for Britain from France is 00 44. When phoning within France add a 0 before the telephone numbers given in this guide. The operator is 12. When phoning France from the UK, the international code is 00 33.

Customs and duty-free
In theory, travellers can import as much duty-free as they like into Britain, as long as it is for the sole use of the importer and is tax-paid in France (or any EU country). Beer, wine and cigarettes are much cheaper in France than in Britain, and a trip to the hypermarket to stock-up on your favourite tipple is well worth it. In practice, however, the authorities have devised certain limits on alcohol and tobacco, beyond which the importer will be asked to prove that the goods are for personal use only.

Electrical voltages
Standard mains voltage is 220 AC at 50 Hz. Generally, however, the two – rather than three-pin plug is in use – so you will need a travel adaptor for electrical items. Adaptors are available from RAC Travel Centres at Dover, Folkestone and Calais.

Insurance
If your home contents insurance and personal medical plan don't cover you and your possessions for travel in France, you will need adequate personal and medical insurance. It is also worth picking up an E111 form from the post office. Most European countries have a reciprocal arrangement which means that EU nationals can gain access to medical help across the Union. Contact RAC Personal Travel Insurance ☎ 0800 550055.

Measures

    1 kilo = 2.2 lbs
    1 litre = 1.75 pints
    1 km = 0.6 miles
To convert miles to kilometres, multiply by 8 and divide by 5. To convert celsius to fahrenheit, approximately, multiply by two and add 30.

Money

The French currency is the franc (F), which equals 100 centimes. There is no limit to the amount of currency which can be carried into France from Britain.
Credit cards are widely accepted, but a difference in the way British and French credit cards are made means that British cards will not always 'swipe'. If this happens, explain that yours is a British card and ask for it to be checked with the bank.
Approximate exchange rate: £1 = 10,50 FF

Public holidays

1 Jan	New Year's Day
30, 31 March	Easter
1 May	Labour Day
8 May	VE Day
18,19 May	Whitsun
14 July	Bastille Day
15 August	Assumption Day
1 November	All Saints' Day
11 November	Remembrance Day
25 December	Christmas Day

Time

French Summer Time starts at 2am on the last Sunday of March and ends at 3am on the last Sunday of October.
France is, therefore, always one hour ahead of Britain.

CLIMATE

Air temp °C	Jan	Feb	Mar	Apr	May	Jun	Jul	Aug	Sep	Oct	Nov	Dec
Paris/Ile de France	7.5	7.1	10.2	15.7	16.6	23.4	25.1	25.6	20.9	16.5	11.7	7.8
Alsace	5.5	5.3	9.3	13.7	15.8	23.0	24.1	26.3	21.2	14.9	7.6	4.7
Aquitaine	10.0	9.4	12.2	19.5	18.0	23.7	27.2	25.7	24.2	19.7	15.4	11.0
Auvergne	8.0	6.4	10.1	15.9	17.1	24.2	27.0	24.5	23.3	17.0	11.0	8.3
Brittany	9.3	8.6	11.1	17.1	16.0	22.7	25.1	24.1	21.2	16.5	12.1	9.3
Burgundy	6.1	5.9	10.3	15.3	15.8	23.8	25.8	26.1	21.2	15.5	9.1	6.2
Champagne-Ardennes	6.2	5.6	8.9	13.8	15.1	22.5	23.8	24.9	19.3	15.0	9.6	6.2
Corsica	12.9	12.2	14.1	16.5	21.0	25.5	25.1	27.9	25.7	21.5	18.1	14.5
Franche-Comté	5.4	4.8	9.8	14.6	15.5	23.0	25.0	26.5	21.8	15.2	9.6	5.8
Languedoc-Roussillon	12.4	11.5	12.5	17.6	20.1	26.5	28.4	28.1	26.1	21.1	15.8	13.5
Limousin	6.1	6.1	9.6	16.1	14.9	22.1	24.8	23.6	21.0	16.2	12.8	8.5
Lorraine	5.5	5.3	9.3	13.7	15.8	23.0	24.1	26.3	21.2	14.9	7.6	4.7
Midi-Pyrénées	10.0	9.0	12.3	18.3	19.1	26.4	27.6	27.2	25.0	19.3	15.5	9.8
Nord/Pas-de-Calais	6.6	5.6	8.3	13.7	14.9	21.5	22.7	24.0	19.3	15.3	8.3	6.9
Normandy	7.6	6.4	8.4	13.0	14.0	20.0	21.6	22.0	18.2	14.5	10.8	7.9
Picardy	6.6	5.6	8.3	13.7	14.9	21.5	22.7	24.0	19.3	15.3	8.3	6.9
Poitou-Charentes	10.0	8.7	11.7	18.2	16.4	22.4	25.3	24.6	22.0	18.4	14.0	9.8
Provence	12.2	11.9	14.2	18.5	20.8	26.6	28.1	28.4	25.2	22.1	16.8	14.1
Rhône Valley	7.4	6.7	10.8	15.8	17.3	25.6	27.6	27.6	23.5	16.5	10.4	7.8
Riviera/Côte d'Azur	12.2	11.9	14.2	18.5	20.8	26.6	28.1	28.4	25.2	22.2	16.8	14.1
Alpes	3.1	3.7	7.9	13.8	15.7	22.4	26.8	25.7	22.7	15.9	10.7	6.3
Val de Loire	7.8	6.8	10.3	16.1	16.4	23.6	25.8	24.5	21.1	16.2	11.2	7.0
Pays de Loire	9.9	8.6	11.3	17.7	16.7	23.3	25.7	24.6	21.8	16.9	12.4	9.5

Source: Direction de la Météorologique de France.

Annual festivals and events

January
- Feast of St-Vincent, Cheilly-les-Maranges, Sampigny and Dezize, Burgundy
- Paris Fashion Shows, Paris

February
- Nice Carnival and Battle of the Flowers, Nice
- Motorcycle Enduro, Le Touquet

April
- Paris Marathon, Paris
- Paris International Fair, Paris
- Le Mans 24 Hour Motorcycle Race, Le Mans
- Festival of Theatre, Dance and Music, Les Andelys, Gisor

May
- Music Festival, Bordeaux
- Film Festival, Cannes
- Monaco Grand Prix, Monaco
- Gipsy Festival, Saintes-Marie-de-la-Mer
- International Tennis Open, Paris
- Jeanne d'Arc Festival, Rouen

June
- William the Conqueror Festival, St-Valéry-sur-Somme
- International Music Festival, Strasbourg
- Le Mans 24 Hour Car Race, Le Mans
- Paris International Air Show, Paris
- Day of Music, Paris
- La Villette Jazz Festival, Paris
- Django Rheinhardt Jazz Festival, Samois-sur-Seine
- French Grand Prix, Nevers Magny-Cours

July
- Bastille Day, celebrations throughout France
- Tour de France
- Avignon Festival, Avignon
- Aix-en-Provence Festival, Aix-en-Provence
- Jazz Festival, Antibes
- Music Festival, Reims

August
- Celtic Festival, Lorient
- Ajacccio Napoleonic Festival, Corsica

September
- Paris Fashion Show, Paris
- Champagne Grape Harvest Celebrations

October
- International Contemporary Art Fair, Paris

- Grand Prix de l'Arc de Triomphe Horse Race, Paris
- Centifolia Perfume Fair, Grasse
- Gastronomic Fair, Dijon
- National Antiques Show, Rouen

November
- Beaujolais Nouveau released at midnight, throughout France
- Three Glorious Days Wine Fair, Burgundy

December
- International Boat Show, Paris

Contact the French Tourist Office in London for a copy of 'Festive France', a regionalised guide to the country's major festivals and events.

Shopping

One look at the French reveals that this is a nation with a passion for clothes. Where there's a passion for clothes, there's a passion for shopping. Every French high street is awash with the big names in European fashion – making window-shopping fun but real shopping expensive. Food shopping can also be entertaining. Most towns and villages hold a morning market selling fresh fruit and vegetables. The supermarkets (*supermarché*) are well-stocked and are good value.

Opening hours
Banks: 9am–12pm, 2–4pm weekdays (closed Saturdays or Mondays)
Supermarkets: 7am–6.30 or 7.30pm
Hypermarkets: 7am–9 or 10pm
Others: 9 or 10am–12pm, 2–6.30pm
Many shops shut on Mondays, some food shops (particularly bakers) open on Sunday mornings.

The French week
French Saturdays are usually treated like weekdays. Mondays are often quiet, with many offices and banks closed.
The working day starts early and finishes late and has an extended break for lunch.

Nightlife

Gallic bright young things are more likely to enjoy live music or each other's conversation in bars or cafés than to pound the dance-floor in clubs.

There are clubs (*boîtes de nuit*), but they are few and far betweeen, and often less successful than those in Britain or the States. Visiting one can be an expensive process and the policy on the door is often completely incomprehensible.

If you do get into a club, you will find that the action doesn't really get going until 11pm. Live music usually takes the form of jazz (which is extremely popular), pop or that very French form of easy-listening made famous by the likes of Edith Piaff.

Food and drink

Food is taken seriously in France, a country where three-hour lunch breaks are considered acceptable and where even roadside cafés are well capable of satisfying the most Epicurean traveller.

Wine, of course, is equally important. Top wine growers achieve cult status and their products make a big difference to the French economy.

Eating and drinking well does not have to cost a fortune (although it can). By avoiding the more touristy areas, travellers will find great food at cheap prices.

Breakfast is normally served in cafés or bars where one can indulge in pastries, croissants or a baguette – normally with strong espresso coffee.

Tea is becoming more widely available, but don't be surprised to be given a cup of hot water, a tea-bag and no milk.

Lunch or dinner in restaurants is an enjoyable, but lengthy, affair. Meals are served at a very leisurely pace, and one is not expected to hurry.

If you are short of time, head for a café or brasserie, or – quicker still – a take-away stall.

Often, the *plat de jour* (daily special) will be the best-value item on the menu. The *prix fixe* or *menu fixe* menus are complete meals at a set price. This will normally be cheaper than choosing dishes *à la carte*.

Wine is drunk at just about any time of day, but particularly as an *apéritif* or during and after a meal.

House wine is almost always cheap and palatable and can be bought by the glass or by the bottle. However, it is usually ordered by the glass (*verre*).

Beer is not drunk in the same manner (or quantity) as it is in Britain. A British-style night in the pub can be quite expensive! The price of drinks varies according to where you sit – at the bar, at a table or outside.

Light Belgian and French lagers are most commonly available. They are served draught (*à la pression*) or by the bottle.

Above: Rhône-Alpes Samoens
Right: The terrace of the 'Café de Flor', Paris

Sport

It is difficult for visitors to participate in sport other than as spectators.

Sports fans will find that football and tennis are popular, as is rugby union and – increasingly – basketball.

If you do feel the need to exercise, the options are usually limited to swimming at a municipal pool, cycling or golf.

Of course, the better hotels often have gyms and tennis courts.

Golf in France

Golfers will find France to be a particularly attractive destination. The sport has been growing in popularity for some time now, and there are many high-quality courses around the country. For a list of these, contact the French Tourist Board in London and ask for their comprehensive *Golf in France* brochure.

In northern France, the Belle Dune club – designed by Jean Manuel Rossi – stands out as one of the best. Spread across some of the most beautiful dunes in Europe, the course offers some challenging holes and great views. Another well-designed course is the Club de Champagne near Villers-Agron. Here, golfers are treated to a complimentary glass of bubbly at the nineteenth hole.

The Club de Saint-Auben near Paris was the first public course to open in France, but it is still capable of testing quite accomplished players. Also in the Ile de France is the Golf National Stadium. This course has been designed with major championships in mind. If you're planning to play in Normandy, try the de Clecy Club. It has been singled out by several commentators as the most attractive course in France.

Brittany and the Loire are well-placed to welcome golfers, with numerous top-class courses. One of the more unusual of these is the Club du Mans, which is within the famous Le Mans 24-hour race track. Another attractive course in this area is the Club de Rhuys. This is a seaside links course, which also happens to be at the heart of a bird sanctuary. The Club Saint-Laurent at Avray has a well-respected championship course.

One of the best clubs in north-east France is the Club de la Largue in Mooslargue. Here you will find a first-class championship course and a Golf Academy. Further south, the Château d'Avoise course – designed by

the English architect Hawtree – has the added advantage of an English-style pub. More upmarket, perhaps, is the Club du Domaine de Divonne, which is one of the oldest and best golf courses in Europe. With breathtaking views across Lake Geneva and Mont Blanc, the course could hardly be better-placed.

In south-west France try the famous Médoc course which has recently been ranked 23rd out of the top 50 courses in Europe. Not surprisingly, sunny Provence and the Côte d'Azur have more than their fair share of great courses. The Pont Royal Golf Club in Mallemort was designed by Severiano Ballesteros and is a wonderful course to play at almost any level. Another well-connected club is the Golf Club de Cannes-Mandelieu at Mandelieu-la-Napoule. This great club was founded in 1891 by the Grand Duke Michael of Russia. This is considered by many to be one of the best courses in the world.

Several tour operators specialise in golfing holidays in France. They include:

A Golfing Experience
17 Rozel Manor, Western Road, Branksome Park, Poole BH13 6EX
☎ 0181 205 7138
Cresta Holidays
Tabley Court, Victoria Street, Altrincham WA14 1EZ
☎ 0161 926 9999
Crystal Holidays
Arlington Road, Surbiton KT6 6BW
☎ 0181 399 5144
Eurodrive
Image House, Station Road, London N17 9LR
☎ 0181 324 4000
Formula International
Archgate, 823-825 High Road, Finchley, London N12 8UB
☎ 0181 446 0126
French Golf Holidays
Horseman Side, Navestock Side, Brentwood CM14 5ST
☎ 01277 374374
Tourplan
CPL House, Ivy Arch Road, Worthing BN14 8BX
☎ 01903 823777

Language

Yes	Oui	Do you speak English?	Parlez-vous Anglais?
No	Non	OK	D'accord
Hello	Bonjour	one	un, une
Goodbye	Au revoir	two	deux
Please	S'il vous plaît	three	trois
Thankyou	Merci	four	quatre
Day	Jour	five	cinq
Week	Semaine	six	six
Month	Mois	seven	sept
Year	Année	eight	huit
Left	Gauche	nine	neuf
Right	Droite	ten	dix
Good	Bon	Sunday	dimanche
Bad	Mauvais	Monday	lundi
Tomorrow	Demain	Tuesday	mardi
Yesterday	Hier	Wednesday	mercredi
Morning	Matin	Thursday	jeudi
Evening	Soir	Friday	vendredi
Afternoon	Aprés-midi	Saturday	samedi
I would like..	Je voudrais…		

Left: For information on winter sports in France, see the introduction to Rhône-Alpes on pages 211–217.

Since 1994, France has been encouraging its
tourist industry to participate in the Bonjour
scheme, which aims to improve the quality
of French tourism services.

That scheme is a nationwide effort to give a
warm welcome and top quality services to
all tourists. Any hotel or company displaying
the 'Bonjour' logo has signed up to meet
certain guidelines on the quality of their
welcome and product. Look for the logo
and expect a warm French welcome.

Motoring
in Europe

preparing for the journey, getting there,
country by country, coming home...
the essential handbook for the
independent motorist abroad

£4.99

RAC

The Story of Champagne

History

Wine has been made in the Champagne region for thousands of years, but the Romans were probably the first outsiders to taste it.

The wine gradually became more widely known, and by the Middle Ages, trade fairs in the Champagne region brought the wine to the attention of traders from all over Europe. At that time, however, Champagne makers could not trap the wine's natural effervescence; Champagne tasted good but it was not bubbly.

A seventeenth century monk, Dom Pérignon, was the first to find a way to contain Champagne's bubbles. As cellarer and steward of the Abbey of Hautvillers, Dom Pérignon was able to spend years tampering with the fermentation process until he successfully mastered the art of brewing Champagne as we know it today – well, more or less. Champagne quickly became popular across Europe and even developed something of a reputation for exclusivity. Champagne is still the favourite tipple of royalty and the rich, but it has also become the drink of celebration.

Page 23: Chamery, Montagne de Reims
Above: The statue of Dom Perignon who mastered the art of brewing Champagne

How champagne is made

Champagne is given its distinctive taste by the conditions in which the area's vines grow: the consistent average temperature, the chalky soil and the amount of rainfall.

Three types of grape are used in Champagne: Pinot Noir, Chardonnay and Meunier. The first gives the wine 'lightness and freshness', the second 'body' and the third 'fruitiness and youth'.

After harvesting and pressing the grapes, a first fermentation transforms the sugar into alcohol. Then Champagnes from different years are combined to form a balanced *cuvée*. Champagne is more than the sum of its parts, and there is no doubt that a successfully-blended Champagne is far superior to its individual constituents. When a particular year's harvest is exceptional, wine might be blended from Champagne only of that year – vintage Champagne. Wine made only from Chardonnay stock is called a *Blancs de Blancs*.

The bottles are then corked for a second fermentation, during which a little sugar and natural Champagne yeast are added. This takes much longer than the first and, during the process, a deposit builds up inside the bottle. The bottles are shaken and turned every day to allow the deposit to slide down the bottle and collect on the cork. The deposit can then be ejected in a process known as the *dégorgement*. Some wine is lost in the *dégorgement*, and this is replaced by a small quantity of extra Champagne and a tiny amount of sugar cane. The exact amount of sugar cane depends on the type of wine which is being made – very dry, dry or *demi-sec*. Each bottle is then re-corked, labelled and shipped.

On 31 December 1999...

Will there be enough Champagne when the clock strikes twelve on the eve of the millennium? The Champagne Information Bureau says 'yes'. But still the rumours of a Champagne drought persist. It now seems likely that these rumours are – at least partly – the result of a handful of rogue speculators' plans to push up the wine's price.

If, however, your palette – and wallet – demand a vintage bottle, you might find that you are running out of time. However, wines from 1988, 1989 and 1990 are still available and are all excellent years.

The Fields of World War I

Warfare and tourism are uneasy partners. It is surprising then, that there has been such a strong resurgence of interest in the sites and strategies of distant battles. One might have expected interest to diminish over time. Not so; battlefield tours now constitute the fastest-growing branch of northern European tourism.

The terror of World War I came to **Picardy** on 31 August 1914, when the German Army marched into Amiens. That September, the French and British Armies halted Germany's advance.

By October, both sides had dug themselves in, to form a Western Front of trenches which stretched across north-east Belgium and France as far as Switzerland.

The monstrous 'War of Attrition' had begun. To gain a real insight into the day-to-day horror of the trenches, visit Camp Terre-Neuve at **Hamel**. It has been preserved, complete with shell holes, as it was left by survivors in 1918.

At 7.30am on 1 July 1916, the Allies launched the Battle of the Somme.

British, Empire and French troops 'went over the top' in a desperate attempt to break the grim deadlock. It was a disaster; 58,000 British soldiers died on the first day. The terrible audit revealed that 600,000 men were lost by each side.

Several mines were simultaneously exploded at the start of the battle. One of the craters from that day, Lochnagar, has been preserved near the village of **La Boiselle**. A monument, designed by Lutyens, stands at **Thiepval**. It commemorates the loss of 73,367 British soldiers.

From **Albert**, a signposted route (the *Route du Souvenir*) guides tourists to the principal sites: the slope of **Beaumont-Hamel**, peppered with shell holes, where so many Scottish Highlanders were killed; the **Bois des Troncs**, taken and lost 18 times in seven days; the memorial to the third Welsh division in **Mametz Wood**; the Ulster Tower near Hamel, commemorating the 36th Irish Division; **Delville Wood**, which was seized by South African troops; the Memorial Park to the Newfoundland Regiment and a blackened tree stump marking the German lines.

In **Pas-de-Calais**, the sombre, but imposing, Vimy Ridge Memorial stands over the

Page 25: A field of poppies in Normandy
Above: The Vimy Canadian Memorial near Lens in northern Picardy showing the shell holes. Vimy was the site of the famous Canadian initiative in April 1917 and the trenches and tunnels have been recreated

trenches, shell holes and underground passages where once the Canadian Corps had prepared to attack Hill 145. The hill was the highest point on the nine-mile Vimy Ridge and a key section in the German defences.

The attack took place on 9 April, 1917. The Canadian troops succeeded where several earlier attempts had failed.

Tributes and stark reminders of the horrendous scenes of World War I are scattered right across northern France. Visitors will always find a reminder which is, for them, the most evocative.

A soldier comforts a dying horse on a monument in **Chipily**, which commemorates the 250,000 horses killed in the fighting. Froissy, near **Cappy**, still has the narrow gauge railway track which supplied the front lines.

There are numerous reminders that young men from across the globe fought in the bitter trenches of World War I: at **Ayette** there is a cemetery for Indian and Chinese war dead, and in the village of **Souchez** there is a graveyard for Muslim, Hindu and Buddhist soldiers. A memorial to the 2nd Australian Division stands at **Mont St-Quentin**.

See page 48 for information about the World War II battlegrounds of Normandy.

Practical information

Museums
LA TARGET, Neuville St Vaast (D937Arras–Béthune). Covers 1914–18 and 1939–45 ☎ 3 21 59 17 76, open: daily 9am–8pm.
HISTORIAL DE LA GRANDE GUERRE, Péronne (place du Château) ☎ 3 22 83 14 18 open: 18 Jan–Apr and Oct–19 Dec, Tue–Sun 10am–6pm; May–Sep, daily 10am–6pm.
MUSEE NOTRE-DAME-DE-LORETTE, Souchez (Ablain–St Nazaire) ☎ 3 21 45 15 80, open: daily 9am–8pm.

War graves information
American Memorial Commission ☎ 3 23 66 87 20
Commonwealth War Graves Commission in France, Beaulains ☎ 3 21-71 03 24
Secretary of State for Veterans, War Cemetaries Service, Comiegne ☎ 3 44-40 06 90
Service for the Care for German Cemeteries, Chaulnes ☎ 3 22-85 47 57

Battlefield tours
Major and Mrs Holt's Battlefield Tours, Golden Key Building, 15 Market Street, Sandwich, Kent CT13 9DA
Middlebrook-Hodgson, 48 Linden Way, Boston, Lincs PE21 9DS

Above: A World War I British Cemetery near Mons in the valley of the Somme, in northern Picardy

Free yourself

If you're travelling in Europe,
RAC Motoring Assistance
provides rapid help in the event
of breakdown, fire, accident,
theft or illness. In addition, our
Personal Travel Insurance
covers you for lost luggage,
theft of personal belongings,
personal injury or cancellation.
Call us on **0800 550 055**

RAC

www.rac.co.uk

Brittany

QUIMPER St-BRIEUC St-MALO VANNES
B R E T A G N E

Breton culture has enjoyed something of a renaissance over the past few years.

It is an appealing mix of Celtic and French. With a language of its own, and a history of independence, some Bretons still see the rest of France as another country.

However Breton nationalism is, for the most part, a very sedate movement which goes no further than the occasional use of the native tongue and a certain feeling of ambivalence towards Paris.

After the Côte d'Azur, Brittany has the most popular stretch of coast in France.

This series of beautiful sandy beaches – which are more impressive than those on the Riviera – is a great reason to visit for a summer seaside break.

The coast is equally attractive during winter, when storms and strong seas conspire to lend the area a rugged but romantic quality. **St-Malo**, an old walled town on the north coast which guards both the sea and the mouth of the Rance River, gives the impression of being shaped by just such violent weather. Squat and huddled, the town is a fortified maze of ancient streets and ramparts.

By far the best view of this defiant town can be seen by boat. As the walls around St-Malo were built primarily to defend the town from sea-born attack, it is from this angle that they seem most impressive. Ironically, much of the wall is a modern-day replica, as St-Malo suffered heavy bomb damage during World War II.

Inland and south of St-Malo is **Rennes** – the capital of Brittany and its cultural hub. Much of the city was destroyed by fire in the eighteenth century. Ambitious architects set about creating a city which could compete with Paris. For this reason, Rennes is far grander than other typical Breton towns – despite the fact that it can hardly be said to rival Paris for architectural interest. The oldest part of Rennes lies between the Vilaine River and the canal. Here you will find the Palais de Justice, once home to the Breton parliament – which is one of very few significant buildings to have survived the fire of 1720.

The Musée de Bretagne offers a useful introduction to the complexities of Breton culture.

In the same building, the Musée des Beaux-Arts displays an outstanding collection of art from the Renaissance to modern art.

Rennes also boasts a delightful labyrinth of shopping streets – a useful antidote to all that cerebral activity!

Moving further west along the 'nose of France', one reaches Dinard and Dinan. The two places are very different.

Dinard is a former fishing village, which has developed at a furious rate over the last 40 years to become a major resort.

Plush hotels and bars help Dinard to make a more lucrative catch than fish, namely tourists. Despite this change in tactics, Dinard has managed to retain much of its charm and it still occupies a prime location opposite the more sober St-Malo.

Dinan has consistently avoided the sort of development which Dinard has embraced. The town has one of the best-preserved citadels in France. It is completely encased within the original walls, behind which perfectly-preserved streets wind their way between beautiful medieval buildings.

Reaching out into the Atlantic, the western

Page 29: A popular riverside restaurant in Dinard
Left: Rennes' St Michael's Square

Finistère region ends at **Brest** – an alluring old town which is fiercely proud of its distinguished maritime history.

In fact, the Maritime Museum here is one of the finest in France. Brest has a calendar of exciting maritime events and festivals throughout the year.

Slightly further south is the **Pointe du Raz**, which is the westernmost tip of France. Usually, such a tenuous claim to fame would mean that the place in question had little to offer. That certainly isn't the case for the Pointe du Raz, which is as beautiful as anywhere in Brittany and which offers fantastic views across the coast.

Another popular port of call is **Quimper**, which is thought to be the oldest city in Brittany.

It was probably founded sometime before the seventh century by an enterprising bishop from England.

Quimper is a pleasant and surprisingly quiet place with a magnificent cathedral and a particularly good art museum.

It is a peaceful place, to be enjoyed simply by exploring at random. Even a brief trip round the alleys and narrow streets of the city centre will reveal some lovely old buildings and atmospheric cafés.

This is the place to try those famous Breton pancakes (*crêpes*) – Quimper prides itself on producing the best in Brittany.

During the week preceding the last Sunday in July, Quimper hosts the Cornouailles Music Festival. With traditional Breton bands and performing artists taking to every stage in town, this has become a highly popular event and it can be difficult to find a hotel room.

Nearby **Concarneau** makes a pleasant excursion. It sits on the south coast between two stretches of immaculate beach.

The town itself is a draw due to its remarkable sea-defences. Early residents of Concarneau were forced to protect their town against high seas. Their solution was to build a giant fortification, known as La Ville Close, which is as unusual as it is beautiful.

Lorient, the fourth-largest city in Brittany, is a less exciting destination for tourists.

The city is shaped by the enormous natural harbour in which it sits. In fact, the harbour has also shaped Lorient's history. An ideal base for shipping, the city became a centre for imperial trade with Asia. However, few reminders of that wealth remain.

During World War II, Lorient became a major German U-boat base and was bombed heavily by the Allied air forces.

That said, there is one very compelling reason to visit Lorient: from the first Friday in August, the city stages an Inter-Celtic Festival, which attracts over 250,000 Celts from all over the world. It has become a focus for Celtic solidarity and a 10-day party of impressive proportions.

Just 10 km from Lorient lie the Carnac Stones – a carefully-arranged collection of some 2,000 obelisks, which date back to before Stonehenge or the Pyramids.

There are two great mysteries attached to these. First, how and why did they get there? Second, why are they not more famous? The Stones are probably arranged in relation to the moon. Whatever the reasoning behind them, they make a spectacular sight.

Belle-Ile, an hour's ferry trip from Quiberon, is also worth visiting.

This little island is dominated by its citadel. A maximum-security prison until 1961, this 'Alcatraz of France' is now open to the public. It is an extraordinary place.

The island is lovely and the view of the Breton coast from the ferry on the return trip is itself a good enough reason to visit.

If you're on the trail of Breton history, it is essential to visit **Vannes**. This ancient town is simply bulging with seemingly semi-collapsed, but beautiful, old houses among a dense web of attractive cobbled streets.

It is here that the Bretons agreed to the Act of Union with France in 1532.

Left: Rue du Jerzual

Festivals in Brittany

May
- Festival of Travel Writers, St-Malo

July
- Festival des Tombées de la Nuit, Rennes
- Embroidery Festival, Pont-l'Abbé
- Medieval Festival, Josselin
- Festival de Suscino, Sarzeau
- Music and Theatre on the Port, Brest (every Thur from 18 July until 5 September)
- Pancake Festival, Gourin (3rd weekend)
- Festival of Sea Shanties, Quiberon (3rd week)
- Apple Tree Festival, Fouesnant
- Cornouailles Music Festival, Quimper
- Jazz Festival, Vannes

August
- Inter-Celtic Festival, Lorient (early)
- Fête des Filets Bleus, Concarneau (11–18)
- Fête de Saint-Loup, Guingamp (week of 15)

What to do in Brittany
- Stand at the westernmost point of France, Pointe du Raz, and enjoy a stunning panorama across the Breton coast.
- Examine the mysterious Carnac Stones which pre-date even Stonehenge, but which still baffle the experts.
- Ponder escape plans from the labyrinthine citadel on the island of Belle-Ile, which was once the 'Alcatraz of France' but which is now open to the public.
- Join the riotous Inter-Celtic Festival in Lorient in early August.
- Indulge in a delicious Breton pancake (*crêpe*) in Quimper, the oldest city in Brittany which is now famous for producing the best pancakes in France.
- Visit La Cohue, the building in Vannes in which the Act of Union between France and Brittany was ratified in 1532.
- Enjoy a traditional seaside break along the beautiful coast of Finistère.

Getting there

By road
Rennes is a 3 hour drive from Paris along the Oceane Motorway (A11). From Rennes, dual carriageways (no tolls) link most major towns in Brittany.
- Traffic information ☎ 2-99 32 33 33

By rail
Eurostar travels from London via Lille to Rennes. There are hourly TGV departures from Paris Montparnasse to Rennes, Brest and Quimper.
By TGV:
- Paris to Rennes takes 2 hours 30 mins
- Lille to Rennes takes 3 hours 45 mins
- Lyon to Rennes takes 4 hours 25 mins

By boat
To the islands:
- Conquet, Brest to Ouessant, Molene ☎ 2 98 80 24 68
- Roscoff to Batz ☎ 2 98 61 77 75 (15 mins)
- Vannes to Arz ☎ 2 97 66 92 06 (15 mins)
- Vannes, Lorient, Quiberon to Belle-Ile ☎ 2 97 46 60 00 (45 mins)
- Quiberon to Houat, Hoëdic ☎ 2 97 50 06 90
- Concarneau, Benodet, Loctudy to Glenan ☎ 2 98 57 00 58 (1 hour)

By air
Brest International Airport (☎ 2 98 32 01 00, Fax: 2 98 84 87 32) is 6 miles north-east of Brest. Get from the airport to Brest by taxi. For car hire at Brest International Airport, contact:
- Avis ☎ 2 98 44 63 02
- Budget ☎ 2 98 41 70 60
- ADA ☎ 2 98 44 44 88).

Rennes-Saint-Jacques International Airport (☎ 2 99 29 60 00, Fax: 2 99 29 60 29) is about 5 miles south-west of Rennes. Get to and from the airport by airport taxi (☎ 2 99 30 79 79 or 2 99 68 84 45). For car hire at Rennes-Saint-Jacques International Airport, contact:
- Avis ☎ 2 99 29 60 22
- Europcar ☎ 2 99 51 60 61
- Hertz ☎ 2 99 54 26 52

BENODET Finistère   1C

★★★ Hôtel Armoric
3 rue Penfoul, 29950 Bénodet
📞 02 98 57 04 03 Fax 02 98 57 21 28
English spoken

A charming family hotel close to the beaches and marina. It is tranquil, with a bar, terrace and very pretty flower-filled garden. From Quimper go to Fouesnant and then Bénodet.

30 bedrs, all ensuite, ⊩ P 20 CC MC Visa Amex ⊰ ▸
3km 🖾 🖊 🖾 ⅲ
RAC 10 %

★★ Hôtel Bains de Mer
rue Kerguelen, 29950 Bénodet
📞 02 98 57 03 41 Fax 02 98 57 11 07
English spoken
Closed 15 Nov-14 Mar
Comfortable well-appointed hotel with good facilities in the centre of Bénodet, close to the port. The restaurant offers traditional menus and seafood specialities whilst the grillroom offers pizzas as well as grills.

32 bedrs, all ensuite, P 8 DB 260-320 B 35 ✕ 75-150
CC MC Visa Amex ⊰ ▸ 5km 🖊 🖾 ℘

BREHAT, ILE DE Côtes d'Armor   1A

★★ Hôtel Bellevue
Le Port Clos, 22870 Ile de Bréhat
📞 02 96 20 00 05 Fax 02 96 20 06 06
English spoken
Closed 4 Jan-5 Feb
Some of the rooms have a sea view. From Pointe de L'Arcouest, take the boat to Port Clos. The restaurant overlooks the harbour and specialises in seafood.

17 bedrs, all ensuite, ⊩ P DB 430-530 B 40-52 ✕ 115-175 CC MC Visa 🖊 ⅲ

BRELIDY Côtes d'Armor   1C

★★★ Château de Brélidy
22140 Brélidy
📞 02 96 95 69 38 Fax 02 96 95 18 03
English spoken

A beautiful 16th century château standing in 10 hectares of parkland, with woods and river. Rooms furnished in keeping with the period. On N12 exit after Guingamp and go towards Bégard/Lannion, after roundabout in Bégard take D15 towards Brélidy.

10 bedrs, all ensuite, ⊩ P 10 DB 420-790 B 50 ✕ 145-185 CC MC Visa Amex 🖾 ▸ 7km 🖊 🖾 7km ⅲ ⅋

BREST Finistère   1C

★★★ Hôtel de la Paix
32 rue Algésiras, 29200 Brest
📞 02 98 80 12 97 Fax 02 98 43 30 95
English spoken
Located in the heart of Brest, a few steps away from St-Louis covered market, near the post office, town hall, conference centre and the famous rue de Siam. Take motorway N12 towards the coast to Brest.

25 bedrs, all ensuite, ⊩ P DB 280-310 B 35 No restaurant CC MC Visa Amex ▸ 15km 🖾 🖊 🖾 ⅲ ℘
RAC 10 %

★★ Otelinn
45 rue du Vieux St-Marc, 29000 Brest
📞 02 98 42 52 00 Fax 02 98 41 96 62
English spoken
A splendid stopover in a green environment, in front of the harbour and of the beaches of the 'Moulin Blanc', where you'll taste specialities of the chef de cuisine.

40 bedrs, all ensuite, ⊩ P 20 DB 265-335 B 40 ✕ 80-180 CC MC Visa Amex ▸ 🖾 🖊 🖾 ⅲ ℘ ⅊

BRIEC Finistère   1C

★★ **Hôtel du Midi**
64 rue du Général de Gaulle, 29510 Briec
📞 02 98 57 90 10 Fax 02 98 57 79 82
English spoken
The Logis de France hotel-restaurant du Midi is located 15 km from Quimper, 60 km from Roscoff. It has 14 rooms with modern comfort and quality cuisine.

14 bedrs, all ensuite, **P** 8 **DB** 260-280 **B** 38 ✕ 78-150
((MC Visa ▸ 🖾 📠 ⅲ 🗷

BUBRY Morbihan   1C

Hôtel Coet Diquel
56310 Bubry
📞 02 97 51 70 70 Fax 02 97 51 73 08
English spoken
A charming inn in the heart of Brittany, set in a 2 hectare park crossed by a river, with an indoor swimming pool and a tennis court.

20 bedrs, all ensuite, ⚓ **P** **DB** 260-340 **B** 40 ✕ 85-192
((MC 🖾 ▸ 🖾 📠 🗷 ⅲ ৬
RAC 10 %

CARNAC Morbihan   1C

★★★ **Hôtel Armoric**
53 av de la Poste, 56340 Carnac
📞 02 97 52 13 47 Fax 02 97 52 98 66
English spoken
Closed Dec-Mar
From Auray, drive into the town centre, pass the church and follow signs to 'Plage'. The hotel is located on the left hand side after the Post Office. The restaurant offers traditional cuisine with an emphasis on seafood.

25 bedrs, all ensuite, ⚓ **P** 25 **DB** 330-480 **B** 42 ✕ 70-160 ((MC Visa Amex ▸ 6km 🖾 📠 🗷 ⅲ 🗷
RAC 10 %

★★ **Hôtel Ibis Thalasso**
av Atlantique, 56340 Carnac
📞 02 97 52 54 00 Fax 02 97 52 53 66
English spoken

Situated between the sea and the salt baths, the hotel has direct access to thalassotherapy centre, has rooms with a balcony, children's club during school holidays and is open all year. Towards Carnac Plage, 15 km from Auray, 60 km from Lorient.

119 bedrs, all ensuite, ⚓ **P** 120 **DB** 390-600 **B** 43
✕ 125 ((MC Visa Amex 🖾 🖾 📠 ▸ 🖾 📠 🗷 ⅲ ৬
RAC 10 %

CHATEAUBOURG Ille et Vilaine   1D

★★★ **Hôtel Pen'Roc**
La Peinière, 35220 St-Didier
📞 02 99 00 33 02 Fax 02 99 62 30 89
English spoken

An attractive, modern 'Silence' hotel built in local style and situated between Rennes and Paris in a quiet rural setting. Take the motorway Paris to Rennes A81/N157, then exit Châteaubourg D857 and go 7.5 km to St-Didier (D33).

33 bedrs, all ensuite, ⚓ **P** 80 **DB** 350-520 **B** 48 ✕ 105-330 ((MC Visa Amex 🖾 🖾 📠 ▸ 15km 🗷 ⅲ 🗷 ৬

CHATEAUGIRON Ille et Vilaine   1D

★ **Auberge du Cheval Blanc**
7 rue de la Madeleine, 35410 Châteaugiron
📞 02 99 37 40 27 Fax 02 99 37 59 68
English spoken
Closed Sun eve and Mon
Set in a small pleasant city with character. It has a castle, old houses, picturesque streets and walks. Located 14 km from Rennes, direction Angers and 25 km from La Guerche de Bretagne, direction Rennes.

11 bedrs, 6 ensuite, ⚓ **P** 14 **DB** 155-245 **B** 30 ✕ 68-172 ((MC Visa 📠 ▸ 18km 📠 🗷 2km ⅲ 🗷 ৬
RAC

COMBOURG Ille et Vilaine   1D

★★★ Hôtel Château et Voyageurs
place Châteaubriand, 35270 Combourg
📞 02 99 73 00 38 Fax 02 99 73 25 79
English spoken
Closed 15 Dec-1 Jan
A delightful hotel near the lake and château on the edge of town. Located between the roads to Dinan and Rennes. The hotel has typical Breton restaurant with a fireplace and serves seafood and fish specialities.

35 bedrs, all ensuite, ↟ P DB 250-650 B 47 ✕ 92-280
℃ MC Visa Amex ▸ 10km 🔲 🔲 🔲 ▦

LE CONQUET Finistère   1C

★★ Hôtel Pointe Ste-Barbe
29217 Le Conquet
📞 02 98 89 00 26 Fax 02 98 89 14 81
English spoken
Closed 11 Nov-18 Dec
An exceptional situation beside the sea and harbour with direct access to the beach. Located 25 km west of Brest on the D789. With panoramic restaurant of high repute.

49 bedrs, 37 ensuite, P 50 DB 199-644 B 39 ✕ 100-464
℃ MC Visa Amex ▸ 10km 🔲 🔲 ▦ 🖉 ♿

CROZON Finistère   1C

★★ Hôtel Moderne
61 rue Alsace Lorraine, 29160 Crozon
📞 02 98 27 00 10 Fax 02 98 26 19 21
English spoken
A small, comfortable hotel with rustic furnishings. It has a well-known restaurant and a good wine cellar.

34 bedrs, 26 ensuite, ↟ P DB 250-338 B 37 ✕ 84-200
℃ MC Visa ▸ 🔲 🔲 🖉

Bonjour '98 France welcomes the world
Since 1994, France has been encouraging its tourist industry to participate in the Bonjour scheme, which aims to improve the quality of French tourism services. That scheme has been enhanced for 1998 to include the Football World Cup. 'Bonjour 98 – France welcomes the world' is a nationwide effort to give a warm welcome and top quality service to visiting football fans and tourists alike.
Any hotel or company displaying the 'Bonjour' logo has signed up to meet certain guidelines on the quality of their welcome and product. Look for the logo and expect a warm French welcome.

DINAN Côtes d'Armor   1D

★★★ Château La Motte Beaumanoir
35720 Pleugueneuc
📞 02 99 69 46 01 Fax 02 99 69 42 49
English spoken

A beautifully situated château, surrounded by ornamental lakes in 24 hectares of grounds, with traditionally furnished rooms having lake views. From Pleugueneuc, take St-Malo road and just outside the village take Plesder exit.

8 bedrs, all ensuite, ↟ P DB 700-1,000 B included
No restaurant ℃ MC Visa ⅔ ▸ 13km 🔲 🔲 🔲
R∂C 10 %

★★ Hôtel Le Manoir de Rigourdaine
22490 Plouër-sur-Rance
📞 02 96 86 89 96 Fax 02 96 86 92 46
English spoken
Closed 15 Nov-3 Apr

This recommended hotel is a charming, stone-built, old house with beams and an open fireplace.Set in extensive grounds with wonderful views of the Breton estuary. Leave N137(St-Malo/Rennes) just after Châteauneuf and take N176 towards Dinan and St-Brieuc.

19 bedrs, all ensuite, ↟ P 25 DB 290-420 B 38 ℃ MC
Visa ▸ 19km 🔲 🔲 ♿

★★ Hôtel Les Alleux

Route de Ploubalay, 22100 Dinan
☎ 02 96 85 16 10 Fax 02 96 85 11 40
English spoken

Quiet, comfortable hotel in a large green park. 1 km north of Dinan follow Ploubalay road. Traditional cuisine and personalised welcome.

31 bedrs, all ensuite, ⋔ P DB 280-300 B 32-35 ✗ 65-165 ℂℂ MC Visa Amex ▸ ▨ ▨ ▦ ♪ ♿
RAC

★★ Hôtel de la Tour de l'Horloge

5 rue Chaux, 22100 Dinan
☎ 02 96 39 96 92 Fax 02 96 85 06 99
English spoken
Dating from the 18th century, the hotel is cosy and friendly, with comfortable, up-to-date accommodation. It stands in the centre of Dinan, close to the clock tower, the old town and tourist office.

12 bedrs, all ensuite, ⋔ P DB 295-335 B 35 No restaurant ℂℂ MC Visa Amex ▸ 10km ▨ ♪
RAC 5 % in low season

DINARD Ille et Vilaine 1D

★★ Hôtel Altair

18 bd Paul Féart, 35800 Dinard
☎ 02 99 46 13 58 Fax 02 99 88 20 49
English spoken
Close to the beach, this hotel is a graded building with character. It has a garden terrace and renowned cuisine. English and French channels on TV.

21 bedrs, all ensuite, ⋔ P DB 190-490 B 35 ✗ 88-200 ℂℂ MC Visa Amex ▸ 6km ♪

★★★ Hôtel des Bains

20 rue du Poncel, 22770 Lancieux
☎ 02 96 86 31 33 Fax 02 96 86 22 85
English spoken

Set 200 m from the main beach, this refurbished hotel was once a family mansion. An ideal starting point for excursions along the Emerald Coast. On the D168 from Dinard.

12 bedrs, all ensuite, ⋔ P 16 DB 340-500 B 35-38 ℂℂ MC Visa Amex ▸ 3km ▨ ▨ ♪ ♿
RAC 10 % except Aug

ERDEVEN Morbihan 1C

★★ Auberge du Sous-Bois

route de Pont-Lorois, 56410 Erdeven
☎ 02 97 55 66 10 Fax 02 97 55 68 82
English spoken
Closed 1 Oct-31 Mar

A typical Breton hotel, modern and comfortable, set amid pines. Erdeven is on D781 between Lorient and Carnac. The restaurant is a large, country-style room with grilled dishes prepared in the open fireplace.

21 bedrs, all ensuite, ⋔ P DB 180-380 B 45 ✗ 66-185 ℂℂ MC Visa Amex ▸ 15km ▨ ▨ 10 ♕

LA FORET-FOUESNANT Finistère　1C

★★ Hôtel Beauséjour
place de la Baie, 29940 La Forêt-Fouesnant
☎ 02 98 56 97 18 Fax 02 98 51 40 77
English spoken
Closed 15 Oct-15 Mar
*A wonderful setting near a beautiful bay, close to
Concarneau in southern Brittany.The restaurant
offers regional, fish-based cuisine.*

25 bedrs, 18 ensuite, ⍭ P 20 DB 180-320 B 35-80
✗ 75-250 ((MC Visa ▸ 1km ▨ ▣ ⠿ ⟊
RAC 5 %

★★★★ Hôtel Manoir du Stang
29940 La Forêt-Fouesnant
☎ 02 98 56 97 37 Fax 02 98 56 97 37
English spoken
Closed 1 Oct-30 Apr

*Dating from the 15th century, a family-run manor
house overlooking water and surrounded by 40
hectares of beautifully landscaped parkland.
Traditionally furnished with some fine antiques.*

24 bedrs, all ensuite, P 50 DB 500-920 B 45 ✗ 160-180
▸ ▨ ▨ ▣ ⠿ ⟋
RAC **Breakfast in low season**

FOUESNANT Finistère　1C

★★ Hôtel Belle Vue
Plage de Cap Coz, 29170 Fouesnant
☎ 02 98 56 00 33 Fax 02 98 51 60 85
English spoken
Closed 2 Nov-1 Mar

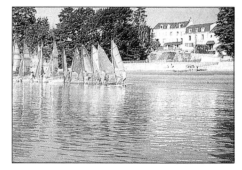

*A family hotel situated in front of the sandy beach of
Cap Coz, between Concarneau and Bénodet.
Children are welcome. From motorway N165, exit
Coat-Conq and take D44 to Fouesnant.*

19 bedrs, 12 ensuite, P 25 DB 180-370 B 39 ✗ 89-175
((MC Visa Amex ▸ 5km ▨ ▣

★★ Hôtel Pointe Mousterlin
Pointe de Mousterlin, 29170 Fouesnant
☎ 02 98 56 04 12 Fax 02 98 56 61 02
English spoken
*Two long sandy beaches reach a rocky plateau for the
pleasure of both swimmers and anglers. The hotel
offers an unimpeded view of the ocean. For people
who prefer solid ground there are two 18 hole golf
courses 6 km from the hotel.*

52 bedrs, all ensuite, P 100 DB 265-450 B 42 ✗ 90-200
((MC Visa Amex ⊞ ▦ ▸ 6km ▨ ▨ ▣ ⠿ ⟊

GUINGAMP Côtes d'Armor　1C

★★ Manoir du Cleuziou
22540 Louargat
☎ 02 96 43 14 90 Fax 02 96 43 52 59
Closed 1 Jan-31 Mar

*Experience the charm, relaxation and gourmet
cuisine in an original 16th century Breton manor.
Now completely restored, the hotel is surrounded by a
park and is just 10 minutes drive west of Guingamp
on N12.*

28 bedrs, all ensuite, ⍭ P 30 DB 320-480 B 40 ✗ 120-
225 ((MC Visa Amex ⊰ ▸ 7km ▨ ▨ ▣ ⠿ ⟋
RAC 5 %

LAMBALLE Côtes d'Armor　1D

★★ Auberge Manoir des Portes
la Poterie, 22400 Lamballe
☎ 02 96 31 13 62 Fax 02 96 31 20 53
English spoken

The hotel is in the countryside, 10 minutes from the beach, and close to Mont-St-Michel, St-Malo and the 'Côte de Granit Rose'. Situated 2 km east of Lamballe this hotel provides dining in the garden.

16 bedrs, all ensuite, ⚡ **P** **DB** 405-560 **B** 42-50 ✕ 110-300 ⊄ MC Visa Amex 🖼 ▸ 🔲 🖾 ♨
RAC 7 %

LESCONIL Finistère   1C

★★ Hôtel Atlantic
11 rue Jean Jaures, 29740 Lesconil
📞 **02 98 87 81 06 Fax 02 98 87 88 04**
English spoken
Set in a lovely garden in this small Breton fishing village, the hotel is 28 km south of Quimper. Restaurant offers traditional and gourmet cuisine. From Quimper, drive towards Pont-l'Abbé and then towards Plobannalec-Lesconil.

23 bedrs, all ensuite, ⚡ **P** 20 **DB** 200-320 **B** 35 ✕ 85-220 ⊄ MC Visa Amex ▸ 20km 🔲 🔲 🖾 ♨ ⌀

LORIENT Morbihan   1C

★★ Hôtel Astoria
3 rue Clisson, 56100 Lorient
📞 **02 97 21 10 23 Fax 02 97 21 03 55**
English spoken
A modern hotel with comfortable rooms, close to the church in the town centre.

34 bedrs, all ensuite, ⚡ **P** 34 **DB** 210-290 **B** 30 No restaurant ⊄ MC Visa Amex ▸ 5km 🔲 🖾 ⌀

LOUDEAC Côtes d'Armor   1D

★★ Hôtel des Voyageurs
10 rue de Cadélac, 22600 Loudéac
📞 **02 96 28 00 47 Fax 02 96 28 22 30**
English spoken
A very comfortable, town centre hotel with a restaurant renowned for its seasonal fish specialities. About 100 m from the church.

28 bedrs, all ensuite, ⚡ **P** 8 **DB** 220-300 **B** 34-45 ✕ 70-250 ⊄ MC Visa Amex ▸ 🔲 🖾 ♨ ⌀
RAC 10 %

PLOERMEL Morbihan   1D

★★★ Hôtel Le Cobh
10 rue des Forges, 56800 Ploërmel
📞 **02 97 74 00 49 Fax 02 97 74 07 36**
English spoken
An old Breton house, close to a magnificent church in the centre of Ploërmel. Monsieur Cruaud, member of the Académie Culinaire de France, offers a warm welcome and a restaurant specialising in traditional local cuisine. Ploërmel is on the N24.

12 bedrs, all ensuite, ⚡ **P** **DB** 140-300 **B** 40 ✕ 50-900 ⊄ MC Visa ⋛ ▸ 2km 🔲 🖾 ♨

★★ Hôtel Relais du Porhoet
11 place de l'Eglise, 56490 Guilliers
📞 **02 97 74 40 17 Fax 02 97 74 45 65**
English spoken
Situated in the typical Breton village of Guilliers, this hotel is a comfortable and convenient stop-over point. The restaurant has lots of character and offers tempting cuisine with seafood specialities. From Ploërmel go north on D766 then left onto D13.

12 bedrs, 11 ensuite, ⚡ **P** **DB** 210-250 **B** 35 ✕ 62-188 ⊄ MC Visa Amex ▸ 13km 🔲 🖾 ♨ ⌀

PONT-L'ABBE Finistère   1C

★★ Hôtel de Bretagne
24 place de la République, 29120 Pont-l'Abbé
📞 **02 98 87 17 22 Fax 02 98 82 39 31**
English spoken
A charming, quietly situated, family hotel, with a restaurant offering mainly fish or seafood, just a few minutes from the Bay of Audierne. A welcoming apéritif is offered on arrival.

18 bedrs, all ensuite, **P** 8 **DB** 260-400 **B** 40 ✕ 120-240 (lunch 75 FF except Sunday) ⊄ MC Visa Amex ▸ 18km 🖾 ⌀
RAC **Free drink on arrival**

PONTIVY Morbihan   1C

★★ Hôtel Le Vieux Moulin
56930 St-Nicolas-des-Eaux
📞 **02 97 51 81 09 Fax 02 97 51 83 12**
English spoken
Closed Feb
A Logis de France hotel, with a restaurant offering local specialities, situated on the side of the River Blavet. From Pontivy take the D768 towards Baud, then turn right on to the D1.

10 bedrs, all ensuite, **P** **DB** 285 **B** 34 ✕ 72-162 ⊄ MC Visa ▸ 10km 🔲 🔲 🖾
RAC 15 %

QUIMPER Finistère   1C

★★★ Hôtel Tour d'Auvergne
13 rue Réguaires, 29000 Quimper
☎ 02 98 95 08 70 Fax 02 98 95 17 31
English spoken
Traditional town centre hotel, with a secure private car park and a restaurant overlooking a flower-filled patio.

41 bedrs, 28 ensuite, ⚹ P 50 DB 450-550 B 55 ✕ 125-250 ℂℂ MC Visa Amex ► 10km ☒ ⠿
RƆC 10 %

RENNES Ille et Vilaine   1D

★★ Hôtel Garden
3 rue Duhamel, 35000 Rennes
☎ 02 99 65 45 06 Fax 02 99 65 02 62
English spoken
This hotel combines the charm of the countryside with all the pleasures of the town. Follow signs for the town centre, then stations and Brittany National Theatre.

24 bedrs, 20 ensuite, P 5 DB 240-310 B 33 No restaurant ℂℂ MC Visa Amex ► 8km ☑ ☒ ⠿

★★ Hôtel Les Forges
Noyal-sur-Vilaine, 35530 Rennes
☎ 02 99 00 51 08 Fax 02 99 00 62 02
English spoken

A warm, welcoming inn with a relaxing atmosphere, located 10 km from Rennes towards Paris. In the restaurant the chef, André Pilard, will invite you to enjoy gourmet cuisine made with fresh fish and other local products

11 bedrs, all ensuite, P 10 DB 225-310 B 35 ✕ 95-198 ℂℂ MC Visa Amex ► 15km ⠿

> When parking your car ensure you are not facing oncoming traffic. This will help you when you return to your car.

RIEC-SUR-BELON Finistère   1C

★★★ Domaine de Kerstinec
Route de Moëlan-sur-Mer, 29340 Riec-sur-Belon
☎ 02 98 06 42 98 Fax 02 98 06 45 38
English spoken
Closed 2-10 Jan

The hotel, standing on the banks of the Belon river, is famous for its wonderful oysters and is close to the painters' city, Pont-Aven. Access via D24, Moëlan-sur-Mer to Riec-sur-Belon road.

18 bedrs, all ensuite, P DB 320-650 B 45 ✕ 89-310 ℂℂ MC Visa ► 15km ☑ ☒ ⠿ ⅁

SABLES-D'OR-LES-PINS Côtes d'Armor   1D

★★ Hôtel Morgane
Sables-d'Or-les-Pins, 22240 Fréhel
☎ 02 96 41 46 90
English spoken
Closed 1 Oct-31 Mar
A centrally situated hotel, with a view of the sea and a family atmosphere, close to beach and wood. Facilities include French and English TV and a flower garden. 30 km from St-Malo and Dinard.

20 bedrs, all ensuite, P 20 DB 250-350 B 40 No restaurant ℂℂ MC Visa ► 1km ☑ ☒ ⅁
RƆC 10 %

ST-BRIEUC Côtes d'Armor   1D

★★ Hôtel du Chêne Vert
A Plérin, 22190 St-Brieuc
☎ 02 96 79 80 20 Fax 02 96 79 80 21
English spoken
A quiet hotel, in verdant surroundings, with spacious, modern bedrooms, bar, sitting rooms, terrace and a restaurant offering a traditional cuisine with marine aromas.

75 bedrs, all ensuite, ⚹ P DB 298-368 B 38-48 ✕ 75-160 ℂℂ MC Visa Amex ► ☒ ☒ ⠿ ⌗ ⅁

★★★ Hôtel Ajoncs d'Or

10 rue des Forgeurs, 35400 St-Malo
📞 02 99 40 85 03 Fax 02 99 40 80 70
English spoken
Closed 11 Nov-25 Feb

Situated in the heart of the 'Corsair city', close to harbour station. The Hôtel Ajoncs d'Or offers you comfortable rooms and a warm welcome by the proprietors, Mr and Mrs Robin.

22 bedrs, all ensuite, ⅺ P DB 430-580 B 46 No restaurant ⅭⅭ MC Visa Amex ► 30km 🔲 🔲 🔲 🔲 10km ⅲ
RAC **10 % on rooms high season**

★★★ Hôtel Alba

17 rue des Dunes, 35400 St-Malo
📞 02 99 40 37 18 Fax 02 99 40 96 40
English spoken

A comfortable, charming hotel overlooking the sea. Good Breton restaurants in town. Follow the signs for Thermes Marins.

22 bedrs, all ensuite, ⅺ P 10 DB 390-780 B 45-50 No restaurant ⅭⅭ MC Visa Amex ► 15km ⅲ 🔲
RAC **10 %**

★★★ Hôtel Brocéliande

43 chaussée du Sillon, 35400 St-Malo
📞 02 99 20 62 62 Fax 02 99 40 42 47
English spoken
Closed 15 Nov-23 Dec

Facing the 'Emerald Coast', hotel is a warm, refined family home. Situated between the old town and the thermal sea baths and overlooking the beach.

9 bedrs, all ensuite, P 9 DB 300-550 B 50 No restaurant ⅭⅭ MC Visa Amex ► 7km 🔲
RAC **Free breakfast for twin-share**

★★★ Hôtel Elizabeth

2 rue des Cordiers, 35400 St-Malo
📞 02 99 56 24 98 Fax 02 99 56 39 24
English spoken
Small, comfortable and refined apartments with stylish furniture in Louis XIII to XV settings. Go to Porte-St-Louis, then take second road on the right.

17 bedrs, all ensuite, P 8 DB 400-680 B 54 ⅭⅭ MC Visa Amex ► 12km 🔲 🔲 ⅲ ⅙
RAC **10 %**

★★★ Hôtel La Cité

26 rue Ste-Barbe, BP77, 35412 St-Malo
📞 02 99 40 55 40 Fax 02 99 40 10 04
English spoken
Inside the town wall. Enter by the main gate, Porte-Vincent and turn right near the ramparts. The hotel , built in 1990 in an 18th century style, is quiet and comfortable with many rooms offering a sea view. Beach is just 50 m away.

41 bedrs, all ensuite, ⅺ P 20 DB 400-600 B 46-50 ✕ 130-195 ⅭⅭ MC Visa Amex ► 10km 🔲 ⅲ 🔲 ⅙
RAC **10 %**

★★★ Hôtel La Malouinière des Longchamps

35430 St-Jouan-dès-Guerets
02 99 82 74 00 Fax 02 99 82 74 14
English spoken
Closed 20 Nov -20 Mar

At the gateway to the privateer town, Blandine and Francis Goger welcome you to their charming, house of character, La Malouinière des Longchamps, and invite you to relax in its family atmosphere.

9 bedrs, all ensuite, **P** 12 **DB** 298-495 **B** 48-62 **CC** MC Visa Amex 10km
RAC 5 % high season

★★ Hôtel La Rance

15 quai Sebastopol, 35400 St-Malo
02 99 81 78 63 Fax 02 99 81 44 80
English spoken
A delightful hotel with bay views, only 5 minutes from the ferry terminal. Follow the signs for the Tour Solidor, museum about Cape Horn and the hotel is close by.

11 bedrs, all ensuite, **P** 11 **DB** 300-505 **B** 47-48 No restaurant **CC** MC Visa Amex 15km

★★ Hôtel Quic en Groigne

8 rue d'Estrées, 35400 St-Malo
02 99 20 22 20 Fax 02 99 20 22 30
Situated inside the walled city, this quiet, comfortable hotel is close to the beaches and only a few minutes walk from the ferry terminal for Portsmouth.

15 bedrs, all ensuite, **P** 6 **DB** 340-420 **B** 32 No restaurant **CC** MC Visa 15km

★★★ Hôtel du Guesclin

8 place du Guesclin, 35400 St-Malo
02 99 40 47 11 Fax 02 99 56 10 49
English spoken

Situated in front of the old city walls to the south of the Port and 50 m from beach. Renovated in 1995-96 and featuring 3 leisure rooms, gym, sunbeds and spa.

22 bedrs, all ensuite, **P** 60 **DB** 220-480 **B** 28-39 **CC** MC Visa Amex
RAC 10 % low season

★★★★ Le Grand Hôtel Thermes

Grande Plage du Sillon, B.P.32, 35401 St-Malo Cédex
02 99 40 75 75 Fax 02 99 40 76 00
English spoken
Closed 4-31 Jan

Situated on the Grande Plage du Sillon this renovated hotel overlooks the sea and is close to the historical walled city of Saint Malo. Take N137 Rennes to St Malo and on arriving at St Malo follow the signs Thermes Marins.

185 bedrs, all ensuite, **P** **DB** 450-1,500 **B** 70 ✕ 130-295 **CC** MC Visa Amex 25km 10km

LA TRINITE-SUR-MER Morbihan 1C

★★ Hôtel Domaine du Congre

D781, St-Philibert, 56470 La Trinité-sur-Mer
02 97 55 00 56 Fax 02 97 55 19 77
English spoken
A comfortable hotel with a friendly atmosphere, new tennis courts, swimming pool and gardens; restaurant specialises in grills with seafood to order. Set back from the road, 2 km from the beach and the famous marina.

23 bedrs, all ensuite, **P** **DB** 285-355 **B** 36 ✕ 95 **CC** MC Visa Amex 12km

Normandy

Every year, thousands of British travellers invade France through the Norman ports of Le Havre or Dieppe. If the locals sometimes seem disconcerted by their burgeoning tourism industry, it might be because this area of France is used to invasions of an altogether deadlier nature. As the closest French province to Britain, Normandy has had to be the 'buffer zone' in a climate of Anglo-French hostility which only ended comparatively recently.

Now, of course, Britain and France are on good terms, and the last British invasion on Norman soil was in support of France on D-Day in 1944. (See page 48.)

This turbulent past has bequethed Normandy immense historical interest – although the region's gentle and attractive character seems entirely at odds with war and battle. The most exciting historic feature in Normandy is the Bayeux tapestry, which was, in fact, embroidered in England.

This 70-metre-long medieval work has almost single-handedly taught us all we know about the early years of this millennium in Europe. In particular, it has provided much information on the Norman invasion of Britain which climaxed in Hastings in 1066.

The visitors' centre is organised so that by the time you see this legendary wall hanging, you are well-schooled in its significance and are ready to be impressed. The town of **Bayeux** also boasts the splendid Cathédral Notre-Dame, which was consecrated shortly after the Battle of Hastings. This is one of best-preserved medieval cathedrals in France and is well worth a thorough tour. Make sure you see the crypt which is, unusually, entirely intact. Bayeux was close to the centre of the early stages of the D-Day landings. The Musée de la Bataille de Normandie displays a clear exhibition on the mechanics and realities of that daring attack.

For a more sobering reminder, visit the elegant cemetery, just yards from the museum. This is the final resting place for just some of the British soldiers who died during Operation Overlord.

Between Bayeux and Caen is the wonderful Château de Fontaine-Henry. Don't miss this gem of French Renaissance architecture.

Caen, to the east of Bayeux and the capital of the Calvados region, is another historic medieval city. William the Conqueror is buried here in the splendid Abbaye aux Hommes, which he had built to hold his tomb. His wife (and cousin) is buried in the equally impressive Abbaye aux Dames. Much of the rest of old Caen was destroyed during the War. There are old town areas,

Page 43: A street in Rouen with the tower of St Quen in the background
Above: The Bayeux tapestry

with beautiful half-timbered houses, but these are mostly convincing reconstructions. Visit the Musée de la Paix to find out more about those dark years. This is, probably, the best war (or peace) museum in France. The happier history of European painting is revealed in a fine collection of works from the fifteenth to the nineteenth centuries at the Musée des Beaux-Arts. Flemish, Venetian and French masters are all well-represented. Art lovers will also be impressed by the famous Musée des Beaux Arts in the otherwise dull port of **Le Havre**. This magnificent gallery displays works by Monet, Boudin and Courbet.

Following World War II, Le Havre was almost entirely rebuilt to the ambitious designs of architect Auguste Perret. Although you will admire the bravery of the scheme, it is hard to escape the rather unpleasant sensation of being trapped in an architectural experiment. The port itself is colossal – the second largest in France.

A far more attractive port can be found at **Dieppe**. Eighteenth-century elegance – with touches of twentieth-century decline – has left Dieppe a pleasant and easy-to-enjoy coastal town. The restaurants here are particularly good.

For a laid-back visit to the coast, head for the seaside resort of **Honfleur**. The appeal of Honfleur is simply that it is a perfectly preserved and peaceful Normandy town. For a seaside town, however, there is one problem: Honfleur has no beach. Strangely, visitors hardly seem to notice.

To the east of Le Havre lies **Rouen**, a beautiful but industrial city which is bisected by the Seine.

The Rive Gauche (left of the river) is the heart of industry in Rouen. This is a major port and a hard-working city.

The Rive Droite (right of the river) is more appealing to travellers. Half-timbered houses crowd around tiny streets, which lead to a steady stream of alluring sights, cafés and leafy squares.

Like so much of Normandy, Rouen was almost flattened in the War. However, the restoration process has been so successful that it is impossible to tell whether one is looking at an original building from the

seventeenth century or a 1960s fake. Rouen is the 'City of One Hundred Towers'. Climb the belfry next to the clock tower on the rue du Gros-Horloge to find the reason; Rouen's skyline is dominated my a mass of spires and towers.

A more morbid side to the city can be found in the Aître St-Maclou – a cemetery for plague victims. There is an air of doom about this place, which can be frightening or fascinating. The houses of the inner courtyard are decorated with motifs of the 'Dance of Death'. Stranger still is the resident cat, which is mummified!

Head for the imposing Palais de Justice which makes a beautiful and safely secular excursion after an eerie hour spent at Aître St-Maclou. Work started on the Palais de Justice in the late fifteenth century and it is by far the most impressive non-religious building in Rouen.

There are some unusual museums in Rouen, for example the Musée Jeanne d'Arc, the Musée de l'Education and the Musée de la Céramique (Rouen is well-known for its pottery). For a final view across Rouen, drive out to the Corniche on the Côte Ste-Catherine. From here, the panorama is unbeatable.

Right: Sailors from the quiet little seaside town of Honfleur were among the first of the French to colonize Canada

On the western tip of Normandy, close to the border with Brittany, **Mont St-Michel** sits quietly astounding visiting tourists. It is, without doubt, an incredible sight and one not to be missed. Like its Cornish equivalent, Mont St-Michel is a part-time island (depending on the tide).

The island appears to grow into a mass of medieval buildings until, towards the peak, a stunning Gothic abbey rises above the streets below to form a pyramid.

The colour of the abbey matches exactly the colour of the island, adding to the illusion that they are the same thing.

Naturally, such a jewel is a powerful magnet to tourists who crowd into the island's tiny streets in huge numbers.

Another problem is the fact that tacky gift shops have been allowed to smother the lower areas of the island.

However, the abbey rises above all this, and it seems that no amount of commercialism can deaden the effect.

Festivals in Normandy

May
- Spring Festival, Mont St-Michel
- Jazz Festival, Coutances

June
- Joan of Arc Festival, Rouen
- Festival of the Sea, Music Festival, Le Perche

July
- Norman Festival, Gavray
- Hunting Festival, Beaumesnil

August
- Festival of Sailors, Berville-sur-Mer

September
- Holy Cross Fair, Lessay
- Cheese Festival, Neufchatel en Bray
- Music Festival, Orne

October
- Apple Festival, Vimoutiers

November
- Herring Festival, Dieppe

Above: Mont St-Michel at sunset

D-Day

A decision reached in Quebec in 1943 was to lead to the most daring operation of World War II and, more importantly, to the defeat of Nazi Germany.

The decision was to launch a full-scale invasion of occupied France in the spring of 1944. Immense secrecy surrounded the operation, which was code-named Overlord.

After rigorous training around the coast of Britain, the attack took place on the beaches of Normandy on the nights of the 5 and 6 June: D-Day.

Rather than attempt to take an established port, the Allies had developed an ingenious system of mobile, prefabricated piers which would allow them to create two artificial ports from which a surprise attack could be launched.

On the night of the mission, three airborne divisions were dropped on land to seize strategic positions which would later help the bulk of the landing force to reach shore in safety.

A staggering 120,000 men and 20,000 vehicles landed on five beaches along the Normandy coast.

The Allies then proceeded to link up those five beaches to form an 80-km-long base from which to attack deeper into France.

From this position of strength, and despite a fierce counter-attack by the Germans, the British, Canadian and American troops pushed forwards to capture Caen and Cherbourg. The British and Canadian troops moved north, while the Americans moved south to form a circle around the 7th German Army.

The Germans eventually capitulated in the Falaise Valley after three months of intense and bloody fighting and the Allies marched into Paris.

TOURIST INFORMATION

- **Normandy Tourist Office (France)**
  Le Doyenné, 14 rue Charles Corbeau, 27000 Evreux
  ☏ 2 32 33 79 00
- **Normandy Tourist Board (Britain)**
  The Old Bakery, 44 Bath Hill, Keynsham, Bristol BS18 1HG
  ☏ 0117 986 0386

Below: This cemetery at Ranville is a reminder of those who died during the allied invasion of occupied France

Getting there

By road

Normandy has a fast and well-developed road network with quick motorway links from Caen and Rouen to Paris.
For coach travel contact: Compagnie Normandie d'Autobus (CNA) 📞 2 35 52 92 29 or Bus Verts 📞 2 31 44 77 44.

By rail

Direct connections between Paris Montparnasse and Granville, Alencon and Rouen, and between Paris St-Lazare and Cherbourg, Le Havre and Dives Cabourg. By TGV: Lyon to Rouen takes 3 hours 45 mins

By boat

Granville, Cartaret, Portbail or Flamanville to the Channel Islands and Sercq 📞 2 33 50 16 36 or 2 33 50 05 04.

By air

Caen-Carpiquet International Airport is about 4 miles west of Caen.

For car hire at the airport, contact:
* CITER 📞 2 31 84 18 83
* Europcar 📞 2 31 84 61 61

Deauville-Saint-Gatien Airport (📞 2 31 65 65 65, Fax 2 31 65 46 46) is 3 miles east of Deauville.
For car hire 📞 2 31 65 65 65.

Le Havre-Octeville Airport (📞 2 35 54 65 00, Fax 2 35 54 65 29) is 3 miles north-west of Le Havre.
For car hire, contact:
* Avis 📞 2 35 53 17 20
* Europcar 📞 2 35 25 21 95
* Hertz 📞 2 35 19 01 19

Rouen-Vallee de Seine Airport (📞 2 35 79 41 00, Fax 2 35 80 48 67) is 7 miles south-east of Rouen.
For car hire, contact:
* Avis 📞 2 35 70 95 12
* Europcar 📞 2 32 08 39 09

Above: Take a trip to Giverny at Vernon (near Rouen) and you really will feel like you have stepped into a Claude Monet masterpiece. His series of waterlily paintings capture the mood of these gardens incredibly well. The gardens are well-maintained and are quite stunning. It is also possible to explore the painter's house and studio. The walls are decorated not with French impressionist paintings but with Japanese prints, and each room is themed entirely around one colour.

AGON-COUTAINVILLE Manche   1B

★★★ Hôtel Neptune
promenoir Jersey, 50230 Agon-Coutainville
☎ 02 33 47 07 66
English spoken
Closed 30 Sep-1 Apr
Hôtel Neptune, situated in the town centre, has a lovely view of the beach and sea. There is an 18 hole golf course, spa, horse-back riding and casino.

11 bedrs, all ensuite, ✦ P DB 350-420 B 49 No restaurant ℂℂ MC Visa Amex ▶ 1km 🗎 ⊠

ALENCON Orne   2C

★★ Hôtel du Grand Cerf
21 rue St-Blaise, 61000 Alençon
☎ 02 33 26 00 51 Fax 02 33 26 63 07
English spoken

Situated in the heart of Alençon, the hotel is an historic building with much character and warmth. The newly renovated bedrooms and suites offer all modern-day comforts.

20 bedrs, all ensuite, ✦ P DB 280-340 B 35 ✖ 80-240 ℂℂ MC Visa Amex ▶ 2km ⊠ 🗎 ⊠ ⫴ ✿
RAC 10 %

ARGENTAN Orne   2C

★★ Hôtel Faisan Doré
Fontenai-sur-Orne, 61200 Argentan
☎ 02 33 67 18 11 Fax 02 33 35 82 15
English spoken
A pretty, half-timbered inn with landscaped gardens, on the road to Flers. The 'Norman Inn' offers regional specialities including marbré de foie gras aux pommes and boeuf ficelle et sa créme de camembert.

15 bedrs, all ensuite, P DB 265-350 B 40 ✖ 95-295 ℂℂ MC Visa Amex ▶ 10km ⊠ ⫴
RAC 10 %

★★ Hôtel Renaissance
20 av 2e-Division-Blindée, 61200 Argentan
☎ 02 33 36 14 20 Fax 02 33 36 65 50
English spoken
A hotel in the town centre, serving a traditional cuisine in a dining room overlooking a flower-filled garden.

11 bedrs, all ensuite, ✦ P 40 DB 217-265 B 35 ✖ 92-228 ℂℂ Visa Amex ▶ 15km ⊠ ⫴ ✿
RAC 5 %

ARROMANCHES-LES-BAIN Calvados   2A

★★ Hôtel Victoria
24 chemin de l'Eglise, 14117 Tracy-sur-Mer
☎ 02 31 22 35 37 Fax 02 31 21 41 66
English spoken
Closed 1 Oct-3 Apr

A renovated 19th century manor house set in parkland with lovely gardens and situated 2 km from Arromanches, towards Bayeux. Complimentary continental breakfast with RAC guide (except bank holidays) and a restaurant specialising in fish and seafood nearby.

14 bedrs, all ensuite, P 16 DB 290-570 B 40-45 No restaurant ℂℂ MC Visa ▶ 7km ⊠ 10km ✿ ♿
RAC Complimentary breakfast

BAGNOLES-DE-L'ORNE Orne   2C

★★ Hôtel Beaumont
26 bd Le Meunier de Raillère, 61140 Bagnoles-de-l'Orne
☎ 02 33 37 91 77 Fax 02 33 38 90 61
English spoken
Closed 1 Dec-end Feb

Comfortable Logis de France hotel dating from the turn of the century. Set behind the church in peaceful surroundings but only 5 minutes' walk from the town centre. Bar and tea room. Restaurant with typical French and gourmet cuisine.

38 bedrs, all ensuite, ✝ **P** **DB** 205-360 **B** 35 ✕ 95-260 ℂℂ MC Visa Amex ⊩ 1km 🚗 🖼 ⅲ 🔊
R∂C 20 %

★★ Hôtel Le Cheval Blanc
place de l'Eglise, 61140 La Chapelle-d'Andaine
📞 **02 33 38 11 88**
English spoken
An attractive Logis de France hotel. La Chapelle-d'Andaine lies 5 km south-west of Bagnoles on the Domfront to Alençon road (D176). The restaurant has earned a good reputation offering traditional and regional specialities.

10 bedrs, 8 ensuite, **P** 20 **DB** 150-260 **B** 30 ✕ 55-210 ℂℂ MC Visa Amex ⊡ ⌿ ⊞ 🖼 🔲 🖼
R∂C 5 %

★★★ Manoir du Lys
Route de Juvigny-sous-Andaine, 61140 Bagnoles-de-l'Orne
📞 **02 33 37 80 69 Fax 02 33 30 05 80**
English spoken
Closed 5 Jan-14 Feb

Set on the edge of the forest, by the golf course, a Norman manor surrounded by apple trees and rhododendrons, not forgetting the deer and the chanterelle and cepe mushrooms. 50 km from Alencon on the Juvigny road.

25 bedrs, all ensuite, ✝ **P** 20 **DB** 300 **B** 60 ✕ 140-300 ℂℂ MC Visa Amex ⊡ ⌿ ⊞ ⊩ 🔲 🚗 🖼 ⅲ 🔊

BARFLEUR Manche 1B

★★ Hôtel Moderne
50760 Barfleur
📞 **02 33 23 12 44 Fax 02 33 23 91 58**
Just 50 m from the harbour in this small, pretty town. Traditional French cooking and some wonderful seafood specialities are served in the dining or banquetting rooms.

7 bedrs, 5 ensuite, ✝ **P** 5 **DB** 150-250 **B** 29 ✕ 105-200 ℂℂ MC Visa 🚗 ⅲ 🔊
R∂C 5 %

BARNEVILLE-CARTERET Manche 1B

★★★ Hôtel La Marine
11 rue de Paris, Carteret, 50270 Barneville-Carteret
📞 **02 33 53 83 31 Fax 02 33 53 39 60**
English spoken
Closed 11 Nov-20 Feb
A pretty, comfortable hotel, in the village centre and right beside the sea. Carteret is a beautiful little fishing port with fine sandy beaches and dunes. Located close to a direct ferry connection with Jersey. Just west of Barneville-Carteret.

31 bedrs, all ensuite, **P** 13 **DB** 398-620 **B** 50 ✕ 140-400 ℂℂ MC Visa Amex ⊩ 2km 🚗 🖼 ⅲ

BAYEUX Calvados 1B

★★★ Château de Goville
D5, 14330 Le Breuil-en-Bessin
📞 **02 31 22 19 28 Fax 02 31 22 68 74**
English spoken

18th century hotel set in a 5 hectare park, with warm atmosphere, original furnishings and beautiful decor. From Bayeux take D5 towards Le Rolay Lettry for 14 km, the hotel is to the left at the end of the park.

10 bedrs, all ensuite, ✝ **P** **DB** 595-695 **B** 60 ✕ 140-250 ℂℂ MC Visa Amex ⊩ 12km 🚗 🖼 ⅲ 🔊

★★ Château du Baffy
Colombiers-sur-Seulles, 14480 Creully
📞 **02 31 08 04 57 Fax 02 31 08 08 29**
English spoken
The château and its villa Mathilda are set in wooded parkland which the restaurant overlooks. Between Creully and Douvres on D176, near the village centre.

35 bedrs, all ensuite, ✝ **P** **DB** 490-560 **B** included ✕ 125-195 ℂℂ MC Visa Amex ⊞ ⊩ 15km 🔲 🚗 🖼 ⅲ 🔊 🔊

★★★ Hôtel Churchill

14 rue St-Jean, 14404 Bayeux
☎ 02 31 21 31 80 Fax 02 31 21 41 66
English spoken
Closed 15 Nov-14 Mar

Highly recommended, the hotel is in a quiet street opposite the tourist office in the centre of Bayeux near the tapestry museum and cathedral. Complimentary continental breakfast on presentation of this guide on your arrival, except bank holidays.

32 bedrs, all ensuite, **P** **DB** 290-530 **B** 42-57 ✕ 75-135 **CC** MC Visa Amex ► 7km 🖼 🖋 ♿
RAC **Free continental breakfast**

★★ Hôtel La Ranconnière

Route d'Arromanches, 14480 Crépon
☎ 02 31 22 21 73 Fax 02 31 22 98 39
English spoken

A converted 14th century manor house with period furniture. From Bayeux, take D12 towards Ouistreham; from Sommervieu, D112 and Crépon is 7 km.

42 bedrs, all ensuite, �🐾 **P** 120 **DB** 295-580 **B** 48 ✕ 98-280 **CC** MC Visa Amex ► 🖼 ⚑ 🖋 ♿

Don't forget to mention the guide
When booking, please remember to tell the hotel that you chose it from the
RAC France for the Independent Traveller

★★★ Hôtel Le Lion d'Or

71 rue St-Jean, 14400 Bayeux
☎ 02 31 92 06 90 Fax 02 31 22 15 64
English spoken

A former 17th century coaching inn, full of character. Heading for the town centre, turn into rue de Crèmel by the railway station. Keep on this road towards the town centre and the hotel is on the right.

25 bedrs, all ensuite, **P** 20 **DB** 350-480 **B** 50-60 ✕ 100-230 **CC** MC Visa Amex ► 9km 🖼 ⚑ 🖋
RAC **8 %**

★★ Hôtel Reine Mathilde

23 rue Larcher, 14400 Bayeux
☎ 02 31 92 08 13 Fax 02 31 92 09 93
English spoken
Closed 15 Dec-10 Feb

In the town centre, situated opposite the post office and town hall and 150 m from the cathedral, the hotel is very quiet with comfortable, individually decorated rooms. Take the N13 towards 'Bayeux centre-ville'.

16 bedrs, all ensuite, **P** **DB** 275-295 **B** 32 ✕ 49-99 **CC** MC Visa Amex ► 8km
RAC **15 % 15 Nov-15 Mar**

★★ Hôtel d'Argouges

21 rue St-Patrice, 14400 Bayeux
☎ 02 31 92 88 86 Fax 02 31 92 69 16
English spoken

In the heart of the historic and artistic city of Bayeux, with its world famous 11th century tapestry, museums and cathedral. The rooms overlook a courtyard, park and flower garden. From Caen go towards Cherbourg, then 'centre-ville'.

25 bedrs, all ensuite, ✝ P 25 DB 200-420 B 39 ℂℂ MC Visa Amex ▸ 10km ▣
RAC 20 % 1 Nov-31 Mar

The hotel is built within a 12th century medieval castle, surrounded by its ramparts. Take the D900 from Cherbourg.

18 bedrs, 16 ensuite, ✝ P 20 DB 275-390 B 40 ✕ 79-170 ℂℂ MC Visa Amex ▸ 15km ▣ ▣ ⠿

LA BOUILLE Seine Maritime　　　2A

★★ Hôtel Bellevue
13 quai Hector-Malot, 76530 La Bouille
📞 02 35 18 05 05 Fax 02 35 18 00 92
English spoken
Closed 20-27 Dec

A pleasing, traditional hotel in a quiet position opposite the River Seine. From Rouen, drive south-west on A13 for 15 km. Exit for Maison Brulée, turn right after 500 m to the village and the river.

20 bedrs, all ensuite, P DB 190-350 B 38 ✕ 110-240 ℂℂ MC Visa ▸ 15km ▣ ▣ ⠿ ∅
RAC 10 %

BRICQUEBEC Manche　　　1B

★★★ Hôtel Vieux Château
4 cours du Château, 50260 Bricquebec
📞 02 33 52 24 49 Fax 02 33 52 62 71
English spoken

BRIONNE Eure　　　2A

★★ Hôtel Soleil d'Or
27550 La Riviere-Thibouville
📞 02 32 45 00 08 Fax 02 32 46 89 68
English spoken
Situated 5 km south of Brionne towards Beaumont-le-Roger, on the right. The restaurant has a gourmet cuisine with regional specialities and an extensive wine and Calvados list.

12 bedrs, all ensuite, P DB 320-585 B 40 ✕ 98-235 ℂℂ Visa Amex ▸ 15km ▣ ▣ ⠿ ♿
RAC 10 %

CAEN Calvados　　　2A

★★ Hôtel Campanile
bd du Bois, 14200 Hérouville-St-Clair
📞 02 31 95 29 24 Fax 02 31 95 74 87
English spoken
A pleasant situation in quiet countryside. Between Ouistreham car ferry and Caen, on the main road.

66 bedrs, all ensuite, P 70 DB 280 B 34 ✕ 66-109 ℂℂ MC Visa Amex ▸ 2km ▣ ⠿ ♿
RAC 8 % in Dec

★★ Hôtel Climat de France
av Montgomery, quartier du Mémorial, 14000 Caen
📞 02 31 44 36 36 Fax 02 31 95 62 62
English spoken
A modern hotel with secure parking, near the Mémorial museum in Caen. Travelling on the north ring road towards Cherbourg, take the Mémorial or Cruelly exit and the hotel is 400 m from Mémorial. Special offer in Jul/Aug - 3 nights 690 FF.

72 bedrs, all ensuite, ✝ P 90 DB 280-305 B 35 ✕ 95-115 ℂℂ MC Visa Amex ▸ 7km ▣ ⠿ ∅ ♿
RAC 10 %

CARENTAN Manche — 1B

★★ Hôtel Aire de la Baie
50500 Carentan
☎ 02 33 42 00 99 Fax 02 33 71 06 94
English spoken
A quiet countryside hotel, ideal as a stopover for British visitors and only 40 minutes from the ferry in Cherbourg. On the N13, exit St-Lô towards Les Veys. The restaurant offers a large choice of hors d'oeuvre and fish specialities.

40 bedrs, all ensuite, ⊮ P 50 DB 260-300 B 37 ✕ 55-158 ℂℂ MC Visa Amex ▸ ☑ ☒ ⧣ ∅ ⅋
RƏC 10 %

CAUDEBEC-EN-CAUX Seine Maritime — 2A

★★ Normotel La Marine
18 quai Guilbaud, 76490 Caudebec-en-Caux
☎ 02 35 96 20 11 Fax 02 35 56 54 40
English spoken

T. V. Satellite

A hotel located in the Seine valley in the centre of Haute Normandie. Its restaurant 'La Marine' - with a panoramic view of the Seine and Pont de Brotonne - will offer you traditional and regional cuisine.

31 bedrs, all ensuite, ⊮ P 20 DB 260-430 B 35 ✕ 78-240 ℂℂ Visa Amex ▸ ☑ ☒ ⧣ ∅ ⅋

CHERBOURG Manche — 1B

Hôtel La Lorette
Cap Lévi, 50840 Fermanville
☎ 02 33 44 49 49 Fax 02 33 44 16 15
English spoken
Closed Jan

A small family-run hotel right on the coast at Cap Lévi. From Cherbourg drive east on the D116. Turn left (north) after 12 km to Fermanville and Cap Lévi or take the pretty coast road through Bretteville.

6 bedrs, all ensuite, ⊮ P 40 DB 195-220 B 30 ✕ 90-145 ℂℂ MC Visa Amex ▸ 6km ☑ ☒ ⧣ ∅
RƏC 5 %

★★ Hôtel Louvre
2 rue H Dunant, 50100 Cherbourg
☎ 02 33 53 02 28 Fax 02 33 53 43 88
English spoken
Closed 2 Dec-1 Jan
A hotel in the town centre with private parking, lifts and family rooms. From ferry: towards town centre, turn right after bridge and follow quays, turn left twice after statue.

42 bedrs, 37 ensuite, ⊮ P 15 DB 280-360 B 36 No restaurant ℂℂ MC Visa Amex ▸ 2km ☒ ∅ ⅋
RƏC 8 % on room rate

CLECY Calvados — 2A

★★★ Hôtel Le Moulin du Vey
14570 Clécy
☎ 02 31 69 71 08 Fax 02 31 69 14 14
English spoken
Closed 11 Nov-28 Dec
Beautiful old mill with 2 annexes in an enchanting setting on the banks of the River Orne - take the D133A over Pont-du-Vey. The restaurant is truly a gourmet delight, overlooking the river and with a shady terrace.

25 bedrs, all ensuite, ⊮ P 80 DB 395-540 B 50 ✕ 135-360 ℂℂ MC Visa Amex ▸ 3km ☑ ☒ ⧣

CONDE-SUR-NOIREAU Calvados — 2A

★★ Hôtel Le Cerf
18 rue de Chêne, 14110 Condé-sur-Noireau
☎ 02 31 69 40 55 Fax 02 31 69 78 29
English spoken
Closed 11 Nov
From Caen, take first left in Condé-sur-Noireau. The classic restaurant offers regional cuisine.

9 bedrs, all ensuite, ⊮ P DB 204-224 B 32 ✕ 69-180 ℂℂ MC Visa Amex ▸ 5km ☒
RƏC 5 %

DEAUVILLE Calvados — 2A

★★ Hôtel Helios
10 rue Fossorier, 14800 Deauville
☎ 02 31 14 46 46 Fax 02 31 88 53 87
English spoken

The hotel is right in the centre of Deauville, in a quiet area between the beach and the racecourse, a few minutes' walk from the casino, the C.I.D. (International Congress Centre) and the sea-water therapy institute.

45 bedrs, all ensuite, **P DB** 380-460 **B** 46 **CC** MC Visa Amex ᴣ ▸ 3km 🖾 🐾 ᴖ
RAC 8 %

★★★ Hôtel Marie-Anne
142 av de la République, 14800 Deauville
📞 **02 31 88 35 32 Fax 02 31 81 46 31**
English spoken
Located in the heart of Deauville, the hotel is furnished and equipped to a high standard and offers a warm welcome and attentive service.

25 bedrs, all ensuite, ⊷ **P DB** 250-900 **B** 25-60 ✕ 70 **CC** MC Visa Amex ᴣ ▸ 3km 🖾 ⁂ ᴖ
RAC 10 %

★★★ Hôtel de l'Amirauté
Touques, 14800 Deauville
📞 **02 31 81 82 83 Fax 02 31 81 82 93**
English spoken

A very comfortable hotel with excellent facilities. Ideal for those wishing to keep fit.

230 bedrs, all ensuite, ⊷ **P** 150 **DB** 630-850 **B** 62 ✕ 160-220 **CC** MC Visa Amex 🗐 ᴣ 🖾 🕮 🖸 ▸ 3km 🖾 🖾 🖾 ⁂ ᴖ
RAC 15 %

★★★ Hôtel Aguado
30 bd Verdun, 76200 Dieppe
📞 **02 35 84 27 00 Fax 02 35 06 17 61**
English spoken
Facing the sea in the town centre, the hotel has been totally renovated and has a warm and friendly atmosphere. It is very comfortable, attractive accommodation and has good facilities. There are restaurants within walking distance.

57 bedrs, all ensuite, **P DB** 340-445 **B** 45 No restaurant **CC** MC Visa ▸ 4km 🖾 🖾 ⁂ ᴖ

★★ Auberge de la Selune
2 rue St-Germain, 50220 Ducey
📞 **02 33 48 53 62 Fax 02 33 48 90 30**
English spoken
Highly recommended (1996) as being extremely comfortable and tremendous value for money. The hotel is in a quiet, green setting by the River Selune, famous for its salmon fishing. South of Avranches and only 15 km from Mont-St-Michel.

20 bedrs, all ensuite, **P** 6 **DB** 280-310 **B** 40 ✕ 78-200 **CC** MC Visa Amex 🗐 ⁂ ᴖ

Hôtel Moulin de Ducey
1 Grande rue, 50220 Ducey
📞 **02 33 60 25 25 Fax 02 33 60 26 76**
English spoken
A haven of peace situated 15 km from Mont-St-Michel. Come and sleep, rocked by the chanting of the water.

28 bedrs, all ensuite, ⊷ **P DB** 380-495 **B** 50 No restaurant **CC** MC Visa Amex ▸ 30km 🗐 🖾

★★★ Hôtel Dormy House
Route du Havre, 76790 Etretat
📞 **02 35 27 07 88 Fax 02 35 29 86 19**
English spoken
Closed 5 Jan-15 Mar
A typical old manor house, set on the cliff top in 4 hectares of attractive parkland. It offers peace and quiet, wonderful views and comfortable accommodation. With a bar and panoramic terrace. Walking distance from beach and town. On D940 from Le Havre.

49 bedrs, all ensuite, ⊷ **P** 60 **DB** 260-850 **B** 50-70 ✕ 189-245 **CC** MC Visa Amex ▸ 🗐 🖾 2km ⁂ 🐾

★★★ Manoir de Beaumont
76260 Eu
☎ 02 35 50 91 91
English spoken
*A charming, peaceful manor furnished with
antiques. With a beautiful view and near the forest,
sea and a restaurant. Take Eu access by D49, turn
on your left and take Beaumont road through forest
of Eu (2 km).*

4 bedrs, all ensuite, ♞ P 10 DB 300 B included
No restaurant ⚒ 🏫 🎿 ▸ 30km 🏌 🎿 2km ⛷
RAC 250 FF for 2, breakfast included.

★★ Hôtel de France
29 rue St-Thomas, 27000 Evreux
☎ 02 32 39 09 25 Fax 02 32 38 38 56
English spoken
*An elegant, provincial building in a quiet location
and offering a traditional, high quality service. With
a superb restaurant overlooking a river and gardens
and serving outstanding classic and contemporary
cuisine.*

15 bedrs, all ensuite, ♞ P 8 DB 265-335 B 36 ✗ 155-
205 ₢ MC Visa Amex ▸ 2km ⛷ ⚘
RAC 10 %

★★★ Hôtel Le Galion
5 rue Victor Hugo, 61100 Flers
☎ 02 33 64 47 47 Fax 02 33 65 10 10
English spoken
*A charming hotel in a quiet street, close to the town
centre.*

30 bedrs, all ensuite, ♞ P 685 DB 250-275 B 35 No
restaurant ₢ MC Visa Amex ▸ ⛷ ⚙ ⚘ ♿

★★★ Hôtel La Beaumonderie
20 route de Coutances, 50290 Breville-sur-Mer
☎ 02 33 50 36 36 Fax 02 33 50 36 45
English spoken

*In a 2 hectare park overlooking the sea and the
Channel Islands. A charming house where General
Eisenhower established his HQ. With a swimming
pool and gourmet restaurant.*

12 bedrs, all ensuite, ♞ P DB 280-870 B 50-80 ✗ 110-
245 ₢ Visa Amex 🏊 ⚒ 🅿 ▸ 1km 🏌 🎿 ⛷ 1km ⚙ ♿
RAC 10 %

★★ Hôtel Ibis
rue 129e Régiment Infanterie, 76600 Le Havre
☎ 02 35 22 29 29 Fax 02 35 21 00 00
English spoken
*Situated in the centre of Le Havre, 300 m from the
railway station and car ferry terminal. The
restaurant has à la carte or fixed-price menus, with
seafood specialities.*

91 bedrs, all ensuite, ♞ P DB 360 B 35 ✗ 55-95 ₢
MC Visa Amex ▸ 20km ⛷ ⚙ ♿

★★★ Hôtel Le Marly
121 rue de Paris, 76600 Le Havre
☎ 02 35 41 72 48 Fax 02 35 21 50 45
English spoken
*A recently renovated, traditional hotel that is
comfortable, light and airy. Good facilities and
conveniently situated just 200 m from the ferries and
close to the new bridge. Excellent choice of
restaurants and pizzerias nearby. Follow signs from
the port*

37 bedrs, all ensuite, ♞ P DB 340-420 B 42 No
restaurant ₢ MC Visa Amex ▸ 20km 🎵 ⛷ ⚙
RAC 10 %

★★ Hôtel Richelieu
132 rue Paris, 76600 Le Havre
☎ 02 35 42 38 71 Fax 02 35 21 07 28
English spoken
*A comfortable, 2 star hotel in the town centre and
close to the ferry harbour. Open 7 days a week, 24
hours a day.*

79 bedrs, all ensuite, P DB 245-320 B 30 No
restaurant ₢ MC Visa Amex ▸ 🎵 ⛷ ⚙
RAC 10 %

★★★ Hôtel Le Cheval Blanc
2 quai des Passagers, 14600 Honfleur
☎ 02 31 81 65 00 Fax 02 31 89 52 80
English spoken
Closed Jan

A 15th century hotel, with 2 restaurants and well renovated rooms with harbour views, occupying a wonderful situation in the picturesque town of Honfleur. An ideal spot for individual or groups of artists

33 bedrs, all ensuite, ⭐ **P** **DB** 449-629 **B** 16 **CC** MC Visa ▸ 7km 🖼 ⚙ ⌀

ISIGNY-SUR-MER Calvados   **2A**

★★ Hôtel de France
15 rue Emile Demagny, 14230 Isigny-sur-Mer
📞 02 31 22 00 33 **Fax** 02 31 22 79 19
English spoken
Closed 15 Nov-15 Feb
On the wartime landing beaches circuit, a comfortable, attractive hotel with quiet rooms surrounding a flowered courtyard. The seafood specialities include oysters, mussels in cream sauce, turbot and halibut dishes.

19 bedrs, all ensuite, ⭐ **P** **DB** 220-280 **B** 32 ✕ 69-185 **CC** MC Visa Amex ↗ ▸ 30km 🖼 ⚙ 🖼 ⚙ ⌀ ♿
RAC 10 % on room rate

LOUVIERS Eure   **2A**

★★★ Hôtel La Haye-le-Comte
4 route de la Haye-le-Comte, 27400 Louviers
📞 02 32 40 00 40 **Fax** 02 32 25 03 85
English spoken
Closed 31 Nov-29 Mar

A peaceful, 16th century manor house, with its own helipad, set in a 5 hectare park between Paris and Deauville. Take D133 from Louviers towards

Neubourg, on outskirts of Louviers turn left to hotel 700m on right.

16 bedrs, all ensuite, ⭐ **P** 16 **DB** 350-510 **B** 50 ✕ 100-190 **CC** MC Visa Amex ▸ 9km 🖼 🖼 ⚙ ⌀ ♿
RAC 10 % in Apr, Oct & Nov

★★★★ Hôtel Moulin de Connelles
Départmentale No 19, 27430 Connelles
📞 02 32 59 53 33 **Fax** 02 32 59 21 83
English spoken
Closed Jan

A 19th century manor house with half-timbered walls in 3 hectares of quiet grounds on the Seine. Facilities for sailing or water skiing nearby. From motorway A13 exit Louviers, towards St-Pierre-du-Vauvray, over the Seine, left at Connelles.

13 bedrs, all ensuite, ⭐ **P** 40 **DB** 600-950 **B** 70 ✕ 140-295 **CC** MC Visa Amex ↗ ▸ 6km 🖼 ⚙ 🖼 ⚙
RAC 5 %

★★★ Relais Mercure Val de Reuil-Louviers
Lieu dit "Les Clouets", 27100 Val de Reuil
📞 02 32 59 09 09 **Fax** 02 32 59 56 54
Come and discover the warm, friendly atmosphere at the Relais Mercure Val-de-Reuil. Conveniently located near both the Val-de-Reuil industrial park and the Bord forest reserve. From Rouen take A13 towards Paris.

58 bedrs, all ensuite, ⭐ **P** **DB** 295-395 **B** 48 ✕ 80-140 **CC** MC Visa Amex ↗ ▸ 🖼 🖼 ⚙ ♿

LUC-SUR-MER Calvados   **2A**

★★★ Hôtel Thermes et du Casino
14530 Luc-sur-Mer
📞 02 31 97 32 37 **Fax** 02 31 96 72 57
English spoken
Closed 1 Nov-9 Apr
A 3 star hotel situated close to the beach. Follow D514 out of Caen along the coast road for 24 km.

48 bedrs, all ensuite, ⭐ **P** 40 **DB** 360-490 **B** 45 ✕ 125-360 **CC** MC Visa Amex 🖼 ↗ 🖼 🖼 ▸ 🖼 ⚙ ♿

LYONS-LA-FORET Eure   2B

★★★ Hôtel La Licorne
Place Benserade, 27480 Lyons-la-Forêt
☎ 02 32 49 62 02 Fax 02 32 49 80 09
English spoken
Closed 15 Dec-20 Jan
*Located in the centre of the Lyons forest, in the heart
of a typical Normandy village, La Licorne offers
delicious, traditional French cuisine and comfortable,
personalised rooms for a quiet stay.*

12 bedrs, all ensuite, **P** 20 **DB** 400-750 **B** 60 ✕ 147-190
CC MC Visa Amex ▸ 🖬 🖾 ⅲ &

LE MONT-ST-MICHEL Manche   1D

★★★ Hôtel de la Digue
50116 Le Mont-St-Michel
☎ 02 33 60 14 02 Fax 02 33 60 37 59
English spoken
Closed 16 Nov-31 March
*The hotel is located 2 km from the nightly illuminated
Mont-St-Michel, at the start of the famous dyke on the
D976. Restaurant offers panoramic views of Mont-St-
Michel and seafood specialities.*

35 bedrs, all ensuite, **P DB** 340-440 **B** 50 ✕ 88-200 **CC**
MC Visa Amex ▸ 20km 🖾

★ Manoir du Gué de Beauvoir
5 route du Mont-Saint Michel, 50170 Beauvoir
☎ 02 33 60 09 23
English spoken
Closed 30 Sep-Apr
*A former manor house situated in the small village of
Beauvoir on the road to Mont-St-Michel. In a quiet
location by the River Coueson that seperates Brittany
from Normandy. Walk along the river to Mont-St-
Michel.*

20 bedrs, 8 ensuite, **P** 30 **DB** 150-260 **B** 29 **CC** MC Visa
🖬 🖾 ⅲ

MORTAGNE-AU-PERCHE Orne   2C

★★ Hostellerie Genty-Home
4 rue Notre Dame, 61400 Mortagne-au-Perche
☎ 02 33 25 11 53 Fax 02 33 25 41 38
English spoken
*A comfortably elegant hostellerie situated near the
church of Notre Dame in the centre of this pretty
town. The restaurant, with tasteful Louis XV/XVI -style
dining room, is known for its inventive cuisine. From
Paris, take N12 west towards Alençon.*

8 bedrs, all ensuite, ♰ **P DB** 230-295 **B** 35-40 ✕ 84-
169 **CC** MC Visa Amex ▸ 15km 🖬 🖾 ⅲ ⋗

★★ Hôtel du Tribunal
4 place du Palais, 61400 Mortagne-au-Perche
☎ 02 33 25 04 77 Fax 02 33 83 60 83
English spoken

*A tasteful 13th century building with lots of beams,
studs and local stone. The flower-covered terrace and
bedrooms have a garden view. Mortagne-au-Perche is
renowned for its black puddings. From Alençon,
travel east on N12.*

11 bedrs, all ensuite, ♰ **P DB** 220-320 **B** 40 ✕ 90-190
CC MC Visa ▸ 15km 🖾 ⅲ

MORTAIN Manche   1D

★★ Hôtel de la Poste
50140 Mortain
☎ 02 33 59 00 03 Fax 02 33 69 53 89
English spoken
Closed half term Feb, Oct

*This centrally located hotel offers stylish comfortable
rooms equipped with TV and telephone. The patio
lounge and many of the bedrooms have a
commanding view over the picturesque Cance Valley.
Fax and minitel are available.*

26 bedrs, all ensuite, ♰ **P** 20 **DB** 180-400 **B** 40 ✕ 100-
200 **CC** MC Visa 🖾 🖾 🖬 🖾 ⅲ
RAC 5 %

OUISTREHAM Calvados   2A

★★ Relais Mercure Côte de Nacre
37 rue Dunes, 14150 Ouistreham
☎ 02 31 96 20 20 Fax 02 31 97 10 10
English spoken

A new hotel, 500 m from sandy D-Day beaches, with all modern facilities and a restaurant offering traditional cuisine and fish dishes. Opposite car ferry terminal. 10 minutes from Caen, 30 km from Arromanches and Bayeux and 2 hours from Paris

50 bedrs, all ensuite, ✱ P 60 DB 305-350 B 38 ✗ 50-140 ⓒ MC Visa Amex ► 6km 🖼 ⊞ ♠ ♿
RAC 10 % on room rate

PONT-AUDEMER Eure 2A

★★ Auberge du Cochon d'Or
Place du Gnl de Gaulle, 27210 Beuzeville
☎ 02 32 57 70 46 Fax 02 32 42 25 70
English spoken
Closed 16 Dec-15 Jan

A charming family-run hotel with rooms overlooking flower gardens and an elegant restaurant offering personalised and traditional cuisine. Beuzeville is between Pont-Audemer and Pont-l'Evêque on the N175; hotel is opposite town hall in village centre.

20 bedrs, 18 ensuite, P 20 DB 200-335 B 35 ✗ 81-240 ⓒ MC Visa ► 12km 🖼 ♠

★★★★ Hôtel Belle Isle-sur-Risle
112 route de Rouen, 27500 Pont-Audemer
☎ 02 32 56 96 22 Fax 02 32 42 88 96
English spoken
A charming mansion, with gourmet restaurant, winter garden, and satellite TV in all rooms, set in 5 acres of century-old trees on an island in the Risle river. From Le Havre take A131 then D810 to Pont-Audemer. Convenient for Deauville and Honfleur.

19 bedrs, all ensuite, ✱ P DB 550-1,250 B 75 ✗ 189-380 ⓒ MC Visa Amex 🖼 ⊰ 🖼 🖼 ► 18km 🖼 🖼 🖼 ⊞

PONT-L'EVEQUE Calvados 2A

★★★ Hôtel Le Clos Saint-Gatien
Saint-Gatien-des-Bois, 14130 Pont-l'Evêque
☎ 02 31 65 16 08 Fax 02 31 65 10 27
English spoken
A prize-winning hotel conversion, from a 17th century working farm, set in gardens with on-site sport and health amenities. Take the Deauville N177 exit from A13 then turn onto the D579 Honfleur road; St-Gatien-des-Bois is 18 km along.

58 bedrs, all ensuite, ✱ P DB 280-860 B 60 ⓒ MC Visa Amex 🖼 ⊰ 🖼 🖼 ► 2km 🖼 🖼 ⊞ ♿

PONTORSON Manche 1D

★★ Hôtel Le Sillon de Bretagne
N175 Bree-en-Tanis, 50170 Pontorson
☎ 02 33 60 13 04 Fax 02 33 70 91 75
English spoken
An old house, with a restaurant offering Norman and seafood specialities, set in a pleasant rural surroundings. From Mont-St-Michel take D976 south to Pontorson; Bree-en-Tanis is 4 km from Pontorson.

7 bedrs, all ensuite, ✱ P DB 180-220 B 89 ✗ 80-200 ⓒ MC Visa Amex ► 🖼 ♠ 5 ♨

REVILLE Manche 1B

★★ Hôtel au Moyne de Saire
Village de l'Eglise, 50760 Réville
☎ 02 33 54 46 06 Fax 02 33 54 14 99
English spoken
Closed Feb
A quiet, comfortable Logis de France hotel, 5 minutes from the beach, with a garden and a restaurant offering regional cuisine and seafood specialities. 3 km from St-Vaast on the Barfleur road.

11 bedrs, 4 ensuite, ✱ P 20 DB 155-375 B 30 ✗ 80-200 ⓒ MC Visa ► 10km 🖼 ♠

ROUEN Seine Maritime 2A

★★★ Hôtel Dieppe
Place B. Tissot, 76000 Rouen
☎ 02 35 71 96 00 Fax 02 35 89 65 21
English spoken

A typically traditional, fully renovated hotel, with a restaurant offering delectable Norman cuisine, founded and managed by the Gueret family since 1880. Centrally located in a district known for art and painting. Follow signs to Gare SNCF.

41 bedrs, all ensuite, ✱ P 20 DB 510-610 B 50 ✗ 118-218 ⓒ MC Visa Amex ► 5km ⊞ ♠
RAC 10 %

★★★ Hôtel La Bertelière
St-Martin-du-Vivier, 76160 Rouen
☎ 02 35 60 44 00 Fax 02 35 61 56 63
English spoken
*A warm, comfortable hotel, with fully equipped rooms
and 2 restaurants offering regional specialities, just
10 minutes from central Rouen. From Rouen take
N28 towards Amiens for 10 km and exit at Bihorel/St-
Martin-du-Vivier (D43), then right onto D443.*

44 bedrs, all ensuite, **P** 120 **DB** 480-580 **B** 60 ✕ 160 **CC**
MC Visa Amex ▶ 5km ⌧ &
RAC Kir (champagne cocktail) offer

★★ Hôtel Québec
18 rue Québec, 76000 Rouen
☎ 02 35 70 09 38 Fax 02 35 15 80 15
*A conveniently situated hotel, on the right bank of the
river in the centre of Rouen, just a few minutes from
the cathedral and the old town. (There is a charge for
parking).*

38 bedrs, 30 ensuite, **P** 4 **DB** 205-320 **B** 32-36 No
restaurant **CC** MC Visa Amex ▶ 5km ⌧ 5km

★★ Hôtel Versan
3 rue Jean Lecanuet, 76000 Rouen
☎ 02 35 07 77 07 Fax 02 35 70 04 67
English spoken
*A charming, centrally situated hotel, completely
redecorated in 1996, with soundproofed rooms. From
the town centre go to the Hôtel de Ville and turn left,
the Hôtel Versan is immediately on the left.*

32 bedrs, all ensuite, ⊁ **P** 8 **DB** 339 **B** 39 No restaurant
CC MC Visa Amex ⚏ ♫ &
RAC 10 %

★★ Hôtel de Bordeaux
9 place de la République, 76000 Rouen
☎ 02 35 71 93 58 Fax 02 35 71 92 15
English spoken
*A centrally situated hotel, with good facilities in all
rooms, standing between the River Seine and the
cathedral. Restaurants nearby.*

48 bedrs, all ensuite, **P** **DB** 195-330 **B** 35 No
restaurant **CC** MC Visa Amex ▶ ⚏
RAC 10 %

Roads that are marked with the Crafty
Bison (*Bison Fute*) sign are shortcuts
which avoid the busiest roads. Crafty
Bison maps are available from
Crafty Bison information centres, which
are scattered along most major routes, or
from tourist boards.

★★ Hôtel Le Clos Normand
Les Pieds dans l'Eau, 14750 St-Aubin-sur-Mer
☎ 02 31 97 30 47 Fax 02 31 96 46 23
English spoken

*A seafront hotel close to the D-Day beaches, with a
restaurant offering seafood and regional specialities.
From Le Havre take A13, head for Douvre-la-
Délivrance and follow signs to St-Aubin-sur-Mer.*

32 bedrs, 31 ensuite, ⊁ **P** 14 **DB** 200-600 **B** 38 ✕ 70-
280 **CC** MC Visa Amex ♫ ⌧ ⚏ &
RAC 10 % with 4 nights stay

★★ Hôtel Cygne
Rue Waldeck, Rousseau, 50600 St-Hilaire-du-Harcouët
☎ 02 33 49 11 84 Fax 02 33 49 53 70
English spoken
Closed 3 Jan-15 Feb
*A warm welcome awaits you at this characterful
hotel with all modern facilities and a reputation for
gourmet cuisine.*

30 bedrs, all ensuite, ⊁ **P** 8 **DB** 290-330 **B** 37 ✕ 75-210
CC MC Visa Amex ♫ ⌧ ⚏ ♫ &
RAC 10 %

★★ Hôtel Bains
8 allée Clémenceau, 50530 St-Jean-le-Thomas
☎ 02 33 48 84 20 Fax 02 33 48 66 42
English spoken
Closed 1 Nov-1 Apr

In the bay of the nightly illuminated Mont-St-Michel, between Granville and Avranches. Run by family for 4 generations. Near 1000 year old seaside village, St-Jean-le-Thomas, Eisenhower's headquarters in the war. On the D911.

30 bedrs, 27 ensuite, ♀ **P** 50 **DB** 155-350 **B** 33 ✕ 50-185 **CC** MC Visa Amex ⤴ ▸ 15km ⊠ ▣ 15km ⋕ ✎
RAC 50% off rooms in Oct, 10% restaurant

★★ Hôtel Marquis de Tombelaine
50530 Champeaux
☎ 02 33 61 85 94 **Fax** 02 33 61 21 52
English spoken
Closed Jan

Just across the bay from Mont-St-Michel, which is visible from the hotel. Essentially, the hotel is a good restaurant with rooms. ✓

6 bedrs, all ensuite, ♀ **P** **DB** 280 **B** 32 ✕ 98.50-350 **CC** Visa Amex ▣ ⤴ ▨ ▦ ▷ ▸ ⊠ ▨ ▣ ▨ 17km ⚬

ST-VAAST-LA-HOUGUE Manche 1B

★★ Hôtel France et Fuchsias
50550 St-Vaast-la-Hougue
☎ 02 33 54 42 25 **Fax** 02 33 43 46 79
English spoken
Closed 3 Jan-22 Feb
A family-run hotel in a pretty provincial-style building with beautiful gardens; close to Tatihou island. From Valognes, take the N802 towards Quettehou and then the D1 towards St-Vaast-la-Hougue.

33 bedrs, 29 ensuite, ♀ **P** 3 **DB** 155-430 **D** 42-45 ✕ 80-270 **CC** MC Visa Amex ▸ 18km ⊠ ▣ ▨ ⋕

★★★ Hôtel La Granitière
74 rue du Maréchal Foch, 50550 St-Vaast-la-Hougue
☎ 02 33 54 58 99 **Fax** 02 33 20 34 91
English spoken
Closed 15 Feb-30 Mar
An impressive granite building with marble floors, rich wall coverings and splendid objets d'art. There are some unusual stained-glass windows and the elegant rooms are spacious, refined and comfortable.

9 bedrs, 8 ensuite, ♀ **P** 10 **DB** 285-560 **B** 42 ✕ 85-190 **CC** MC Visa Amex ▸ 8km ▨ ⋕

SEES Orne 2C

★★ Hôtel Ile de Sées
Mace, 61500 Sées
☎ 02 33 27 98 65 **Fax** 02 33 28 41 22
English spoken

An attractive, peaceful hotel situated just south of N138/N158 junction. The traditional restaurant offers classic and regional cuisine. Meals are served on the terrace in fine weather.

16 bedrs, all ensuite, **P** 50 **DB** 290-350 **B** 35 ✕ 103-175 **CC** MC Amex ▨ ⋕

THURY-HARCOURT Calvados 2A

★★★ Relais de la Poste
2 route de Caen, 14220 Thury-Harcourt
☎ 02 31 79 72 12 **Fax** 02 31 39 53 55
A typically French, riverside hotel with pleasant rooms and apartments and creepers covering the walls around shuttered windows. Restaurant offers seafood specialities. South from Caen on D562 to Thury-Harcourt.

12 bedrs, all ensuite, **P** **DB** 300-620 **B** 45 ✕ 95-370 ▣ ▸ 7km ▨

LE TREPORT Seine Maritime 2B

★★ Hôtel de la Gare
20 place de la Gare, 76260 Eu
☎ 02 35 86 16 64 **Fax** 02 35 50 86 25
English spoken
This hotel has art deco interior and all rooms have modern facilities. A 3 km walk through the forest will take you to the sea. Restaurant offers traditional cuisine and fish specialities.

20 bedrs, all ensuite, ♀ **P** 10 **DB** 300-350 **B** 38 ✕ 90-210 **CC** MC Visa Amex ▨

TROUVILLE-SUR-MER Calvados 2A

★★★ Hôtel Beach
1 quai Albert, 14360 Trouville-sur-Mer
☎ 02 31 98 12 00 Fax 02 31 87 30 29
English spoken
Closed Jan

Sea-facing hotel, close to the town centre, directly linked to the casino and health centre. 2 hours drive from Paris on A13, then N177 to Trouville.

110 bedrs, all ensuite, **P** ℂ MC Visa Amex ⊰ ⊦ 10km ◪ ◪ ⫴ ⌀ ⌖

★★ Hôtel Les Sablettes
15 rue P. Besson, 14360 Trouville-sur-Mer
☎ 02 31 88 10 66 Fax 02 31 88 59 06
Closed Dec-Jan

This comfortable, town-centre, hotel offers a warm welcome, elegant décor and French TV; close to the casino, beach and car park.

18 bedrs, 12 ensuite, ⊁ **P DB** 280-360 **B** 33 No restaurant ℂ MC Visa ⊰ ⊦ ◪ ◪

★★★ Hôtel Mercure
Place Foch, 14360 Trouville-sur-Mer
☎ 02 31 87 38 38 Fax 02 31 87 35 41
English spoken
Town centre hotel close to the beach and the casino; 2 hours drive from Paris on A13, then N177 to Trouville.

80 bedrs, all ensuite, ⊁ **P DB** 370-600 **B** 57 ✕ 100-150 ℂ MC Visa Amex ⊦ 8km ◪ 2km ⫴ ⌀ ⌖
RAC **15 %**

VALOGNES Manche 1B

★ Hôtel de l'Agriculture
16 rue Léopold Delisle, 50700 Valognes
☎ 02 33 95 02 02 Fax 02 33 95 29 33
English spoken
A pretty, creeper clad building with many fine interior features and a restaurant offering speciality cuisine, including homard grillé farci and soupe de poisson. From Valognes central square, head towards the station (Carteret road), turn second left.

34 bedrs, 14 ensuite, ⌖ **P** 15 **DB** 150-280 **B** 35-40 ✕ 75-200 ℂ MC Visa ⊦ 15km ◪ ⫴ ⌀
RAC **5 % 15 Sep-31 Mar**

VERNEUIL-SUR-AVRE Eure 2C

★★★★ Hostellerie Le Clos
98 rue de la Ferté Vidame, 27130 Verneuil-sur-Avre
☎ 02 32 32 21 81 Fax 02 32 32 21 36
English spoken
Closed 13 Dec-20 Jan

Situated in a fortified town, this charmingly original Norman country house will transform your stay into a dream; lovely gardens and a restaurant offering fine regional cuisine and excellent service. Close to N12.

10 bedrs, all ensuite, ✝ **P** 20 **DB** 700-900 **B** 80 ✗ 180-330 **CC** MC Visa Amex 🗙 🖾 ▶ 7km 🗙 🗾 🖾 ‖ ⌀ ♿

★★ Hôtel Le Saumon
89 place de la Madeleine, 27130 Verneuil-sur-Avre
☎ **02 32 32 02 36 Fax 02 32 37 55 80**
English spoken

Nadine and Alain Simon welcome you at this former posthouse. Situated in the heart of Verneuil, next to the Madeleine Tower (a 16th century church) in a square with timber framed houses and small boutiques.

29 bedrs, all ensuite, ✝ **P DB** 210-290 **B** 40 ✗ 65-260 **CC** MC Visa ▶ 7km 🗾 🖾 ♿

★★ Hôtel Moulin de Balisne
RN 12, 27130 Balines
☎ **02 32 32 03 48 Fax 02 32 60 11 22**
English spoken

A quiet, comfortable former mill standing in 25 acres, with two rivers, two lakes and a restaurant offering simple regional dishes and fish and vegetarian specialities. 4 km east of Verneuil, towards Paris, to the right of N12.

12 bedrs, all ensuite, ✝ **P** 60 **DB** 350-450 **B** 50 ✗ 150-300 **CC** MC Visa Amex ▶ 4km 🗙 🗾 🖾 ‖ ⌀
RAC 10 % on rooms & dinner 3 nights

★★★ Hôtel Résidence du Lac
Center-Parcs "Les Bois-Francs", 27130 Verneuil-sur-Avre
☎ **01 42 18 12 12 Fax 01 42 18 12 01**
English spoken
Large nicely decorated double bedrooms, with views of lake and forest and equipped with radio, TV and direct telephone. Bathrooms have double washbasin, jacuzzi. Beds made and towels supplied. Hairdresser and dry cleaning service.

88 bedrs, all ensuite, **P DB** 1,350-1,990 4 nts Mon-Thu or 3 nts Fri-Sun **B** 62.50 **CC** MC Visa Amex 🗙 🗾 🗙 🖾 ▶ ▶ 4km 🗙 🗙 🖾 🖾 ‖ ⌀ ♿

VILLEDIEU-LES-POELES Manche   **1B**

★★ Hôtel St-Pierre et St-Michel
12 place de la République, 50800 Villedieu-les-Poêles
☎ **02 33 61 00 11 Fax 02 33 61 06 52**
English spoken
Closed Jan-Feb
Charming 19th century hotel, with a highly acclaimed restaurant, located in the town centre. Villedieu-les-Poêles is Between St-Lô and Avranches.

23 bedrs, 21 ensuite, ✝ **P DB** 180-320 **B** 35 ✗ 115-225 **CC** MC Visa 🗙 ▶ 🗾 🖾 ‖ ♿
RAC 8 %

★★ Manoir de l'Acherie
50800 Ste-Cécile
☎ **02 33 51 13 87 Fax 02 33 61 89 07**
English spoken
A small, characterful hotel set in the Normandy countryside. Restaurant has a rustic dining room with an open fire and offers regional and speciality cuisine. From Villedieu travel 3 km on the N175, then turn right on to D554.

14 bedrs, all ensuite, **P DB** 250-330 **B** 38 ✗ 90-225 **CC** MC Visa Amex ▶ 20km 🗾 🖾 12km ‖ ⌀ ♿

Picardy and Nord/Pas-de-Calais

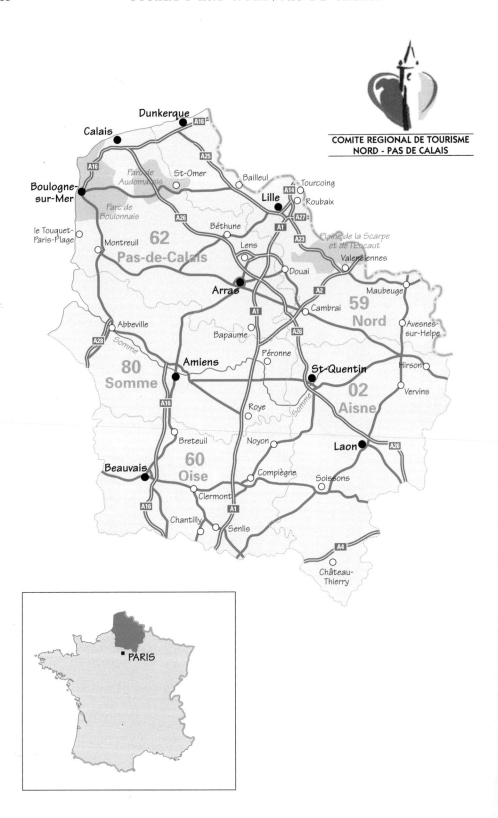

Dunkerque
Calais
St-Omer
Bailleul
Tourcoing
Boulogne-
sur-Mer
Parc de
Audomarois
Lille
Roubaix
Parc de
Boulonnais
le Touquet-
Paris-Plage
Montreuil
Béthune
Lens
Plaine de la Scarpe
et de l'Escaut
62
Pas-de-Calais
Valenciennes
Douai
Arras
A2
Maubeuge
59
Nord
Cambrai
Avesnes-
sur-Helpe
Abbeville
Bapaume
Péronne
Hirson
Somme
80
Somme
Amiens
Roye
St-Quentin
Vervins
02
Aisne
Somme
Breteuil
Noyon
Laon
60
Oise
Beauvais
Compiègne
Soissons
Clermont
Chantilly
Senlis
Château-
Thierry

PARIS

With three major passenger ports and a close proximity to Britain, northern France is an important gateway to continental Europe. However, Picardy and Nord/Pas-de-Calais have trouble holding on to their visitors, who prefer to head for more distant destinations – not least because of the terrible first impression one gets from arriving at the ports of Calais or Dunkerque. It is, however, rather unfair to dismiss northern France as nothing more than a hurdle to be jumped in the race to a more exciting holiday spot. Travellers would do well to explore the area before moving on.

Dunkerque is the northernmost port in France and a centre for heavy industry. The town witnessed bitter fighting during World War II and, of course, the legendary withdrawal of 350,000 Allied troops in May 1940.

The Musée des Beaux-Arts is the place to find out more about that desperate, but extraordinary, event.

World War I features more strongly than World War II in the history of northern France. It was here that the horrific battle of attrition was fought from the trenches in 1914–18.

Visit the Great War Museum in Peronne or take the Tour of the Memorials to the Great War from Albert to gain a better understanding of those terrible years.

Away from the constant loading and off-loading of some nine million British ferry passengers every year, **Calais** offers glimpses of an unusual past.

Edward III took Calais during the Hundred Years' War, and the town remained in English hands for over 200 years. Britain attacked Calais again in the 1940s – this time to prevent Nazi Germany from using the port to launch an invasion of the British Isles.

Calais is now littered with giant hypermarkets which daytrippers use to fill their cars with cheap cigarettes and alcohol. These enormous places make every effort to encourage a fast flow of money across the Channel. Expect to find extra-wide shopping trolleys, English-speaking employees and very low prices.

Pages 64–65: At Calais visit the impressive Hôtel de Ville and Rodin's Burghers of Calais statue. The Burghers were six local officials who offered their lives to Edward III to protect their fellow townspeople.

Above: Picardy is littered with magnificent châteaux. Each has a distinct character and all are steeped in European history. Visit the sixteenth-century Troissereux near Beauvais; Château Compiègne; Château Vic-sur-Aisne; the enormous Château de Coucy; and the painstakingly-restored Château Guise and Château Chantilly (pictured here).

The attractive walled port of **Boulogne** provides a better introduction to France than the more austere Calais or Dunkerque. The old port is frenetic and engaging, with centre stage given to a lively fish market for which the town is famous. Seafood here is a treat. Try eating at one of the many excellent restaurants in the Ville Basse area. The most entertaining attraction in Boulogne is the futuristic Nausicaa sea centre on the boulevard Sainte Beuve.

Look out for the remains of a Roman temple to Diana and a suitably odd statue of the Virgin Mary. Another history lesson can be gleaned from the town's excellent Château-Musée on the rue de Bernet. This surprisingly diverse museum houses exhibits on just about every subject from Alaskan zoology to Zambian art.

A less obvious destination for travellers is **Lille**, an enormous industrial city near the Belgian border. Lille epitomises modern

Above: Rue de Béthune, in Lille – something of a shoppers' paradise. You are almost bound to succumb to temptation in the magnificent Galleries d'Euralille, which manage to make shoppers feel more like they are in work of art than a massive shopping complex.

industrial France. It is a vibrant, but sometimes strained, city which has more to attract the tourist than one might at first suppose. The very fact that it is not a particularly popular place for tourists only adds to its appeal.

Old money has bequeathed the city a collection of splendid buildings, giving the centre an air of grandeur and affluence. Here you will find some of the best restaurants in northern France and a flourishing cultural life. Don't miss the exceptional Musée d'Art Moderne, with works by Miro, Picasso and Laurens.

The City Fathers have been keen to encourage progressive modern architecture in Lille. Striking new buildings stand alongside the older face of the city. This eclectic mish-mash of styles helps to create the image of a dynamic city – and reveals the extent to which Lille has changed over the course of the twentieth century.

A less demanding detour between Calais and Paris is Amiens.

Like so many towns in northern France, **Amiens** was badly damaged during World War II. Whatever delights the town offered prior to 1939 are now just memories – except one. The stunning Cathédrale Notre-Dame is billed as the biggest Gothic structure in France. It has a simple, but very beautiful, interior, which feels all the more impressive when one considers how lucky Amiens is that its jewel survived six years of war. Take the guided tour around the sixteenth-century choir stalls.

Writer Jules Verne spent many years in Amiens (a claim made by several French towns, but which is, in this case, quite true) and there is a charming museum of his life on rue Dubois.

Another Cathédrale Notre-Dame stands in the lovely town of **Laon**, which overlooks Champagne from its perch in the Picardy hills. This cathedral is older and architecturally more interesting than its bigger sister in Amiens.

Don't admire the cathedral from afar; the interior is even more impressive than the intricate exterior.

The 'old town' area of Laon has survived the rigours of the twentieth century fairly intact. Wander in the streets around the cathedral, and you will find enticing boutiques and pretty streets encased by what is left of a once-mighty series of ramparts.

Food and drink in northern France

Northern France is famous for 'natural' ingredients and wholesome dishes.

The sea offers lotte de mer, sole and John Dory. The area is also well-known for excellent scallops, crab, shrimp and oysters. Cream, butter and cheese provide the tasty if rather fattening, base for many northern French recipes.

Norman cheeses, such as Livarot and Pont-l'Evêque, have been popular since the Middle Ages. Camembert – at just 200-years-old – is a relative newcomer.

Rouen is famous for its special style of roast duckling, which has earned devotees all over the world. Tripe sausages (*andouillette*) from Nord are savoured all over France. Sadly, one would seldom guess that some of the finest vegetables in France are grown in Artois and Picardy. The splendid cauliflowers from St-Omer and carrots from St-Valery are now rarely served.

But Picardy does have quite an array of distinctive dishes. Be warned: these recipes are gorgeous but, usually, very rich! *Flamiche Picarde*, for example, is a sort of leek pudding made with eggs and cream. *Rissoles* are puff-pastry envelopes crammed with deep-fried meat and covered in a cream sauce.

There are also some unusual soups, including pumpkin, tripe, beer and frog. Cider is produced across the region. In Calvados, cider is further distilled to form the strong schnapps of the same name. It is often at least 50 percent in strength, and is drunk at almost every opportunity!

Getting there

By road

Most visitors to this part of northern France will arrive at the port of Calais. From Calais the A16 takes travellers towards Paris, the A26 heads for Reims. The A1 links Paris and Lille.

By rail

Paris Gare du Nord has high-speed TGV links with most major towns in Picardy and Nord/Pas-de-Calais. By TGV:

• Calais to Paris takes 1 hour 30 mins
• Lille to Lyon takes 3 hours, there is a Eurostar service on this route.

By air

Picardy is north of Paris. Many visitors will arrive at *Paris Charles de Gaulle Airport* (☎ 1 48 62 12 12), which is about 10 miles north-east of the capital and a 20 minute drive from southern Picardy.

For car hire at Paris Charles de Gaulle, contact:

• Avis ☎ 1 48 64 39 65
• Europcar ☎ 1 48 62 33 33

Charter flights from Manchester and Dublin land at *Beauvais Tille Airport* (☎ 3 44 45 01 05, Fax: 3 44 45 44 54), which is about two miles north of Beauvais.

Lille Lesquin Airport (☎ 3 20 49 68 68, Fax: 3 20 49 68 10) is four miles south of Lille. For car hire here, contact:

• Avis ☎ 3 20 87 59 56
• Budget ☎ 3 20 87 54 90

TOURIST INFORMATION

• **Nord/Pas-de-Calais**
  6 Place Mendes, Lille 59800
  ☎ 3 20 14 57 57
  Fax: 3 20 14 57 58
• **Picardy**
  Bld Mail Albert Ier, Amiens
  80 000
  ☎ 3 22 91 10 15
  Fax: 3 22 97 92 96

Left: Gâteau Battu is one of the sweeter delicacies of Normandy

ABBEVILLE Somme   2B

★★ Hôtel de France
19 place du Pilori, 80100 Abbeville
☎ 03 22 24 00 42 Fax 03 22 24 26 15
English spoken

Situated near a pretty park with flowers and a stream. The hotel is peaceful and relaxing but only two minutes from the pedestrian area in the heart of the city. Comfortable; suite with jacuzzi available. 15 km from the sea, between Calais and Paris.

69 bedrs, all ensuite, ♈ P DB 300-400 B 40-50 ✕ 70-98 ⊄ MC Visa Amex ▶ 3km 🖫 🖾 ⚏ ⊘ ⚲
RAC 10 %

AIRE-SUR-LA-LYS Pas de Calais   2B

★★★★ Hostellerie des Trois Mousquetaires
Château du Fort de la Redoute, 62120 Aire-sur-la-Lys
☎ 03 21 39 01 11 Fax 03 21 39 50 10
English spoken
Closed mid Dec-mid Jan

Restful, friendly 19th century château with gardens, parkland, lakes and views over the Lys valley. Good restaurant with regional specialities, dishes cooked in beer and a wide selection of hot desserts. Off the N43.

33 bedrs, all ensuite, P DB 495-595 B 55 ✕ 120-250 ⊄ MC Visa Amex ▶ 20km 🖾 ⚏

★★ Hôtel du Lion d'Or
5 av Carnot, 62120 Aire-sur-la-Lys
☎ 03 21 39 03 76 Fax 03 21 38 21 13

This hotel is situated near the junction of D157 (Boulogne) and N43 (Calais), south of Arques. The restaurant specialises in a range of traditional fish dishes.

7 bedrs, 4 ensuite, ♈ P DB 150-180 B 40-50 ✕ 60-200 (plus à la carte) ⊄ MC Visa 🖫 🖾 🖾 ⊘ ⚲

ALBERT Somme   2B

★★ Hôtel Basilique
3 rue Gambetta, 80300 Albert
☎ 03 22 75 04 71 Fax 03 22 75 10 47
English spoken
Closed 2 weeks Aug & Christmas
Comfortable family-run hotel in the centre of Albert, close to the town park. The restaurant offers a good choice of speciality dishes from regional and house cuisine.

10 bedrs, all ensuite, ♈ P DB 290-300 B 34 ✕ 78-150 (children's menu 52 FF) ⊄ MC Visa ▶ 17km 🖾 🖾 12km ⚏

★★★ Hôtel Le Royal Picardie
av du Général Leclerc, 80300 Albert
☎ 03 22 75 37 00 Fax 03 22 75 60 19
English spoken
Purpose built to offer every comfort in stunning, contemporary surroundings.There is a choice of extremely pretty, light and airy dining rooms for the gourmet with cuisine invitingly presented.

24 bedrs, all ensuite, ♈ P 80 DB 275-305 B 35 ✕ 78-220 ⊄ MC Visa Amex ▶ 15km 🖫 🖾 🖾 ⚏ ⊘ ⚲

★ Hôtel de Paix
43 rue Victor Hugo, 80300 Albert
☎ 03 22 75 01 64 Fax 03 22 75 44 17
English spoken
Closed 15 Feb-30 Feb
A warm welcome is assured at this hotel/restaurant situated in the heart of the Great War's battlefields.

14 bedrs, 8 ensuite, ♈ P 4 DB 148-248 B 28 ✕ 79-159 (plus à la carte) ⊄ MC Visa ▶ 🖾 ⚏ ⊘
RAC 5 %

AMIENS Somme   2B

★★ Hôtel de Normandie
1 bis rue Lamartine, 80000 Amiens
☎ 03 22 91 74 99 Fax 03 22 92 06 56
English spoken
A charming hotel, situated in a quiet town centre street, with car park, 3 minutes from the station and 5 minutes from the cathedral.

28 bedrs, 20 ensuite, ♈ P DB 250-275 B 30 ⊄ MC Visa Amex 🖼 🖻 ▶ 5km 🖾 ⚏ ⊘
RAC 10 %

★★★ Novotel

Route de Roye, 80440 Boves
☏ 03 22 46 22 22 Fax 03 22 53 94 75
English spoken
A quiet, modern hotel offering air-conditioned rooms, a garden area, swimming pool and family rooms. The restaurant is open until midnight. From the city centre follow Paris A1 or Longueau.

94 bedrs, all ensuite, ⊶ **P DB** 470-490 **B** 55 (plus à la carte) **CC** MC Visa Amex ⋛ ⊦ 10km 🖵 🖾 ⠿ ⌀ ⅊

ARDRES Pas de Calais   2B

★★ Hôtel La Chaumière

67 av de Rouville, 62610 Ardres
☏ 03 21 35 41 24
English spoken
This is a town centre hotel with terrace and garden, situated 17 km from Calais on N43.

12 bedrs, all ensuite, ⊶ **P** 8 **DB** 190-290 **B** 30 No restaurant **CC** MC Visa ⊠ ⊦ 10km ⅀ 🖵 🖾 ⠿ ⅊
RAC 10 % low season

ARRAS Pas de Calais   2B

★★ Hôtel Les 3 Luppars

49 Grand'Place, 62000 Arras
☏ 03 21 07 41 41 Fax 03 21 24 24 80
English spoken

A 15th century, town centre house with convenient parking and ensuite rooms. A friendly welcome is guaranteed in this town famous for its history and fine arts.

42 bedrs, all ensuite, ⊶ **P DB** 260 **B** 35 No restaurant **CC** MC Visa Amex ▦ ⊦ 2km 🖾 ⠿ ⌀
RAC 10 % on room rate

BAILLEUL Nord   2B

★★★ Belle Hôtel

19 rue de Lille, 59270 Bailleul
☏ 03 28 49 19 00 Fax 03 28 49 22 11
English spoken

With 31 individual, well decorated, rooms this typical old Flemish house was refurbished in 1991. Set in the heart of the Mont des Flandres in a quiet town centre locality it is ideal for groups. Mountain biking, horse riding organised. Calais 1 hour.

31 bedrs, all ensuite, ⊶ **P** 40 **DB** 390-540 **B** 45-55 No restaurant **CC** MC Visa Amex 🖾 ⠿ ⌀ ⅊

Hôtel Pomme d'Or

27 rue d'Ypres, 59270 Bailleul
☏ 03 28 49 11 01 Fax 03 28 49 22 11
English spoken
Closed 1-23 Aug
The restaurant can take up to 170 people and the hotel has 7 rooms of which 5 are ensuite. Groups and seminars are most welcome and regional and traditional cuisine is offered. Lille 10 minutes, Calais 1 hour.

7 bedrs, 5 ensuite, ⊶ **P DB** 120-270 **B** 32 ✕ 69-145 **CC** MC Visa Amex ⠿

BAPAUME Pas de Calais   2B

★★ Hôtel de la Paix

Avenue A. Guidet, 62450 Bapaume
☏ 03 21 07 11 03 Fax 03 21 07 43 66
A small and friendly hotel with a stunning interior and all creature comforts. Lovely dining rooms offer a good choice of classic and gastronomic cuisine.

12 bedrs, all ensuite, ⊶ **P** 15 **DB** 290-340 **B** 42 ✕ 99-240 **CC** MC Visa Amex ⊦ 15km 🖵 🖾 15km ⠿
RAC 5 %

BEAUVAIS Oise   2B

★★ Hôtel du Palais

9 rue St-Nicholas, 60000 Beauvais
☏ 03 44 45 12 58 Fax 03 44 45 66 23
English spoken
Comfortable hotel just two minutes walk from the cathedral in Beauvais.

15 bedrs, 10 ensuite, **P DB** 175-238 **B** 27-30 **CC** MC Visa Amex ⅀ ⋛ 🖾 ▦ 🖵 ⊦ ⅀ 🖾 🖵 🖾 ⠿ ⅊
RAC 5 %

BERGUES Nord   2B

★★ **Hôtel Commerce**
Rue du Mont de Piété, 59380 Bergues
☎ 03 28 68 60 37 Fax 03 28 68 70 76
English spoken

Attractive hotel next to the church and museum in this fortified town. Large banqueting hall and ample parking. Access by A16 motorway from Calais, A25 Lille-Dunkerque motorway. 10 km from Malo-les-Bains beach.

15 bedrs, 9 ensuite, ★ **P** **DB** 150-300 **B** 32 No restaurant **CC** MC Visa ▸ 4km 🚗 ✈ ⅲ ♪

BETHUNE Pas de Calais   2B

★★★★ **Hôtel Chartreuse du Val St-Esprit**
1 rue de Fouquières, 62199 Gosnay
☎ 03 21 62 80 00 Fax 03 21 62 42 50
English spoken
Built in 1792 on the site of a 14th century monastery, restored and converted into a luxurious hotel in 1986 with its own brasserie. Leave A26 at exit 6 and follow signs to 'Les Chartreuses'.

56 bedrs, all ensuite, ★ **P** **DB** 460-1,500 **B** 60 ✕ 285-365 **CC** MC Visa Amex ▸ 🚗 ✈ ⅲ ♪ ♿
RƎC 10 %

BOULOGNE-SUR-MER Pas de Calais   2B

★★★ **Hôtel Cléry Château d'Hesdin**
62360 Hesdin-l'Abbé
☎ 03 21 83 19 83 Fax 03 21 87 52 59
English spoken
Closed Jan

An elegant hotel, completely renovated and redecorated in 1996, with lovely grounds. The restaurant offers fresh, light traditional cuisine.

21 bedrs, all ensuite, **P** **DB** 330-745 **B** 55 ✕ 135-175 **CC** MC Visa Amex ▸ 7km 🚗 ✈ 7km ⅲ

CALAIS Pas de Calais   2B

★★★ **Holiday Inn Garden Court**
bd Alliés, 62100 Calais
☎ 03 21 34 69 69 Fax 03 21 97 09 15
English spoken

In the town centre overlooking the harbour and sea. 5 min from ferry terminal and Channel Tunnel. Comfortable and modern hotel offering excellent family rates. There is limited underground parking at the hotel, so check availability at reception first.

65 bedrs, all ensuite, ★ **P** **DB** 570-670 **B** 65 ✕ 95-150 **CC** MC Visa Amex 📺 ▸ 15km 🚗 ✈ ⅲ ♪ ♿
RƎC 10 %

★★ **Hôtel Climat de France**
digue Gaston Berthe, 62100 Calais Plage
☎ 03 21 34 64 64 Fax 03 21 34 35 39
English spoken
Just a few minutes from the ferry, the Channel Tunnel and the TGV Gare Frethun. The restaurant overlooks the seafront and mussels are a speciality.

44 bedrs, all ensuite, ★ **P** 80 **DB** 290-350 **B** 35 ✕ 98-138 **CC** MC Visa Amex 🚗 ⅲ ♪ ♿
RƎC 8 %

★★★ **Hôtel George V**
36 rue Royale, 62100 Calais
☎ 03 21 97 68 00 Fax 03 21 97 34 73
English spoken
A quiet and comfortable town centre hotel. Follow Calais-Nord signs from the car ferry terminal and the brown arrow marked George V.

42 bedrs, all ensuite, ★ **P** **DB** 310-380 **B** 42 ✕ 95-160 **CC** MC Visa Amex ▸ 15km ✈ ⅲ ♪ ♿
RƎC 5 %

★★★ Hôtel Meurice
5 rue Edmond Roche, 62100 Calais
☎ 03 21 34 57 03 Fax 03 21 34 14 71
English spoken
*Situated in the centre of Calais, but in a particularly
quiet residential quarter near Richelieu park. The
hotel has a long tradition of quality and service.
Suites are also available.*

39 bedrs, all ensuite, **P DB** 390-500 **B** 86 ✕ 80-300 **CC**
MC Visa Amex ⊠ ⋨ ↾ 20km ⊠ ⊠
RAC 5 %

★★ Hôtel Pacific
40 rue du Duc de Guise, 62100 Calais
☎ 03 21 34 50 24 Fax 03 21 97 58 02
English spoken
*Located 5 minutes from the ferry. A small family-run
hotel in the town centre. Very quiet with comfortable
rooms, moderate prices, private bar and a car park.
Close to restaurants.*

19 bedrs, 9 ensuite, ↾ **P** 6 **DB** 145-290 **B** 30 **CC** MC
Visa Amex
RAC 10 % on a stay of 2 nights

★★ Hôtel du Golf
Digue Gaston Berthe, 62100 Calais
☎ 03 21 96 88 99 Fax 03 21 34 75 48
English spoken
*The hotel overlooks the sea and is conveniently
situated near the ferry port, Channel Tunnel and
A26. From the town centre take the road to La Plage.
There are restaurants nearby and self-catering
facilities available for stays of a week or more.*

31 bedrs, all ensuite, **P** 50 **DB** 290-350 **B** 35 ✕ 98-138
CC MC Visa Amex ↾ 10km ⊠ ⁑ ℘ ⅏
RAC 8 %

★★★ Métropol Hôtel
45 quai du Rhin, 62100 Calais
☎ 03 21 97 54 00 Fax 03 21 96 69 70
English spoken
Closed 20 Dec-4 Jan
*A quiet hotel behind the railway station in the town
centre. Situated 5 minutes from the ferry and
Channel Tunnel.*

40 bedrs, all ensuite, ↾ **P** 13 **DB** 300-380 **B** 48 No
restaurant **CC** MC Visa Amex ↾ ⊠ ℘ ⅏
RAC 15 %

CAP GRIS-NEZ Pas de Calais   **2B**

★★ Hôtel Les Mauves
Audinghen, 62179 Cap Gris-Nez
☎ 03 21 32 96 06
English spoken
Closed Nov 15-end Mar
*A small, charming hotel with comfortable rooms, in a
leafy setting, 500 m from the sea. Located between*

*Calais and Boulogne-sur-Mer on D191; exit D940 at
Audinghen or take exit 7 from A16.*

16 bedrs, 13 ensuite, **P** 15 **DB** 220-520 **B** 41 ✕ 118-230
CC MC Visa ↾ 12km ⊠

CHANTILLY Oise   **2B**

★★★ Hôtel Relais d'Aumale
Montgrésin, 60560 Chantilly
☎ 03 44 54 61 31 Fax 03 44 54 69 15
English spoken

*Former hunting lodge set in the heart of the Chantilly
forest. Charming hotel with comfortable, well-
appointed accommodation.*

24 bedrs, all ensuite, ↾ **P** **CC** MC Visa Amex ↾ 5km
⊠ ⊠ ⁑ ⅏
RAC 5 %

COMPIEGNE Oise   **2B**

★★★ Auberge à la Bonne Idée
St-Jean-aux-Bois, 60350 Compiègne
☎ 03 44 42 84 09 Fax 03 44 42 80 45
English spoken
*In the heart of the Compiègne forest, the hotel dates
back to the 17th century. Located in the centre of St-
Jean-aux-Bois on the D85, just 10 minutes drive from
the A1.*

24 bedrs, all ensuite, ↾ **P** **DB** 380-480 **B** 55 ✕ 130 **CC**
MC Visa Amex ↾ 8km ⊠ ⁑ ⅏

Hôtel Relais Brunehaut
3 rue de l'Eglise, 60350 Chelles
☎ 03 44 42 85 05 Fax 03 44 42 83 30
Closed 1 Jan-30 Apr
*A former mill restored to working order. This hotel is
situated in a pretty garden full of flowers in the heart
of this picturesque village. Located 16 km from
Compiègne.*

6 bedrs, all ensuite, ↾ **P** 10 **DB** 270-350 **B** 40-45
✕ 140-220 **CC** Visa ↾ 15km ⊠ ⊠ ℘ ⅏

★★★ Hôtel de Harlay
3 rue Harlay, 60200 Compiègne
☎ 03 44 23 01 50 Fax 03 44 20 19 46
English spoken
The hotel occupies an exceptional riverside position in this historic town. It has easy access and is opposite the main bridge.

21 bedrs, all ensuite, ⊼ P No restaurant ℂℂ MC Visa Amex

★★★ Europe'Hôtel
13 rue Leughenaer, 59140 Dunkerque
☎ 03 28 66 29 07 Fax 03 28 63 67 87
English spoken
In the heart of Dunkerque, this hotel has comfortable rooms and a piano bar. The restaurant has an à la carte menu.

116 bedrs, all ensuite, ⊼ P 20 DB 390 B 49 (plus à la carte) ℂℂ MC Visa Amex ⊞
Rac 10 % on room rate

★★ Hôtel L' Hirondelle
46 av Faidherbe, Malo-les-Bains, 59240 Dunkerque
☎ 03 28 63 17 65 Fax 03 28 66 15 43
English spoken
A modern, comfortable Logis de France hotel in the town centre and only 2 minutes from the beach.

42 bedrs, 39 ensuite, ⊼ P 2 DB 265-315 B 28 ✗ 65-150 ℂℂ MC Visa Amex ⊠ ▸ ⊠ ⊞ ⌀ ⅋

★★ Hôtel Trianon
20 rue Colline, Malo-les-Bains, 59240 Dunkerque
☎ 03 28 63 39 15 Fax 03 28 63 34 57
A traditional hotel located just 100 m from the beach. Follow directions to the beach and then to the casino.

12 bedrs, 8 ensuite, ⊼ P 1 DB 190-245 B 28 No restaurant ℂℂ MC Visa ▸ 4km ⊿ ⊠

★★★ Welcome Hôtel
37 rue Poincaré, 59140 Dunkerque
☎ 03 28 59 20 70 Fax 03 28 21 03 49
English spoken
Set right in the centre of town, only 20 minutes walk from the sea. With a large Parisian brasserie-style restaurant with live music at weekends.

39 bedrs, all ensuite, ⊼ P DB 390 B 48 ✗ 65-238 ℂℂ MC Visa Amex ▸ 10km ⊞ ⌀ ⅋
RaC 10 %

★★★★ Château de Bellinglise
Route de Lassigny, 60157 Elincourt
☎ 03 44 96 00 33 Fax 03 44 96 03 00

English spoken

16th century manor in 640 acres of wooded parkland with own helipad. Unique, individually decorated rooms. 1 hour from Paris on the A1 (North), take exit 11 at Ressons sur Matz, go eastwards & follow Château de Bellinglise signs- 11 km on D15 to Elincourt.

35 bedrs, all ensuite, ⊼ P 70 DB 860-1,710 B 85 ✗ 220-350 ℂℂ MC Visa Amex ▦ ▸ 5km ⊠ ⊿ ⊠ ⊞ ⌀

★★ Hôtel Le Clos du Montvinage
8 rue Albert Ledent, 02580 Etréaupont
☎ 03 23 97 91 10 Fax 03 23 97 48 92
English spoken
Closed 4-23 Aug
Experience the charm and tranquillity of this hotel on the banks of the River Oise. From Vervins, go north on N2 for 7 km to Etréaupont.

19 bedrs, all ensuite, P DB 335-390 B 39-49 ✗ 90-190 ℂℂ MC Visa Amex ꝫ ▸ ⊠ ⊿ ⊠ ⊞ ⌀ ⅋
RaC Apértif offered

★★ Hôtel Champagne Picardie
41 rue A Godin, 02120 Guise
☎ 03 23 60 43 44
English spoken
Closed Feb
Former home of the aristocracy, the hotel is set in park-like gardens in the town centre. With carefully-prepared and good simple food on offer.

12 bedrs, all ensuite, P 12 DB 240-290 B 25 ✗ 60-140 ℂℂ MC Visa ⌀

Don't forget to mention the guide
When booking, please remember to tell the hotel that you chose it from the
RAC France for
the Independent Traveller

HARDELOT Pas de Calais   2B

★★★ Hôtel du Parc-Intercontinental Reso
av Francois 1er, 62152 Hardelot
☎ 03 21 33 22 11 Fax 03 21 83 29 71
English spoken
Closed 1-18 Jan
The hotel lies in the heart of the Hardelot forest. Close to the beach, it has two golf courses and an equestrian centre. Rooms are of the highest standard, most having a balcony or terrace overlooking the forest. Between Boulogne and Le Touquet.

81 bedrs, all ensuite, ⚓ P 70 DB 545-1,200 B 57 ✖ 135-180 ℂℂ MC Visa Amex ⌖ ⊞ 🖩 ▸ 1km 🔲 ▣ ▣ ‖‖ ♫ ♿

HAZEBROUCK Nord   2B

★★ Auberge de la Forêt
La Motte-au-Bois, 59190 Hazebrouck
☎ 03 28 48 08 78 Fax 03 28 40 77 76
English spoken
Closed 22 Dec-16 Jan

A comfortable hotel, renowned for its fine cuisine and wine cellar, in the heart of the Nieppe forest in French Flanders. Follow N43 from Calais to Arques. La Motte-au-Bois is south of Hazebrouck, 15 km from Arques on N42.

12 bedrs, all ensuite, ⚓ P 15 DB 240-320 ✖ 135-275 ℂℂ MC Visa ▣ ‖‖ ♫

LAON Aisne   2B

★★★★ Château de Barive
Ste-Preuve, 02350 Liesse
☎ 03 23 22 15 15 Fax 03 23 22 08 39
English spoken
Closed 22 Dec-30 Jan

The château, with gourmet restaurant offering regional specialities, stands in a quiet, secluded 500 hectare estate. From Laon take exit 13 to Sissonne, then on the Ste-Preuve road look out for a left turn to the château.

15 bedrs, all ensuite, P DB 480-880 B 65 ✖ 130-330 ℂℂ MC Visa Amex ⌖ 🖩 ▸ 18km 🔲 ▣ ▣ ‖‖

★★★ Hôtel Mercure
Golf de l'Ailette, 02860 Chamouille
☎ 03 23 24 84 85 Fax 03 23 24 89 20
English spoken

A comfortable hotel, with lovely views, in a peaceful, lakeside setting. Restaurant has lake views and excellent wines at reasonable prices. From A26 south of Laon, take Parc Nautique de l'Ailette exit and follow signs to Chamouille and Golf de l'Ailette.

58 bedrs, all ensuite, ⚓ P DB 450-550 B 52 ✖ 90-160 ℂℂ MC Visa Amex ⌖ ▣ 🔲 ▣ ▣ ‖‖ ♫ ♿

LUMBRES Pas de Calais   2B

★★★★ Hôtel Moulin de Mombreaux
62380 Lumbres
☎ 03 21 39 62 44 Fax 03 21 93 61 34
English spoken
Closed 20-29 Dec

Les Hauts de Montreuil ★★★

21/23, rue P. Ledent
62170 Montreuil-sur-Mer
Tel. 03 21 81 95 92
Fax. 03 21 86 28 83

"Write down in gold letters a moment of your existence in the book of your life"

Close to the walls, a few yards from the town centre, this old building of the walled city will help you discover the charm of bygone days.

Between seaside and countryside, on the edge of the Côte d'Opale, witness time passing by in an original 16th century setting.

The 27, tastefully decorated 3 star rooms will allow you to relax privately.

We also have a private indoor car park.

The gourmet restaurant's menu offers you gourmand pleasures with a series of dishes in which flavours, traditions and rural accents blend with originality, love and talent. Our only ambition is to please you.

We will take you with pleasure on a tour of the 16th century vaulted cellar, cheese maturing cellar, rare vintage wine, spirit and regional product shop.

A summer terrace and a romantic fountain, a wine bar and snooker are available for your pleasure.

J. M. Gaudry, 'Maitre Cuisinier de France' offers you fresh regional produce in this 18th century mill's dining room. Its 24 hotel rooms are built over the river in the middle of a flower garden. From A26, take junction 3 St Omer towards Boulogne.

24 bedrs, all ensuite, ★ P 80 DB 530-680 B 58 ✕ 220-560 CC MC Visa Amex ▶ 📧 ⊡ ⊞ 🌙 ᕷ
RAC 10 %

MONTREUIL Pas de Calais   2B

★★★ Auberge de la Grenouillère
La Madelaine-sous-Montreuil, 62170 Montreuil-sur-Mer
📞 03 21 06 07 22 Fax 03 21 86 36 36
English spoken
Closed 16 Dec-1 Feb
Picardy-style farmhouse set on the River Canche, at the foot of the ramparts of Montreuil-sur-Mer. The highly acclaimed restaurant has a rustic atmosphere and offers specialities including cuisses de grenouilles and crêpes.

4 bedrs, all ensuite, ★ P 15 DB 380-550 B 50 ✕ 150-400 CC MC Visa Amex ▶ 15km ⊡ ⊠ 🌙 ᕷ

★★ Hôtel de France
2 rue du Petit Coquempot, 62170 Montreuil-sur-Mer
📞 03 21 06 05 36 Fax 03 21 06 05 36
English spoken
Closed 15 Nov-15 Feb

An historically important, charmingly original 16th century coaching inn, renovated and decorated in individual style by owners, featuring award winning flowered courtyard and terrace bar. Located in centre of Montreuil off N1. Weekend groups welcome.

14 bedrs, 11 ensuite, P 10 DB 350-480 B 45 ✕ 96-160 CC MC Amex ▶ 10km ⊠ ⊡ ⊠ ⊞ 🌙

★★★ Les Hauts de Montreuil
21-23 rue Pierre Le Dent, 62170 Montreuil-sur-Mer
📞 03 21 81 95 92 Fax 03 21 86 28 83
English spoken
Closed 4 Jan-6 Feb
A 16th century building with summer terrace and romantic fountain, a gourmet restaurant (4 menus à la carte), regional cheese maturing, vaulted wine and spirit cellar and a shop with regional products for tasting and purchase.

27 bedrs, all ensuite, ★ P DB 430-500 B 60 ✕ 100-245 CC MC Visa Amex ▶ 12km ⊠ ⊞
RAC 10 %

NOYON Oise   2B

★★ Hôtel Le Cèdre
8 rue de l'Evêché, 60400 Noyon
☎ 03 44 44 23 24 Fax 03 44 09 53 79
English spoken

Situated close to the cathedral, in the beautiful heart of an old French city in central Picardy, this quiet, comfortable hotel offers several activities. Access via A1, junction 12 or via A26, junction 12. Indoor car park for guests.

34 bedrs, all ensuite, ★ P DB 350 B 38 ✕ 80-130 (Buffet 38 FF) ₵₵ MC Visa Amex ▸ ▣ ▣ ⅲ ∅ ₺
RAC 10 %

PERONNE Somme   2B

★★ Hostellerie de Remparts
21 rue Beaubois, 80200 Péronne
☎ 03 22 84 01 22 Fax 03 22 84 31 96
English spoken

A small attractive hotel with a range of accommodation, including suites, and a restaurant offering gourmet cuisine. East of A1/E15 and N17; take Maurepas exit 13.1.

16 bedrs, 15 ensuite, ★ P DB 220-450 B 35-40 ✕ 95-280 ₵₵ MC Visa Amex ▸ ▣ ▣ ⅲ ∅
RAC 10 %

★★ Hôtel St-Claude
42 pl Louis Daudre, 80200 Péronne
☎ 03 22 84 46 00 Fax 03 22 84 47 57
English spoken
This characterful, town centre, hotel with bar and restaurant, is close to the historic sites of the Great War. Situated at the crossroads of the Paris-Lille and Amiens-St-Quentin motorways.

15 bedrs, 14 ensuite, ★ P 20 DB 220-280 B 35-40 ✕ 65-170 ₵₵ MC Visa Amex ▣ ▣ ⅲ ∅
RAC 10 %

POIX-DE-PICARDIE Somme   2B

★★ Hôtel Le Cardinal
place de la République, 80290 Poix-de-Picardie
☎ 03 22 90 08 23 Fax 03 22 90 18 61
English spoken

A completely refurbished 16th century hotel, with a warm atmosphere and traditional cuisine, situated in the centre of the town. Ideally situated on the way to Beauvais, Paris and the south-west of France on the N29 Amiens/Rouen road.

35 bedrs, all ensuite, ★ P DB 260 B 33 ✕ 78-195 ₵₵ MC Visa Amex ▣ ⟲ ▸ ▣ ▣ ⅲ ∅

RANCOURT Somme   2B

★★ Hôtel Le Prieuré
N17, 80360 Rancourt
☎ 03 22 85 04 43 Fax 03 22 85 06 69
English spoken
A beautiful, imposing hotel, with an atmospheric restaurant, conveniently situated between Bapaume and Péronne in the heart of historic Picardy; just a few minutes drive from the Bapaume exit on A26 from Calais.

27 bedrs, all ensuite, ★ P 60 DB 290 B 35 ✕ 99-240 ₵₵ MC Visa Amex ▸ 30km ▣ ▣ ⅲ

ROYE Somme   2B

★★ Hôtel Central
36 rue Amiens, 80700 Roye
☎ 03 22 87 11 05 Fax 03 22 87 42 74
English spoken
A small hotel, with a neo-classical restaurant specialising in regional cuisine and seafood, situated in the town centre. Access: Take Roye exit from junction 12 of A1(Paris-Lille).

8 bedrs, all ensuite, ♒ P DB 260-320 B 30 ✕ 88-210
《 MC Visa Amex ⊞

★★ Hôtel des Lions
Route de Rosières, 80700 Roye
☎ 03 22 79 71 00 Fax 03 22 79 71 01
English spoken

A quiet, peaceful, countryside hotel with a restaurant offering traditional cuisine and regional specialities. Leave A1 at exit 12 and hotel at Roye is about 300 m further along.

43 bedrs, all ensuite, ♒ P 50 DB 270-320 B 40 ✕ 95-150 《 MC Visa Amex ⊞ ♪ ♿
RAC 10 %

ST-GOBAIN Aisne   2B

★★ Hôtel Les Roses de Picardie
11 rue Clémenceau, 02410 St-Gobain
☎ 03 23 52 88 74
English spoken
St Gobain is a small town of 2300 inhabitants situated in the heart of a magnificent 6000 hectare forest. The town and the forest are a favourite place for the tourists in Aisne. Take N44 south turn on to D13 for St-Gobain. Private car park for guests.

12 bedrs, 8 ensuite, ♒ P DB 180-230 B 25 《 MC Visa Amex ⊞ ♪ ♿
RAC 10 %

ST-OMER Pas de Calais   2B

★★★★ Hostellerie St-Hubert
1 rue du Moulin, 62570 Hallines
☎ 03 21 39 77 77 Fax 03 21 93 00 86
English spoken

Attractive château, situated in a green park and renovated at the end of the 19th century in 'La Belle Epoque' style. Hallines is ten minutes drive south-west of St-Omer.

9 bedrs, 8 ensuite, P 30 DB 400-800 B 50 ✕ 180-250
《 MC Visa ▶ 8km ▣ ▣ ⊞

ST-POL-SUR-TERNOISE Pas de Calais   2B

★★ Hôtel Le Lion d'Or
74 rue d'Hesdin, 62130 St-Pol-sur-Ternoise
☎ 03 21 03 10 44 Fax 03 21 41 47 87
English spoken

Comfortable hotel situated in the heart of Ternois, between Montreuil and Arras. Restaurant with traditional cuisine and candlelight dinners. 5 km from motor-race circuit. 20 km from the site of the Battle of Agincourt.

16 bedrs, all ensuite, ♒ P 10 DB 240-300 B 35 ✕ 88-200 《 MC Visa ▣ ▣ ⊞ ♪
RAC 10 %

ST-QUENTIN Aisne   2B

★★ Hôtel Ibis
14 place de la Basilique, 02100 St-Quentin
☎ 03 23 67 40 40 Fax 03 23 62 69 36
English spoken
On a pretty square opposite the basilica and close to the pedestrian streets. Air- conditioned restaurant Le Diamand offers refined traditional cuisine.

49 bedrs, all ensuite, ♒ P DB 320-380 B 36 ✕ 79-150
《 MC Visa Amex ▶ 5km ▣ ⊞ ♪ ♿
RAC 5 %

★★★ Hôtel Mémorial
8 rue Comédie, 02100 St-Quentin
☏ 03 23 67 90 09 Fax 03 23 62 34 96
English spoken

*Highly recommended. Elegant townhouse offering a
range of beautifully presented accommodation
ranging from large bedrooms to self-contained suites
and apartments. In the town centre close to the library.*

9 bedrs, 7 ensuite, ⊬ P 10 DB 280-650 B 45-60 CC MC
Visa Amex ▸ 3km ▣ ⠿ ⌀

*A small hotel in the town centre not far from the
town hall. St-Quentin is 35 km north of Loan on the
A26 Calais to Reims motorway.*

18 bedrs, all ensuite, ⊬ P 15 DB 280-400 B 40-60 No
restaurant CC MC Visa Amex ▣ ⌀ ♿
RAC 10 %

★★★ Hôtel des Canonniers
15 rue des Canonniers, 02100 St-Quentin
☏ 03 23 62 87 87 Fax 03 23 62 87 86
English spoken
Closed 2nd/3rd week in Aug

SECLIN Nord   2B

★★★ Auberge du Forgeron
17 rue Roger Bouvry, 59113 Seclin
☏ 03 20 90 09 52 Fax 03 20 32 70 87
English spoken
Closed 3-21 Aug
*A typical inn, with one of the best cellars in northern
France. Restaurant specialises in regional cuisine
prepared by a member of the 'Académie Culinaire'.
10 km from Lille, leave A1 at junction 19. Close to
A25 and A27.*

19 bedrs, 16 ensuite, P B 40 ✕ 120-300 CC MC Visa
Amex ▸ 8km ▣ ▣ ⠿ ♿

SENLIS Oise   2B

★★ Hôtel Ibis
60300 Senlis
☎ 03 44 53 70 50 Fax 03 44 53 51 93
English spoken

*From A1 motorway, take exit 8 towards the town
centre. 35 km from Paris and 5 minutes from the
Astérix theme park.*

92 bedrs, all ensuite, 🛌 P 80 DB 295-305 B 35 ✕ 55-95
CC MC Visa Amex ⏸ 🖼 ⁂ ♬ ⓑ

LE TOUQUET Pas de Calais   2B

★★★★ Grand Hotel Park Plaza
4 bd de la Canche, 62520 Le Touquet-Paris-Plage
☎ 03 21 06 88 88 Fax 03 21 06 87 87
English spoken
*Quietly situated on the River Canche, this luxury
hotel, with tastefully furnished rooms or suites, offers
excellent conference and business facilities and is
only a short walk from the town centre and beaches.
35 km south of Boulogne off N940.*

135 bedrs, all ensuite, 🛌 P 100 DB 550-1,450 B 70-90
✕ 90-160 CC MC Visa Amex ⏸ 🔲 ⏸ 1km 🔲 1km 🖼
0.50km ⁂ ♬ ⓑ
RAC 10 %

★★★ Hôtel Bristol
17 rue Jean Monnet, 62520 Le Touquet-Paris-Plage
☎ 03 21 05 49 95 Fax 03 21 05 90 93
English spoken
Closed 6-26 Jan
*A charming, fully renovated hotel with a colourful
history and comfortable 3 star accommodation. All
the rooms have private bathrooms and direct dial
telephones; English and French TV also available.
Located near the beach and the open-air market.*

46 bedrs, all ensuite, 🛌 P DB 450-630 B 45-70 No
restaurant CC MC Visa Amex ⏸ 🖼 ⁂ ♬ ⓑ

★★★★ Hôtel Holiday Inn Resort
av Maréchal Foch, 62520 Le Touquet-Paris-Plage
☎ 03 21 06 85 85 Fax 03 21 06 85 00
English spoken
*A bright, modern 4 star hotel with attractive
swimming pool and tennis court, situated at the edge*

*of the forest but close to the centre of Le Touquet.
From Boulogne road D940 take Le Touquet-N39-exit .*

88 bedrs, all ensuite, 🛌 P 55 DB 530-630 B 65 ✕ 145
CC MC Visa Amex 🔲 🖼 ⏸ 🔲 🖼 ⁂ ♬ ⓑ

★★ Hôtel Logis de France Les Cèdres
62176 Camiers
☎ 03 21 84 94 54 Fax 03 21 09 23 29
English spoken
Closed 16 Dec-15 Jan
*The hotel is situated close to the Ste-Cécile beach at
Hardelot: 8 km from Le Touquet off the D940
Boulogne to Le Touquet road.*

29 bedrs, 23 ensuite, 🛌 P 15 DB 235-295 B 35 ✕ 80-
138 CC MC Visa Amex ⏸ 6km 🖼 ⁂ ♬ ⓑ

★★★ Hôtel Manoir
62520 Le Touquet-Paris-Plage
☎ 03 21 06 28 28 Fax 03 21 06 28 29
English spoken
Closed 4 Jan-2 Feb

*Overlooking its own golf course, Le Manoir Hôtel
offers the ideal holiday venue for those seeking luxury
and seclusion. Coming from Etaples, turn left at the
third set of traffic lights in Le Touquet. Hotel is on the
right.*

42 bedrs, all ensuite, 🛌 P 80 DB 790-1,110 B included
✕ 150-195 CC MC Visa Amex ⏸ 🔲 🔲 🖼 ⁂

★★★★ Westminster Hôtel
5 av du Verger, 62520 Le Touquet
☎ 03 21 05 48 48 Fax 03 21 05 45 45
English spoken
Closed 1 Jan-15 Feb

*A hotel with a good reputation and a great tradition;
situated between town and forest, 500 m from the
beach and 150 m from the Convention Centre.
Award winning restaurant, large entrance hall, cosy
lounges and American bar.*

115 bedrs, all ensuite, 🛌 P 50 DB 680-1,150 B 75
✕ 115-360 CC MC Visa Amex 🔲 🔲 ⏸ 1km 🖼 ⁂ ♬ ⓑ

VALENCIENNES Nord — 2B

★★★ Grand Hôtel
8 place de la Gare, 59300 Valenciennes
☎ 03 27 46 32 01 Fax 03 27 29 65 57
English spoken

An extraordinary former 16th century posthouse restored to perfection and now graded as an historic monument. Open fires, brick floors and large, heavily beamed and luxuriously appointed rooms. Centrally situated in old town with private courtyard behind.

98 bedrs, all ensuite, ♻ P DB 430-590 B 52 ✕ 100-250 ℂℂ MC Visa Amex ▣ ▸ 15km ▣ ⅲ ✈
RAC 8 %

VERVINS Aisne — 3A

★★★ Hôtel Tour du Roy
45 rue du Général Leclerc, 02140 Vervins
☎ 03 23 98 00 11 Fax 03 23 98 00 72
English spoken

A splendid manor house steeped in history and overlooking the old city of Vervins. Hand painted bathrooms and stained-glass windows. Rooms overlook terraces, park or landscaped square. On the N2 in the centre of Vervins. A glass of champagne on arrival.

18 bedrs, all ensuite, ♻ P 25 DB 400-800 B 70 ✕ 180-350 ℂℂ MC Visa Amex ▸ 6km ▣ ▣ ▣ ⅲ ✈ ♿
RAC 10 %

VILLERS-COTTERETS Aisne — 2B

★★★ Hôtel Le Régent
26 rue du Général Mangin, 02600 Villers-Cotterêts
☎ 03 23 96 01 46 Fax 03 23 96 37 57
English spoken

A charming, centrally located, 18th century posthouse offering elegant, period atmosphere and all modern comforts.

17 bedrs, all ensuite, ♻ P 20 DB 258-390 B 31-45 No restaurant ℂℂ MC Visa Amex ▸ ▣ ⅲ ✈ ♿

WIMEREUX Pas de Calais — 2B

★★ Hôtel Centre
78 rue Carnot, 62930 Wimereux
☎ 03 21 32 41 08 Fax 03 21 33 82 48
English spoken
Closed 15 Dec-15 Jan
From Boulogne-sur-Mer, follow the coast road 5 km north to Wimereux. The hotel is in the main street. Restaurant has 1920s décor and specialises in seafood.

25 bedrs, all ensuite, ♻ P 15 DB 235-315 B 35 ✕ 99.50-170 ℂℂ MC Visa ▸ 2km ▣ ⅲ ✈
RAC 5 % on Fri & Sat

★★ Hôtel Paul et Virginie
19 rue Général de Gaulle, 62930 Wimereux
☎ 03 21 32 42 12 Fax 03 21 87 65 85
English spoken
Closed 8 Dec-21 Jan
A quiet hotel, with restaurant specialising in seafood, just north of Boulogne-sur-Mer. Wimereux is on the N940 and the hotel is signposted in the town.

15 bedrs, 11 ensuite, P DB 200-290 B 39 ✕ 100-174 ℂℂ MC Visa ▸ 1km ▣

WISSANT Pas de Calais — 2B

★★ Hôtel Bellevue
10 rue Paul Crampbell, 62179 Wissant
☎ 03 21 35 91 07 Fax 02 31 85 60 87
English spoken
Closed 15 Nov-15 Mar
A fully renovated hotel, with a safe park for children, situated 200 m from the village centre. Large private parking area.

30 bedrs, all ensuite, P 40 DB 350-650 B 50 ✕ 100-200 ℂℂ MC Visa Amex ▸ 13km ▣ ▣ ⅲ

★ Hôtel de Normandy
2 place de Verdun, 62179 Wissant
☎ 03 21 35 90 11 Fax 03 21 82 19 08
English spoken
Closed Dec
This hotel and restaurant, in the heart of the last village on the coast where fish is still caught in the traditional way, offers gourmet cuisine made with local produce.

27 bedrs, 18 ensuite, P DB 530-680 ✕ 90-180 ℂℂ Visa ▸ 13km ▣ ▣

Loire

COMITÉ RÉGIONAL
DU TOURISME

Région des Pays de la Loire

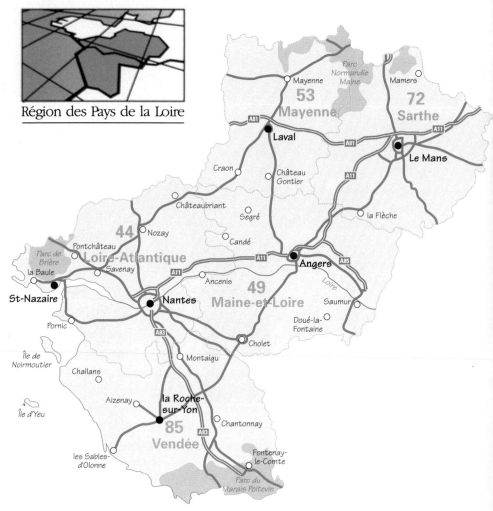

Pays-de-la-Loire

Loire Valley

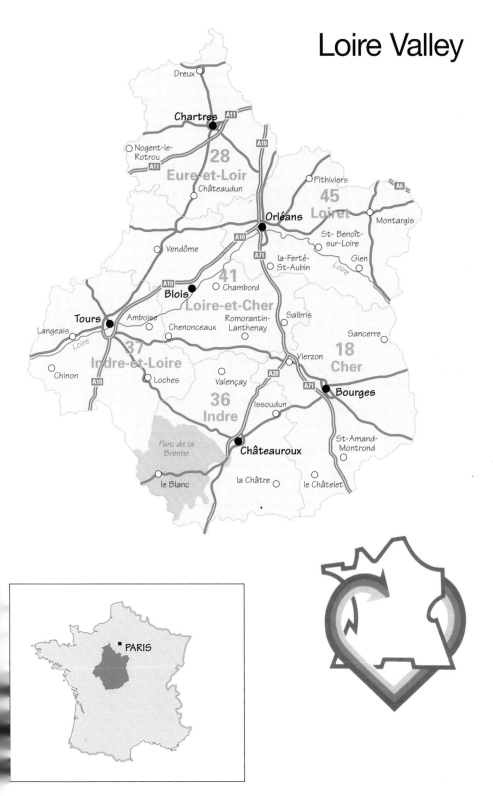

Dreux

Chartres A11

Nogent-le-
Rotrou
A11

A10

28
Eure-et-Loir

Châteaudun

Pithiviers

A6

45
Loiret

Orléans

Montargis

St-Benoît-
sur-Loire

Vendôme

A10

A71

la-Ferté-
St-Aubin

Gien

Loire

41
Chambord

Blois

Loire-et-Cher

Amboise

Salbris

Tours

Langeais

Loire

Chenonceaux

Romorantin-
Lanthenay

Sancerre

37
Indre-et-Loire

Vierzon

18
Cher

Chinon

A10

Loches

Valençay

A20

A71

Bourges

36
Indre

Issoudun

St-Amand-
Montrond

Parc de la
Brenne

Châteauroux

le Blanc

la Châtre

le Châtelet

PARIS

Stretching from the Ile de France to the Atlantic Ocean, the Loire Valley and Western Loire form an enormous splash of châteaux, vineyards and rolling hills which dominates the west of central France.

Despite shaping and naming the region, the River Loire itself plays a surprisingly small role in the day-to-day life of the area.

The Loire is the longest river in France, but it is not used for shipping or boating. It has carved a beautiful route through the region, and its banks are well-worth exploring.

Equally striking is the enormous number of châteaux scattered across the Loire. There are almost too many. Don't try to see every one or you will suffer a severe overdose.

Orléans is just near enough to Paris for frenzied commuters to dart there everyday to work. However, such a close relationship with the capital does have its downside: Orléans is rather eclipsed by Paris.

Ignore what snobbish Parisians might tell you, and visit Orléans. This is, after all, the historic city which Joan of Arc saved from the English in May 1429.

Naturally, Joan of Arc is hero-worshipped in Orléans – particularly during May when she is honoured with her own festival.

A local look-a-like is dressed in armour and triumphantly paraded through the streets.

Visit the Maison de Jeanne d'Arc, where her life is documented in an entertaining way.

Another hive of Joan of Arc memorabilia can be found in the lovely Cathédral Ste-Croix. Stained-glass windows in the nave tell the story of her life in the form of a sort of early cartoon strip.

For a complete break from sieges and chain-mail, head for the city's surprisingly impressive Musée des Beaux-Arts.

A short drive south from Orléans takes the traveller to the Abbey of Saint-Benoît-sur-Loire and, slightly further on, the Château of Sully-sur-Loire. Both make interesting stop-off points. The abbey was founded in 651 and it became a significant centre of worship in Charlemagne's time.

Visit on a Sunday to catch a traditional Gregorian service.

More imposing is the magnificent Château of Sully-sur-Loire which occupies an island in the river. The castle has a certain solidity and shine which makes it difficult to believe that it dates back to the fourteenth century. It was designed by Charles V's architect and, in the eighteenth century, was home to Voltaire during his exile.

Impressive though the Château of Sully-sur-Loire undoubtedly is, the finest and largest castle in the Loire is to the west at Chambord. The Disney-like Château de Chambord can fairly be described as breathtaking. Its roof has been likened to a city skyline on a single building. It is said to

Page 83: Orléans Cathedral of the Holy Cross
Above: The Loire and beyond it Orléans

Above: Detail of the entrance at the cathedral at Chartres

be based on a design by Leonardo da Vinci, although it displays many obviously French features. It is now a UNESCO World Heritage Site. If you see just one château in the Loire, see this one.

For an architectural feat of a more saintly nature, head north to **Chartres**. Here you will find another UNESCO World Heritage Site – this one motivated by religion rather than a young king's terrific ego. The cathedral at Chartres is a stunning testament to the inventiveness of medieval architecture. Completed in 1260, it is as immense as it is geometrically confusing.

Sitting south of Orléans on the A71, motorists often zip past Bourges on their way from the land of châteaux to the Massif Central.

Bourges is not a particularly exciting town, but it is worth a visit thanks to its exceptional cathedral which is, arguably, as impressive as that of Chartres. The Cathédral Saint-Etienne is a masterpiece of Gothic logic. Rather than allowing the mandatory flying buttresses to intrude on the interior, the simple design leaves a clear, vast and singularly impressive central space which never fails to hush its visitors.

Bourges itself is a quietly attractive town. Julius Caesar is said to have considered it the most beautiful in Gaul. Explore the old town area which is nestled to the north of the cathedral. References to royal financier Jacques Coeur are plastered all over the town. Coeur built a splendid palace for himself in Bourges – on the proceeds of a vast business empire – and made himself something of a local hero in the process. Like Bourges, **Tours** is often treated as a convenient base from which to explore nearby châteaux and vineyards, but is itself seldom explored by travellers. The town's Musée du Compagnonnage is a good place to go to get a feel for why there are so many châteaux in the Loire region. Next door, the Musée des Vins tackles the more important question of how wine has been produced through the ages.

Tours' cathedral, Saint-Gatien, is one of the most underrated in France. It crams just about every whim of the Gothic period into its intricate facade. The effect is dazzling, especially at night when the cathedral is lit to great effect.

If you do intend to use Tours as a base for châteaux-spotting, your first stop ought to be the château at **Chinon**. Although this is not the most exciting castle in the Loire, it does have five-star historic pedigree. It was here that a young Joan of Arc met Charles VII. Charles was hiding from Henry V of England. The English had taken Paris and with it the French throne. Joan of Arc somehow persuaded Charles to let her have an army. The rest is history.

Travelling west from Tours will take you to the livelier town of **Angers**. Don't be put off by the town's nickname, 'Black Angers', which has no sinister connection, but merely refers to the colour of the local stone.

This is a town in which to take it easy. You won't have to walk far to find great restaurants, quiet cafés and attractive streets. There are, though, two sights in Angers that really should not be missed. Look for the Tapestry of the Apocalypse in the Château d'Angers. Dating back to the 1370s, this must have been the medieval equivalent of a video-nasty. It depicts scenes from the Book of Revelations and is clearly designed to leave its viewers feeling distinctly uneasy. However, there is an antidote. In the Hôpital St-Jean hangs a more recent tapestry, Le Chant du Monde, which is Jean Lurçat's answer to the Tapestry of the Apocalypse. Lurçat died in 1966, before he could finish his magnum opus, but his intentions are clear. After some initial concerns about nuclear war, the tapestry appears to develop an increasingly happy tone, eventually becoming an uninhibited celebration of life. You are liable to come away singing.

Another enjoyable town is **Nantes**, although it does seem to be suffering from an acute identity crisis.

It is in the Loire region, but feels as though it ought to be in Brittany – and with good reason. Its Château des Ducs, or the Château of Duchesse Anne, was the birthplace of one of the last rulers of an independent Brittany. Jules Verne was also born in Nantes and there is a museum dedicated to him on rue de l'Hermitage.

Below: The Château de Chenonceau is an elegant Renaissance creation which spans the River Cher and is surrounded by its own delightful gardens. Chenonceau is visibly less draughty and oppressive than some of the other châteaux in the area. This is perhaps why it became the favoured residence of the ladies of the Royal Court.

Getting there – Pays de Loire

By road
The A11 is the fast road from Paris to Nantes via Le Mans and Angers. Paris is also linked to Tours by the A10. Other major arteries are the A81 between Le Mans and Laval and the A83 between Nantes and Les-Sables d'Olonne.

By rail
Pays de Loire is well-served by high-speed TGV trains from Paris Gare Montparnasse:
* Paris to Le Mans takes 1 hour
* Paris to Nantes takes 2 hours
* Paris to Angers takes 1 hour 30 mins
* Lyon to Le Mans takes 3 hours

By air
Nantes Atlantique International Airport (☎ 2 40 84 80 00, Fax: 2 43 84 99 11) is 6 miles south-west of Nantes.
For car hire contact:
* Ada ☎ 2 40 84 83 48
* Avis ☎ 2 40 84 81 01
* Budget ☎ 2 40 84 81 07

Getting there – Loire Valley

By road
The A10 motorway links Paris and Bordeaux via Tours and Orléans. The A71 links Orléans to Clermont-Ferrand. The A20 links Vierzon to Limoges.

By rail
By TGV:
* Tours to Paris Gare Montparnasse takes 1 hour 20 mins
* Tours to Lille takes 2 hours 30 mins
* Tours to Lyon takes 3 hours 15 mins
* Chatres to Paris Gare Montparnasse takes 1 hour 10 mins
* Blois to Paris Gare Austerlitz takes 1 hour 30 mins
* Bouges to Paris Gare Austerlitz takes 2 hours 5 mins
* Orléans to Paris Gare Austerlitz takes 1 hour

By air
Tours-Saint-Symphorien Airport (☎ 2 47 49 37 00, Fax: 2 47 42 59 45) is about 4 miles north-east of Tours. Get to Tours by taxi (☎ 2 47 20 30 40 or 2 47 49 29 29).

TOURIST INFORMATION

* **Loire Valley Tourist Office**
  5 rue St-Pierre Lantin, Orléans
  ☎ 2 38 70 32 74
  Fax: 2 38 70 33 80
* **Western Loire Tourist Information**
  2 rue de la Loire, BP 2171-44204, Nantes
  ☎ 2-40 48 24 20 Fax: 2-40 08 07

AMBOISE Indre et Loire 2C

★★ Hôtel La Brèche
26 rue J Ferry, 37400 Amboise
☎ 02 47 57 00 79 Fax 02 47 57 65 49
English spoken
Closed 20 Dec-mid Jan
A charming, gourmet stop in a relaxing setting. Delicate and thoughtful cuisine satisfying all your desires. Food served in garden in season. Specialities include saumon fumé de la maison and foie gras maison.

13 bedrs, 10 ensuite, **P** 8 **DB** 160-310 **B** 35 ✕ 75-170 ℂℂ MC Visa ➤ 10km ⊠ ⊞ ⋒

ANGERS Maine et Loire 2C

★★★★ Château des Briottières
49330 Champigné
☎ 02 41 42 00 02 Fax 02 41 42 01 55
English spoken

The château, with restaurant offering traditional French cuisine, is situated between Angers and Sablé, Durtal and Le Lion d'Angers. From Paris take A11 towards Nantes, take exit 11 for Durtal, drive for 27 km to Champigné: château is 4 km on.

9 bedrs, all ensuite, ✝ **P DB** 750-1,110 **B** 50 ✕ 300 (inc wine and coffee) ℂℂ MC Visa ⤜ ➤ 4km ▣ ⊠ ⊞

★★ Hôtel Climat de France
rue du Château-d'Orgemont, 49100 Angers
☎ 02 41 66 30 45 Fax 02 41 66 76 08
English spoken
The hotel has a cordial atmosphere and is just 5 minutes from the city centre, in the direction of Cholet and Poitiers. The restaurant offers good wines and regional cuisine; specialities include sandre au beurre blanc and rillauds tièdes.

42 bedrs, all ensuite, ✝ **P** 50 **DB** 280 **B** 35 ✕ 62-130 ℂℂ MC Visa Amex ➤ 5km ⊠ ⊞ ⋒ ⅁

★★ Hôtel Saint Julian
9 place Ralliement, 49100 Angers
☎ 02 41 88 41 62 Fax 02 41 20 95 19
English spoken
Family hotel situated in the main square opposite the theatre and close to the château, cathedral and museums.

34 bedrs, 33 ensuite, ✝ **P DB** 225-295 **B** 32 No restaurant ℂℂ MC Visa Amex ➤ 5km ⊠ ⋒ RℬC **10 %**

★★ Hôtel du Mail
8 rue des Ursules, 49100 Angers
☎ 02 41 25 05 25 Fax 02 41 86 91 20
English spoken

We offer absolute calm in a 17th century building situated in the heart of the city, with an indoor private car park for motorbikes and bicycles. Easy access from A11(exit Angers-Centre) and TGV.

27 bedrs, 25 ensuite, ✝ **P** 20 **DB** 185-320 **B** 35-39 No restaurant ℂℂ MC Visa Amex ➤ 5km ⊠ 5km

★★★ Quality Hôtel de France
8 place de la Gare, 49100 Angers
☎ 02 41 88 49 42 Fax 02 41 86 76 70
English spoken
On the A11 motorway, take the castle exit, drive on, take the first right and carry on to the railway station, the hotel faces it. The Bouyer family will help you appreciate the sweetness of life in this region.

56 bedrs, 55 ensuite, **P** 20 **DB** 380-550 **B** 50 ✕ 65-220 ℂℂ MC Visa Amex ➤ 5km ▣ ⊠ ⊞ ⋒ ⅁ RℬC **10 %**

ARGENTON-SUR-CREUSE Indre 4B

Château de Bouesse
36200 36200 Bouesse
☎ 02 54 25 12 20 Fax 02 54 25 12 30
English spoken
Closed mid Nov-mid Mar

A medieval château three hours south of Paris on the N20 and a few minutes east of Argenton-sur-Creuse on the D927. Formerly the fortress home of one of Joan of Arc's top generals, the castle is being painstakingly restored by an English couple.

11 bedrs, all ensuite, **P DB** 350-480 **B** 55 ✕ 95-210 **CC** MC Visa Amex ▸ 25km 🖵 ⚡ ⛟

★★ Hôtel Le Cheval Noir

27 rue Auclert-Descottes, 36200 Argenton-sur-Creuse
📞 02 54 24 00 06 **Fax** 02 54 24 11 22
English spoken
A town centre hotel with a family atmosphere, 25 km south on the N20 from Châteauroux. Turn right in town, heading towards Gargilesse Le Pèchereau.

20 bedrs, all ensuite, ☂ **P DB** 230-320 **B** 35 ✕ 90-160 (plus à la carte) **CC** MC Visa ⚡ ⛟ ⌁ ♿

★★ Manoir de Boisvillers

11 rue Moulin de Bord, 36200 Argenton-sur-Creuse
📞 02 54 24 13 88 **Fax** 02 54 24 27 83
English spoken
Closed 1 Dec-5 Jan
In the heart of Argenton, this is an 18th century manor situated on the river, in an area steeped in Roman history. Very quiet and charming with fully equipped, personalised rooms.

14 bedrs, 13 ensuite, ☂ **P** 14 **DB** 240-380 **B** 45 No restaurant **CC** MC Visa Amex ⌁ ▸ 20km 🖵 ⚡
RƎC 10 %

★★★★ Castel Marie-Louise

1 av Andrieu, BP 409, 44504 La Baule
📞 02 40 11 48 38 **Fax** 02 40 11 48 35
English spoken
Closed 4 Jan-13 Feb

A charming Belle-Epoque manor set in attractive shaded grounds overlooking the bay. Following the esplanade, the hotel is just after the Grand Casino. The restaurant will satisfy the most demanding palates with its gourmet and traditional haute-cuisine.

31 bedrs, all ensuite, ☂ **P DB** 810-1,900 **B** 100 ✕ 220-480 **CC** MC Visa Amex ⌁ ⚡ ⚙ ▸ ⚡ ⚡ ⛟ ♿

★★★ Hôtel Bellevue Plage

27 bd Océan, 44500 La Baule
📞 02 40 60 28 55 **Fax** 02 40 60 10 18
English spoken
Closed mid Nov-mid Feb
Ideally situated facing the sea, in the centre of La Baule bay, the hotel offers a warm welcome and good facilities including a private car park.

35 bedrs, all ensuite, ☂ **P DB** 500-830 **B** 55 ✕ 125-290 **CC** MC Visa Amex ⚡ ⚙ ▸ ⚡ ⛟
RƎC 10 % except Jul & Aug

★★★ Hôtel La Concorde

1 avenue de la Concorde, 44500 La Baule
📞 02 40 60 23 09 **Fax** 02 40 42 72 14
English spoken
A pleasant, family-run hotel, facing the sea and the beach.

47 bedrs, all ensuite, **P** 75 **DB** 350-560 **B** 46 No restaurant **CC** MC Visa Amex ⚡

Hôtel Le Clémenceau

42 avenue Georges Clemenceau, 44500 La Baule
📞 02 40 60 21 33 **Fax** 02 40 42 72 46
English spoken
A traditional hotel, near the railway station and a few minutes walk from the beach. Located 70 km from Nantes.

16 bedrs, all ensuite, ☂ **P DB** 260-390 **B** 35 ✕ 75-135 **CC** MC Visa ⌁ ▸ ⚡ ⌁
RƎC 5 %

★★ Hôtel Villa Flornoy

7 av Flornoy, 44380 Pornichet
📞 02 40 11 60 00 **Fax** 02 40 61 86 47
Closed 31 Oct-1 Mar
In 'Grand Villa' style, built at the turn of the century and standing in a quiet avenue close to the beach and the markets. This handsome building has a flower garden and sun terrace. From La Baule drive east along the coast road for 2 km to Pornichet.

21 bedrs, all ensuite, **P DB** 350-510 **B** 40 ✕ 105-135 **CC** MC Visa
RƎC 10 %

★★ Hôtel Welcome

7 av des Impairs, 44504 La Baule
📞 02 40 60 30 25 **Fax** 02 40 24 37 30
English spoken
Closed 5 Nov-25 Mar
Well appointed hotel with pleasant atmosphere. Situated 30 m from the sea, between the casino and shopping centre.

18 bedrs, all ensuite, ☂ **P DB** 340-450 **B** 38 **CC** MC Visa Amex ▸ 7km 🖵 ⚡
RƎC 20 % except Jul-Aug

BEAUGENCY Loiret   2D

★★★ Hôtel L'Abbaye
2 quai de l'Abbaye, 45190 Beaugency
☎ 02 38 44 67 35 Fax 02 38 44 87 92
English spoken
A most attractive 17th century abbey, overlooking the River Loire and ideally located for visiting the Loire châteaux. The gourmet restaurant has dining rooms with open fires and flagstone floors.

17 bedrs, all ensuite, ♭ P 14 DB 520-580 B 45 ✕ 190
℃ MC Visa Amex ▶ 6km 🖥 🖾 ⌀

★★★★ Hôtel La Tonnellerie
12 rue des Eaux-Bleues, Tavers, 45190 Beaugency
☎ 02 38 44 68 15 Fax 02 38 44 10 01
English spoken
Closed Jan-Feb

At the entrance of Sologne, in the heart of the châteaux region, lies the discreet charm of an old manor house. Situated 3 km from Beaugency towards Blois. The restaurant offers nouvelle and classic cuisine served in the 'winter garden' or on the terrace.

20 bedrs, all ensuite, ♭ P DB 450-1,240 B 65 ✕ 95-
260 ℃ MC Visa Amex ⦚ ▶ 9km 🖾 🖥 🖾 ⌗
RAC 10 %

BEAUMONT-SUR-SARTHE Sarthe   2C

★★ Hôtel du Chemin de Fer
place de la Gare, 72170 Beaumont-sur-Sarthe
☎ 02 43 97 00 05 Fax 02 43 33 52 17
English spoken
Closed winter/All Saints day

Traditionally furnished Logis de France hotel with attractive, shady garden. On N138, between Alençon and Le Mans. At the traffic lights, follow the D26 on to the small railway station. The hotel is close to the level crossing.

15 bedrs, 12 ensuite, ♭ P 50 DB 215-388 B 31.50
✕ 89-250 ℃ MC Visa Amex ▶ 🖾 🖾 ⌗ ⌀

LE BLANC Indre   4B

★★ Hôtel L'Ile d'Avant
Route de Châteauroux, 36300 Le Blanc
☎ 02 54 37 01 56 Fax 02 54 37 38 06
English spoken
Closed 20 Dec-15 Jan
A relaxing stop-over on the holiday road between Poitiers and Châteauroux and Blois and the Périgord.

15 bedrs, all ensuite, ♭ P 50 DB 210-285 B 35 ✕ 62-
140 ℃ MC Visa ▶ 🖾 ⌗ ⌀ ⌔

BLOIS Loir et Cher   2D

★★ Hôtel La Caillère
36 route des Montils, 41120 Candé-sur-Beuvron
☎ 02 54 44 03 08 Fax 02 54 44 00 95
English spoken
Closed 2 Jan-28 Feb

A hotel, set in the heart of châteaux country, where all rooms have a view of the large garden. From Blois, take the south bank of the River Loire towards Amboise for 19 km.

14 bedrs, all ensuite, ♭ P 20 DB 300-360 B 45 ✕ 98-
278 ℃ MC Visa Amex ▶ 8km 🖾 ⌗ ⌀ ⌔
RAC 5 %

★★ Hôtel Le Monarque
61 rue Porte Chartraine, 41000 Blois
☎ 02 54 78 02 35 Fax 02 54 74 82 76
English spoken
A charming hotel in the heart of Blois, capital city of the Loire châteaux region, with a simple and refined atmosphere to calmly enjoy.

25 bedrs, 22 ensuite, P 6 DB 195-350 B 30 ✕ 70-160
(plus à la carte) ℃ MC Visa ▶ 15km 🖾 ⌀
RAC

BONNEVAL Eure et Loire   2D

★★★ Hostellerie de Bois Guibert
Guibert, 28800 Bonneval
☎ 02 37 47 22 33 Fax 02 37 47 50 69
English spoken

A 17th century country manor house surrounded by wooded parkland with a modern comforts. On N10, just outside Bonneval.

14 bedrs, all ensuite, ♀ P 50 DB 250-550 B 50 ✗ 145-325 ℂ MC Visa Amex ► ✦ ⅲ ♫

BOURGES Cher   2D

★★★★ Château de la Verrerie
18700 Aubigny s/Nere
☎ 02 48 81 51 60 Fax 02 48 58 21 25
English spoken
Closed 15 Dec-15 Jan

Comfort and tranquillity in this elegant, renaissance château which overlooks a lake in the middle of a forest. Set 32 km from Gien, going south on D940 to Aubigny-sur-Nère then D89. Follow signs to the château.

12 bedrs, all ensuite, ♀ P 250 DB 880-1,100 B 60-80 ✗ 98-380 ℂ MC Visa Amex ► ⊠ ⬛ ✦ ⅲ
RƎC 10 %

★★★ Hôtel d'Angleterre
1 place des Quatre Piliers, 18000 Bourges
☎ 02 48 24 68 51 Fax 02 48 65 21 41
English spoken

Quiet and comfortable, the hotel has been fully renovated and is not far from the cathedral in the old town.

31 bedrs, all ensuite, ♀ P 10 DB 430 B 42 ✗ 90-130 ℂ MC Visa Amex ► 2km ✦ ⅲ ♫ ♿

BUZANCAIS Indre   4B

★★ Hôtel L'Hermitage
Route d'Argy, 36500 Buzançais
☎ 02 54 84 03 90 Fax 02 54 02 13 19
English spoken

Situated between Loches and Châteauroux, L'Hermitage is located in a quiet park on the Indre river bank. Ideal place for good food lovers, indoor parking available.

12 bedrs, all ensuite, ♀ P DB 290-340 B 30 ✗ 90-295 ℂ MC Visa ► 7km ⬛ ✦ 7km
RƎC 5 % 15 Oct-15 Apr

★★ Hôtel Le Croissant
53 rue Grande, 36500 Buzançais
☎ 02 54 84 00 49 Fax 02 54 84 20 60
English spoken
Small, modern hotel in the town centre. An award-winning restaurant with a characterful dining room offering Lorraine and Alsace specialties.

14 bedrs, 12 ensuite, P DB 225-265 B 32 ✗ 85-240 ℂ MC Visa ⊡ ⊰ ✦ ▦ ▯ ⊠ ✦ ⅲ ♿

CHAMBORD Loir et Cher   2D

★★★ Château de Nanteuil
Huisscau-sur-Cosson, 41350 Vineuil
☎ 02 54 42 61 98 Fax 02 54 42 37 23
English spoken
Closed Jan
Between Blois and Chambord on the D33, a country house now run as a hotel by the owner, in the heart of Loire valley châteaux country. Meals served on the riverside terrace. With a 7 hectare wooded park, ideal for an after dinner stroll.

7 bedrs, all ensuite, ♀ P DB 280-400 B 35 ✗ 100-190 ℂ MC Visa ► 10km ⬛ ✦ ⅲ ♿

★★★★ Château des Marais
27 rue de Chambord, 41500 Muides-sur-Loire
☎ 02 54 87 05 42 Fax 02 54 87 05 43
English spoken
Closed 15 Sep-15 May

This hotel is situated on a 12 hectare property surrounded by a shaded park. Very calm and quiet. 4 rooms are in the 17th century 'Maison of Mai'. From Chambord, 6 km north on the route 'Francois 1er' to Muides, then follow signs.

12 bedrs, all ensuite, ♂ P 15 DB 280-350 B 35 ✕ 59-150 ℂℂ MC Visa ⊰ ▶ 10km 🔲 🔲 🖾 ⌀

★★ Hôtel Le Champalud
Promenade du Champalud, 49270 Champtoceaux
☎ 02 40 83 50 09 Fax 02 40 83 53 81
English spoken

The hotel is close to the church square and Champalud public gardens in this historic town on the River Loire. East of Nantes off the A11 and N23, exit Ancenis.

16 bedrs, 11 ensuite, ♂ P 20 DB 190-270 B 34-38 ✕ 61-250 ℂℂ MC Visa ▶ 4km 🔲 🔲 🖾 ⊞
RⱭC 10 % low season

★★ Hôtel Mirwault
Route de Mirwault, 53200 Château-Gontier
☎ 02 43 07 13 17 Fax 02 43 07 82 96
English spoken
Closed 1 Jan-15 Mar

A quiet hotel on the banks of the River Mayenne with all bedrooms having a view of the river and the château opposite.

11 bedrs, all ensuite, ♂ P 20 DB 250-285 B 35 ✕ 80-170 ℂℂ MC Visa ▶ 12km 🔲 🖾 ⊞ ⌀ ♿
RⱭC 5 %

★ Hôtel de la Gare
170 av Jean Jaurès, 72500 Château-du-Loir
☎ 02 43 44 00 14 Fax 02 43 44 11 79
A friendly hotel/restaurant situated halfway between Le Mans and Tours, with a restaurant offering freshwater fish, game and home-made desserts.

16 bedrs, 10 ensuite, ♂ P 8 DB 200-250 B 25 ✕ 58-150 ℂℂ MC Visa ▶ 2km 🔲 🖾 ⌀

★★ Hôtel du Parc La Capitainerie
1 square du Général de Gaulle, 45110 Châteauneuf-sur-Loire
☎ 02 38 58 42 16 Fax 02 38 58 46 81
English spoken
Closed Feb
A traditional hotel, once a meeting place for the hunt, close to the tourist route of the châteaux of the Loire Valley.

12 bedrs, all ensuite, ♂ P 12 DB 280-387 B 36 ✕ 120-273 ℂℂ MC Visa ▶ 10km 🔲 🖾 ⊞

Hôtel Sarthe
49330 Châteauneuf-sur-Sarthe
☎ 02 41 69 85 29
English spoken
Closed 3 weeks in Oct
A family hotel beside the River Sarthe, near to the centre of town. Between Le Mans and Tour: from Angers, take N23 to Seiches then on to Durtal and D859 for 20 km westward.

7 bedrs, all ensuite, P 20 DB 200-300 B 30 ✕ 70-210 ℂℂ MC Visa ⊰ 🖾 ▶ 8km 🔲 🔲 🖾 ⌀
RⱭC Apértif drinks offered

★★ Auberge Arc en Ciel
Route de Montlucon, La Forge-de-l'Ile, 36330 Châteauroux
☎ 02 54 34 09 83 Fax 02 54 34 46 74
English spoken
Closed 22 Dec-4 Jan

An attractive setting beside the River Indra and near an oak forest. Ten minutes from the town centre on the D943 leading to Châtre. The restaurant is 20 m from the hotel.

24 bedrs, 18 ensuite, **↿ P** 50 **DB** 205-225 **B** 25 No restaurant **CC** MC ▶ ⊠ ⠿ ♪
RAC 5 %

CHENONCEAUX Indre et Loire   2C

★★ Hostel du Roy
rue du Dr Bretonneau, 37150 Chenonceaux
☎ 02 47 23 90 17 Fax 02 47 23 89 81
English spoken
Closed 16 Nov-15 Feb
A village centre hotel, with a garden, close to the château. From A10, exit at Amboise or Blois. Gourmet restaurant offers excellent meat, fish and game specialities.

37 bedrs, 24 ensuite, **↿ P** 17 **DB** 130-256 **B** 30 ✕ 65 **CC** MC Visa Amex ▶ 20km ⊡ ⊠ ⠿ ♿

★★ Hôtel Cheval Blanc
Place de l'Eglise, 37150 Bleré
☎ 02 47 30 30 14 Fax 02 47 23 52 80
English spoken
In the centre of Touraine and its chateaux. Guests will be pleasantly surprised by the atmosphere and the quality of the cuisine. Close to Chenonceaux - 5 km.

12 bedrs, all ensuite, **P** 12 **DB** 300-420 **B** 38 ✕ 95-270 **CC** MC Visa Amex ⊰ ⊡ ⊠

CHINON Indre et Loire   2C

★★ Best Western Hôtel de France
47 place du Général de Gaulle, 37500 Chinon
☎ 02 47 93 33 91 Fax 02 47 98 37 03
English spoken

Renovated 16th century building combining comfort with a respect for tradition. In the heart of the medieval Vieux-Chinon and the Loire Valley, an ideal centre for exploring the 'Garden of France'. View of the château and easy access.

30 bedrs, all ensuite, **P DB** 340-400 **B** 45 ✕ 98-165 **CC** MC Visa Amex ▶ 15km ⊠
RAC 5 %

★★ Chris'Hôtel
12 place Jeanne d'Arc, 37500 Chinon
☎ 02 47 93 36 92 Fax 02 47 98 48 92
English spoken
In a quiet square, this highly recommended hotel is near the ancient part of Chinon and has private parking, very pleasant, friendly atmosphere and some excellent rooms finely decorated in Louis XV style.

33 bedrs, all ensuite, **↿ P** 5 **DB** 190-380 **B** 40 **CC** MC Visa Amex ▶ 15km ⊡ ⊠ ⠿
RAC Oct-Apr 20% & May-Sept 10%

★★ Hôtel Diderot
4 rue Buffon, 37500 Chinon
☎ 02 47 93 18 87 Fax 02 47 93 37 10
English spoken
Closed 20 Dec-10 Jan

Highly recommended, a few yards from Place Jeanne d'Arc, this interesting 18th century building features half-timbered walls, an especially fine staircase, a walled courtyard and family atmosphere.

27 bedrs, all ensuite, **P** 1 **DB** 300-400 **B** 40 No restaurant **CC** MC Visa Amex ▶ ⊠ ⠿ ♿
RAC 20 % 1 Nov-15 Mar

CHOLET Maine et Loire   2C

★★★ Hôtel Le Belvédère
Au Lac de Ribou, 49300 Cholet
☎ 02 41 65 46 75 Fax 02 41 65 46 77
English spoken
Closed 29 Jul-21 Aug & 24 Feb-2 Mar
A charming hotel in very nice countryside on the edge of Cholet, with a view of the lake. Follow directions towards Maulévrier then Ribou leisure centre.

8 bedrs, all ensuite, **↿ P DB** 295-360 **B** 38 ✕ 100-200 **CC** Visa Amex ▶ ⊠ ⊡ ⊠ ⠿

★★ Hôtel Le Vert Galant

rue J de Saymond, 49510 Jallais

☎ 02 41 64 20 22 Fax 02 41 64 15 17

A quiet, country hotel set between Beaupréau and Chemillé, 16 km north of Cholet. Nantes and Angers are both 43 km away.

29 bedrs, all ensuite, **P** 100 **DB** 220-300 **B** 30-35 ✕ 40-220

COMBREUX Loiret   2D

★★ Hôtel La Croix Blanche

45530 Combreux

☎ 02 38 59 47 62 Fax 02 38 59 41 35

English spoken

Quietly situated, on the bank of the Canal d'Orléans, in a forest 35 km from Orléans. A welcoming apéritif is offered on arrival. Restaurant (closed Tue evenings and Wed) specialises in fish.

7 bedrs, all ensuite, ⚡ **P** **DB** 280 ✕ 125-200 **CC** MC Visa ▸ 🖊 🖾 ⚌ 🐾

RAC 8 %

DESCARTES Indre et Loire   2C

★★ Hôtel Moderne

15 rue Descartes, 37160 Descartes

☎ 02 47 59 72 11 Fax 02 47 92 44 90

English spoken

Closed 20 Dec-5 Jan

A nice, family hotel with all comforts, in the birthplace of philosopher, Descartes. Situated near the Loire castles and Futuroscope and in splendid surroundings.

11 bedrs, all ensuite, ⚡ **P** 10 **DB** 250-305 **B** 30 ✕ 20-200 **CC** MC Visa ▸ 🖊 🖾 🐾

DORDIVES Loiret   2D

★★ Hôtel César

8 rue de la République, 45680 Dordives

☎ 02 38 92 73 20 Fax 02 38 92 76 67

English spoken

Situated 1 hour south of Paris and Eurodisney, between Montargis and Nemours. Exit A6 for

Dordives, set 200 m from N7 but with very quiet, safe car park in the gardens.

18 bedrs, 12 ensuite, ⚡ **P** 18 **DB** 130-260 **B** 15-40 ✕ 90-250 **CC** MC Visa ꜛ ▸ 🖾 🖊 🖾 ⚌ 🐾 ⚘

RAC on fax booking after agreement

LA FLECHE Sarthe   2C

★★ Auberge du Port des Roches

Le Port des Roches, 72800 Luché-Pringé

☎ 02 43 45 44 48 Fax 02 43 45 39 61

English spoken

Closed Sun eve, Mon and Feb

This inn with a terrace is in the countryside overlooking the River Loir. From Luché follow D13 towards Mansigne for about 1.8 km, then turn on to D124. The hotel is 800 m ahead on the right.

12 bedrs, 10 ensuite, ⚡ **P** 15 **DB** 240-300 **B** 32 ✕ 115-190 **CC** MC Visa 🖊 🖾

RAC 8 % on room rate

★★ Hôtel de l'Image

50 rue Grollier et bd Montréal, 72200 La Flèche

☎ 02 43 94 00 50 Fax 02 43 94 47 19

Closed 15 Dec-15 Jan

La Flèche is approximately 40 km south of Le Mans on N23.

20 bedrs, 16 ensuite, ⚡ **P** 30 **DB** 200-350 **B** 32 ✕ 72-150 **CC** MC Visa 🖊 🖾 ⚌

RAC 5 % on room rate, show card

FONTEVRAUD-L'ABBAYE Maine et Loire   2C

Hostellerie du Prieuré St-Lazare

Abbaye Royale de Fontevraud, B.P.14, 49590 Fontevraud-l'Abbaye

☎ 02 41 51 73 16 Fax 02 41 51 75 50

English spoken

Closed 22 Dec-28 Feb

A comfortable relaxing hotel, situated on the site of the royal abbey of Fontevraud, the finest and largest in the western Christian world. Located 16 km from Saumur on the D947 and serving good local cuisine

52 bedrs, all ensuite, **P** **DB** 430-480 **B** 55-65 ✕ 98-280 **CC** MC Visa Amex ▸ 🖾 ⚌ 🐾

RAC 10 %

HÔTEL LA CROIX BLANCHE

Opposite L'Abbaye in a rural 16th century setting, good local cuisine made by the boss and his staff. Breakfast on the Terrace – Crêperie. Comfortable and finely decorated bedrooms and Conference rooms.

49590 FONTEVRAUD
FRANCE
TEL: 02 41 51 71 11
FAX: 02 41 38 15 38

★★ Hôtel La Croix Blanche ✓
7 place du Plantagenêt, 49590 Fontevraud-l'Abbaye
☏ 02 41 51 71 11 Fax 02 41 38 15 38
Closed 2-11 Nov & 11 Jan-6 Feb
Opposite the abbey, in a rustic 16th century surrounding, the hotel offers regional cuisine cooked by the proprietor and his team and breakfast on the terrace. With a crêperie, meeting room and rooms with all comforts, it surrounds a flower garden.

21 bedrs, all ensuite, ⚓ P 21 DB 290-450 B 37 ✕ 99-245 ℂℂ MC Visa Amex ▸ 3km ⁂ ♪ ♿
R∂C 5 %

GENNES Maine et Loire 2C

★★★ Hôtel Jeanne de Laval
rte Nationale, 49350 Les Rosiers-sur-Loire
☏ 02 41 51 80 17 Fax 02 41 98 04 18
A third generation family hotel with large comfortable rooms and terrace overlooking a flowery garden. A high quality of traditional cuisine is offered in this comfortable and quiet establishment.

10 bedrs, all ensuite, P 20 B 55 ✕ 180-420 ▦ ⌃ ▨ ▦
▣ ▨ ⁂ ♪ ♿
R∂C

GIEN Loiret 2D

★★ Hôtel Anne de Beaujeu
10 rte Bourges, 45500 Gien
☏ 02 38 29 39 39 Fax 02 38 38 27 29
English spoken
A comfortable, family run hotel close to the River Loire. In Gien, take D940 towards Bourges and the hotel is close to the old bridge.

30 bedrs, all ensuite, ⚓ P DB 320 B 35 No restaurant
ℂℂ MC Visa Amex ▸ 18km ▨ ▧ ♪ ♿
R∂C 7 %

★★ Hôtel La Poularde
13 quai de Nice, 45500 Gien
☏ 02 38 67 36 05 Fax 02 38 38 18 78
English spoken
A small hotel with spacious rooms. Opposite the River Loire close to the Anne de Beaujeu château and offering traditional cuisine carefully prepared by the chef, Joël Danthu.

9 bedrs, all ensuite, P DB 270-290 B 35-40 ✕ 90-235
ℂℂ MC Visa Amex ▧ 2km ⁂

★★★ Hôtel Rivage
1 quai Nice, 45500 Gien
☏ 02 38 37 79 00 Fax 02 38 38 10 21
English spoken
Closed Feb-Mar
A provincial, warm inn on the Loire river bank in the locality of the first Loire chateâu and the Gien earthenware museum. From Orléans follow direction Nevers. Offering refined and inventive cuisine.

19 bedrs, all ensuite, ⚓ P 20 DB 370-525 B 48 ✕ 145-390 ℂℂ MC Visa ▸ 20km ▨ ⁂

INGRANDES-SUR-LOIRE Maine et Loire 2C

★★ Hôtel Le Lion d'Or
26 rue du Pont, 49123 Ingrandes-sur-Loire
☏ 02 41 39 20 08 Fax 02 41 39 21 03
English spoken
Closed 15-28 Feb

Situated between Angers and Nantes, Le Lion d'Or dates from 1660 and was the first hotel in Ingrandes. Enjoy peace and relaxation in renovated, modern rooms, close to the River Loire.

16 bedrs, 10 ensuite, ⚓ P 12 DB 160-260 B 25 ✕ 65-180 ℂℂ MC Visa Amex ▸ ▧ ♪

LAMOTTE-BEUVRON Loir et Cher · 2D

★★★ Hôtel La Croix Blanche de Sologne
41600 Chaumont-sur-Tharonne
📞 02 54 88 55 12 Fax 02 54 88 60 40
English spoken

One of France's oldest hotels, in a quiet village setting, north-west of Lamotte-Beuvron on D922. Restaurant renowned for Sologne and Périgord specialities.

18 bedrs, all ensuite, ✈ P 35 DB 340-580 B 45 ✕ 118-250 CC MC Visa Amex ▶ 8km 🔲🔲🔲 3km ⅲ ✐ ♿
RAC 10 %

LANGEAIS Indre et Loire · 2C

★★★ Hôtel Le Castel de Bray et Monts
Bréhémont, 37130 Langeais
📞 02 47 96 70 47 Fax 02 47 96 57 36
English spoken

An unusual and rather eccentric 18th-century manor house, with interesting rooms in the main house and in a converted chapel in the grounds overlooking the vineyard. From Langeais, cross the Loire and turn right (west) along the southern bank for 3 km.

12 bedrs, all ensuite, ✈ P DB 295-630 B 48 ✕ 125-285 🔲 ▶ 10km 🔲🔲🔲 ⅲ ✐

★★★★ Relais du Vieux Château d'Hommes
Hommes, 37340 Savigné-sur-Lathan
📞 02 47 24 95 13 Fax 02 47 24 68 67
English spoken

In the heart of the Loire Valley and its vineyards, a 15th century château with comfortable rooms. Restaurant specialities include aspèrges à la crème and terrine de lapin. North of Langeais on the D57 to Hommes, then right to Savigné.

5 bedrs, all ensuite, ✈ P 15 DB 485-585 B included ✕ 135-150 CC MC Visa ⌣ ▶ 10km 🔲🔲 ⅲ ♿

LOCHES Indre et Loire · 2C

★ Grill Motel
Rue des Lézards, BP 221, 37600 Loches
📞 02 47 91 30 40 Fax 02 47 91 30 35
English spoken
Closed 20 Dec-12 Jan
A modern hotel set in large gardens overlooking Loches and the castle. Restaurant offers traditional dishes and barbeque grills and salads served on the terrace in summer. Access via N143 south-east of Tours.

27 bedrs, all ensuite, ✈ P DB 175 B 30 ✕ 49-80 CC MC Visa 🔲🔲🔲🔲🔲🔲🔲 ⅲ ✐ ♿
RAC **Drink offered**

★★ Hôtel Luccotel
Rue des Lézards, 37600 Loches
📞 02 47 91 30 30 Fax 02 47 91 30 35
English spoken
Closed 20 Dec-12 Jan
Set in the middle of a green park, overlooking the historic city of Loches, the Luccotel offers an exceptional panorama. The proximity of the Loire châteaux and natural sites invite you to explore.

42 bedrs, all ensuite, ✈ P DB 245-330 B 36 ✕ 90-230 CC MC Visa 🔲🔲🔲🔲🔲🔲🔲 ⅲ ✐ ♿
RAC **Drink offered on the house**

LUÇON Vendée · 4A

★ Grand Hôtel du Croissant
Place des Acacias, 85400 Luçon
📞 02 51 56 11 15

English spoken
Closed mid Oct
A traditional family-run inn offering a warm welcome and refined, beautifully presented cuisine using fresh local ingredients. Reasonably priced and easily accessible via N137. 20 km from the Atlantic coast.

40 bedrs, 20 ensuite, ✝ **P** 10 **DB** 140-252 **B** 30-32 ✕ 62-120 **CC** MC Visa ▸ ▣ ▣ ⫶⫶ ⌀

Le Château
85450 Moreilles
📞 02 51 56 17 56 Fax 02 51 56 30 30
English spoken

A country house with a warm atmosphere, nice, family furniture and rural cuisine. Located half way between England and Spain on the N137, within 30 minutes of La Rochelle and close to the Marais Poitevin reserve. Only Euro/Travellers cheques accepted.

3 bedrs, all ensuite, ✝ **P** 8 **DB** 400-600 **B** 55 ✕ 195 ⅃ ▣ 3km ⫶⫶
RAC **5 %**

★★ Hostellerie du Maine
17 av de Saumur, 72800 Le Lude
📞 02 43 48 31 31 Fax 02 43 94 19 74
English spoken
The Hostellerie du Maine, set in a wooded area close to the Loire châteaux, offers you a friendly welcome with local 'Sarthois' cuisine.

24 bedrs, 22 ensuite, ✝ **P** **DB** 160-240 **B** 32 ✕ 75-210 **CC** MC Visa ▸ ▣ ▣ ⫶⫶ ⌀ ⌀
RAC **5 %**

★★ Le Vedaquais
Place de la Liberté, 72500 Vaas
📞 02 43 46 01 41 Fax 02 43 46 37 60
English spoken
Closed 1-4 Jan
A centrally located hotel, pleasantly situated in orchards, in the square of a small village on the Loire river bank.

8 bedrs, all ensuite, ✝ **P** 10 **DB** 230-250 **B** 28 ✕ 85-220 **CC** MC Visa ▸ 30km ▣ ▣ ▣ ⌀ ⌀
RAC **10 %**

★★ Hôtel Bon Laboureur
1 rue Paul Beit, 72600 Mamers
📞 02 43 31 15 10 Fax 02 43 31 15 25
English spoken
A quality hotel/restaurant, centrally situated on a quiet street, with moderate prices and a variety of regional speciality dishes. Private car park for guests.

9 bedrs, all ensuite, ✝ **P** 4 **DB** 205-230 **B** 30 ✕ 50-180 **CC** MC Visa Amex ▸ 12km ▣ ▣ 1km ⫶⫶ ⌀

★★★ Hôtel Chantecler
50 rue de la Pelouse, 72000 Le Mans
📞 02 43 24 58 53 Fax 02 43 77 16 28
English spoken

A friendly hotel, with a contemporary style dining room with mosaic floors and lots of mirrors, quietly situated in the town centre between the SNCF station and the congress hall.

35 bedrs, all ensuite, **P** **DB** 345-365 **B** 45 ✕ 80-200 **CC** MC Visa Amex ▸ 6km ▣ 3km ⌀

★★★ Hôtel Concorde
16 avenue du Général Leclerc, 72000 Le Mans
📞 02 43 24 12 30 Fax 02 43 24 85 74
English spoken
This centrally located hotel, a few minutes from the station and the old town, has been fully renovated and offers traditional French cuisine and attractive, comfortable accommodation with good facilities.

55 bedrs, all ensuite, ✝ **P** **DB** 480-700 **B** 55 ✕ 95-205 **CC** MC Visa Amex ▸ 5km ▣ ▣ ⫶⫶ ⌀
RAC **10 %**

★★ Motel Papéa
RN 23, Bener, 72530 Yvre-l'Evêque
☎ 02 43 89 64 09 Fax 02 43 89 49 81
English spoken

This hotel has separate, self-contained chalets, each with full facilities including a covered car park. Located 5 minutes from the centre of Le Mans at Bener on N23. Exit No 6 from A11, Le Mans-Est, then left at lights. Good restaurant next door.

21 bedrs, all ensuite, ➤ P 21 DB 200-275 B 30-35 **CC**
MC Visa ▸ 5km 🅿 🅰 ⌀
RAC **10 %**

MAYENNE Mayenne　　　　　　　2C

★★ Grand Hôtel
2 rue A de Loré, 53100 Mayenne
☎ 02 43 00 96 00 Fax 02 43 32 08 49
English spoken
A 150 year old hotel with modern day comforts, ideally situated in the town centre, close to the River Mayenne. Restaurant offers gourmet and regional cuisine with fish specialities.

27 bedrs, all ensuite, ➤ P 40 DB 215-389 B 40-42
✗ 89-199 **CC** MC Visa Amex ▸ 20km 🅿 🅰 ⛬ ⌀
RAC **8 %**

LA MENITRE Maine et Loire　　　2D

★★ Hôtel au Bec Salé
Le Port St-Maur, 49250 La Menitre
☎ 02 41 45 63 56 Fax 02 41 45 67 88
English spoken
Closed 2 Jan-2 Feb
Situated on the famous Loire châteaux road, between Angers and Saumur on the D952.

11 bedrs, all ensuite, ➤ P DB 230-270 B 35 ✗ 69-170
CC MC Visa Amex ▸ 🅿 🅰 ⌀ ♿
RAC **10 % on presentation of guide**

MISSILLAC Loire Atlantique　　　1D

★★★★ Hôtel de la Bretesche
44780 Missillac
☎ 02 51 76 86 96 Fax 02 40 66 99 47
English spoken
Closed 1-28 Feb

This 14th century, lakeside château, set on the edge of an 18 hole golf course, was completely renovated in 1996. From Missillac, drive towards La Baule and the hotel is on the right, 500 m from the village.

29 bedrs, all ensuite, ➤ P 30 DB 420-1,200 B 65
✗ 160-380 **CC** MC Visa Amex ⌀ 🅿 🅿 🅰 ⛬ ⌀ ♿
RAC **10 % on bed and breakfast**

MONTBAZON Indre et Loire　　　2C

★★★★ Château d'Artigny
37250 Montbazon
☎ 02 47 34 30 30 Fax 02 47 34 30 39
English spoken
Closed 1 Dec-10 Jan

Imposing château, set in beautiful parkland, offering every comfort and excellent facilities. Gourmet cuisine with seafood and meat specialities.

53 bedrs, all ensuite, ➤ P DB 680-1,670 B 90 ✗ 290-450 **CC** MC Visa Amex ⌀ 🅿 🅿 ▸ 17km 🅿 🅰 ⛬

★★ Hôtel Le Moulin Fleuri
route du Ripault, 37250 Montbazon
📞 02 47 26 01 12 **Fax** 02 47 34 04 71
English spoken
Closed 1 Dec-9 Jan
A converted mill with restaurant, offering 30-variety cheeseboard and a magnificent wine list, in a delightful setting on the Loire châteaux route. From Tours off N10, towards Azay-le-Rideau.

12 bedrs, 8 ensuite, ⍢ **P** 20 **DB** 195-290 **B** 46 ✕ 175-304 **((** MC Visa Amex ▸ 12km 🔲 🖼 3km ⑪

MONTOIRE-SUR-LE-LOIR Loir et Cher   **2C**

★★ Hôtel Le Cheval Blanc
place de la Libération, 41800 Troo
📞 02 54 72 58 22 **Fax** 02 54 72 55 44
Closed Nov
A comfortable 2 star hotel with a restaurant specialising in seafood. From Vendôme go west on the D917 to Montoire-sur-le-Loir, then Troo.

9 bedrs, all ensuite, ⍢ **P** 30 **DB** 270-360 ✕ 125-300 (plus à la carte) **((** MC Visa ▸ 30km 🔲 🖼 ⑪ ⍥

★★ Hôtel du Cheval Rouge
1 place Foch, 41800 Montoire-sur-le-Loir
📞 02 54 85 07 05 **Fax** 02 54 85 17 42
English spoken
Closed 11-27 Nov /19 Jan-5 Feb
A traditional, old French hotel with plenty of charm and a restaurant offering gourmet cuisine. Located 19 km west of Vendôme on the D917.

15 bedrs, 9 ensuite, ⍢ **P** 10 **DB** 150-265 **B** 31 ✕ 126-245 **((** MC Visa Amex 🔲 ⑪ ⍥
RAC 10 % winter only

MONTREUIL-BELLAY Maine et Loire   **2C**

★★ Splendid'Hôtel
rue Dr Gaudrez, 49260 Montreuil-Bellay
📞 02 41 53 10 00 **Fax** 02 41 52 45 17
English spoken

Beautiful hotel, dating from the 15th and 17th centuries, set in a pretty village full of flowers. Rooms, some with a view of the 12th-century château, are

decorated in Louis XV or rustic-style. Restaurant offers traditional cuisine. 15 km from Saumur.

60 bedrs, 55 ensuite, ⍢ **P** **DB** 180-450 **B** 38-48 ✕ 80-220 **((** MC Visa 🔲 🛇 🖼 📺 ▸ 15km 🔲 🖼 ⑪ ⍥ ⅙
RAC 10 % except Jul-Aug

MONTRICHARD Loir et Cher   **2C**

★★★ Hôtel de la Tête Noire
24 rue de Tours, BP3, 41401 Montrichard
📞 02 54 32 05 55 **Fax** 02 54 32 78 37
English spoken
A pretty hotel with comfortable rooms, an attractive dining room and a flower-filled terrace overlooking the river. Montrichard is a small, friendly town on the River Cher, ideal for visiting nearby Loire Valley châteaux.

36 bedrs, 30 ensuite, ⍢ **P** 10 **DB** 195-330 **B** 36 ✕ 96-260 **((** MC Visa ▸ 17km 🔲 🖼 ⑪

NANTES Loire Atlantique   **1D**

★★★ Hôtel Astoria
11 rue Richebourg, 44000 Nantes
📞 02 40 74 39 90 **Fax** 02 40 14 05 49
English spoken
Closed 4 weeks in August
A family-run hotel close to the park, the cathedral, the ducal château and the Musée Beaux Arts. Indoor secured car-park available to guests. Member of the 'Bonjour Campaign'. 80 km from Angers.

45 bedrs, 42 ensuite, ⍢ **P** 18 **DB** 290-350 **B** 38 No restaurant **((** MC Visa ⑪ ⍥ ⅙

★★★ Hôtel Mercure
RN 165, 44360 Vigneux-de-Bretagne
📞 02 40 57 10 80 **Fax** 02 40 57 13 30
English spoken
To find the hotel drive from Nantes towards La Baule-Vannes-Brest and take the Vigneux exit. From Brest go towards Nantes, and take the St-Etienne exit.

88 bedrs, all ensuite, ⍢ **P** **DB** 420-520 **B** 51 ✕ 80-150 **((** MC Visa Amex 🛇 🖼 📺 ▸ 🔲 🖼 ⑪ ⍥ ⅙
RAC 10 %

★★ Hôtel Otelinn
45 rue Batignolles, Beaujoire, 44300 Nantes
📞 02 40 50 07 07 **Fax** 02 40 49 41 40
English spoken
The Otelinn has a restaurant which specialises in fish, poultry and grills. From Nantes follow signs to Beaujoire stadium; the hotel is opposite.

60 bedrs, all ensuite, ⍢ **P** 60 **DB** 265-325 **B** 40 ✕ 70-180 **((** MC Visa Amex 🖼 ▸ 2km 🔲 🖼 ⑪ ⍥ ⅙

NEUVILLE-AUX-BOIS Loiret — 2D

★★★ L'Hostellerie
48 place du Général Leclerc, 45170 Neuville-aux-Bois
☎ 02 38 75 50 00 Fax 02 38 91 86 81
English spoken

A modern, comfortable, family hotel, set in a typical village square, offering traditional hospitality and a restaurant with an excellent reputation. 20 km north of Orléans on D97 or from Paris, exit A10 at Artenay. Special weekend rates available.

32 bedrs, all ensuite, ♉ P 30 DB 335-390 B 40 ✕ 85-185 ⊞ ▸ ▨ ▣ ⠿ ⚲ ⅋ ♿
RAC 10 % on meals & drinks

NOIRMOUTIER-EN-L'ILE Vendée — 1D

★★★ Hôtel Fleur de Sel
85330 Noirmoutier-en-l'Ile
☎ 02 51 39 21 59 Fax 02 51 39 75 66
English spoken
Closed 2 Nov-mid Feb

Set in a quiet island location between the port and beaches, this hotel has attractively flowered and exotic gardens and an excellent, garden-side restaurant known for its seafood specialities. Approach island on D948.

35 bedrs, all ensuite, ♉ P 50 DB 350-630 B 50 ✕ 125-170 ⅭⅭ MC Visa Amex ⚑ ▨ ▣ ▸ 40km ▨ ▣ ⠿ ♿
RAC 5 % except Jul-Aug

ONZAIN Loir et Cher — 2D

★★★ Château des Tertres
route de Monteaux, 41150 Onzain
☎ 02 54 20 83 88 Fax 02 54 20 89 21
English spoken
Closed 11 Nov-4 Apr

Situated near the Loire's most sumptuous chatêaux, this 19th century residence, with comfortable, personalised rooms, overlooks a vast 5 hectare park planted with rare species of trees.

14 bedrs, all ensuite, P 14 DB 400-520 B 44 No restaurant ⅭⅭ MC Visa Amex ▸ 5km ▨ 3km

ORLEANS Loiret — 2D

★★ Hôtel L'Escale du Port-Arthur
205 rue de l'Eglise, 45160 St-Hilaire-St-Mesmin
☎ 02 38 76 30 36 Fax 02 38 76 37 67
English spoken
Closed 4-24 Feb
A, 3 cheminées, Logis de France hotel, standing on the banks of the Loire, with a dining room overlooking the river. Access via A71 motorway, junction Olivet or D951. 7 km from Orléans on the left bank of the Loire.

20 bedrs, all ensuite, ♉ P 60 DB 283-325 B 37 ✕ 108-230 ⅭⅭ MC Visa Amex ▸ 6km ▣ ▨ ⠿ ⚲
RAC 5 %

★★ Hôtel Le Rivage
635 rue Reine Blanche, 45160 Olivet
☎ 02 38 66 02 93 Fax 02 38 56 31 11
English spoken
Closed 26 Dec-20 Jan

Set in peaceful countryside on the banks of the River Loire and in the midst of châteaux country and with a shady terrace. Olivet is just south of Orléans. Serving refined cuisine, beautifully presented and using fresh seasonal produce.

17 bedrs, all ensuite, **⋔ P** 40 **DB** 370-490 **B** 50-55 **✕** 155-300 **CC** MC Visa Amex **▶** 10km 🔲 🔲 🔲 ⚏ ⚐

★★★ Orléans Parc Hôtel
55 route d'Orléans, 45380 La Chapelle-St-Mesmin
📞 02 38 43 26 26 Fax 02 38 72 00 99
English spoken
Closed 24 Dec-2 Jan

A quiet, comfortable 19th century house set on the side of the Loire in 8 acres of land. From A71, exit Orléans-Centre then take N152 to La Chapelle-St-Mesmin.

33 bedrs, all ensuite, **⋔ P** 50 **DB** 420-580 **B** 42-45 **✕** 198-238 **CC** MC Visa Amex **▶** 🔲 🔲 ⚏ ⚐ ♿

OUCQUES Loir et Cher 2D

★★ Hôtel du Commerce
9 rue de Beaugency, 41290 Oucques
📞 02 54 23 20 41 Fax 02 54 23 02 88
English spoken
A hotel restaurant with well equipped rooms, each one decorated in a different style. 160 km from Paris on the A10; take exit Meungs/Loire or Blois

12 bedrs, all ensuite, **P** 3 **DB** 250-300 **B** 40 **✕** 95-265 **CC** MC Visa Amex **▶** 5km

PORNIC Loire Atlantique 1D

★★ Hôtel Relais St-Gilles
7 rue F de Mun, 44210 Pornic
📞 02 40 82 02 25
English spoken
Closed 10 Oct-31 Mar
A 19th century posthouse, quietly situated close to the Pornic castle, within easy reach of the lively harbour and beaches.

28 bedrs, 24 ensuite, **⋔ P** 8 **DB** 230-350 **B** 34-35 **✕** 100-120 **CC** MC Visa **▶** 1km

POUANCE Maine et Loire 2C

★★ Hôtel Porte Angevine
Route de Craon, 49420 Pouancé
📞 02 41 92 68 52 Fax 02 41 92 47 54
From St Malo: take N137 to Rennes, D163 to Châteaubriant, N171 to Pouancé and D775 towards Segré. Centrally situated for all of the many attractions of the 'Pays-de-la-Loire'.

18 bedrs, all ensuite, **P** 100 **DB** 230 **B** 30 **✕** 62-170 🔳 ⚏ 🔲 ▶ 🔲 🔲
RƏC 10 %

POUZAUGES Vendée 1D

★★ Auberge de la Bruyère
18 rue du Dr Barbanneau, 85700 Pouzauges
📞 02 51 91 93 46 Fax 02 51 57 08 18
English spoken
A new, hillside, hotel with wonderful views of countryside. From Nantes, take N137, turn on to D960B at Chantonnay following signs for Pouzauges and Bressuire. From the centre of Pouzauges, go towards La Pommeraie. The hotel is 300 m beyond the church.

28 bedrs, all ensuite, **⋔ P** 15 **DB** 305-365 **B** 38 **✕** 80-175 **CC** MC Visa Amex 🔳 🔲 ⚏

LA ROCHE-SUR-YON Vendée 4A

★★ Hôtel Marie Stuart
86 rue Louis Blanc, 85000 La Roche-sur-Yon
📞 02 51 37 02 24 Fax 02 51 37 86 37
English spoken
A centrally situated, comfortable and friendly, family-run hotel, dating from the 1880s and set in the heart of picturesque Vendée.

14 bedrs, all ensuite, **P DB** 289 **B** 33-37 **✕** 79-135 **CC** MC Visa Amex **▶** 4km 🔲 ⚏

Electrical voltages

Standard mains voltage is 220 AC at 50 Hz. Generally, however, the two – rather than three-pin plug is in use – so you will need a travel adaptor for electrical items. Adaptors are available from RAC Travel Centres at Dover, Folkestone and Calais.

SABLE-SUR-SARTHE Sarthe   2C

★★★ Grand Hôtel de Solesmes
16 place Dom-Guéranger, 72300 Sablé-sur-Sarthe
☎ 02 43 95 45 10 Fax 02 43 95 22 26
English spoken

Located 3 km from Sablé-sur-Sarthe, The Grand Hôtel is ideally placed for exploring Western France; the Loire châteaux, vineyards, Mont-St-Michel and Chartres cathedral. A range of trips available every day.

34 bedrs, all ensuite, ⋔ P 10 DB 450 B 50 ✕ 130-200 ℀ MC Visa Amex 📶 ▶ 🔲 🔳 🖾 ⛟

ST-AMAND-MONTROND Cher   5A

★★★ Auberge Moulin de Chameron
18210 Bannegon
☎ 02 48 61 83 80 Fax 02 48 61 84 92
English spoken
Closed 1 Mar-15 Nov
A warm welcome is assured at these former mill buildings, converted into a hotel in 1972. The mill equipment is still in place in a small museum; the comfortable rooms are in a separate building. Bannegon lies between Nevers and St-Amand-Montrond.

13 bedrs, all ensuite, ⋔ P 18 DB 350-515 B 51-85 ✕ 130-190 ℀ MC Visa Amex ⇗ ▶ 🖾 ⛟

★★ Hôtel Le Noirlac
215 rte de Bourges, 18200 St-Amand-Montrond
☎ 02 48 96 80 80 Fax 02 48 96 63 88
English spoken
Closed 22 Dec-1 May
A warm, welcoming, modern hotel with a restaurant making full use of locally grown produce. From N144 drive towards Bourges, take A71 exit and the hotel is is quietly situated 2 km from the town centre.

43 bedrs, all ensuite, ⋔ P 80 DB 320 B 38 ✕ 95-145 ℀ MC Visa Amex ⇗ 🔲 ▶ 🖾 🔳 🖾 ⛟ ⛓

★★ Hôtel de la Poste
9 rue du Dr Vallet, 18200 St-Amand-Montrond
☎ 02 48 96 27 14 Fax 02 48 96 97 74
A former Relais de Poste dating from 1585, the hotel has quiet, comfortable rooms and a gourmet restaurant offering regional fish and game specialities. St-Amand-Montrond is 45 km south of Bourges: leave the A7 at junction 8.

20 bedrs, 18 ensuite, P 15 DB 190-300 B 39 ✕ 98-240 ℀ MC Visa Amex ▶ 25km 🖾 ⛟ 🗡 ⛓
RAC 5 %

ST-JEAN-DE-MONTS Vendée   4A

★★ Auberge de la Chaumière
103 av d'Orouet, lieu-dit Orouet, 85160 St-Jean-de-Monts
☎ 02 51 58 67 44 Fax 02 51 58 98 12
English spoken
When arriving at St-Jean-de-Monts, follow directions to Sables d'Olonne, then D38 6 km to the south-east to Orouet.

37 bedrs, all ensuite, ⋔ P 40 DB 250-450 B 37 ✕ 80-220 ℀ MC Visa Amex 🔲 🔳 ▶ 6km 🖾 🖾 🗡 ⛓
RAC 10 % high season on rooms

★★ Hôtel Robinson
28 bd Général Leclerc, 85160 St-Jean-de-Monts
☎ 02 51 59 20 20 Fax 02 51 58 88 03
English spoken

Comfortable hotel with garden and terrace. Close to town centre and 900 m from beach. Half-board, full-board and weekend breaks available.

80 bedrs, 72 ensuite, ⍭ P 80 **DB** 210-380 **B** 37-38 ✕ 74-230 ℂℂ MC Visa Amex 🔲 🔀 ▸ 1km 🔳 🔲 ⁂ ♬ ♿ ㄖㄋㄈ

A recently renovated posthouse, with comfortable, air-conditioned and soundproofed accommodation, that has stood on the Paris to Madrid road (N10) for many centuries.

19 bedrs, all ensuite, ⍭ P **DB** 320-450 **B** 50-60 ✕ 108-240 ℂℂ MC Visa Amex ▸ 1km 🔳 🔲 ⁂ ♬ ♿ ㄖㄋㄈ **8 %**

ST-SYMPHORIEN-LE-CHATEAU Eure et Loire 2D

★★★★ **Château d'Esclimont**
28700 St-Symphorien-le-Château
☎ **02 37 31 15 15 Fax 02 37 31 57 91**
English spoken

A superb 16th century château with a moat, lake, landscaped gardens and 150 acres of wooded parkland. From Paris, take A11 and exit at Ablis, take a right turn off N10 after 6 km.

53 bedrs, all ensuite, ⍭ P 150 **DB** 980-1,900 **B** 95 ✕ 260-495 ℂℂ MC Visa Amex 🔲 ▸ 17km 🔲 🔳 🔀 ⁂ ♬

STE-MAURE-DE-TOURAINE Indre et Loire 2C

★★★ **Hostellerie Hauts de Ste-Maure**
2 av Charles de Gaulle, 37800 Ste-Maure-de-Touraine
☎ **02 47 65 50 65 Fax 02 47 65 60 24**
English spoken
Closed Feb

SALBRIS Loir et Cher 2D

★★★ **Domaine de Valaudran**
av de Romorantin, 41300 Salbris
☎ **02 54 97 20 00 Fax 02 54 97 12 22**
English spoken

A charming hotel situated in a park. From the N20, drive west towards Romorantin for 2 km. Turn off at the first roundabout after the toll booth.

31 bedrs, all ensuite, ⍭ P 60 **DB** 465-595 **B** 70-80 ✕ 120-350 ℂℂ MC Visa Amex 🔲 ▸ 25km 🔲 🔳 ⁂ ♬ ♿ ㄖㄋㄈ **10 % on room rate Jan-May**

★★★ **Hôtel du Parc**
8 av d'Orléans, 41300 Salbris
☎ **02 54 97 18 53 Fax 02 54 97 24 34**
English spoken
A relaxing stop-over, with a private car park, close to a wooded park. For Salbris: drive south, towards Périgord, from Orléans on the A71 or N20.

27 bedrs, 23 ensuite, ⍭ P 30 **DB** 220-450 **B** 45 ✕ 100-240 ℂℂ MC Visa Amex ▸ 1km 🔲 🔳 ⁂ ♬ ㄖㄋㄈ **10 %**

SAULGES Mayenne   2C

★★★ Hôtel L'Ermitage
53340 Saulges
☎ 02 43 90 52 28 Fax 02 43 90 56 61
English spoken
Closed Feb

*A picturesque, quiet hotel in the heart of the Mayenne
countryside. Excellent facilities and lovely gardens.
Belongs to Relais du Silence chain.*

36 bedrs, all ensuite, ⊬ P 15 DB 340-530 B 53 ✕ 100-
250 ℂℂ MC Visa Amex ♨ ⊞ ▦ ▸ 20km ▨ ⊠ 3km
▦ ♿ 10 ☕

SAUMUR Maine et Loire   2C

★★★★ Château-Hôtel Prieuré
Chênehutte-les-Tuffeaux, 49350 Gennes
☎ 02 41 67 90 14 Fax 02 41 67 92 24
English spoken
Closed Jan-Feb

*Exceptionally situated 16th century manor house
with great views, quiet rooms and contemporary
residences in the park. Restaurant with panoramic
views. From Saumur, towards St-Hilaire-St-Florent
then take D751 for 6 km.*

35 bedrs, all ensuite, ⊬ P DB 500-1,600 B 85-130
✕ 235-400 ℂℂ MC Visa Amex ♨ ▣ ▸ ⊗ ▨ ⊠ ▦ ✂ ♿
RAC 10 %

★★★ Hôtel Anne d'Anjou
32 quai Mayaud, 49400 Saumur
☎ 02 41 67 30 30 Fax 02 41 67 51 00
English spoken
*A classic 18th century building, overlooking the river,
situated between the River Loire and Château de
Saumur. An extremely comfortable hotel with some
stunning features and a charming illuminated
interior courtyard.*

45 bedrs, all ensuite, P 14 DB 420-560 B 48 ✕ 160-350
ℂℂ MC Visa Amex ▸ 15km ▨ ⊠ ▦ ♿

Hôtel Clos des Bénédictins
2 rue des Lilas, 49400 St-Hilaire-Saint-Florent
☎ 02 41 67 28 48 Fax 02 41 67 13 71
English spoken

The hotel is situated on a hill, close to the Cadre Noir, overlooking Saumur, the Loire and the Loire chateaux and cellars.

22 bedrs, all ensuite, ✦ **P** **DB** 300-550 **B** 58 ✗ 120-390 ℂℂ MC Visa Amex ⌁ ⌁ ▣ ▣ ▥ ⌁ ♿

★★★ Hôtel Loire
Rue du Vieux Pont, 49400 Saumur
☎ **02 41 67 22 42 Fax 02 41 67 88 80**
English spoken

A very quiet hotel situated on the Loire river bank, opposite the château and Mairie of Saumur. Indoor parking, and a quality restaurant offering regional cuisine.

44 bedrs, all ensuite, **P** 40 **DB** 430-590 **B** 48 ✗ 85-198 ℂℂ MC Visa Amex ⌁ 4km ▣ ▣ ▥ ♿
RAC 10 %

★★★ Hôtel St-Pierre
8 rue Haute-St-Pierre, 49400 Saumur
☎ **02 41 50 33 00 Fax 02 41 50 38 68**
English spoken
A stylish, luxurious 17th century hotel in the historic town centre. Quiet rooms with designer bathrooms. Saumur can be reached on either side of the river from Tours, on N152 and D7. New deal: 8 nights in apartment with breakfast - 5000 FF.

16 bedrs, all ensuite, ✦ **P** **DB** 580-1,600 **B** 47-57 No restaurant ℂℂ MC Visa Amex ⌁ 5km ▣ ▣ ⌁ ♿
RAC 10 %

TOURS Indre et Loire 2C

★★★ Château de Beaulieu
67 rue de Beaulieu, 37300 Joué-les-Tours
☎ **02 47 53 20 26 Fax 02 47 53 84 20**
English spoken
Enjoy a relaxing, gourmet holiday with Jean-Pierre Lozay (master cook of France) at this delightful 18th century manor house, situated in the heart of the Loire châteaux, 5 km south-west of Tours. Access by D86 and then D207.

19 bedrs, all ensuite, **P** 100 **DB** 380-750 **B** 50-80 ✗ 195-480 ℂℂ MC Visa Amex ⌁ 4km ▣ ▣ 2km ▣ ▥ ⌁
RAC Special price in low season

★★ Château de la Loire
12 rue Gambetta, 37000 Tours
☎ **02 47 05 10 05 Fax 02 47 20 20 14**
English spoken
Closed 7 Dec-22 Feb
This hotel has a warm, welcoming atmosphere and is situated in a quiet area near the old town and the town hall. Rue Gambetta is just off rue Nationale.

30 bedrs, all ensuite, ✦ **P** 10 **DB** 190-280 **B** 38 No restaurant ℂℂ MC Visa Amex ⌁ 10km ▣ ⌁ ♿
RAC 10 %

★★ Hôtel Ariane
8 avenue du Lac, 37300 Joué-les-Tours
☎ **02 47 67 67 60 Fax 02 47 67 33 36**
English spoken
Closed 20 Dec-5 Jan

Two conference rooms, each seating up to 30 people, are available in this new hotel. Nearby facilities include 18 hole golf course, water sports, squash and a children's playground.

32 bedrs, all ensuite, ✦ **P** 35 **DB** 259-289 **B** 32-37 No restaurant ℂℂ MC Visa ⌁ ⌁ ▣ ▣ ▥ ⌁ ♿

★★ Hôtel Cygne
6 rue Cygne, 37000 Tours
☎ **02 47 66 66 41 Fax 02 47 20 18 76**
English spoken
A charming 18th century hotel, centrally located in a quiet street near the theatre, castle and cathedral; five minutes from the station.

18 bedrs, all ensuite, ✦ **P** 6 **DB** 240-390 **B** 35 No restaurant ℂℂ MC Visa Amex ⌁ 5km ▣ ▣ ⌁

Facilities for the Disabled
Hotels do their best to cater for disabled visitors. However, it is advisable to contact the hotel direct to ensure it can provide for a particular requirement.

★★ Hôtel Mirabeau

89 bis bd Heurteloup, 37000 Tours
📞 02 47 05 24 60 Fax 02 47 05 31 09
English spoken
A centrally located 19th century building with period furnishings. Close to the Loire and the Mirabeau bridge. From the A10 motorway, take exit 12 to Tours-Centre.

25 bedrs, all ensuite, ⊁ P DB 250-310 B 29-39 No restaurant CC MC Visa Amex ⌖ 3km 🖾
RAC 10 %

VIERZON Cher   2D

★★ Hôtel Arche

Forum République, 18100 Vierzon
📞 02 48 71 93 10 Fax 02 48 71 83 63
English spoken

Modern, quiet and comfortable hotel, with a panoramic view of the Berry canal, set in the centre of Vierzon. Restaurant offers French regional cuisine and grill specialities. Free enclosed parking.

40 bedrs, all ensuite, P 40 DB 235-290 B 35 ✕ 75-120 CC MC Visa Amex ⌖ 2km 🖾 🖾 ⊞ ⌀ ⛟

★★★ Hôtel Continental

104 bis avenue E. Vaillant, 18100 Vierzon
📞 02 48 75 35 22 Fax 02 48 71 10 39
English spoken

A quiet hotel with spacious bedrooms, charming atmosphere and à la carte restaurant specialising in traditional French cuisine. Leave motorway at Vierzon-Nord exit, hotel 1 km.

37 bedrs, 30 ensuite, ⊁ P 37 DB 160-270 B 35 ✕ 20-50 (plus à la carte) CC MC Visa Amex ⌖ 2km 🖾 ⊞ ⌀

VILLENY Loir et Cher   2D

★★★ Hôstellerie de Chênes Rouges

41220 Villeny
📞 02 54 98 23 94 Fax 02 54 98 23 99
English spoken
Closed 1 Feb-8 Mar

A fine hostelry, close to Chambord and Cheverny in the Sologne region, offering comfort and elegance in woodland setting. Meals may be served by the fireside or swimming pool. Fishing in the lake, walking in the peace of the forest. 90 minutes from Paris.

10 bedrs, all ensuite, ⊁ P 15 DB 650-800 B 75 ✕ 175-205 CC MC Visa Amex ⋩ ⌖ 15km 🖾 🖾 🖾 ⊞ ⌀ ⛟
RAC 10 %

VOVES Eure et Loire   2D

★★★ Hôtel Quai Fleuri

15 rue Texier-Gallas, 28150 Voves
📞 02 37 99 15 15 Fax 02 37 99 11 20
English spoken
A warm, welcoming, renovated former mill, with a relaxed atmosphere and a panoramic terrace, set in wooded parkland between Chartres and Orléans.

17 bedrs, all ensuite, ⊁ P 12 DB 345-440 B 45 ✕ 75-225 CC MC Amex 🖾 ⊞ ⌀ ⛟

Paris and
Ile de France

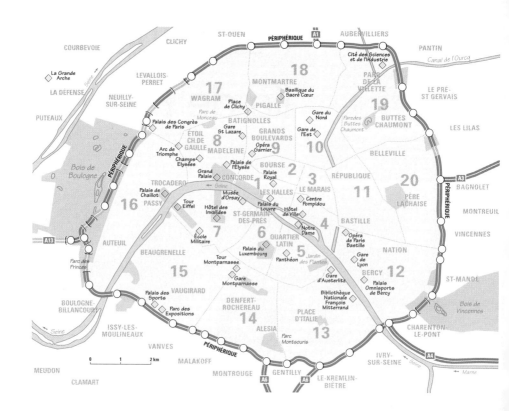

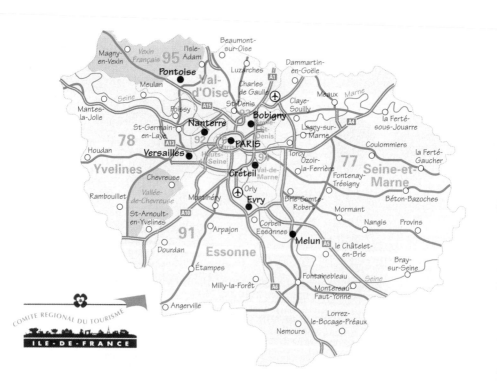

Paris defeats every cynic. With so much hyperbole and superlative poured over the French capital, the more jaded traveller might secretly hope to despise the city. But it can't be done. Paris is wonderful. Like any great city, Paris can at first appear to be almost overwhelming. Take this 'moveable feast' in stages – you can always come back for more.

Getting about in Paris is most easily done by a combination of metro-riding and walking. Driving is almost pointless (and, often, death-defying) and the buses can be rather confusing. The metro is extensive, efficient and fairly cheap. Lines are named according to their final stop. So, for example, the Château de Vincennes line becomes the Grande Arche de la Défense when travelling in the opposite direction. With this information, a metro map and some stout shoes, one can begin to explore Paris. The names and numbers of the *arrondissements* are provided on the map opposite.

The **Eiffel Tower** (open daily 9am–midnight in summer, 9.30am–11pm in winter) is a good place to start, the reason being that the commanding view from the top is the best way to get a feel for the layout of the city. With the help of perspective and 1,053 feet, Paris becomes a perfect scale model. The tower itself is truly stunning. It was built to a design by Monsieur Eiffel in 1889 for the World's Fair. After an initially sceptical reaction from the French people, Eiffel managed to wow the world with the then tallest structure on Earth. Queues for the alarming lift ride to the top can be long, but the wait is well-rewarded. Visit the tower at night for an irresistibly romantic view across the shimmering capital.

After relaxing in the exquisitely-manicured Champ de Mars park behind the Eiffel Tower, one can cross the Seine to make the long, but scenic, walk along the riverside to the **Place de la Concorde**. This imposing and rather manic convergence of avenues is in the process of being turned into a giant sundial as part of the French plans to mark the millennium. The giant obelisk from Luxor, which stands in the centre of the place, will be the pointer.

Page 109: The Seine, the bridges of Paris and Ile de la Cité
Above left: A view of the bridge Alexander III and the Eiffel Tower
Above right: The Eiffel Tower viewed from the top of the Garnier's Paris Opera

From here, ultra-expensive boutiques line the exclusive Champs-Elysées all the way to the Arc de Triomphe (open daily 10am–5.30pm Apr–Sep, 10am–5pm Oct–Mar).

The **Champs-Elysées** has little to offer the visitor, except a vague sense of the great wealth Paris has accumulated over the years. The **Arc de Triomphe**, similarly, is impressive for its grandeur but is hardly entertaining – unless, of course, you decide to cross the road for a closer look.

If you do, you will be an unwitting player in the biggest lottery in Europe. The stakes are high: Parisians tear around their triumphal arch with no regard for pedestrians.

Back at the Place de la Concorde, one can continue the Seine-side walk east through the delightful **Jardins des Tuileries**. These expansive gardens are perfect for lying back to watch the whirl of Paris life flash past. Patrons at the over-priced, but laid-back, cafés are constantly serenaded by particularly accomplished buskers.

The gardens are a useful place to prepare for the mayhem which is the **Musée National du Louvre** (open Mon, Wed–Sun 9am–6pm). This is arguably the best art museum in the world, and its size is staggering. It would take years to see everything it has to offer – particularly as only a fraction of its collection can be on display at any one time. The crowds can be frustrating, so it is definitely a good idea to get there early. Most visitors head straight for the main displays, such as the Mona Lisa and the Venus de Milo, but these works are just the beginning.

Around the corner is the much more manageable **Musée de l'Orangerie** (Mon, Wed–Sun 9.45am–5.15pm). This is a beautiful and restful gallery with magnificent works by many of the most influential Impressionist masters. Paintings from Monet's beautiful Nymphéas series are wrapped around the walls of this museum. A short walk north from the Louvre will take you to the **Forum des Halles**. This is the place for shopping, although it can seem slightly sterile after a day spent exploring

Above: The Louvre Museum with the Pyramide

the more traditional boutiques of Paris. More exciting is the extraordinary **Centre Pompidou** (Mon, Wed–Fri noon–10pm, Sat, Sun 10am–10pm). Renzo Piano and Richard Rogers' then controversial design can now hardly fail to be mentioned in any discussion of the merits of modern architecture. The striking inside-out design has defied all critics (and there have been many) by becoming one of the most visited buildings in France.

As a modern art gallery, it is brilliant. As a spectacle, it is fascinating. The front plaza of the Centre is packed with buskers and street artists, creating a carnival-like atmosphere. Continuing the walk along the Seine from the Louvre, leads to the ever-trendy **Marais** district. Bursting with boutiques, cafés and colour, Le Marais is the perfect place to

spend half a day wandering aimlessly through the city's stylish streets.

Anyone with even a passing interest in Picasso should visit the **Musée Picasso** (Mon, Wed–Sun 9.30am–6pm or 5.30pm in winter), which is the largest collection of the man's work and personal memorabilia anywhere in the world.

This is also a great area in which to eat. Restaurants, from the romantic to the riotous, jostle for attention along the banks of the Seine. Some of the more attractive and more touristy eateries can be found on or around the **Ile de la Cité**. This is the bigger of two islands which force the mighty Seine temporarily to split into two.

Another masterpiece is the beautiful Sainte-Chapelle.

Left: Paris was born on the Ile de la Cité. So was Quasimodo. The breathtaking Cathédral de Notre-Dame towers over the island. Brave the steep stairs in the tower to enjoy one of the finest views in Paris.

Left: Montmartre with the Sacré-Coeur dominating the skyline

A rather more macabre afternoon can be spent at **La Conciergerie** (open daily 9.30am–6.30pm Apr–Sep, 10am–4pm Oct–Mar), the oldest, but now defunct, prison in Paris. Marie-Antoinette was one of many victims of the French Revolution to await the chop in La Conciergerie. The ex-gaol now boasts an interesting display on those turbulent years.

Ile St Louis, which is connected by bridge to the Ile de la Cité, must be the best address in Paris. There is not a great deal to do here, but the beautiful houses and streets, which are home to just 6,000 Louisiens, are worth seeing.

On the opposite side of the Seine from Le Marais is the **Latin Quarter**, so named because of the Latin-speaking university which stood here until 1789.

This bookish theme runs right through the area. Victor Hugo, Jean-Jacques Rousseau and Voltaire are all buried here in the Panthéon.

Dusty bookshops are squeezed in between a glut of Greek and Arab restaurants.

If you're in Paris for the art, don't overlook the excellent **Musée d'Orsay** (Tue–Sun 9am–6pm in summer, 10am–6pm in winter), which deals with painting and sculpture from the mid nineteenth century to the outbreak of World War I. Look out for works by Renoir, Monet, Van Gogh and Cézanne. Take time to explore the Latin Quarter. This part of the Left Bank has a very different feel from the monumental and upmarket boulevards of the opposite side of the river. Head here for cheap restaurants and a rather appealing 'village' atmosphere.

Another village in Paris is **Montmartre**. With the church of **Sacré-Coeur** dominating the local skyline, and with a sense of isolation from the rest of the city, Montmartre has become one of the most visited sights in Paris. This immense popularity has caused the character of the area to change. Once a thriving artists' community, Montmartre now appears to be geared solely towards relieving tourists of their hard-earned francs.

Certainly the centre of the village, place de Tertre, is overcrowded with tourists and the caricaturists. But don't be put off. Like so many of Paris' more patronised attractions, a few steps away from the centre of the action will take the traveller to more genuine treats. Walk away from place de Tertre in any direction – but especially towards the seedy, but exciting, **Pigalle** district – and you will find all the benefits of Montmartre's hill-top perch and charming streets.

Pigalle itself is an interesting area. Like London's Soho, strip joints rub shoulders with some great restaurants and lively bars.

Few cities have had quite the same influence over European culture as Paris. One way to gauge the extent of this is to visit the Père Lachaise cemetery on the boulevard de Ménilmontant.

The inventory of dead cultural icons buried here reads like the guest list to the best party of all time. Oscar Wilde, Chopin, Proust, Balzac and Bizet are just a few of the better-known names to be found on the headstones of this elegant cemetery.

Most visitors to Père Lachaise are there to see Jim Morrison's grave, just follow the graffiti to find it.

Day trips from Paris in the Ile de France

Disneyland Paris
Considering the uneasy nature of the relationship between the French people and American culture, it is hard to understand why Disney chose to build its European arm in France.

Talk to a French person about Disneyland, and they will invariably make disparaging noises and roll their eyes. Ignore them.

Disneyland – like its counterparts in California and Florida – is fantastic fun. Kids and adults alike will love the sheer escapism of the place.

It is extremely efficiently-run and the employees make every effort to please.

The queues can be a headache, so go before the school term ends if you possibly can.

Head for the dare-devil Indiana Jones and Thunder Mountain rides. Younger children will love Fantasyland.

Slick son et lumiere-style performances take place throughout the day and are worth waiting around for.

Food and drink can be expensive so you might appreciate taking a packed lunch with you.

Drive to Disneyland Paris (20 miles from Paris) along the A4 or take the RER to Marne-la-Vallée-Chessy.

Giverny
Monet's famous house and gardens (below) are within reach of Paris and are described in this guide on page 49.

Left: Césars Tower in Provins

The Palace of Versailles

Just 10 miles from Paris, Versailles makes a popular and highly rewarding excursion. It is a masterpiece of one-upmanship.

Louis XIV was determined to build a palace which would out-do Vaux-le-Vicomte – the stately home of his finance minister, Nicholas Fouquet (see page 118).

Most agree that Louis' pad has the edge. So enormous is the palace that visitors often feel rather daunted.

Take a guided tour to get a real feel for the place. Perhaps the most impressive room in the building is the famous Hall of Mirrors. This is where the Versailles Treaty was signed in the aftermath of World War I. Many historians consider it one of the most significant acts of the twentieth century.

You can visit the bedchamber where Louis XIV died and where Louis XVI and Marie-Antoinette faced the revolutionary mob in 1789.

Also open are the private apartments of Marie-Antoinette; and the room where the Swiss Guards confronted the revolutionaries in a desperate attempt to save the King.

Outside, the 250-acre formal gardens stand as testament to the green-fingered geometry of André Le Nôtre. Various kings continued to add to the gardens, so now they are littered with strange follies and majestic summer houses (which would, to most people, be considered châteaux in their own right).

Drivers should use the N185 to reach Versailles. Otherwise take the RER to Versailles-Rive Gauche or the train from Gare St-Lazare.

Below: The fountain at the Palace of Versailles

Fontainebleau

Fontainebleau is further from Paris than Versailles (43 miles), but still it attracts hordes of Parisian day-trippers.

They come as much for the preposterous château as for the enormous forest, which is a favoured playground for the capital's stressed-out office workers.

The château is amazing, but it is also ridiculous. Built in the sixteenth century, Fontainebleau was a prize of Italianate architecture. However, successive kings, and even emperors, have added to it so that now it is an enormous, conflicting jumble of styles. It is, however, a unique and amusing place, which will reward anyone willing to make the journey.

Drive via the A6 and N7 or take a train from the Gare de Lyon.

Auvers-sur-Oise

Just 22 miles from Paris, Auvers-sur-Oise provides an accessible excursion from the capital. This is where the brilliant, but deeply troubled, Vincent Van Gogh lived out the last two months of his life before his suicide in July 1890.

Van Gogh rented a cheap and depressing room above an inn. His time here was short, but prolific, and the perfectly-preserved room is highly evocative. If you are not already familiar with Van Gogh's work from this period, go to the Musée d'Orsay before visiting Auvers-sur-Oise.

It is quite amazing to see his subject-matter just days or even hours after seeing his work.

Drive via the A15 and N184 or take a train from the Gare du Nord or Gare St-Lazare.

Left: Even though Fontainebleau Palace is 43 miles from Paris, the astounding building and impressive gardens are well worth a visit

Vaux-le-Vicomte

The spectacular château at Vaux-le-Vicomte (which is 37 miles from Paris) is overshadowed only by the intriguing story which surrounds it.

Nicholas Fouquet was one of the richest and most influential men in France in the seventeenth century.

He became the finance minister, a role which he used to further his own business career as much as to sort out the temperamental French economy.

At the height of his fortune, he built the vast Vaux-le-Vicomte. Then, unfortunately, he made a mistake.

He organised what historians have described as the most excessive party in the history of Europe. The 23-year-old King, Louis XIV, was invited.

Louis was outraged by what he saw. Fouquet's gargantuan display of wealth and self-satisfaction threatened his authority. The King's action was ruthless but decisive. He had Fouquet arrested and tried for fraud. The disgraced minister was sentenced to solitary confinement and his possessions confiscated by the crown.

It was this jealousy that prompted Louis XIV to commission Versailles – the most extravagant château he could imagine.

The best time to see Fouquet's dream home is on one of the many evenings when the château is lit up beautifully by strategically-placed candles.

Drive via the A6 and Melun or take the train to Melun from the Gare de Lyon, followed by a taxi to the château.

TOURIST INFORMATION
- **Paris Tourist Office**
  127 avenue des Champs-Elyseés, 75008 Paris
  ☎ 1 49 52 53 54
- **Ile de France Tourist Office**
  26 avenue de l'Opéra, 75001 Paris
  ☎ 1 42 60 28 62

Getting there

By road
The major arteries from Paris include:
- A13 to Caen
- A1 to Lille
- A4 to Strasbourg
- A5 to Langres
- A6 to Lyon
- A10 to Bordeaux
- A11 to Nantes

By rail
Each major train station in Paris serves a different region of France:
- Gare Montparnasse for Brittany and southern Normandy
- Gare St-Lazare for northern Normandy
- Gare du Nord for northern France
- Gare de l'Est for Strasbourg and Champagne
- Gare de Lyon for the Alps, Burgundy and southern France
- *Gare d'Austerlitz* for south-west France.

By air
Paris Orly Airport (◘ 1 49 75 52 52) is around 4 miles south of Paris. Get to Paris by taxi, Air France airport shuttle, Orlybus, Jetbus, RER line C or RER line B.
For car hire contact:
- Avis ◘ 1 49 75 44 91
- Budget ◘ 1 49 75 56 00
- Europcar ◘ 1 49 75 47 47

Paris Charles de Gaulle Airport (◘ 1 48 62 12 12) is about 10 miles north-east of the capital. Get into Paris by taxi, Air France airport shuttle, Roissybus or RER line B.
Car hire at Paris Charles de Gaulle, contact:
- Avis ◘ 1 48 64 39 65
- Europcar ◘ 1 48 62 33 33

Below: The popular Château de Courances
Far left: The splendid Vaux-le-Vicomte Palace

BARBIZON Seine et Marne   2D

★★★ Hôtel La Dague
5 Grand Rue, 77630 Barbizon
☎ 01 60 66 40 49 Fax 01 60 69 24 59
English spoken
*A large rustic manor, set in the 'Village of Painters',
on the edge of Fontainebleau Forest. Located 50 km
from Paris by A6 motorway. 5 km from the château
and Fontainebleau. The gourmet meals are served
outside in summer.*

25 bedrs, 23 ensuite, ⊨ P 15 DB 350-450 B 48-60
✕ 140-260 ₵₵ MC Visa ▶ 8km 🖾 🖳 🖂 ⊞ ℘
RAC 10 %

BOULOGNE-BILLANCOURT Hauts de Seine   3B

★★★ Hôtel Acanthe
9 rondpoint Rhin et Danube, 92100 Boulogne-
Billancourt
☎ 01 46 99 10 40 Fax 01 46 99 00 05
English spoken
*Situated 8 km from Opera Garnier and opposite the
metro, the hotel offers bright, well designed and air-
conditioned accommodation, a summer garden and
easy access to motorway A13 to Normandy.*

69 bedrs, all ensuite, ⊨ P 14 DB 785-860 B 75 ₵₵ MC
Visa Amex ▶ 🖂 ⊞ ఉ
RAC 10 %

CERGY-PONTOISE Val d'Oise   2B

★★★ Hôtel Astrée
3 rue des Chênes Emeraude, bd de l'Oise, 95000
Cergy
☎ 01 34 24 94 94 Fax 01 34 24 95 15
English spoken
*A warm and friendly welcome in a comfortable and
refined setting. With a bar, air-conditioning and a
free car park. Motorway A15, junction 10, Cergy
centre in front of building #3.*

55 bedrs, all ensuite, ⊨ P 48 DB 500-780 B 45 No
restaurant ₵₵ MC Visa Amex ▶ 2km 🖂 ⊞ ℘ ఉ
RAC Free breakfast

Telephoning France
When telephoning France from the United
Kingdom dial 00 33 and omit the initial 0
of the French code.
Telephoning the United Kingdom
When telephoning the United Kingdom
from France dial 00 44 and omit the initial
0 of the United Kingdom code.

CHARENTON Val de Marne   3B

★★★ Hôtel Atria Paris Charenton
5 place des Marseillais, 94227 Charenton
☎ 01 46 76 60 60 Fax 01 49 77 68 00
English spoken

*Situated close to the Bois de Vincennes. From the
Paris ring road (Périphérique) go to Charenton-
Centre. The Métro station Liberté is 20 m away. Close
to the leisure centre.*

133 bedrs, all ensuite, ⊨ P ₵₵ MC Visa Amex 🖾 🖳
⊞ ℘ ఉ

FONTAINEBLEAU Seine et Marne   2D

★★★ Hostellerie Moulin de Flagy
2 rue du Moulin, 77940 Flagy
☎ 01 60 96 67 89 Fax 01 60 96 69 51
English spoken
Closed 13-25 Sep & 20 Dec-22 Jan

*Hotel and restaurant closed Sunday evenings and
Mondays*

10 bedrs, all ensuite, ⊨ P 20 DB 330-500 B 52 ✕ 160-
250 (plus à la carte) ₵₵ MC Visa Amex ▶ 3km 🖳 🖂
10km ఉ

★★ Hôtel Ibis
18 rue Ferrare, 77300 Fontainebleau
☎ **01 64 23 45 25** Fax **01 64 23 42 22**
English spoken

Newly renovated, the hotel is set in large gardens at the edge of the forest and is just 3 minutes from the château. With light, spacious rooms and a family atmosphere it is a good stop-over on the way south and within easy reach of central Paris.

20 bedrs, 18 ensuite, ⟵ P DB 305-335 B 35 ✕ 50-65 CC MC Visa Amex ▶ 34km ▣ ▣

An attractive, modern hotel in the centre of town, 5 minutes walk from the famous château and 45 minutes from Paris. French regional cuisine served on the patio in summer.

81 bedrs, all ensuite, ⟵ P 30 DB 220-370 B 39 ✕ 55-95 CC MC Visa Amex ▶ 1km ▣ ⠿ ⌁ ♿

★★★ Hôtel de Londres
Place du Gal de Gaulle, 77300 Fontainebleau
☎ **01 64 22 20 21** Fax **01 60 72 39 16**
English spoken
Closed 21 Dec-5 Jan
Family owned since 1850, the hotel, with comfortable rooms and antique furniture, has an enviable position opposite the palace's main entrance.

12 bedrs, all ensuite, P DB 450-850 CC MC Visa Amex ▶ 2km ▣ ⌁

★★★ Hôtel Le Vieux Logis
5 rue Sadi Carnot, ThOmery, 77810 Fontainebleau
☎ **01 60 96 44 77** Fax **01 60 70 01 42**
English spoken

★★★★ Hôtel de l'Aigle Noir
27 place Napoléon Bonaparte, 77300 Fontainebleau
☎ **01 60 74 60 00** Fax **01 60 74 60 01**
English spoken

Set in the Seine Valley and forest, this establishment has 14 double bedrooms, a swimming pool, patio and golf within 6 km. 'Fine cuisine gastronomique dans un cadre lumineux et raffiné'. Located 50 min from Paris and 5 min from Fountainbleau.

14 bedrs, all ensuite, ⟵ P DB 400 B 50 ✕ 155-240 CC MC Visa Amex ⤴ ▶ 7km ▣ ▣ ▣ ⠿ ⌁

A 16th century town-house near the gardens of Fontainebleau, with 56 individually decorated rooms and apartments. Gourmet restaurant and piano-bar 'Le Montijo' and indoor pool and gym. Ideal for weekends and seminars. Close to Paris.

56 bedrs, all ensuite, ⟵ P DB 790-2,000 B 90 ✕ 180-450 CC MC Visa Amex ▣ ▣ ▣ ▶ 1km ▣ ▣ ▣ ⠿ ⌁ ♿
RAC 10 %

★★ Hôtel Victoria
112 rue de France, 77300 Fontainebleau
☎ **01 60 74 90 00** Fax **01 60 74 90 10**
English spoken

GRESSY Seine et Marne 2B

★★★★ Manoir de Gressy
77410 Gressy
☎ 01 60 26 68 00 Fax 01 60 26 45 46
English spoken
Closed 20 Dec-5 Jan

*A charming 17th century manor house,
reconstructed as a luxury hotel. From central Paris,
head towards Charles de Gaulle airport, follow signs
to Soisson then A104 and N2. Exit at Airport/Mitry,
then follow signs to Gressy.*

85 bedrs, all ensuite, ✝ **P** 100 **DB** 950-1,250 **B** 85
✗ 185 (plus à la carte) **CC** MC Visa Amex ⊰ 🏋 ▸
15km 🔲 ✈ ♯ ⌀ ⅄
RƏC 10 % off bed & breakfast

GUIGNES Seine et Marne 2D

★★★ Hôtel La Chaum'Yerres
1 av Libération, 77390 Chaumes-en-Brie
☎ 01 64 06 03 42 Fax 01 64 06 36 15
English spoken

*A small hotel offering excellent service and a warm
welcome, comfortable rooms (3 with jacuzzi) and a
pretty garden. In the heart of the village and with the
river flowing past. Situated just north-east of Guignes
and only 40 km from Paris.*

10 bedrs, all ensuite, ✝ **P** **DB** 290-580 **B** 48 ✗ 180-255
CC MC Visa Amex ▸ 10km 🔲 ✈ ♯ ⌀ ⅄
RƏC 10 % on room rate

MARNE-LA-VALLEE Seine et Marne 3B

★★★ Golf Hôtel
15 av du Golf, 77600 Bussy-St-Georges
☎ 01 64 66 30 30 Fax 01 64 66 04 36
English spoken
*The hotel, peacefully situated next to an 18 hole golf
course, has its own outdoor, heated swimming-pool, 2
tennis courts and private access to the golf links. 27
km from Paris and 10 minutes from Disneyland.*

94 bedrs, all ensuite, ✝ **P** 100 **DB** 530-580 **B** 55-60
✗ 68-155 **CC** MC Visa Amex ⊰ 🕑 ▸ 🔲 ✈ ♯ ⌀ ⅄
RƏC 10 %

★★★ Saphir Hôtel
Aire des Berchères, 77340 Pontault-Combault
☎ 01 64 43 45 47 Fax 01 64 40 52 43
English spoken

*A light, spacious hotel with excellent, friendly service
and all the comforts and facilities, including 20
suites, of a 4-star establishment. Set in landscaped
gardens between Paris and Disneyland. Leave A4 at
Pontault-Combault.*

180 bedrs, all ensuite, ✝ **P** **DB** 440-550 **B** 52 ✗ 77-160
CC MC Visa Amex ⊰ 🏋 📟 🕑 ▸ 2km 🔲 ✈ ♯ ⌀ ⅄

MEUDON Hauts de Seine 3B

★★★ Hôtel Forest Hill
40 avenue du Mar de Lattre, Meudon La Forêt, 92365
Meudon
☎ 01 46 30 22 55 Fax 01 46 32 16 54
English spoken

Meudon is south-west of Paris, close to the Vélizy Shopping Centre, with easy access to the heart of the capital via the Porte de Sévres or the Porte de St-Cloud.

157 bedrs, all ensuite, ⊬ P 100 DB 420-920 B 40-55 ✕ 79-134 ℂℂ MC Visa Amex ⫶ 🖾 🖾 🖾 ⅲ 𝒫 ⅃
RaC 20 %

NEAUPHLE-LE-CHATEAU Yvelines 2D

★★★ Hôtel Le Verboise
78640 Neauphle-le-Château
☎ 01 34 89 11 78 Fax 01 34 89 57 33
English spoken
Closed 4-17 Aug & 20-27 Dec

A large, elegant 19th century residence set in its own 3 hectare park. The restaurant offers speciality cuisine including salade de langoustine, gaspacho de homard and barbue au jus de viande. 20 minutes from Paris: west of Versailles on N12.

20 bedrs, all ensuite, ⊬ P DB 490-590 B 68 ✕ 155-235 ℂℂ MC Visa Amex ⥃ 2km 🖾 🖾 ⅲ

NEMOURS Seine et Marne 2D

★★ Hôtel L'Ecu de France
Restaurant Le Victor Hugo, 3 rue de Paris, 77140 Nemours
☎ 01 64 28 11 54 Fax 01 64 45 03 65
English spoken
An inviting Logis de France hotel, with traditional cuisine and an excellent cellar, which has been welcoming travellers since 1384. Exit A6 or N7 and drive towards Nemours centre. The hotel is close to the church in the centre of town.

25 bedrs, 20 ensuite, ⊬ P DB 219-259 B 28-38 ✕ 99-275 ℂℂ MC Visa Amex ⥃ 15km 🖾 🖾 ⅲ 𝒫

★★ Hôtel Les Roches
av L. Pelletier, St-Pierre-lès-Nemours, 77140 Nemours
☎ 01 64 28 01 43 Fax 01 64 28 04 27
English spoken
Closed 1 Feb-1 Apr
A hotel in a verdant setting, providing quality service and quiet, comfortable rooms. The restaurant, a regional 'value for money' award winner, offers fine

creative cuisine. 70 km from Paris, 12 km from Fontainebleau on N7.

15 bedrs, 13 ensuite, ⊬ P DB 220-270 B 30 ✕ 90-290 ℂℂ MC Visa ⥃ ⥃ 10km 🖾 🖾 🖾 𝒫
RaC 10 %

ORGEVAL Yvelines 2B

★★★★ Hôtel Moulin d'Orgeval
rue de l'Abbaye, 78630 Orgeval
☎ 01 39 75 85 74 Fax 01 39 75 48 52
English spoken

A luxurious former abbey, standing in beautiful grounds, with a renowned restaurant offering facilities for the disabled. From A13, exit at Poissy-Villennes then turn right towards Orgeval, and look for signs

14 bedrs, all ensuite, ⊬ P 50 DB 680-800 B 60 ✕ 140-350 ℂℂ MC Visa Amex ⥃ 🖾 ⥃ 3km 🖾 🖾 🖾 ⅲ 𝒫 ⅃
RaC 5 %

PARIS II 3B

★★★ Hôtel Baudelaire Opéra
61 rue Sainte-Anne, 75002 Paris
☎ 01 42 97 50 62 Fax 01 42 86 85 85
English spoken

The Hôtel Baudelaire is superbly located in the centre of Paris, within easy walking distance of most main attractions and shops. On arriving in Paris, follow the signs to either the Louvre or Opéra. The hotel is between the two.

29 bedrs, all ensuite, P DB 595-650 B 38 No restaurant ℂℂ MC Visa Amex 𝒫
See advert on next page

Hôtel Baudelaire Opéra ★★★

There's nowhere better to explore Paris from!
We are a 3 star hotel right in the middle of Paris (2nd arrondissement), within easy walking distance of most of the major attractions – including the Louvre, Opéra, main department stores and direct train access for EuroDisney.

A warm welcome awaits you – comfortable en-suite rooms (cable TV), reasonable prices and a friendly atmosphere. The hotel is English-owned, so please feel free to call, write or fax in English or French!

**61 RUE SAINTE-ANNE, 75002 PARIS
TEL: +33 (0)1 42 97 50 62
FAX: +33 (0)1 42 86 85 85**

A charming hotel, with beautiful, well equipped rooms furnished with wood, wrought iron, Louvre mouldings and balconies. Fantastic location between the Luxembourg Gardens and the Latin Quarter. Sigmund Freud stayed here in 1885.

26 bedrs, all ensuite, **P DB** 790-1,050 **B** 50 No restaurant **CC** MC Visa Amex ▦ ◢ ㋡ **RAC 8 %**

PARIS VI   3B

★★★ Holiday Inn Paris
St-Germain-des-Prés, 92 rue de Vaugirard, 75006 Paris
📞 **01 42 22 00 56 Fax 01 42 22 05 39**
English spoken

PARIS III   3B

★★★★ Hôtel Pavillon de la Reine
28 pl des Vosges, 75003 Paris
📞 **01 42 77 96 40 Fax 01 42 77 63 06**
English spoken

In the historic Marais district on the romantic Place des Vosges, this air-conditioned hotel has individually decorated rooms with antique furniture, some overlooking flower-filled courtyards.

55 bedrs, all ensuite, ⊁ **P** 20 **DB** 1,850-2,300 **B** 110-135 No restaurant **CC** MC Visa Amex ▶ ▨ ◢ ㋡

PARIS V   3B

★★★ Hôtel des Jardins du Luxembourg
5 impasse Royer-Collard, 75005 Paris
📞 **01 40 46 08 88 Fax 01 40 46 02 28**
English spoken

A completely renovated hotel, fully air-conditioned with a restaurant, bar and private underground garage. Located on the left bank in the famous quarter of St-Germain-des-Prés.

134 bedrs, all ensuite, ⊁ **P** 130 **DB** 880-1,050 **B** 75 ✗ 100-250 **CC** MC Visa Amex ▦ ◢ ㋡

★★★ Hotel des Deux Continents
25 rue Jacob, 75006 Paris
📞 **01 43 26 72 46 Fax 01 43 25 67 80**
Situated in the heart of St-Germain-des-Prés, a quiet charming hotel with air-conditioned bedrooms and a cosy atmosphere.

41 bedrs, all ensuite, **P DB** 715-815 **B** 45

★★★★ Hôtel Relais Christine
3 rue Christine, 75006 Paris
📞 **01 40 51 60 80 Fax 01 40 51 60 81**
English spoken

Set in the heart of St-Germain-des-Prés, on the left bank of the River Seine, this 16th century hotel, formerly a cloister, offers a warm welcome. The air-conditioned rooms are individually decorated in warm-coloured fabrics and antique furniture.

51 bedrs, all ensuite, ♍ **P** 20 **DB** 1,850-2,700 **B** 110-135 **CC** MC Visa Amex ▶ ☒ ⅲ ♬
RaC **Upgrade with availability**

★★★ Hôtel Relais St-Sulpice
3 rue Garancière, 75006 Paris
☎ 01 46 33 99 00 Fax 01 46 33 00 10
English spoken

Formerly a nobleman's private house, this quiet hotel, located close to the Luxembourg Gardens in the St-Germain quarter, offers air-conditioned rooms and views of the St Sulpice church. Private parking available for guests.

26 bedrs, all ensuite, **P** **DB** 920-1,250 **B** 50 No restaurant **CC** MC Visa Amex ▨ ♬ ら
RaC **8 %**

★★ Hôtel Welcome
66 rue de Seine, 75006 Paris
☎ 01 46 34 24 80 Fax 01 40 46 81 59
English spoken
This hotel is situated in the heart of Saint-Germain-des-Prés, 15 minutes walk from the Louvre and the Musée d'Orsay and close to Odéon metro station.

30 bedrs, all ensuite, **P** **DB** 440-545 **B** 40 No restaurant **CC** MC Visa

★★★ Hôtel de Seine
52 rue de Seine, 75006 Paris
☎ 01 46 34 22 80 Fax 01 46 34 04 74
English spoken

This hotel, situated on the corner of rue de Seine and rue Jacob in the heart of St-Germain-des-Prés, offers comfortable rooms, a family atmosphere and a convenient location for guests to enjoy the area's bustling day and night life.

30 bedrs, all ensuite, **P** **DB** 820-1,090 **B** 45 No restaurant **CC** MC Visa

PARIS VII   3B

★★★ Hôtel Les Jardins d'Eiffel
8 rue Amélie, 75007 Paris
☎ 01 47 05 46 21 Fax 01 45 55 28 08
English spoken

A completely renovated hotel with a garden, situated in a residential area close to the Eiffel Tower and Les Invalides.

80 bedrs, all ensuite, ♍ **P** **DB** 670-970 **B** 60 No restaurant **CC** MC Visa Amex ▶ 10km ☒ ⅲ ♬ ら

PARIS VIII   3B

★★★ Hôtel Centre Ville Matignon
3 rue de Ponthieu, 75008 Paris
☎ 01 42 25 73 01 Fax 01 42 56 01 39
English spoken

Charming, art deco hotel, located close to the Champs-Elysées. All the bedrooms are equipped with minibar, TV and safe.

25 bedrs, all ensuite, ♍ **P** **DB** 690-890 **B** 55 No restaurant **CC** MC Visa Amex ♬
RaC **10 %**

★★★ Hôtel Elysée
12 rue des Saussaies, 75008 Paris
📞 01 42 65 29 25 Fax 01 42 65 64 28
English spoken

*A charming air-conditioned hotel with all modern
facilities. Within easy reach of the Champs-Elysées,
the shopping area of Faubourg-St-Honoré, theatres
and gourmet restaurants. Suites also available.*

32 bedrs, all ensuite, **P DB** 720-1,280 **B** 65 No
restaurant **CC** MC Visa Amex 🏊
RAC **20 %**

★★★★ Hôtel Napoléon
40 av de Friedland, 75008 Paris
📞 01 47 66 02 02 Fax 01 47 66 82 33
English spoken
*An Empire-style hotel, close to the Arc de Triomphe
and Champs-Elysées, offering friendly and efficient
service. Public parking nearby.*

102 bedrs, all ensuite, 🛏 **P DB** 1,500-2,100 **B** 110 No
restaurant **CC** MC Visa Amex ▶ ⅲ ᕦ
RAC

★★★ Hôtel Résidence Monceau
85 rue du Rocher, 75008 Paris
📞 01 45 22 75 11 Fax 01 45 22 30 88
English spoken

*Quietly situated in the Etoile-Montmartre-Opéra-St-
Lazare area, this 3 star tourist hotel offers classic
comfort a warm atmosphere and 51 spacious rooms.
Close to the Parc Monceau and the lively market on
the rue de Lévis.*

51 bedrs, all ensuite, **P DB** 720-890 **B** 50 No
restaurant **CC** MC Visa Amex 🏊 ᕦ
RAC **10 %**

★★★★ Hôtel Sofitel Paris Arc de Triomphe
14 rue Beaujon, 75008 Paris
📞 01 53 89 50 50 Fax 01 53 89 50 51
English spoken

*Situated close to the Champs-Elyseés and Etoile, in the
heart of Paris, this luxurious and trendy former
mansion has been entirely renovated in an 18th
century style. Restaurant 'Le Clovis' offers refined
cuisine in an elegant setting.*

135 bedrs, all ensuite, 🛏 **P DB** 2,200-3,150 **B** 120
✕ 250-500 **CC** MC Visa Amex ▶ 🖪 ⅲ 🏊 ᕦ
RAC **15 %**

L'OUEST HOTEL

★ ★

Reasonably Priced ✔
Central Position ✔
Comfortable Rooms ✔
Easy Parking ✔

L'Ouest Hôtel is in the 8th arrondissement, 10 minutes' walk from Monmartre and from the Champs Elysées and on to the Tuileries ... the Louvre ...
And when your legs give out, the métro is there at St-Lazare.

**L'Ouest Hôtel
3 rue du Rocher
75008 Paris
Tel: 01 43 87 57 49
Fax: 01 43 87 90 27**

See under Paris VIII

★★ L'Ouest-Hôtel
3 rue du Rocher, 75008 Paris
☎ 01 43 87 57 49 Fax 01 43 87 90 27
English spoken

This hotel is located in the heart of the business centre, next to the St-Lazare station, between Monmartre and the Champs-Elysees.

53 bedrs, all ensuite, **P DB** 460-510 **B** 30 No restaurant **CC** MC Visa Amex

PARIS IX · 3B

★★★ Hôtel du Pré
10 rue P.Sémard, 75009 Paris
☎ 01 42 81 37 11 Fax 01 40 23 98 28
English spoken

A fully renovated hotel, situated in central Paris between the Opéra, Gare du Nord and Sacré Coeur. From Autoroute du Nord exit via Porte de la Chapelle to the Gare du Nord, then turn right down rue La Fayette to the hotel.

145 bedrs, all ensuite, **⊀ P DB** 460-580 **B** 50 No restaurant **CC** MC Visa Amex

PARIS XI · 3B

★★★ Hôtel Home Plazza Bastille
74 rue Amelot, 75011 Paris
☎ 01 40 21 22 23 Fax 01 47 00 82 40
English spoken
The largest Suite Hotel de Charme, close to place des Vosges and the Bastille in the historic centre of Paris. With 1,500 square metres of private gardens and terrace. Easy access to Disneyland, 30 minutes away.

290 bedrs, all ensuite, **⊀ P** 40 **DB** 1,180 **B** 65 **✗** 75-210
CC MC Visa Amex **⊞** ⌀ ♿
RAC 50 %
See advert on next page

★★★ Hôtel Home Plazza St-Antoine
289 bis rue du Fg St-Antoine, 75011 Paris
☎ 01 40 09 40 00 Fax 01 40 09 11 55
English spoken
A Suite Hotel de Charme establishment, with private courtyard, in the historic centre of Paris. Only 30 minutes from Paris Disneyland.

90 bedrs, all ensuite, **⊀ P** 20 **DB** 880-1,480 **B** 65 **CC**
MC Visa Amex **⊞** ⌀ ♿
RAC 50 %
See advert on next page

All Suite Hotel Home Plazza Bastille
74. rue Amelot 750111 PARIS
Tel. : 33 1 40 21 22 23 – Fax. : 33 1 47 00 82 40
290 rooms. Metro St Sébastien Froissart
Close to Place des Vosges, Historic Marais area and
Opera Bastille.

All Suite Hotel Home Plazza St Antoine
289. Bis rue di Fg St Antoine 750111 PARIS
Tel. : 33 1 40 09 40 00 – Fax. : 33 1 40 09 11 55
90 rooms.
Near Opera Bastille, close to Express Metro Nation
(15 min. to Etoile / 30 min. to Disneyland Paris®)

- The Largest Suite Hotel De Charme in the Historic Centre of Paris. Garden View.
- Junior Suites and 4 Beds Suites with Wet-Bar and Fully equipped kitchenette.
- 1,500 sq. metres of Private Gardens and Terraces.
- Private Garage. Restaurant / Bar.

(Amex, Euro/Mastercard, Visa, Dinner's)
Multilingual Reception.

Private Courtyard All Suite Hotel Home Plazza Bastille

SPECIAL RATES : 50 % discount on rack rates
from 13.7.98 to 31.8.98 incl. (minimum stay of 3 nights)
▷ SINGLE : 407 FF – DOUBLE : 414FF / 614FF
QUADRUPLE : 740FF / 940FF
Net rates upon our availability+ City tax.
Per room / per day

Family rooms All Suite Hotel Home Plazza Bastille & St Antoine

---

PARIS XII   **3B**

★★★ Hôtel Le Relais de Lyon
64 rue Crozatier, 75012 Paris
📞 01 43 44 22 50 Fax 01 43 41 55 12
English spoken

Built in 1984, this modern 5-storey hotel, with period furnishing, is situated close to the Bastille and Gare de Lyon in a quiet part of east-central Paris. Free garaging for guests.

34 bedrs, all ensuite, **P** 7 **DB** 386-492 **B** 40 No restaurant **CC** MC Visa Amex ⚎ ✗

★★ Nouvel Hôtel
9 rue d'Austerlitz, 75012 Paris
📞 01 43 42 15 79 Fax 01 43 42 31 11
English spoken
A comfortable hotel, with fully equipped and soundproofed rooms, ideally situated between Gare de Lyon and Gare d'Austerlitz. 10 minutes to Omnisports de Bercy and place de la Bastille. Three stops to Etoile and two stops to the Opéra on the métro.

24 bedrs, all ensuite, **P** **DB** 380 **B** 30 No restaurant **CC** MC Visa Amex

---

PARIS XIII   **3B**

★★ Hôtel Arts
8 rue Coypel, 75013 Paris
📞 01 47 07 76 32 Fax 01 43 31 18 09
English spoken
A comfortable hotel, situated in a quiet residential street, close to the place d'Italie-Gobelins métro station.

37 bedrs, all ensuite, 🐾 **P** **DB** 290-360 **B** 30 No restaurant **CC** MC Visa Amex ✗

PARIS XIV   **3B**

★★ Hôtel Ariane Montparnasse
35 rue Sablière, 75014 Paris
📞 01 45 45 67 13 Fax 01 45 45 39 49
English spoken

A new two star hotel in a quiet location ten minutes from the Montparnasse train station and RER Denfert-Rochereau. Five minutes from Porte d'Orléans.

30 bedrs, all ensuite, ⋔ P DB 350-560 B 35 No restaurant ℂℂ MC Visa Amex ⚌ ⚘
RAC 10 %

★★ Hôtel Istria
29 rue Campagne Première, 75014 Paris
☎ 01 43 20 91 82 Fax 01 43 22 48 45
English spoken

Set in a very quiet street, in the artists' Montparnasse area, near the TGV station and within walking distance of St-Germain-des-Prés, the Latin Quarter and Luxembourg Gardens. Access: Périphérique-Sud exit Pte Orléans towards Montparnasse.

26 bedrs, all ensuite, ⋔ P DB 540-590 B 40 No restaurant ℂℂ MC Visa ⚘
RAC 10 % Bed & Breakfast

★★★ Hôtel Mercure Paris Montparnasse
20 rue de la GaÔté, 75014 Paris
☎ 01 43 35 28 28 Fax 01 43 27 98 64
English spoken
A modern hotel, with authentic bistro, on the left bank, near Montparnasse TGV station and within walking distance of St-Germain-des-Prés, Latin Quarter and Luxembourg Gardens. Access: Périphérique-Sud exit Pte Orléans towards Montparnasse.

185 bedrs, all ensuite, ⋔ P 45 DB 900-1,080 B 72 ℝ 130-175 ℂℂ MC Visa Amex ⚌ ⚘ ♿
RAC 10 %

★★★ Abaca Messidor Hôtel
330 rue de Vaugirard, 75015 Paris
☎ 01 48 28 03 74 Fax 01 48 28 75 17
English spoken

The countryside in the heart of Paris - it's a delightful luxury. The nearest métro station is Convention on line 12. Secure car parking available opposite hotel.

72 bedrs, all ensuite, ⋔ P DB 470-855 B 70 No restaurant ℂℂ MC Visa Amex ⚌ ⚘
RAC 10 %

★★ Hôtel Fondary
30 rue Fondary, 75015 Paris
☎ 01 45 75 14 75 Fax 01 45 75 84 42
English spoken
A traditional, centrally situated hotel, just 20 minutes from the Champs-Elysées. The nearest Métro station is Emile Zola.

20 bedrs, all ensuite, ⋔ P DB 385-405 B 38 No restaurant ℂℂ MC Visa Amex

★★★ Hôtel Forest Hill Paris Balard
1 bd Victor, 75015 Paris
☎ 01 40 60 16 16 Fax 01 40 60 03 40
English spoken

A comfortable hotel, close to the Balard métro station and 100m from the Aquaboulevard de Paris and Porte de Versailles exhibition centre. Restaurant 'Le Beverly' is known for its good food and magnificent buffet.

130 bedrs, all ensuite, ⋔ P DB 595-1,695 B 40-68 ✕ 79-134 ℂℂ MC Visa Amex ⊢ ⚌ ⚘ ♿
RAC 20 %

★★ Hôtel Le Farmus
94 bd Garibaldi, 75015 Paris
☎ 01 47 34 49 74 Fax 01 40 65 95 76
English spoken

A completely renovated hotel, with restaurant offering French regional specialities, situated on the left bank of the River Seine close to the Eiffel Tower and Les Invalides. A great base for shopping trips. Public parking nearby.

25 bedrs, all ensuite, ✞ P DB 430 B 40 ℂℂ MC Visa Amex ♬
RAC 10 %

★★ Hôtel Lecourbe
28 rue Lecourbe, 75015 Paris
☎ 01 47 34 49 06 Fax 01 47 34 64 65
English spoken

An elegant hotel with an interesting history and charming, flower-filled, private courtyard.

47 bedrs, all ensuite, ✞ P DB 450-500 B 49 No restaurant ℂℂ MC Visa Amex ⋕ ♬
RAC 10 %

★★ Hôtel Lilas Blanc Grenelle
5 rue de l'Avre, 75015 Paris
☎ 01 45 75 30 07 Fax 01 45 78 66 65

A quiet, comfortable hotel situated in the centre of the 15th district. Its 32 personalised bedrooms are harmoniously decorated and fully equipped with the latest comforts. Visitor tax included in the price.

32 bedrs, all ensuite, ✞ P DB 405-435 B 35 No restaurant ℂℂ MC Visa Amex ▸ 18km ♬
RAC 5 %

PARIS XVI   3B

★★★★ Hotel Saint James Paris
43 av Bugeaud, 75116 Paris
☎ 01 44 05 81 81 Fax 01 44 05 81 82
English spoken

The Hotel Saint James (formerly the St James' club) was completely renovated in 1987 and offers quiet, spacious bedrooms individually decorated in a mixture of traditional and modern styles. Patrons restaurant and bar. The only 'chateau hotel' in Paris.

48 bedrs, all ensuite, ✞ P 15 DB 1,900-2,150 B 110-135 ✗ 350 ℂℂ MC Visa Amex ⊞ ▦ ▸ ▣ ⋕ ♬

★★★★ Hôtel Garden Elysée
12 rue St-Didier, 75016 Paris
☎ 01 47 55 01 11 Fax 01 47 27 79 24
English spoken

A charming hotel, with a peaceful garden, situated in a quiet residential area close to the Champs-Elysées.

48 bedrs, all ensuite, P 4 DB 1,700 B 95 No restaurant ℂℂ MC Visa Amex ⋕ ♿
RAC 10 %

★★ Hôtel Hameau de Passy
48 rue de Passy, 75016 Paris
☎ 01 42 88 47 55 Fax 01 42 30 83 72
English spoken

A recently renovated hotel with a small garden and a private garage nearby. Situated in a residential area, between Muette and Passy métro stations, close to the Eiffel Tower.

32 bedrs, all ensuite, ⍾ P DB 500-630 B included
No restaurant ℂℂ MC Visa Amex 🖾 🖉 ⅃
RAC 5 %

★★★★ Le Parc Westin Demeure Hôtels
55-57 av Raymond Poincaré, 75116 Paris
☎ 01 44 05 66 66 Fax 01 44 05 66 00
English spoken

This hotel, situated between l'Etoile and the Trocadéro in the heart of the 16th district, has been completely renovated and decorated in the English style. Restaurant 'Le Relais du Parc' offers traditional cuisine and views of the interior garden.

120 bedrs, all ensuite, ⍾ P 4 DB 2,300-2,650 B 140 ℂℂ
MC Visa Amex 🖾 ⫶⫶ ⅃

★★★ Hôtel Acacias Etoile
1 rue Acacias, 75017 Paris
☎ 01 43 80 60 22 Fax 01 48 88 96 40
English spoken

A charming hotel, with a private garden, quietly situated close to the Arc de Triomphe.

37 bedrs, all ensuite, ⍾ P DB 650-700 B 48 ℂℂ MC
Visa Amex ▸ 🖾
RAC 10 %

★★★ Hôtel Centre Ville Etoile
6 rue des Acacias, 75017 Paris
☎ 01 43 80 56 18 Fax 01 47 54 93 43
English spoken

An elegantly charming hotel situated between the Champs-Elysées and the Porte Maillot.

30 bedrs, all ensuite, ⍾ P DB 590-790 B 55 No
restaurant ℂℂ MC Visa Amex 🖉
RAC 10 %

★★ Hôtel Flaubert
19 rue Rennequin, 75017 Paris
☎ 01 46 22 44 35 Fax 01 43 80 32 34
English spoken

An inn-style hotel, built around a small garden, only 10 minutes walk from the Arc de Triomphe. Exit the Périphérique at Porte Courcelles, the hotel is situated on rue Rennequin close to avenue Wagram.

37 bedrs, all ensuite, ⍾ P 10 DB 480-550 B 40 No
restaurant ℂℂ MC Visa Amex 🖉 ⅃
RAC 15 % 10%/15%

PARIS XVIII   3B

★★★★ Hôtel Terrass
12 rue Joseph-de-Maistre, 75018 Paris
☎ 01 46 06 72 85 Fax 01 42 52 29 11
English spoken

A traditional, luxury-class, hotel quietly situated in the heart of picturesque Montmartre.

101 bedrs, all ensuite, P 10 DB 1,080-1,730 B 70
✗ 130-170 ₵₵ MC Visa Amex ⅲ
RAC 5 %

★★ Hôtel Utrillo
7 rue A Bruant, 75018 Paris
☎ 01 42 58 13 44 Fax 01 42 23 93 88
English spoken

Situated in the heart of Montmartre, with a nice view from the top floor, the hotel serves a generous buffet breakfast. The nearest métro stations are Abbesses and Blanche.

30 bedrs, all ensuite, P DB 390-450 B 40 ₵₵ MC Visa Amex ▣

PARIS XIX   3B

★★★ Hôtel Forest Hill La Villette
28 avenue Corentin Cariou, 75019 Paris
☎ 01 44 72 15 30 Fax 01 44 72 15 80
English spoken

A 3 star hotel, with a brasserie and gourmet restaurant, situated to the north of the city, close to Cité des Sciences and the stunning 'Géode'. Porte de la Villette is the nearest métro station.

260 bedrs, all ensuite, ⊁ P 1,000 DB 595-1,695 B 40-68
✗ 79-134 ₵₵ MC Visa Amex ⅲ ⌔ &
RAC 20 %

ROISSY Val d'Oise   3B

★★ Hôtel Ibis Parc d' Expositions
Villepinte, BP 60069, 95972 Roissy CDG Cedex
☎ 01 48 63 89 50 Fax 01 48 63 23 10
English spoken

A hotel at the entrance of the Villepinte exhibition centre, on the northern outskirts of Paris. 5 minutes from Roissy-Charles de Gaulle airport, 15 minutes from Asterix theme park, 30 minutes from Disneyland Paris via Fancilenne dual carriageway.

124 bedrs, all ensuite, ⊁ P DB 249-598 B 39 ✗ 55-135
₵₵ MC Visa Amex ⅲ &

ROLLEBOISE Yvelines   2B

★★★ Château de la Corniche
5 route de la Corniche, 78270 Rolleboise
☎ 01 30 93 21 24 Fax 01 30 42 27 44
English spoken
Closed 20 Dec-6 Jan

This historic château, overlooking the Seine, was formerly the home of King Leopold II. 58 km from Paris, 30 km from Versailles and 8 km from Giverny.

*From Paris take A13 exit 13. From Vernon take the
N15, on the right just after Bonnières.*

35 bedrs, all ensuite, ✝ P 80 **DB** 400-800 **B** 50-60
✕ 160-360 (plus à la carte) **CC** MC Visa Amex ⊰ ►
8km ▨ ☒ ░ ♫

SACLAY Essonne 3B

★★★ Novotel
rue Charles Thomassin, 91400 Saclay
☎ 01 69 35 66 00 **Fax** 01 69 41 01 77
English spoken
*Situated close to the scenic Chevreuse Valley. Take A10
motorway towards Les Ulis, then N118 exit Saclay.*

136 bedrs, all ensuite, ✝ P **DB** 580-725 **B** 60 ✕ 98
(plus à la carte) **CC** MC Visa Amex ⊰ ☒ ► ▨ ☒ ░ &

ST-GERMAIN-EN-LAYE Yvelines 3B

★★★ Hôtel Forest Hill
10 rue Yvan Tourgueneff, 78380 Bougival
☎ 02 39 18 17 16 **Fax** 02 39 18 15 80
English spoken

*The hotel is located to the west of Paris, close to La
Défense business centre, Versailles and St-Germain,
in a pleasant leafy setting on the banks of the Seine.
Bougival lies close to the N13, about 4 km on the
Paris side of central St-Germain.*

175 bedrs, all ensuite, ✝ P 200 **DB** 490-920 **B** 40-55
✕ 79-134 **CC** MC Visa Amex ⊰ ► ▨ ☒ ░ ♫ &
RAC 20 %

★★★★ Hôtel La Cazaudehore et La
Forestière
1 av Prés Kénnédy, 78100 St-Germain-en-Laye
☎ 01 30 61 64 64 **Fax** 01 39 73 73 88
English spoken
*A stylish hotel located in the heart of the St-Germain
forest, 1.5 km from the town (towards Pontoise) and
20 km from Paris.*

30 bedrs, all ensuite, P 60 **DB** 990 **B** 75 ✕ 290-370 **CC**
MC Visa Amex ► ░ ♫

ST-LEGER-EN-YVELINES Yvelines 2D

★★★ Hôtel Pendragon Oak
78610 St-Léger-en-Yvelines
☎ 01 34 86 30 11 **Fax** 01 34 86 35 08
English spoken

*Situated in the heart of the Rambouillet forest 50 km
from Paris, this charming 18th century hotel has
comfortable rooms, satellite TV (English channels),
English style furniture and a pub open until 1 am,
with English beers.*

26 bedrs, all ensuite, ✝ P 15 **DB** 350-550 **B** 50-60
✕ 159-250 **CC** Visa ⊰ ► ▨ ☒ ☒ ░
RAC 10 %

ST-QUENTIN-EN-YVELINES Yvelines 2D

★★★ Hôtel Auberge du Manet
61 avenue Victor Clairet, 78180 Montigny
☎ 01 30 64 89 00 **Fax** 01 30 64 55 10
English spoken

*30 km from Paris, close to Versailles on the Loire
châteaux route, this former outbuilding of the Port-
Royal abbey has all the charm of an historic residence.
Its refined cuisine is a true taste of the south.*

35 bedrs, all ensuite, ✝ P **DB** 390-550 **B** 56 ✕ 130-180
CC MC Visa Amex ☒ ► ▨ ☒ ☒ ░ ♫ &
RAC 3rd night free
See advert on next page

AUBERGE DU MANET
HOTEL RESTAURANT ★★★

Located in the beautiful Nature Park of Vallée Chevreuse, this elegant manor house offers serenity, charm and superb cuisine featuring specialities from Provence. Ideally located 30 km from Paris, 10 km from Versailles, 120 km from the Loire Castles.

**61 AVENUE DU MANET
78180 MONTIGNY LE BX
FRANCE**
Tel: 01 30 64 89 00 Fax: 01 30 64 55 10

SAVIGNY-SUR-ORGE Essonne   3B

★★ Hôtel Albion
9 avenue de Garigliano, 91600 Savigny-sur-Orge
☎ 01 69 05 05 05 Fax 01 69 05 00 33
English spoken

Hotel with terrace, swimming pool, golf, restaurant with cuisine of Provence. 5 minutes from the motorway A6 (Paris-Lyon), 10 minutes from Orly airport.

54 bedrs, all ensuite, ⌇ P DB 245 B 35 ✕ 69-200 ℃
MC Visa Amex ⌷ ▣ ▸ ▨ ▩ ⵗ ∅ ♿
RAC **8 %**

When parking your car ensure you are not facing oncoming traffic. This will help you when you return to your car.

LES ULIS Essonne   3B

★★★ Hôtel Mercure
3 rue Rio Solado, Courtaboeuf, 91952 Les Ulis
☎ 01 69 07 63 96 Fax 01 69 07 92 00
English spoken
This modern hotel in a pleasant, shady park is a peaceful stop-over point, 1 km off the highway, offering easy access to Paris (20 km). Take Ulis/Courtaboeuf exit from A12 if coming from west or from A10 if coming from south.

108 bedrs, all ensuite, ⌇ P 150 DB 610-930 B 62
✕ 120-150 ℃ MC Visa Amex ⌷ ▸ 6km ▨ ▩ ⵗ ♿
RAC **15 % Jul-Aug & Weekends**

VELIZY-VILLACOUBLAY Yvelines   2D

★★★ Hôtel Holiday Inn
22 av de l'Europe, 78140 Vélizy-Villacoublay
☎ 01 39 46 96 98 Fax 01 34 65 95 21
English spoken

A comfortable, well-equipped hotel opposite the Velizy shopping mall. Ideally situated 10 minutes from Paris, 5 minutes from Versailles in the heart of a famous golf course area. Access via A56 or N118. Exit Velizy Zone d'Emplois.

182 bedrs, all ensuite, ⌇ P 160 DB 895-1,100 B 75
✕ 135-225 ℃ MC Visa Amex ⌷ ▩ ▸ 15km ▨ ⵗ ∅ ♿
RAC **Weekend 50%, Weekdays 25%**

VERSAILLES Yvelines   3B

★★ Hôtel Aérotel
88 rue du Docteur-Vaillant, 78210 St-Cyr-l'Ecole
☎ 01 30 45 07 44 Fax 01 34 60 35 96
English spoken

Experience the peace of the countryside just 30 minutes from Paris in a cosy family-run Relais du Silence hotel just behind the château. Easy access by métro, RER and motorways.

26 bedrs, all ensuite, ⊁ **P** **DB** 250-380 **B** 38 ✕ 60-80 ℂℂ MC Visa ⊰ ▸ 🖾
RAC 10 %

★★★ Hôtel Résidence du Berry
14 rue Anjou, 78000 Versailles
☎ 01 39 49 07 07 **Fax** 01 39 50 59 40
English spoken
A charming hotel completely refurbished in 1997, located in the heart of Versailles. 5 minutes walk from the famous palace and RER railway station. The hotel offers a private garden, a bar and a business centre.

38 bedrs, all ensuite, ⊁ **P** **DB** 430-500 **B** 50 ℂℂ MC Visa Amex ▸ 3km 🖾 ♉

★★★ Novotel
4 bd St-Antoine, BP 88, 78152 Le Chesnay Cedex
☎ 01 39 54 96 96 **Fax** 01 39 54 94 40
English spoken
Five minutes from the Palace of Versailles. From the A13 exit Versailles-Ouest/Notre-Dame/Le Chesnay or, from the A86 exit Versailles-Centre. Charge for covered parking.

105 bedrs, all ensuite, ⊁ **P** 37 **DB** 580-725 **B** 60-75 ✕ 95-120 ℂℂ MC Visa Amex ▸ 4km 🖾 ♯ ⅋

★★★★ Trianon Palace Hôtel
1 bd de la Reine, 78000 Versailles
☎ 01 30 84 38 00 **Fax** 01 39 49 00 77
English spoken
The Trianon Palace is situated on the edge of the former royal domain of Louis XIV, in a 3 hectare park with century-old trees. 15 minutes from Paris

190 bedrs, all ensuite, **P** **DB** 1,400-2,100 **B** 110-140 ✕ 165-610 ℂℂ MC Visa Amex 🖾 🖾 🖾 ▸ 🖾 🖾 ♯ ⅋ ⅋

★★★ Relais Mercure Timing Paris Sud
116 rue Edouard Vaillant, 94807 Villejuif Cedex
☎ 01 47 26 06 06 **Fax** 01 46 77 80 21
The hotel offers 4 hectares of space organised for business, sports and relaxation. Enter Paris through

Porte d'Italie, take N7 towards Villejuif, turn off at the Ford garage and follow the signs.

148 bedrs, all ensuite, **P** 250 **DB** 535 **B** 50 ✕ 115-145 🖾 🖾 🖾 🖾
RAC

★★★ Hôtel Daumesnil-Vincennes
50 avenue de Paris, 94300 Vincennes
☎ 01 48 08 44 10 **Fax** 01 43 65 10 94
English spoken
The hotel Daumesnil-Vincennes offers a warm welcome, a friendly atmosphere and 50 comfortable, air-conditioned rooms. 10 minutes from the centre of Paris (métro Berault, RER Vincennes).

50 bedrs, all ensuite, ⊁ **P** 15 **DB** 420-650 **B** 38-45 No restaurant ℂℂ MC Visa Amex ▸ 🖾 ♉
RAC 10 %

★★ Hôtel du Donjon-Vincennes
22 rue du Donjon, 94300 Vincennes
☎ 01 43 28 19 17 **Fax** 01 49 57 02 04
English spoken
Closed Aug
A quiet hotel only 100 m from the Château de Vincennes. RER, métro and bus station close by.

25 bedrs, all ensuite, **P** **DB** 280-370 **B** 30 ℂℂ MC Visa 🖸 ▸ 5km 🖾 🖾 ♯ ⅄
RAC 10 %

Champagne-Ardennes

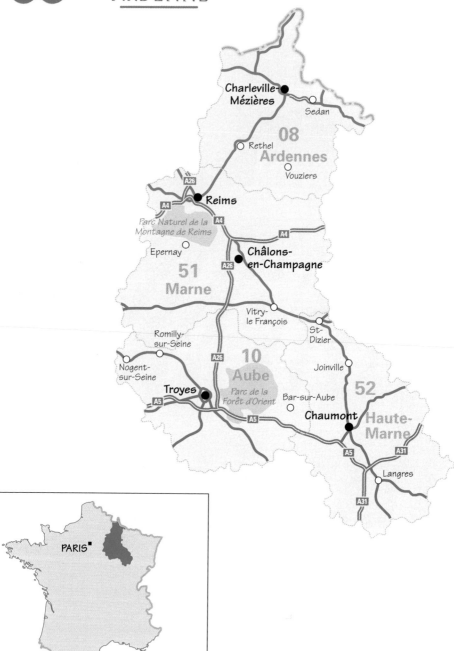

The name 'Ardennes' is taken from the Celtic 'Ar Den' which means 'deep forest'. It's a fair description. The Ardennes Forest dominates the north of this region, particularly around the border with Belgium. It is a breeding ground for myths and legends – as well as wild boars. Further south, the trees thin out to reveal a gentle and open landscape which is now, of course, coated with vineyards.

One of the more unusual treasures of the Ardennes is the zig-zag citadel at **Givet**. This star-shaped fortress is now smoothed by moss, but it still makes an interesting diversion.

Fans of the seditious poet Arthur Rimbaud might want to visit **Charleville**, his birthplace. Rimbaud wrote the great *Le Bateau Ivre* when he was only 17. Visit the well thought out Rimbaud museum to find out more about this boy-genius. More adventurous enthusiasts might want to follow the Rimbaud trail which links places connected to Rimbaud and his travelling companion and fellow poet Verlaine. Ask at the local tourist information office for details of that route.

While Rimbaud was still in his teens France was facing military domination from the north. The Prussian Army had grown to become one of the greatest in the world. When the Prussians swept south through the Ardennes in 1870, Napoleon III's badly-prepared soldiers could do little to turn back the Germanic tide. The final scenes of battle were played out around the medieval fortress at **Sedan**. The site is all the more magnificent for its historical associations.

For a long time, the chalky land of Champagne was quite separate from France. The two were merged, with the union between Joan of Naverre and Champagne and King Philip IV of France. The deal was officially signed and sealed with the coronation of their son, Louis X, in 1314.

Reims is no stranger to coronations. Some 26 Gallic monarchs have been invested here, and many of those graduated to the gallery of statues above Reims cathedral's rose window.

The cathedral is itself a good enough reason to visit the city. To many minds, this is the most impressive Gothic cathedral in France. Since so much of Reims was destroyed during the war, it is fortunate that the cathedral still stands – although how much

of it has been restored is hard to tell. Connoisseurs of bubbly should visit the sprawling cellars of champagne makers such as Tattinger, Pommery and Mumm. You will find some vintage bottles at outrageous prices, but, if you pretend to be interested in buying one, you could well get a free taste of a more recent bottle.

While Reims is the administrative centre of the champagne industry, **Epernay** is its real home. This is where Dom Pérignon first figured out how to trap the wine's natural effervescence. The whole town seems to live for champagne, and many of the best-known names in the business are based here. See pages 140-141 for details of how to visit the most famous champagne houses.

For a complete break from bubbly, head for **Troyes** which is around 60 miles south of Reims. Troyes is a particularly attractive town which has been nicknamed 'the city of a hundred towers'. The wobbly-looking half-timbered houses are charming, and there is also a colourful cathedral and a Museum of

Pages 136–137: Vineyards at Villedomange near Reims
Above: The cathedral at Reims has remarkable architecture, with rich sculptures, including the famous Smiling Angel, and the Rose window (seen above)

Modern Art. If modern art is not your thing, you could always visit the Musée de la Bonneterie. This slightly strange attraction offers an intriguing exhibition on Troyes' distinguished hat making industry.

Travellers often overlook Langres and Colombey-les-Deux Eglises, although both are well worth visiting. **Langres** occupies an enviable position above the River Saône. It is easy to see why the Romans were so keen to build a town here. Modern Langres has retained several interesting reminders of its Gallo-Roman origins, including a vast expanse of medieval wall.

Charles de Gaulle retired to **Colombey-les-Deaux Eglises** and, in the process, put this quiet little village on the world map.

A taste of Champagne

The production of France's most prestigious wine centres on a range of low, vine-planted hills on the Côte d'Ile de France between the Tardenois and the Brie Plateau and the long plain of the Champagne sèche. The heart of the region, where the grapes grow best, focuses on the Montagne de Reims. This is outlined by the Marne River on the south and a curved line drawn between Vincelles, Reims and Ambonnay in the west, north and east respectively.

Only wine made from vines planted within this strictly delineated 84,000 acres and prepared according to a particular process can, by law, be called champagne. Some of this land is owned by the famous *maisons de champagne* (champagne houses), which produce most of the wine. However, much of the land is owned by thousands of smaller growers – *vignerons* – who either sell their grapes to the main houses or make their own champagne. Along the roadsides and in the stone-built villages and towns that dot the area, signs will direct you to visit the *caves* of these small producers.

Touring in Champagne

Drivers can follow the 'Route touristique de champagne' covering the area from Reims to Villenauxe-la-Grande, via Epernay, Dormans and Vertus. If you prefer to take a leisurely cruise on the Marne, the cruise Le Champagne Vallée departs from Cumiéres

Above: A windmill in the Champagne region at Vernezay, near Reims

(☎ 3 26544951). The following minor roads give spectacular views across the wooded Champagne countryside:

- the **D386** from Fismes along the Vesle River
- the **D9** from Reims
- the **D34** down to the Marne
- the **D19** and **D26** around Bouzy in the east.

Champagne cellars

Listed below are the largest champagne houses in Reims and Epernay. Other champagne houses can be visited in Vallée de la Marne, the Côteaux de Sézannais and the Côte des Blancs.

- **De Castellane**
  57 rue de Verdun, Epernay
  ☎ 3 26 51 19 19
- **De Venoge**
  30 av de Champagne, Epernay
  ☎ 3 26 53 34 34
- **Heidsieck**
  51 bld Henry-Vasnier, Reims
  ☎ 3 26 84 43 44
- **Mercier**
  70 av de Champagne, Epernay
  ☎ 3 26 51 22 00
- **Möet et Chandon**
  18 av de Champagne, Epernay
  ☎ 3 26 51 20 00
- **Mumm**
  34 rue du Champ-de-Mars, Reims
  ☎ 3 26 49 59 69
- **Pommery**
  5 place du Général Gourand, Reims
  ☎ 3 26 61 62 55
- **Tattinger**
  9 place St-Nicaise, Reims
  ☎ 3 26 85 45 35

Festivals in Champagne-Ardennes
April
- Festival of art workers and craft market, Sedan

May
- Fête du Boudin Blanc (white sausage fair), Fumay
- Antiques fair and festival of glass making, Launois-sur-Vence

June
- Un été au Petit Bois (theatre, mime, music and dance), Charleville

July
- Medieval festival, Hierges

- Woodcutters' contest, Renwez
- Sound and light show, Vendresse

December
- Saint Nicholas fair and Christmas market, Launois-sur-Vence

Getting there

By road
Major arteries through Champagne-Ardennes include the:
- A26 from Calais to Troyes via Reims
- A4 from Paris to Strasbourg via Metz
- A5 from Paris to Langres via Troyes
- A34 from Reims to Mezières via Charleville
- A31 from Dijon to Metz via Nancy

By rail
TGV rail connections between Strasbourg and Paris, Bâle and Calais and Dijon and Lille.

By air
Reims Champagne Airport (☎ 3 26 07 15 15, Fax: 3 26 07 62 23) is about 5 miles north of Reims.
For car hire contact:
- Avis ☎ 3 26 47 10 08
- Budget ☎ 3 26 77 66 66
- Europcar ☎ 3 26 88 38 38

TOURIST INFORMATION
- Champagne-Ardennes Tourist Office
  5 rue de Gérico, BP 319, 51013 Chalons-en-Champagne Cedex
  ☎ 3 26 21 85 80
  Fax: 3 26 21 85 90

BAR-SUR-AUBE Aube   3C

★★★ Hôtel Le Moulin du Landion
Bar-sur-Aube, 10200 Dolancourt
☎ 03 25 27 92 17 Fax 03 25 27 94 44
English spoken
Closed 1 Dec-5 Feb
*Set in magnificent landscape, the hotel, mill and river
are just over 2 hours from Paris, in this small,
peaceful village. The restaurant has a view of the
turning mill wheel.*

16 bedrs, all ensuite, ⚲ **P** 30 **DB** 390-445 **B** 43 ✗ 99-
315 **CC** MC Visa Amex ⟨ ⌐ 20km 🚲 🖼 ⫴ ⌀ ♿
RAC **15 % except Jun-Sep**

BOURBONNE-LES-BAINS Haute Marne   3C

★★★ Hôtel Jeanne d'Arc
rue Amiral Pierre, 52400 Bourbonne-les-Bains
☎ 03 25 90 46 00 Fax 03 25 88 78 71
English spoken
Closed 20 Nov-1 Mar
*A comfortable and welcoming hotel for three
generations. "Les Armoises" restaurant features
regional cuisine. Located 10 minutes from A31
motorway, junction Montigny-le-Roi.*

30 bedrs, all ensuite, ⚲ **P** 20 **DB** 270-580 **B** 40-52
✗ 90-200 **CC** MC Visa Amex ⟨ ⌐ 40km 🖼 10km ⌀ ♿
RAC **5 % on room rate**

ARMES DE
CHAMPAGNE

*Charming Hôtel***-Restaurant***,
facing the basilica, located in the heart
of the tiny village of L'Epine.
8 km from Châlons en Champagne.
(Motorway A4 exit No 28-Saint-
Étienne au Temple.)*

**31 AV DU LUXEMBOURG,
51460 L'EPINE
TEL: 03 26 69 30 30
FAX: 03 26 69 30 26**

CHALONS-EN-CHAMPAGNE Marne   3A

★★ Hôtel Bristol
77 av P Sémard, 51510 Fagnières
☎ 03 26 68 24 63 Fax 03 26 68 22 16
English spoken
Closed Christmas
*A comfortable hotel with spacious rooms that can
accommodate extra beds for children. From A26 take
St-Gibrien exit and go straight on for 4.6 km.*

24 bedrs, all ensuite, **P** **DB** 220-270 **B** 30-35 No
restaurant **CC** MC Visa ⌐ 15km 🚲 🖼 5km ⌀

★★★ Hôtel aux Armes de Champagne
31 avenue du Luxembourg, 51460 L'Epine
☎ 03 26 69 30 30 Fax 03 26 66 92 31
English spoken
Closed 11 Jan-16 Feb

*Traditional French hostelry, very tastefully decorated
and with good facilities. In the shadow of the basilica
of Notre Dame in pretty L'Epine. 8 km from Châlons-
en-Champagne on N3 to Metz/Verdun.*

37 bedrs, all ensuite, ⚲ **P** **DB** 400-725 **B** 65 ✗ 220-490
CC MC Visa Amex ⌐ 5km 🚲 🖼 20km ⫴ ⌀

CHAOURCE Aube   3C

★★ Hôtel aux Maisons
Maisons-lès-Chaource, 10210 Chaource
☎ 03 25 70 07 19 Fax 03 25 70 07 75
English spoken
*In a small village near the Chaource forest, 30 km
from Troyes. Take the main N71 south from Troyes
turning onto D444. From A6 motorway drive 25 km
following signs for Nitry and Tonnerre.*

14 bedrs, 12 ensuite, ⚲ **P** 50 **DB** 160-250 **B** 30-40
✗ 100-160 **CC** MC Visa Amex ⟨ ⌐ 6km 🚲 🖼 ⫴ ⌀ ♿
RAC **10 %**

CHAUMONT Haute Marne   3C

★★★ Hôtel Grand Terminus Reine
Place du Général de Gaulle, 52000 Chaumont
☎ 03 25 03 66 66 Fax 03 25 03 28 95
English spoken

Find comfort and elegance in this modernised hotel. Close to the railway station in the centre of Chaumont.

63 bedrs, 59 ensuite, **🛏 P DB** 180-460 **B** 40-50 **✕** 98-360 **CC** MC Visa **▸** 18km 🖼 ⅲ ⌀ &

★★ Hôtel Le Grand Val
Route Langres, 52000 Chaumont
📞 03 25 03 90 35 Fax 03 25 32 11 80
English spoken
A modern two star hotel, situated at the the south junction of Chaumont towards Lausanne and Côte d'Azur via Langres (N19). Offers well-prepared meals and a carefully selected wine list.

52 bedrs, 44 ensuite, **P DB** 175-300 **B** 27 **✕** 58-165 **CC** MC Visa Amex 🖼 ⅲ &

★★★ Château d'Etoges
51270 Etoges
📞 03 26 59 30 08 Fax 03 26 59 35 57
English spoken

A renovated 17th century château surrounded by moats, and 12 hectares of gardens. Located in the heart of the Champagne region. Etoges is 20 km south of Epernay on D33.

20 bedrs, all ensuite, **🛏 P** 30 **DB** 600-1,200 **B** 70 **✕** 180-340 **CC** MC Visa Amex **▸** 15km 🖬 🖼 ⅲ ⌀ &
RAC 10 % on room rate except weekend/bank holidays

★★ Hôtel Val St-Hilaire
7 quai des Fours, 08600 Givet
📞 03 24 42 38 50 Fax 03 24 42 07 36
English spoken
Closed 20 Dec-5 Jan

Easy to find, the only hotel in Givet, near the Belgian border, on the waterfront alongside the River Meuse and bordered by a promenade. The hotel opened in 1990, is bright, cheerful and well situated in the heart of the cultural, artistic area of town.

20 bedrs, all ensuite, **🛏 P** 20 **DB** 345 **B** 45 No restaurant **CC** MC Visa Amex **▸** 25km 🖼 ⅲ ⌀ &
RAC 10 %

★★ Hôtel de la Poste
place Grève, 52300 Joinville
📞 03 25 94 12 63 Fax 03 25 94 36 23
English spoken
Well known for its fine cuisine, the hotel is on N67 between Chaumont and St-Dizier. Exit towards Joinville-Est and go to the town centre where there are signs to the hotel and where you will find a shaded car park.

10 bedrs, all ensuite, **🛏 P DB** 250-280 **✕** 80-220 **CC** MC Visa Amex

★★ Auberge des Voiliers
Lac de la Liez, 52200 Langres
📞 03 25 87 05 74 Fax 03 25 87 24 22
English spoken
Closed 1 Feb-15 Mar
Small, warm, welcoming inn overlooking Lake Liez. Take N19 towards Vesoul, after 4 km turn right after the bridge and the inn is 2 km ahead. Restaurant offers traditional regional cuisine. Excellent sailing/boating facilities nearby.

8 bedrs, all ensuite, **P** 3 **DB** 250-450 **B** 35 **✕** 80-200 **CC** MC Visa **▸** 30km 🖬 ⅲ ⌀ &
RAC 10 % 1-15 Oct only

★★ Grand Hôtel de Europe

23 rue Diderot, 52200 Langres
☎ 03 25 87 10 88 Fax 03 25 87 60 65
English spoken
Closed 1-25 Oct & 9-23 May
A 17th century, Logis de France hotel in the centre of town, just a stone's throw from the city walls and the countryside beyond. Attractive wood-panelled restaurant with a good choice of menus.

28 bedrs, 26 ensuite, ➤ P DB 280-320 B 36 ✕ 78-250 CC MC Visa ▸ 30km 🎿

★★ Hôtel Le Cheval Blanc

4 rue de l'Estres, 52200 Langres
☎ 03 25 87 07 00 Fax 03 25 87 23 13
English spoken
Closed second week of Nov
This charming hotel, which was once an abbey, has some vaulted rooms, renowned gourmet cuisine and a nice dining room. A stopover worth discovering.

17 bedrs, all ensuite, ➤ P DB 280-390 B 40 ✕ 115-300 CC MC Visa ▸ 🎿 🖼 ✗

MAGNANT Aube   3C

Hôtel Le Val Moret
Autoroute A5, 10110 Magnant
☎ 03 25 29 85 12 Fax 03 25 29 70 81
English spoken

Motel-style accommodation in Champagne countryside. From A5 take the Chaumont/Troyes exit towards Magnant, 30 km from Troyes.

30 bedrs, all ensuite, ➤ P 60 DB 200-300 B 30 ✕ 79-210 CC MC Visa Amex 🖼 ♨ ✗ ♿

REIMS Marne   3A

★★★★ Grand Hôtel de Templiers

22 rue des Templiers, 51100 Reims
☎ 03 26 88 55 08 Fax 03 26 47 80 60
English spoken
A quiet, relaxing, beautifully presented neo-Gothic residence; the perfect base for sightseeing and touring the surrounding area.

19 bedrs, all ensuite, P 19 DB 950-1,800 B 85 No restaurant CC MC Visa Amex 🖼 ▸ 5km ♨ ♿
RAC 10 %

★★ Grand Hôtel du Nord

75 pl Drouet-d'Erlon, 51100 Reims
☎ 03 26 47 39 03 Fax 03 26 40 92 26
English spoken
A charming, traditional hotel situated in the town centre close to the pedestrian zone, cathedral, museums and champagne cellars. Secured car park close by. Accessible A4 (A26), Reims-Centre exit.

50 bedrs, all ensuite, ➤ P DB 250-320 B 30 No restaurant CC MC Visa Amex ▸ 10km 🖼 5km ♨ ✗
RAC 8 %

★★★ Hôtel Best Western La Paix

9 rue Buirette, 51100 Reims
☎ 03 26 40 04 08 Fax 03 26 47 75 04
English spoken
An attractive hotel, with air-conditioned rooms, warm décor and garden with terrace, situated in the heart of the city close to the cathedral, wine cellars, monuments and shops.

105 bedrs, all ensuite, ➤ P 35 DB 430-650 B 53 CC MC Visa Amex 🏊 ▸ 10km ♨ ✗

★★ Hôtel Bristol

76 place Drouet d'Erlon, 51100 Reims
☎ 03 26 40 52 25 Fax 03 26 40 05 08
English spoken

A fully renovated, traditional hotel in the heart of this historic city, close to cathedral, shops and wine cellars.

40 bedrs, all ensuite, ➤ P DB 270-300 B 30 No restaurant CC MC Visa Amex
RAC 10 % or free breakfast

★★★★ Hôtel Cheval Blanc

rue du Moulin, 51400 Sept-Saulx
☎ 03 26 03 90 27 Fax 03 26 03 97 09
English spoken
Closed 23 Jan-20 Feb
A beautifully situated hotel, run by the same family for 150 years, with a restaurant offering speciality cuisine plus views of the grounds and the river that runs through them. From Reims take N44 south, then D37 to Sept-Saulx.

25 bedrs, all ensuite, ➤ P 25 DB 390-980 B 50 ✕ 180-360 CC MC Visa Amex ▸ 20km 🖼 🎿 🖼 ♨
RAC 8 % on room rate

★★ Hôtel La Maison du Champagne
2 rue du Port, 51360 Beaumont-sur-Vesle
☎ 03 26 03 92 45 Fax 03 26 03 97 59
English spoken
A 2 star hotel with restaurant offering local cuisine and seasonal specialities. From Reims: go south-east on N44 for 10 km.

11 bedrs, all ensuite, **P** 20 **DB** 260-300 **B** 35 ✕ 77-210 **CC** MC Visa Amex ▸ 10km 🎁 ⅲ ⌀

★★ Hôtel Le Bon Moine
14 rue des Capucins, 51100 Reims
☎ 03 26 47 33 64 Fax 03 26 40 43 87
English spoken

A 2 star hotel, situated close to the cathedral, offering a traditional French welcome, good cuisine and car park. Exit Reims-Cathédrale from A4.

10 bedrs, all ensuite, ⚊ **P** **DB** 250 **B** 35 ✕ 59-140 **CC** MC Visa ▸ ⌀
RAC 10 %

★★★ Hôtel Mercure Reims Cathédrale
31 bd P DouMer, 51100 Reims
☎ 03 26 84 49 49 Fax 03 26 84 49 84
English spoken

A centrally situated hotel, close to the cathedral, with a restaurant offering regional cuisine and views over the River Marne. Take Reims-Cathédrale exit from A4 motorway.

124 bedrs, all ensuite, ⚊ **P** **DB** 450-520 **B** 55 ✕ 95-180 **CC** MC Visa Amex 🎁 ▸ ⅲ ⌀ ♿

★★★ New Hôtel Europe
29 rue Buirette, 51100 Reims
☎ 03 26 47 39 39 Fax 03 26 40 14 37
English spoken
A centrally situated hotel, 2 minutes from A4 and A26, with pleasant garden, peaceful surroundings and comfortable rooms.

54 bedrs, all ensuite, **P** 12 **DB** 380-420 **B** 48-55 No restaurant **CC** MC Visa Amex ▸ 12km 🎁 ⅲ ⌀ ♿
RAC 10 %

★★★ Novotel Reims Tinqueux
route de Soissons BP12, 51431 Tinqueux
☎ 03 26 08 11 61 Fax 03 26 08 72 05
English spoken
Closed Nov
A large, contemporary hotel with good facilities and a restaurant offering speciality cuisine including carré d'agneau rôti aux senteurs des Alpilles. Exit Reims-Tinqueux from A4 or A26.

127 bedrs, all ensuite, ⚊ **P** 200 **DB** 470-500 **B** 55 ✕ 87-117 **CC** MC Visa Amex 🏊 🎁 ▸ 5km 🎁 ⅲ ⌀ ♿

REMILLY-AILLICOURT Ardennes   **3B**

★★ Auberge du Port
route Remilly-Bazeilles, 08450 Remilly-Aillicourt
☎ 03 24 27 13 89 Fax 03 24 29 35 58
English spoken
Closed 20 Dec-15 Jan
A quiet, comfortable hotel in verdant surroundings on the banks of the River Meuse. East of Sedan, go through Bazeilles and hotel is 1 km beyond, on the D129 towards Remilly.

20 bedrs, all ensuite, **P** **DB** 320 **B** 40 ✕ 98-215 **CC** MC Visa Amex ▸ 🎁 🎁 ⅲ ⌀
RAC 8 % on room rate

ST-DIZIER Haute Marne   3C

★★★ Hôtel Le Gambetta
62 rue Gambetta, 52100 St-Dizier
☎ 03 25 56 52 10 Fax 03 25 56 39 47
English spoken
Le Gambetta Hotel, situated in the town centre on the borders of Champagne and Lorraine, offers comfortable rooms and a restaurant with quality, traditional cuisine and excellent wines. Indoor and outdoor car park for guests.

63 bedrs, all ensuite, ⛟ P 20 DB 220-480 B 35 ✗ 55-125 ⓒⓒ MC Visa Amex ▦ ⊞ ♫ ໕

TROYES Aube   3C

★★★ Hôtel Relais St-Jean
51 rue Paillot de Montabert, 10000 Troyes
☎ 03 25 73 89 90 Fax 03 25 73 88 60
English spoken

Situated in the heart of the historic, 16th century, pedestrian area of Troyes, this hotel, opened in 1989, offers beautifully conceived, ultra-modern and air-conditioned surroundings with facilities to match.

23 bedrs, all ensuite, ⛟ P 23 DB 480-660 B 60 No restaurant ⓒⓒ MC Visa Amex ▶ 20km ▦ ⊞ ♫ ໕
RAC 5 %

★★ Motel Savinien
87 rue Jean de la Fontaine, 10300 Sainte Savine
☎ 03 25 79 24 90 Fax 03 25 78 04 61
English spoken

Once in town follow the N60 in the direction of Sens; look on the left hand side for an illuminated sign indicating rue Jean de la Fontaine; the motel is located on the right.

60 bedrs, all ensuite, ⛟ P DB 230-250 B 40 ✗ 85-185 ⓒⓒ MC Visa ▣ ⊞ ▦ ▧ ▨ 5km ⊞ ♫ ໕

★★★ Novotel Troyes Aéroport
10600 Barberey
☎ 03 25 71 74 74 Fax 03 25 71 74 50
English spoken
This Novotel, surrounded by pleasant, shady gardens, offers a free stay to under 16s sharing parents' room. From A5: junction 20 for Troyes then follow signs to airport. A26: junction 31 towards Troyes, follow signs to Provins and then signs to airport.

83 bedrs, all ensuite, ⛟ P 100 DB 460-490 B 55-59 ✗ 90-130 ⓒⓒ MC Visa Amex ⊐ ⊞ ▶ 12km ▦ ⊞ ໕
RAC 10 %

VITRY-LE-FRANCOIS Marne   3C

★★★ Hôtel de la Poste
place Royer-Collard, 51300 Vitry-le-François
☎ 03 26 74 02 65 Fax 03 26 74 54 71
English spoken
Closed 20 Dec-5 Jan
A traditional hotel, behind the church, in the town centre. Restaurant offers a varied menu ranging from a simple set menu to traditional local cuisine and seafood specialities. 10 km from Lac du Der, one of Europe's largest artificial lakes.

31 bedrs, 28 ensuite, ⛟ P DB 240-480 B 45-55 ✗ 98-220 ⓒⓒ MC Visa Amex ⊞ ▦ ▶ ▦ ⊞ ♫ ໕

VOUZIERS Ardennes   3A

★★★ Auberge au Pieds des Monts
Hameau de Grivy-Loisy, 08400 Vouziers
☎ 03 24 71 92 38 Fax 03 24 71 96 21
Closed Christmas & New Year
A small inn surrounded by quiet countryside and situated in a village with only 90 habitants. From Calais, take A26 to Reims, then go towards Luxembourg and Vouziers. In Blaise, 3 km before Vouziers, turn left towards Grivy-Loisy.

6 bedrs, all ensuite, P 6 DB 200-300 B 40 ✗ 65-110 ⓒⓒ MC Visa ▶ 20km ▣ ▦ 15km ♫
RAC ½ bottle champagne per couple for 2 nights

AUBERGE DU PIED DES MONTS

**FERME AUBERGE
DU PIED DES MONTS
GRIVY LOISY, 08400 VOUZIERS
TEL: 031 24 71 92 38**

Small inn "guest rooms" in tiny village of 90 inhabitants. Nice, quiet countryside.

From Calais, take A26 to Reims and then towards Luxembourg then towards Vouziers. In Blaise 3 km before Vouziers turn left towards Grivy-Loisi.

Gourmet stay in Champagne-Ardennes for 850FF/person.

◊ 2 nights at the Auberge du Pied des Monts in a comfortable ensuite room.

◊ 2 meals at the Auberge including a gourmet one.

◊ 2 breakfasts.

◊ Champagne cellar tour with sampling in Epernay.

◊ Foie gras producers tour with sampling of special vintage.

Offer valid from 15 March to 15 December 1998

It is recommended to book in advance.

Supplement for single room 250FF.

Lorraine-Vosges/
Alsace

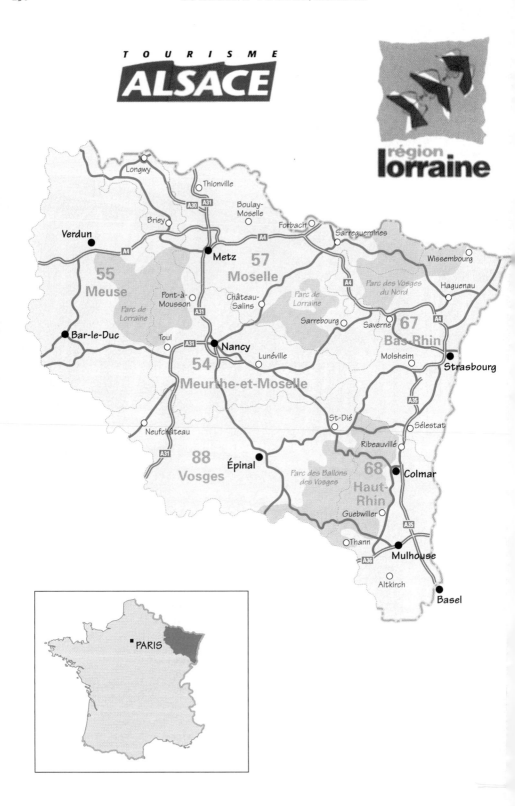

This north-eastern corner of France sits at one of Europe's most complex crossroads. Belgium, Luxembourg and Germany border Lorraine, and the area has played a pivotal role in European history.

Lorraine is both varied and beautiful. The dense and ancient Ardennes Forest to the north contrasts with the Vosges Mountains to the south. Running through it all is the River Moselle.

This century, however, it is the Maginot Line which has come to symbolise Lorraine. After World War I, France was determined to protect herself from attack. The Maginot Line was built across the north-east and was intended to be a solid line of impenetrable defences. It was an ambitious project. From 1930 to 1940 the Line was hailed as an unparalleled feat of engineering. But when France's worst fears were realised during World War II, the Maginot Line failed to hold back the German Army. The Maginot Line 'trail' is a popular tourist route and is well worth exploring.

Bitche, in the east, was a key point on the Line and one can still see the Simershof Fort and eight bunkers which have hardly been touched since 1940. There is also a fascinating Maginot Fortifications Museum (tel 3 87 06 16 16).

Further west, **Metz** is a sort of cross section of defensive design from Roman times to the twentieth century. Once the Roman 'Metis', Metz boasts an exciting legacy of art and architecture from that period. Visit the Musée Archéologique which is housed in the old Roman baths; it offers an outstanding display of Roman sculpture. Most people in Metz are particularly proud of the Eglise St-Pierre-aux-Nonnains, which is the oldest basilica in France; it dates back to the fourth century. Metz was one of three independent Bishoprics (with Toul and Verdun) in the middle ages.

This religious importance is illustrated by the glorious Cathédrale St-Etienne. Go inside to see the dazzling effect of the cathedral's stained glass windows.

Nancy, to the south, is at the very centre of the region – both geographically and culturally. Many of the elegant civic buildings here reflect a penchant for the Rococo style. Only two gates remain of the heavy duty walls which once ringed the city. They are the Porte Notre Dame and the Porte de la Craffe. The latter is kitted out with its own torture chamber.

More enjoyable, perhaps, are the myriad medieval streets which form an attractive tangle through the city-centre. Among this web you will find an appealing mix of colourful bars, cafés and great restaurants. The more traditional face of Nancy is on display in the Musée Lorrai (for information on Metz tel 3 87 55 53 76; for Nancy tel 3 83 35 22 41).

Pages 148–149: Strasbourg's Notre Dame Cathedral by E Steinbach (1384) with the 460 ft spire added by Jean Hultz in 1439

Above: Place Stanislas in Nancy

THE CROSS OF LORRAINE
This simple design with two crossbars is one of the most familiar symbols in Europe. It was first used during the Crusades and was probably created by Godefroy de Bouillon. More recently General de Gualle used the cross to rally the Resistance Movement during World War II.

Toul is a short drive west of Nancy. Its narrow streets are neatly packed behind well-preserved town walls.

All four of the imposing gates are in surprisingly good condition. The cathedral is equally impressive, although much of it is a reconstruction; Toul suffered badly during World War II. **Verdun**, to the north-west, is a familiar name to war historians and the scene of some of the fiercest fighting of World War I. The World Centre for Peace offers a chance to reflect on the tragedy of the two world wars.

Conflict is nothing new to neighbours **Vittel** and **Contrexville**. The two spa towns are locked in bitter rivalry. Both claim to offer the best restorative waters and both bottle the stuff for mass consumption. Vittel is better-known, but no one from Contrexville would ever admit it. Roman baths are on view at **Plombières-les-Bains**, a charming – and peaceful – town in the Vosges.

Alsace

Alsace is a fusion of France and Germany. Locals have a hard time thinking of themselves as French rather than Alsatian. **Strasbourg**, the capital, is a European powerhouse to rival Brussels. This is the home of the European Parliament, the Council of Europe and the European Court of Human Rights.

The centrepiece of this seductive city is the impossibly fine Cathédrale de Notre Dame. The tallest spire was added in the fifteenth century, but the bulk of the cathedral was built during the fourteenth. The sixteenth-century saw the mechanically-minded

Left: Nieder Morschwir in Alsace

Strasbourg's most famous son is Gutenberg, the man who invented the printing press. Gutenberg came to Strasbourg in 1434 from his native Mainz. While working as a goldsmith he was secretly perfecting his revolutionary invention of moveable metal type, the basis of printing techniques from the fifteenth-century to the advent of the computer.

In 1997, America's *Life* magazine commissioned a panel of top academics to name the 100 most influential people of the second millennium. Gutenberg was number one. The Gutenberg press was inspired by Alsatian wine presses and formed the basis of mass printing from the fifteenth to the twentieth century. Locals are also keen to point out that Rouget de l'Isle's *Marseillaise* was first sung in Strasbourg.

Alsations add a rather bizarre but fascinating astronomical clock.

Strasbourg is a delightful city, and one which is easy to enjoy, thanks to the fact that much of its centre is pedestrianized. The rest of the region is shaped by the mighty Rhine river and the Vosges Mountains. The Vosges are home to a series of idyllic mountain villages. Half-timbered houses with flower-filled window boxes crowd around tidy village squares. They give every impression of having changed little in hundreds of years. Drivers might want to follow the carefully signposted *Route des Villages Pittoresque* which links some of the more attractive examples of Alsatian country living.

It is hard to escape military history in Alsace-Lorraine. Even here, in the seemingly unadulterated Vosges, there are reminders of the area's tempestuous past. For example **Wissembourg**, on the German border, was once heavily fortified and is still encased behind strong defensive walls.

If you would rather escape past battles, head for the charming spa towns of

Above left: The main street of Bar-le-Duc, Lorraine
Above right: The window designed by Marc Chagall in Sarrebourg

Pechelbron and **Morsbronn** where relaxation is the only option.

Molsheim is used to a faster pace of life; this is where Ettore Bugatti built his factory in 1909. By the 1920s he was manufacturing the greatest racing cars of all time, including the *Royale*, a frequent winner at Le Mans.

The town of **Selestat** has a slightly more flimsy claim to fame; this is the home of the Christmas tree. Apparently, there is evidence that the good people of Selestat started the tradition back in 1521.

It is hard to avoid the orbit of **Mulhouse** when travelling in Alsace. This is a hard-working city, and one which has little to offer visitors except a taste of industrial France. There are some interesting museums here, including the Musée National de l'Automobile, but these are not really enough to warrant a diversion. More interesting, perhaps, is the Ecomusée du Haut-Alsace which is near **Ungersheim** and is the biggest open air museum in France. It is a collection of some 60 old farm buildings and cottages.

Getting there

By road

The A4 Paris-Strasbourg motorway links the towns of Verdun and Metz with the international road network.

The A31 Luxembourg-Lyon route serves Metz, Nancy, Pont-á-Mousson, Toul and the Vosges Mountains.

Three coach companies operate in the area:
- Alsace Voyages ☎ 3 88 66 28 23
- Circuits d'Alsace ☎ 3 89 41 90 88
- Les Balades Magar ☎ 3 88 54 01 44

By air

Bale-Mulhouse Airport (☎ 3 89 90 31 11, Fax: 3 89 90 25 77) is about 20 miles south-east of Mulhouse. Get to Mulhouse from the airport by taxi (30 mins) or bus (45 mins).

For car hire, try:
- Avis ☎ 3 89 90 29 39
- Europcar ☎ 3 89 69 23 58
- Hertz ☎ 3 89 90 29 40

Strasbourg Entzheim International Airport
(📞 3 88 64 67 67, Fax: 3 88 64 67 64) is
about eight miles south-west of Strasbourg.
Get from the airport to Strasbourg by airport
taxi (📞 3 88 36 13 13) or bus. For car hire,
contact:

- Ada 📞 3 88 64 69 05
- Avis 📞 3 88 68 82 53
- Budget 📞 3 88 52 87 52

Captain Alfred Dreyfus is one of
Mulhouse's most famous sons. He was
falsely accused of spying by the
corrupt and desperate French
government of the 1890s. Denied a
fair trial, and hounded by an anti-
semitic press, Dreyfus was sent to the
infamous Devil's Island. Confined to a
single room cell with almost no light,
he was the only prisoner on the island
from which it is impossible to escape.
Even if Dreyfus had managed the
super-human feat of escaping his cell
and reaching the ocean, he would
have been attacked by sharks. Emile
Zola's open letter, *J'Accuse*, helped
bring Dreyfus' plight to popular
attention. Eventually the government's
cover-up was exposed and Dreyfus
was released. Doctors were amazed
that Dreyfus had survived the ordeal,
but he was a broken man.

TOURIST INFORMATION

- **Alsace Tourist Office**
  6 avenue de la Marseillaise,
  67000 Strasbourg
  📞 3 88 25 01 66
  Fax: 3 88 52 17 06
- **Lorraine Tourist Office**
  3 rue des Tanneurs, 57000 Metz
  📞 3 87 37 02 16
  Fax: 3 87 37 02 19

Food and drink in Lorraine-Alsace

Lorraine's delights include the famous
Vosges honey and strawberries from
Woippy.

Restaurants in Alsace serve *flammkuchen* or
tarte flambée – the local answer to pizza –
at the weekends.

Farmhouses sometimes open up too,
cooking the slabs of delicious pastry and
fried onion in big bread ovens at the back.
Try the Munster cheese – great, hot or cold
– which is often eaten with cumin and a
glass of kirsch.

The tall, narrow flute bottles instantly
identify Alsace wines in a French
supermarket.

Grape varieties include Riesling,
Gewurztraminer, Sylvaner, Pinot Blanc, Gris
and Noir and Muscat d'Alsace.

'Vendanges Tardives' and 'Selection de
Grains Nobles' on labels signify that they are
late-harvested wines, sweeter than most.

Alsace is also the home of the *brasserie*
(brewery) and the place where all the good
French beers are brewed. It is probably the
only region of France where you won't feel
out of place ordering a beer on a hot
summer's day!

*Left: Turned into succulent tarts, Lorraine's mirabelle
plums (shown here), bilberries and redcurrants are also
used to make its delicious jams and traditional preserves
Right: Paté de foie gras en brioche – a rich and tasty
speciality*

ABRESCHVILLER Moselle   3D

★★ Hôtel des Cignognes
74 rue Jordy, 57560 Abreschviller
☎ 03 87 03 70 09 Fax 03 87 03 79 06
English spoken
Located in the middle of a pine forest, ideal for hiking or mountain biking. Exit A4 at Sarrebourg junction and then take D44.

29 bedrs, 27 ensuite, ⊮ P 15 DB 150-310 B 37 ✕ 72-185 ℂℂ MC Visa Amex ⊡ ▦ ▨ ▨ ⅲ ✍
RAC 10 %

BRIEY Meurthe et Meuselle   3A

★★ Hôtel Aster
rue de l'Europe, 54150 Briey
☎ 03 82 46 66 94 Fax 03 82 20 91 76
English spoken
In the heart of the 'Pays Haut-Lorrain', a comfortable hotel in a verdant setting. From motorway A4, exit Jarny, then drive north on the N103 to Briey.

35 bedrs, all ensuite, ⊮ P 35 DB 230-280 B 30 ✕ 70 (plus à la carte) ℂℂ MC Visa Amex ▦ ▨ ⅲ ✍ ♿

BUSSANG Vosges   3D

★★ Hôtel des Sources
88540 Bussang
☎ 03 29 61 51 94 Fax 03 29 61 60 61
English spoken

On the banks of the Moselle, in a quiet environment near the forest. Between Epinal and Mulhouse, towards the source of the Moselle.

11 bedrs, all ensuite, P 11 DB 310-350 B 35 ✕ 100-280 ℂℂ MC Visa ▦ ▨ ▨ 7km ✍
RAC 10 % min 3 nights

★★ Hôtel du Tremplin
8 rue du 3ème RTA, 88540 Bussang
☎ 03 29 61 50 30 Fax 03 29 61 50 89
English spoken
Small, family-run hotel in the centre of Bussang which is in the heart of the Hautes-Vosges, the source of the Moselle river. Good sports facilities nearby.

18 bedrs, 13 ensuite, ⊮ P DB 160-350 B 35 ✕ 75-280 ℂℂ MC Visa Amex ▨ ▨ ▨ ⅲ
RAC 10 % on room rate

COLMAR Haut Rhin   3D

★★ Hôtel Beauséjour
25 rue du Ladhof, 68000 Colmar
☎ 03 89 41 37 16 Fax 03 89 41 43 07
English spoken

A family-run hotel built in 1913, 5 minutes away from old town. Restaurant, with bright dining room and pleasant garden offers traditional and daring cuisine. Pretty rooms with all modern comfort designed for short breaks and business.

44 bedrs, all ensuite, ⊮ P DB 300-520 B 45 ✕ 98-260 ℂℂ MC Amex ▦ ▦ ▸ ▨ ⅲ ✍ ♿
RAC 5 %

★★★★ Hôtel Europe
15 route de Neuf-Brisach, Horbourg-Wihr, 68180 Colmar
☎ 03 89 20 54 00 Fax 03 89 41 27 50
English spoken

A most attractive, modern hotel set in pretty grounds. Spacious, light and airy accommodation, some rooms with jacuzzi. Excellent conference facilities. With a choice of three restaurants including 'L'Eden des Gourmets'.

138 bedrs, all ensuite, ⊁ P 350 DB 590-790 B 65 ✗ 120-375 ⊄ MC Visa Amex ⊠ ⊞ ⊞ ▶ 10km ⊠ ⊿ ⊠ ⊞ ⌀ ⅋

★★★ Hôtel Husseren-les-Châteaux
rue Schlossberg, 68420 Husseren-les-Châteaux
☎ 03 89 49 22 93 Fax 03 89 49 24 84
English spoken

A modern, interesting hotel with individually decorated bedrooms on two levels. It has views over vineyards and the Rhine Valley. Located 6 km south of Colmar on the N83.

38 bedrs, all ensuite, ⊁ P DB 545-900 B 58 ✗ 40-335 ⊄ MC Visa Amex ⊠ ⊞ ⊞ ▶ 22km ⊠ ⊠ ⊞ ⌀ ⅋

★★ Hôtel Ibis
13 route de Neuf-Brisach, 68180 Horbourg-Wihr Colmar
☎ 03 89 23 46 46 Fax 03 89 24 35 45
English spoken
The hotel is a few minutes from Colmar, the historic town in the heart of the vineyards of Alsace and offers easy access to Germany. There are swimming pools and gym nearby and don't forget to visit the superb museum and discover the old city.

86 bedrs, all ensuite, ⊁ P 86 DB 290-390 B 35-36 ✗ 55-95 ⊄ MC Visa Amex ▶ ⊠ ⊞ ⌀ ⅋

★★ Hôtel Rapp
1 rue Weinemer, 68000 Colmar
☎ 03 89 41 62 10 Fax 03 89 24 13 58
English spoken
A cosy hotel in the old town, close to the Place Rapp car park. There is a hammam and a fitness room available. Member of the 'Bonjour Scheme'. There are two restaurants, serving specialities and traditional and regional dishes.

41 bedrs, all ensuite, ⊁ P 3 DB 360-450 B 40-45 ✗ 100-330 ⊄ MC Visa Amex ⊠ ⊞ ⊞ ▶ 8km ⊠ ⊞ ⌀ ⅋

★★★ Hôtel St-Martin
38 Grand'rue, 68000 Colmar
☎ 03 89 24 11 51 Fax 03 89 23 47 78
English spoken
Closed 1 Jan-28 Feb

Tastefully renovated, a former residence with quiet intimate rooms, Louis XVI facade and renaissance turret. In the historic heart of Colmar, between the cathedral and the old customs house. Excellent restaurants close by.

24 bedrs, 16 ensuite, ⊁ P DB 580-650 B 52 No restaurant ⊄ MC Visa Amex ▶ 10km ⊠ ⌀
RAC 10 %

FEY Moselle   3B

★★ Hôtel Les Tuileries
Route de Cuvry, 57420 Fey
☎ 03 87 52 03 03 Fax 03 87 52 84 24
English spoken
The hotel-restaurant Les Tuileries welcomes you in a pleasant setting on the edge of the forest. A charming hotel with personal style mixing comfort and convenience. Seductive restaurant, tasty and varied cuisine. Situated 5 minutes from Metz.

41 bedrs, all ensuite, ⊁ P 100 DB 305-325 B 45 ✗ 115-350 ⊄ MC Visa Amex ⊞ ▶ ⊿ ⊠ ⊞ ⌀ ⅋
RAC 7 % on room rate
See advert on next page

Telephoning France
When telephoning France from the United Kingdom dial 00 33 and omit the initial 0 of the French code

Hôtel Les Tuileries

LES TUILERIES
57420 FEY

5 minutes from Metz, 17 minutes from Nancy, Fey junction on the motorway, the Hôtel-Restaurant 'les Tuileries' welcomes you in a pleasant setting on the edge of the forest. The 41 room hotel will charm you with its personal style, mixing comfort and convenience. The restaurant will seduce you with its studied decor and its tasty and varied cuisine. Also, 5 rooms fully equipped for meetings, seminars, etc.

- **Green park for pleasant walks**
- **Playground area for children • Mountain bikes**
- **Sauna for hotel residents • Boules play area**

**HÔTEL LES TUILERIES
ROUTE DE CUVRY, 57420 FEY FRANCE
TEL: 03 87 52 03 03 FAX: 03 87 52 84 24**

GERARDMER Vosges   3D

★★★ Grand Hôtel Bragard
place Tilleul, 88400 Gérardmer
☎ 03 29 63 06 31 Fax 03 29 63 46 81
English spoken
Traditional hotel, located in town centre, with 7000 sq m park and featuring grand comfort, gastronomic restaurant 'Le Grand Cerf' and Louis XIII bar. From Nancy/Metz take A31 via Epinal and Remiremont.

60 bedrs, all ensuite, ⊁ P 60 DB 400-750 B 60 ✗ 125-400 ℂℂ MC Visa Amex ⅊ 📧 ▸ 40km 🔲 ✈ ⊞ ⌀ ♿

GUEBWILLER Haut Rhin   3D

★★★ Domaine Langmatt
68530 Murbach
☎ 03 89 76 21 12 Fax 03 89 74 88 77
English spoken
Set in 3 hectares and surrounded by lovely countryside in the heart of the National Park des Ballons des Vosges. With refined cuisine and an excellent wine cellar. Located 6km west of Guebwiller off N83 via Buhl.

30 bedrs, all ensuite, P 30 DB 480-720 B 50 ✗ 85-256 ℂℂ MC Visa Amex ☒ ▸ 20km ✈ ⊞ ♿
RAC 5 %

KAYSERSBERG Haut Rhin   3D

★★★ Hôtel Constantin
10 rue du Père Kohlmann, 68240 Kaysersberg
☎ 03 89 47 19 90 Fax 03 89 47 37 82
English spoken

This 18th century renovated, wine grower's house is in the heart of the old city of Kayserberg near the Constantin fountain. A good base for touring Alsace.

20 bedrs, all ensuite, P 15 DB 330-380 B 40 No restaurant ℂℂ MC Visa ☒ ▸ 2km ☒ ✈ ⌀ ♿

★★★ Hôtel Les Remparts
4 rue de la Flieh, 68240 Kaysersberg
☎ 03 89 47 12 12 Fax 03 89 47 37 24
English spoken
On the edge of the historical town, bordering forests and vineyards, the Hotel Les Remparts offers you calm and comfort in its 42 rooms, all with bath, WC, private bar, phone and TV.

40 bedrs, all ensuite, ⊁ P 40 DB 340-440 No restaurant ℂℂ MC Visa Amex 🖾 ▸ ⊞ ♿

LONGUYON Meurthe et Meuselle   3A

★★ Hôtel de Lorraine
place de la Gare, 54260 Longuyon
☎ 03 82 26 50 07 Fax 03 82 39 29 09
English spoken
Closed Jan
A welcoming establishment with old-world charm. An ideal location for exploring Lorraine and discovering its special way of life. Quality French cuisine, breakfast and well facilitated, comfortable rooms, combined with delightful tradition.

14 bedrs, all ensuite, ⊁ P DB 225-290 B 35 ✗ 120-360 ℂℂ MC Visa Amex ▸ ✈ ⊞ ⌀

LUTZELBOURG Moselle   3B

★★ Hôtel au Lion Bleu
176 rue Koëberlé, 57820 Lutzelbourg
☎ 03 87 25 31 88 Fax 03 87 25 42 98
English spoken

The hotel offers an exceptional geographical location. Countryside lovers will enjoy the nearby greenery and pine forest. Delicious traditional and local cuisine. Backeoffe and choucroute au Riesling are specialities that will delight the palate.

26 bedrs, 18 ensuite, ⋔ P 30 DB 160-195 B 30 ✕ 85-178 ℂ MC Visa Amex ⬚ ▣ ▣ ▣ ‼ ⋒ ⅏

MARLENHEIM Bas Rhin   3D

★★★ Hostellerie du Cerf
30 rue du Général de Gaulle, 67520 Marlenheim
📞 03 88 87 73 73 Fax 03 88 87 68 08
English spoken
Closed Mar
This hostellerie, surrounded by vineyards, in the centre of a pretty village, has elegant, comfortable rooms and offers inventive cuisine prepared with the best home grown produce. From Strasbourg, go east on the motorway, then N4 towards Saverne.

18 bedrs, 8 ensuite, ⋔ P DB 300-850 B 60-88 ✕ 250-550 ℂ MC Visa Amex ▸ ▣ ▣ ‼ ⅏
RAC 5 %

METZ Moselle   3B

★★ Hôtel Cécil
14 rue Pasteur, 57000 Metz
📞 03 87 66 66 13 Fax 03 87 56 96 02
English spoken
Closed 25 Dec-2 Jan
This quiet, comfortable, recently renovated hotel is in the town centre, close to the railway station and the A31.

39 bedrs, 36 ensuite, P 10 DB 225-290 B 35 No restaurant ℂ MC Visa Amex ▸ 8km ▣
RAC 10 % on the garage

★★ Hôtel Foch
3 place R.Mondon, 57000 Metz
📞 03 87 74 40 75 Fax 03 87 74 49 90
English spoken
A family-run hotel situated on Metz-Centre exit, only 300 m from the pedestrian centre. It's the ideal starting point for exploring the town and its monuments.

38 bedrs, 32 ensuite, ⋔ P DB 240-298 B 30 No restaurant ℂ MC Visa Amex ▸ ▣ ⅏
RAC 10 %

★★★ Hôtel du Théâtre
Port-St-Marcel, 1-3 rue du Pont-St-Mar, 57000 Metz
📞 03 87 31 10 10 Fax 03 87 30 04 66
English spoken

Situated next to the cathedral in one of the oldest parts of Metz, this riverside, Châteaux et Hôtels Indepentants hotel is part of a redevelopment plan for the old port of St-Marcel. Rooms with views of river or docks and waterside terraces.

36 bedrs, all ensuite, ⋔ P 100 DB 490-990 B 55 ✕ 98-168 ℂ MC Visa Amex ⬚ ▣ ▣ ▸ 3km ▣ ▣ ‼ ⅏
RAC 15 % 25% on suites & apartments

MULHOUSE Haut Rhin   3D

★★★ Hôtel Bristol
18 av de Colmar, 68100 Mulhouse
📞 03 89 42 12 31 Fax 03 89 42 50 57
English spoken
A very comfortable and well furnished hotel, with colour TV and conference facilities, situated in the centre of Mulhouse. Member of the 'Bonjour Campaign'. Access by A36. Groups welcome.

70 bedrs, all ensuite, ⋔ P 40 DB 280-480 B 42 No restaurant ℂ MC Visa Amex ▸ 15km ▣ ▣ ‼ ⅏
RAC 15 % weekend or in Jul/Aug

★★ Hôtel Inter Salvator
29 passage Central, BP 1354, 68100 Mulhouse
📞 03 89 45 28 32 Fax 03 89 56 49 59
English spoken
A quiet hotel offering a warm welcome. Just after the motorway exit Mulhouse-Centre, turn left at the tower, then go towards the station.

53 bedrs, all ensuite, ⋔ P 15 DB 260-330 B 35 No restaurant ℂ MC Visa Amex ▸ 15km ▣ ‼ ⅏
RAC 10 %

★★ Hôtel de Bâle
19 passage Central, 68100 Mulhouse
☎ 03 89 46 19 87 Fax 03 89 66 07 06
English spoken
A well-kept traditional hotel, with a garden, offering a warm welcome. Leave the motorway A36 at Mulhouse-Centre. The hotel is in the town centre opposite the Banque de France.

32 bedrs, 22 ensuite, ✣ **P** **DB** 200-295 **B** 36 No restaurant **CC** MC Visa ☞ 8km ⊠ ⋨
RAC 10 %

★★ Hôtel du Musée
3 rue del'Est, 68100 Mulhouse
☎ 03 89 45 47 41 Fax 03 89 56 60 80
English spoken
Closed 21 Dec-4 Jan

A quiet, comfortable, traditional hotel, with a garden, situated opposite the museum close to the town centre. Leave the motorway at Mulhouse-Centre exit and follow signs first to the station and then 'Musée de l'Impression sur étoffes'.

44 bedrs, 27 ensuite, ✣ **P** 30 **DB** 170-305 **B** 36 No restaurant **CC** MC Visa Amex ⊠ ☞ 15km ⊠ 1km ⋕ ⋨ ⚅
RAC 10 % on room rate

MUNSTER Haut Rhin   3D

★★ Hôtel Le Beau Site
3 rue Principale, Hohrod, 68140 Munster
☎ 03 89 77 31 55 Fax 03 89 77 28 71
English spoken
Closed 15 Nov-15 Feb
Quietly set, hillside hotel with a friendly atmosphere, modern facilities and a large terrace with beautiful views. Family rooms and apartments also available. Take D417 from Colmar to Munster: after Munster turn right and the hotel is on the left.

14 bedrs, all ensuite, **P** 16 **DB** 215-270 **B** 30 ✕ 72-120 **CC** MC Visa ☞ 15km ⊠ ⊠ ⋕ ⋨
RAC Only for groups

NANCY Meurthe et Meuselle   3D

★★★ Hôtel Mercure Nancy Centre Stanilas
5 rue des Carmes, 54000 Nancy
☎ 03 83 35 32 10 Fax 03 83 32 92 49
English spoken

An air-conditioned hotel near the historic town centre, close to the station and 100 m from Place Stanislas. Take exit Nancy-Centre Ville, and follow signs to the station and Place Stanislas.

80 bedrs, all ensuite, ✣ **P** 100 **DB** 400-465 **B** 52 ✕ 90-160 **CC** MC Visa Amex ☞ ⋕ ⋨
RAC 5 %

ORBEY Haut Rhin   3D

★★ Hôtel Saut de la Truite
68370 Orbey
☎ 03 89 71 20 04 Fax 03 89 71 31 52
English spoken
Closed Dec-Feb
This family run hotel, with terrace, garden, traditional and gourmet restaurants, is situated in the centre of Alsace and the Vosges region. An ideal place for a holiday. 20 km from Colmar and 10 km from Kayserberg

22 bedrs, 18 ensuite, ✣ **P** 25 **DB** 210-310 **B** 40 ✕ 85-205 **CC** MC Visa ☞ 12km ⊠ ⊠ ⋕ ⚅
RAC 5 %

★★★ Hôtel au Bois le Sire
20 rue Charles de Gaulle, 68370 Orbey
☎ 03 89 71 25 25 Fax 03 89 71 30 75
English spoken
Closed 4 Jan-5 Feb

A family-run hotel, with gourmet cuisine, standing at the foot of the Vosges mountains. From Kaysersberg take N415 towards St-Die, then left to Orbey.

36 bedrs, all ensuite, **↑ P** 20 **DB** 260-380 **B** 50 ✕ 100-350 (during week, 3 course menu for 53 FF) **CC** MC Visa Amex ⊠ ▸ 10km ☑ ☒ ⅲ &

★★ Hôtel de la Croix d'Or
13 rue de l'Eglise, 68370 Orbey
☎ 03 89 71 20 51 Fax 03 89 71 35 60
English spoken
Closed 6-31 Jan

A family-run hotel, with a rustic-style restaurant serving regional speciality cuisine and standing on a hillside just outside the village. Orbey is 40 km from Gérardmer and 12 km from Kaysersberg. Take N415 towards St-Die, then turn left to Orbey.

19 bedrs, 16 ensuite, **↑ P DB** 250-300 **B** 45 **CC** MC Visa Amex ☒ ▸ 10km ☑ ☒ ⅲ
RAC 10 % except May & Jul-Sep

LA PETITE-PIERRE Bas Rhin　　　　　**3B**

★★ Auberge d'Imsthal
l'Etang d'Imsthal, 67290 La Petite-Pierre
☎ 03 88 01 49 00 Fax 03 88 70 40 26
English spoken
A pretty, lakeside hotel, with a warm atmosphere and attractive rooms, set in tranquil surroundings in the heart of a forest. The restaurant is renowned for its excellent service and fine cuisine.

23 bedrs, 20 ensuite, **↑ P DB** 289-650 **B** 50 ✕ 50-240 **CC** MC Visa Amex ☒ ☒ ▸ ☑ ☒ ⅲ &

★★ Hôtel Les Vosges
67290 La Petite-Pierre
☎ 03 88 70 45 05 Fax 03 88 70 41 13
English spoken
Closed Feb
A traditional hotel, with a renowned well established restaurant, set in the forested region of Alsace. Located 60 km north-west of Strasbourg on A4; turn off at Saverne and take D178 to the village.

32 bedrs, all ensuite, **↑ P DB** 290-490 **B** 52 ✕ 100-290 **CC** MC Visa Amex ☒ ☒ ▸ 30km ☒ ⅲ ⌀ &

★★ Hôtel Vieux Moulin
67320 Graufthal
☎ 03 88 70 17 28 Fax 03 88 70 11 25
English spoken
Closed 7-22 Oct & 12 Jan-3 Feb

A lovely house, with fine traditional and regional cuisine, surrounded by woods and dominated by impressive sandstone cliffs. From the A4, exit Phalsbourg; the village of Petite-Pierre is 8 km further on.

14 bedrs, 7 ensuite, **↑ P** 30 **DB** 225-370 **B** 30 ✕ 50-200 **CC** MC Visa &

★★ Hôtel au Lion d'Or
15 rue Principale, 67290 La Petite-Pierre
☎ 03 88 70 45 06 Fax 03 88 70 45 56
English spoken
Closed Jan
A highly recommended family hotel, with excellent cuisine and good service, set in an ancient hilltop village in northern Alsace. Most of the bedrooms overlook the valley. Take A4; Petite-Pierre is 60 km northwest of Strasbourg..

40 bedrs, all ensuite, **↑ P** 30 **DB** 370-450 **B** 40-55 ✕ 120-250 **CC** MC Visa Amex ☒ ☒ ▸ ☒ ☒ ⅲ ⌀ &

PHALSBOURG Moselle　　　　　**3B**

★★ Hôtel Notre-Dame
57370 Phalsbourg
☎ 03 87 24 34 33 Fax 03 87 24 24 64
English spoken
Closed 10-30 Jan & 22-28 Feb
Set in the heart of the forest in a corner of Lorraine, this secluded hotel, with rustic furniture and modern décor, has a restaurant specialising in Alsacian cuisine. Situated 4km from Phalsbourg, 8km from Saverne; take Phalsbourg exit from N43 or N4.

34 bedrs, all ensuite, **↑ P** 25 **DB** 300-400 **B** 43 ✕ 88-245 **CC** MC Visa Amex ☒ ☒ ☒ ⅲ ⌀ &

REMIREMONT Vosges   3D

★★ Hôtel de la Poste
67 rue Charles de Gaulle, Bd 57, 88202 Remiremont
☎ 03 29 62 55 67 Fax 03 29 62 34 90
English spoken
Closed 1-15 Aug/17 Dec-7 Jan
An old hotel, with a restaurant offering classic and regional cuisine, in picturesque town at the foot of the Vosges mountains.

21 bedrs, 19 ensuite, ⚲ P 10 DB 260-350 B 35 ✕ 92-205 ℂℂ MC Visa Amex ► 20km ▨ ▦ ✗ ⚵
RAC 10 % on room rate

★★ Hôtel du Cheval de Bronze
59 rue Charles de Gaulle, Bd 57, 88202 Remiremont
☎ 03 29 62 52 24 Fax 03 29 62 34 90
English spoken
An old coaching inn, in centre of town, with a small private garden/courtyard. 25 km south of Epinal in the Vosges.

35 bedrs, 31 ensuite, ⚲ P 12 DB 155-325 B 35 No restaurant ℂℂ MC Visa Amex ► 20km ▨ ▨ ▦ ✗
RAC 10 %

RIBEAUVILLE Haut Rhin   3D

★★★ Hôtel La Pépinière
rte de Ste-Marie-aux-Mines, 68150 Ribeauvillé
☎ 03 89 73 64 14 Fax 03 89 73 88 78
English spoken
Closed 18 Nov-Apr

A traditional, chalet-style hotel, set in the middle of the forest, with a restaurant offering panoramic views and creative cuisine. On the Ribeauvillé to Ste-Marie-aux-Mines road.

21 bedrs, all ensuite, ⚲ P 20 DB 360-450 B 48 ✕ 145-360 ℂℂ MC Visa ► 18km ▨ ▨ ▦ ▦
RAC 10 %

RIQUEWIHR Haut Rhin   3D

★★★ Hôtel Le Schoenenbourg
rue du Schoenenbourg, 68340 Riquewihr
☎ 03 89 49 01 11 Fax 03 89 47 95 88
English spoken

A modern hotel in a peaceful setting near vineyards. Just 100 m from the old Riquewihr, a medieval town.

45 bedrs, all ensuite, ⚲ P 45 DB 395-550 B 50 ✕ 190-450 ℂℂ MC Visa Amex ⚵ ▦ ▦ ► 10km ▦ ✗ ⚵

ST-HIPPOLYTE Haut Rhin   3D

★★★ Hôtel aux Ducs de Lorraine
16 route du Vin, 68590 St-Hippolyte
☎ 03 89 73 00 09 Fax 03 89 73 05 46
English spoken
Closed 24 Nov-10 Dec & 10 Jan-14 Feb
An elegant hotel, on the outskirts of the village, with period atmosphere plus rooms with flower bordered balconies and wonderful views of the mountains and vineyards.

40 bedrs, all ensuite, P 20 DB 350-700 B 60 ✕ 110-310 ℂℂ MC Visa ► 18km ▨ ▦ ✗

★★★ Hôtel du Parc
6 rue du Parc, 68590 St-Hippolyte
☎ 03 89 73 00 06 Fax 03 89 73 04 30
English spoken
Closed 6 Jan-6 Feb
A traditional hotel, located on the outskirts of the village, bordering the wine route in the centre of an Alsacian vineyard.

37 bedrs, all ensuite, ⚲ P 30 DB 350-700 B 60 ✕ 125-350 ℂℂ MC Visa Amex ▦ ▦ ► ▦ ▨ ▦ ▦ ✗ ⚵

STE-MENEHOULD Marne   3A

★ Hôtel Commerce
55120 Aubreville
☎ 03 29 87 40 35 Fax 03 29 87 43 69
English spoken
Closed 1-20 Oct
*A peaceful and traditional, family-run, Logis de
France hotel. Leave A4 at the Ste-Menehould exit and
follow the signs to Aubreville which is about 20 km
east.*

8 bedrs, 5 ensuite, 🍴 P 20 DB 160-210 B 25 ✕ 70-120
《 MC Visa 📷 🖼 ⌀

SAVERNE Bas Rhin   3B

Hôtel Chez Jean
3 rue de la Gare, 67700 Saverne
☎ 03 88 91 10 19 Fax 03 88 91 27 45
English spoken
Closed 22 Dec-10 Jan
*A completely refurbished hotel, with summer terrace,
sun room, tea room and 3 restaurants including a
gourmet restaurant. Very comfortable rooms with
radio, TV, safe deposit, hairdryer, heated towel rail.*

25 bedrs, all ensuite, 🍴 P DB 398-468 B 50 ✕ 90-220
《 MC Visa Amex 🖥 ▶ 30km 🖼 ⚌ ⌀

SCHIRMECK Bas Rhin   3D

★★★ Château de Barembach
5 rue du Maréchal de Lattre, 67130 Schirmeck
☎ 03 88 97 97 50 Fax 03 88 47 17 19
English spoken
Closed 5 Jan-5 Feb
*A small, elegant, 19th century château used as the
owners' private home until 1983. Surrounded by
mountains and forests, it has a terrace and a pretty
flower garden.General Patton used it as his
headquarters in 1944. West of Strasbourg on
A35/N420.*

15 bedrs, all ensuite, 🍴 P 15 DB 475-895 B 55 ✕ 145-
398 《 MC Visa Amex ▶ 35km 📷 🖼 ⚌
RAC **10 % 1 Nov-31 Mar**

SEWEN Haut Rhin   3D

★★ Hôtel Les Vosges
68290 Sewen
☎ 03 89 82 00 43 Fax 03 89 82 08 33
Closed 1-26 Dec
*A comfortable family-owned hotel, with an extensive
garden, surrounded by the forests of the Vosges
mountains. On the D466 towards Ballon-d'Alsace.*

17 bedrs, 15 ensuite, 🍴 P DB 250-300 B 35 ✕ 90-260
《 MC Visa Amex ▶ 📷 🖼 ⚌
RAC **5 %**

STRASBOURG Bas Rhin   3D

Hilton Hôtel
av Herranschmidt, 67000 Strasbourg
☎ 03 88 37 10 10 Fax 03 88 36 83 27
English spoken
*A first class hotel, located in a peaceful green area
less than 1 mile from the centre, close to motorway
exit Wacken (right turn at the traffic lights). 24 hour
room service, British club bar and excellent cuisine
will meet highest expectations.*

246 bedrs, all ensuite, P 90 DB 630-1,600 B 93 ✕ 105-
159 《 MC Visa Amex ▶ 🖼 ⚌ ⌀ ♿
RAC **15 % off rack**

★★★ Hôtel Europe
38 rue Fosses des Tanneurs, 67000 Strasbourg
☎ 03 88 32 17 88 Fax 03 88 75 65 45
English spoken
*Full of charm and character this 15th century
posthouse stands next to La Petite France pedestrian
area. A unique 1:50 scale model of Strasbourg
Cathedral is displayed in the reception hall. Direct
access from motorway, exit Place des Halles.*

60 bedrs, all ensuite, P 20 DB 380-890 B 48 No
restaurant 《 MC Visa Amex ▶ 10km 🖼 ⚌ ♿

★★★ Hôtel Le Bristol
4-5 place de la Gare, 67000 Strasbourg
☎ 03 88 32 00 83 Fax 03 88 75 60 78
English spoken

*A recently modernised, soundproofed and air-
conditioned, hotel. Opposite the central station, close
to the town centre.*

37 bedrs, all ensuite, 🍴 P DB 450-600 B 45-65 《 MC
Visa Amex ▶ 10km 🖼 ⚌ ⌀ ♿
RAC **10 %**

★★★ Hôtel des Rohan
17 rue du Maroquin, 67000 Strasbourg
☎ 03 88 32 85 11 Fax 03 88 75 65 37
English spoken
This small, peaceful hotel is situated next to the cathedral in the historic town centre. The bedrooms are furnished in a variety of styles, from rustic to Louis XV and are equipped with every modern convenience. Porters at hand on arrival.

36 bedrs, all ensuite, ♍ P DB 495-795 B 52 No restaurant ⟨⟨ MC Visa Amex ▶ 15km ⊠

★★★ Hôtel du Dragon
2 rue de l'Ecarlate, 67000 Strasbourg
☎ 03 88 35 79 80 Fax 03 88 25 78 95
English spoken

A 17th century house, converted into a stylish hotel, quietly set in the old city near La Petite France. Some rooms have a view of the cathedral and there is a small garden. Many restaurants within walking distance. Approach the hotel via quai-St-Nicolas.

32 bedrs, all ensuite, P DB 495-675 B 60 No restaurant ⟨⟨ MC Visa Amex ▶ 6km ⊠ ⊞ ⋪ ⅙
RƏC 10 %

★★ Hôtel du Rhin
7-8 place de la Gare, 67000 Strasbourg
☎ 03 88 32 35 00 Fax 03 88 23 51 92
English spoken

An imposing hotel, with soundproofed rooms and underground parking, situated opposite the station in the town centre. From the A35, take the Centre-Ville exit and then follow signs to Gare Centrale.

61 bedrs, 54 ensuite, ♍ P 340 DB 200-400 B 35 ⟨⟨ MC Visa Amex ⊞ ⋪ ⅙

★★★ Hôtel d'Angleterre
162 rue de Charmey, 88800 Vittel
☎ 03 29 08 08 42 Fax 03 29 08 07 48
English spoken
A recently renovated hotel, close to the casino and the spa, offering all modern conveniences plus the benefit of a lift, private parking and gardens. Traditional cuisine.

61 bedrs, all ensuite, ♍ P 60 DB 380-480 B 45 ✕ 100-200 ⟨⟨ MC Visa Amex ⊠ ▶ 1km ⊠ ⊞ ⋪ ⅙

★★★ Le Parc Hôtel
67710 Wangenbourg
☎ 03 88 87 31 72 Fax 03 88 87 38 00
English spoken
Closed 4 Nov-23 Dec & 3 Jan-20 Mar

Set in a 1 hectare park and established for 6 generations, the Parc Hotel offers for your enjoyment: a warm, quiet atmosphere, 33 comfortable rooms, a panoramic terrace, children's playground and snooker.

33 bedrs, all ensuite, ♍ P 20 DB 310-429 B 50 ✕ 110-265 ⟨⟨ MC Visa ⊠ ⊠ ⊠ ⊠ ⊠ ⊠ ⊞ ⋪

Poitou-
Charentes

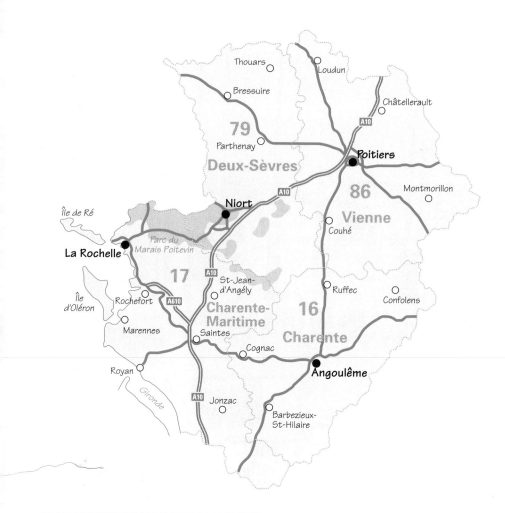

British visitors have long been attracted to the Atlantic west of France. The climate is pleasant and this stretch of coast, though beautiful, is less self-conscious than more southerly resorts.

The centre of this low-key chic is **La Rochelle**, a pretty beachside town which one could hardly fail to enjoy. Like most seaside resorts, La Rochelle is most alive in summer. During the winter months, many of the charming eighteenth-century shop fronts shut until the warm weather returns. Shopping is something which La Rochelle does well; cosy boutiques can be found at almost every turn. But the best place to go is the rue du Palais which runs through the old town to the Porte de la Grosse Horloge - or 'gateway to the big clock tower'. In fact, three towers stand over this monumental portal. Go through the gateway to reach the

sheltered harbour from where boat trips can be taken along the coast. Boats can also be taken to the Ile de Ré where locals head for lazy days on the beach.

If you're travelling with children, or if you just fancy something slightly different, you might take a trip to the Arche de Noé (Noah's Ark) animal park at St-Clément. Another enjoyable excursion is the Baleines lighthouse. This was once a prime whale-spotting site. They are less common now.

Rochefort is not in the same league as La Rochelle, but it is an interesting enough place which is worth some time. Most visitors make a beeline for the Coderie Royale with its International Centre of the Sea and Maison de Pierre Loti. Loti (real name Julien Viaud) was a sort of early Barbara Cartland. His books sold well, and allowed him to kit out his home in the sort

age 165: The old harbour at La Rochelle
bove: The relaxed pace of life at Montmorillon

of quasi-oriental opulence which also provided the settings for many of his stories. With little else to offer the traveller, Rochefort can't compete with the **Ile d'Oléron** to which tourists flock every summer. **Oléron** is an up-and-coming destination, with great beaches and a well-developed tourist infrastructure. Some might say too developed.

Poitiers, some 60 miles north-east of La Rochelle, is a buzzing town which also boasts an impressive legacy of Romanesque art. The principal sights here are the Palais de Justice and Notre-Dame-la-Grande. That said, modern Poitiers will hold your attention with its eclectic collection of cafés and shops.

Few visitors to Poitou-Charentes leave **Cognac** off their itineraries. Cognac has grown rich by producing the expensive tipple which shares its name. There are seven distilleries here and most conduct guided tours and tasting. There's not a lot else to do here, so you might as well sample the stuff. Try: the Otard Distillery at 127 blvd Denfert-Rochereau; Hennessey at 1 rue de la Richonne (☏ 45 82 52 22); Martell in rue de Gate-Bourse (☏ 45 82 44 44); or Remy-Martin at Domaine de Merpins on the D732 (☏ 45 35 76 66).

East of Cognac, the heavily-fortified town of **Angoulême** guards its famous seventeenth-century paper mills. Today, the mills roll out acres of comic strips – including French and Belgian heroes Asterix and Tintin. Cartoons are extremely popular in France, a land where Asterix is a leading national figure. Visit the Centre National de la Bande Dessin et de l'Image which is heaven on earth for comic strip fans – and surprisingly

Above: Get carried away into virtual adventures at the Futuroscope. This European park of the moving image near Poitiers is popular with adults and children alike.

fascinating for everyone else.

Another enjoyable town with a tenuous claim to fame is **Saintes**, which is west of Cognac. This is where the philanthropic Dr Guillotin invented his revolutionary machine for making execution quick and painless. Saintes was also an important stopover for pilgrims heading south to Compostela de la Santiago; earlier it was a Roman stronghold. This intriguing past is illustrated by the town's amphitheatre and Arch of Germanicus.

Saintes is a convenient place from which to launch an exploration of the coastal towns of **Saint-Georges-de-Didome**, **Saujon**, **La Tremblade** and **Marennes**. Head south to find **Talmont**, where an extraordinary Romanesque church stands on stilts out of reach of the waves.

Something a bit different...

For the hire of 2–12 berth self-drive cruisers for one week or more on the Charente River, contact:
- Blakes Holidays, Wroxham, Norwich NR12 8DH (☎ 01603 784131, Fax: 01603 782871)
- Crown Blue Line, 8 Ber Street, Norwich NR1 1EJ (☎ 01603 630513, Fax: 01603 664298)
- French Country Cruises, Andrew Bock Travel, 54 High Street East, Uppingham, Rutland LE15 9PZ (☎ 01572 821330, Fax: 01572 821072)

For cookery courses and wine tours and tastings, French Expressions organise tailor-made tours to Cognac and gastronomic breaks by car/fly drive to châteaux and hotels of character. Contact them at 13 McCrone Mews, Belsize Lane, London NW3 5BB (☎ 0171 431 1312, Fax: 0171 431 4221).

Getting there

By road
The most important route through Poitou Charentes is the A10 which stretches between Paris and La Rochelle via Orleans, Tours, Poitiers and Bordeaux.

By rail
By TGV:
- Paris (Gare Montparnasse) to Poitiers takes 1 hour 30 mins
- Paris to La Rochelle takes 2 hours 51 mins
- Lille to Poitiers takes 3 hours 10 mins
- Lyon to Poitiers takes 3 hours 50 mins
- Bordeaux to Angoulême takes 52 mins

There are also train services from Paris Gare Austerlitz to Cognac, Saintes, Rochefort and Royan.

By air
Angoulême-Brie-Champniers Airport (☎ 5 45 69 88 09, Fax: 5 45 69 81 47) is about 11 miles north of Angoulême. Get into central Angoulême by taxi (☎ 6 07 85 33 98 or 5 45 24 74).

For car hire contact:
- Avis ☎ 5 45 38 94 50
- Europcar ☎ 5 45 95 27 28

La Rochelle-Laleu Airport (☎ 5 46 42 30 26, Fax: 5 46 00 04 84) is 3 miles north-west of La Rochelle. Get to La Rochelle by taxi (☎ 5 46 41 55 55) or bus (every 20 mins).
For car hire contact:
- Europcar ☎ 5 46 41 09 08
- Hertz ☎ 5 46 41 02 31

TOURIST INFORMATION

- **Poitou-Charentes Tourist Office**
  Boite Postale 56, 86002 Poitiers Cedex
  ☎ 5 49 50 10 50
  Fax: 5 49 41 37 28

ANGLES-SUR-L'ANGLIN Vienne   4B

★★★ Hôtel Le Relais du Lyon d'Or
Route de Vicq, 86260 Angles-sur-l'Anglin
📞 05 49 48 32 53 Fax 05 49 84 02 28
English spoken
Closed 1 Jan-end Feb
*A 14th century hotel combining modern comfort with
old-world charm. Personalised bedrooms and service.
The restaurant specialises in fresh regional products.
Take D5 from Chatelleraut or D2 from Chauvigny.*

10 bedrs, all ensuite, ⋔ P 10 DB 275-450 B 40 CC MC
Visa ► 🚗 ⊠ ‖‖ ♫ ⅊

CHATELAILLON-PLAGE Charente Maritime   4A

★★ Hôtel de la Plage
Bd de la Mer, 17340 Châtelaillon-Plage
📞 05 46 56 26 02
English spoken
Closed 1 Oct-31 Mar
*Lounge and rooms overlook the sea, Ile de Ré,
d'Oléron, d'Aix and Fort Boyard. An absolutely safe,
fine sandy beach is opposite the hotel.*

10 bedrs, all ensuite, ⋔ P 10 DB 220-270 B 32 No
restaurant CC MC Visa ► 15km 🚗 ⊠ ♫

★★ Majestic Hôtel
Bd de la Libération, 17340 Châtelaillon-Plage
📞 05 46 56 20 53 Fax 05 46 56 29 24

English spoken
Closed 16 Dec-15 Jan
*Built in 1927, the hotel is decorated in 1920s style
and is only 100 m from the beach. Restaurant offers
seafood specialities. Follow signs for Centre-Ville and
Mairie in Châtelaillon-Plage.*

30 bedrs, 26 ensuite, ⋔ P DB 300-600 B 35 ✕ 60-185
CC MC Visa Amex ► 15km ‖‖ ♫

COGNAC Charente   4B

★★ Domaine du Breuil
104 av R Daugas, 16100 Cognac
📞 05 45 35 32 06 Fax 05 45 35 48 06
English spoken

*A charming hotel restaurant. A 19th century
building set in a landscaped 7 hectare park. Visit the
Cognac storehouses. To find the hotel head for the
town centre and follow the signposts. Serves classic
and regional cuisine.*

24 bedrs, all ensuite, ⋔ P 50 DB 270-370 B 40 ✕ 85-
185 CC MC Visa Amex ► 🚗 ⊠ ‖‖ ♫ ⅊

★★★ Hôtel Aliénor
Avenue d'Angoulême, 16100 Cognac
📞 05 45 35 42 00 Fax 05 45 35 45 02
English spoken
*The hotel has 55 soundproof rooms, each with its own
drawing room, telephone, mini-bar, terrace, jacuzzi
and TV (national and foreign channels). Try the
hotel's restaurant 'La Part des Anges'. With a private
car park for patrons.*

55 bedrs, all ensuite, ⋔ P 80 DB 320-350 B 42 ✕ 85-
140 CC MC Visa Amex ⋛ ► ⊠ ‖‖ ♫ ⅊
RⱭC 10 %

★★ Hôtel Urbis
24 rue Elisée Moushier, 16100 Cognac
📞 05 45 82 19 53 Fax 05 45 82 86 71
English spoken
*A modern hotel with garden and private, locked car
park. Conveniently situated and with very helpful
staff.*

40 bedrs, 39 ensuite, ⋔ P 13 DB 295 B 35 CC MC Visa
Amex ► 5km ⊠ ♫ ⅊

L'ISLE-JOURDAIN Vienne 4B

★★★ Hôtel Val de Vienne
Port-de-Salle, 86150 Le Vigeant
☎ 05 49 48 27 27 Fax 05 49 48 47 47
English spoken
Closed 12 Jan-3 Feb

Beautifully situated on the banks of the River Vienne, each room has a private terrace overlooking the river. From L'Isle-Jourdain take D8 south towards Availles, turn left after 4 km to Port-de-Salles. Hotel well signposted on right.

20 bedrs, all ensuite, ⵂ P 100 DB 420-520 B 45 ✕ 95-250 ₡ MC Visa ⵒ ⵒ 45km ▣ ▣ ⵂ ⵒ ⵂ

LOUDUN Vienne 2C

★★ Hôtel La Roue d'Or
1 av Anjou, 86200 Loudun
☎ 05 49 98 01 23 Fax 05 49 22 31 05
English spoken
A small, comfortable hotel with an attractive dining room and a good choice of set menus and à la carte dishes. Conveniently situated for exploring the surrounding region.

14 bedrs, all ensuite, ⵂ P DB 280 B 35 ✕ 75-220 ₡ MC Visa Amex ⵒ 15km ▣ ⵂ ⵂ

MORTAGNE-SUR-GIRONDE Charente Maritime 4A

★★ Auberge de la Garenne
3 impasse de l'Ancienne Gare, 17120 Mortagne-sur-Gironde
☎ 05 46 90 63 69 Fax 05 46 90 50 93
English spoken
The auberge and bungalow accommodation are set in large, peaceful grounds at the top of the village. The restaurant offers well prepared, traditional cuisine and meals can be taken outside on the terrace in summer. On the D6.

11 bedrs, 6 ensuite, ⵂ P 11 DB 178-238 B 30-32 ✕ 70-200 ₡ MC Visa ⵒ ⵒ ▣ ▣
RAC 5 %

NIORT Deux Sèvres 4B

★★ Hôtel Le Paris
12 avenue de Paris, 79000 Niort
☎ 05 49 24 93 78 Fax 05 49 28 27 57
English spoken
Closed 25 Dec-1 Jan
A comfortable, town centre hotel, with quiet rooms, garage and TV, conveniently situated for restaurants, cinemas, museums and churches as well as the Poitevin marshes. 30 minutes from La Rochelle and 45 minutes from Poitiers, motorway exit 32.

44 bedrs, 22 ensuite, ⵂ P DB 180-350 B 35 No restaurant ₡ MC Visa ⵒ ▣ ▣ ⵂ

★★ Hôtel Les Ruralies
79230 Prahecq
☎ 05 49 75 67 66 Fax 05 49 75 80 29
English spoken

An attractive, comfortable hotel, set in an extraordinary garden in the heart of historic Niort. Regional and country cuisine is served in 'La Mijotière' restaurant and fast food in 'La Pergola' café.

51 bedrs, 50 ensuite, ⵂ P 100 DB 300-350 B 25-35 ✕ 70-120 ₡ MC Visa Amex ⵒ 8km ▣ 8km ▣ 6km ⵂ ⵒ ⵂ

OLERON, ILE DE Charente Maritime 4A

★★ Hôtel Otelinn
17310 St-Pierre-d'Oléron, Oléron
☎ 05 46 47 19 92 Fax 05 46 47 47 19
English spoken
Set in the heart of the island of Oléron, a few minutes away from beaches, forests and numerous cycling circuits.

34 bedrs, all ensuite, ⵂ P 34 DB 245-480 B 40 ✕ 70-200 ₡ MC Visa Amex ▣ ⵒ
RAC 8 %

Don't forget to mention the guide
When booking, please remember to tell the hotel that you chose it from the
RAC France for the Independent Traveller

POITIERS Vienne   4B

★★★ Château Le Clos de la Ribaudière
10 place du Champ de Foire, 86360 Chasseneuil-du-Poitou
☎ 05 49 52 86 66 Fax 05 49 52 86 32
English spoken
A 19th century château, with exceptional décor and a restaurant offering seafood specialities, set in lovely surroundings in a riverside park. From A10 take Futuroscope exit towards Chasseneuil-Centre Village.

41 bedrs, all ensuite, ♀ P DB 320-520 B 50 ✕ 115-285 ℂℂ MC Visa Amex ⊐ ⏚ 8km ☑ ⋏
RAC 10 %

★★ Hôtel Le Saint-Georges
12 Grand'Rue, 86370 Vivonne
☎ 05 49 89 01 89 Fax 05 49 89 00 22
English spoken

A characterful 18th century hotel, recently renovated and situated on the main street (Grande Rue) leading to the centre of Vivonne. The ideal place to savour the delightful, relaxed lifestyle of Poitiers.

26 bedrs, all ensuite, ♀ P DB 230-260 B 30-35 ✕ 75 ℂℂ MC Visa ☑ ⋕ ⋏ ⛨

★★ Hôtel Mondial
86240 Croutelle
☎ 05 49 55 44 00 Fax 05 49 55 33 49
English spoken

A motel-style hotel shaped like a '4' with a swimming pool in the middle. Just 10 minutes from Poitiers town centre and the Futuroscope. Take exit 30 from N10 drive towards Angoulême and the hotel is 200 meters on the right.

40 bedrs, all ensuite, ♀ P 50 DB 305-450 B 38 No restaurant ℂℂ MC Visa Amex ⊐ ⏚ 12km ☑ ⋏ ⋕ ⋏ ⛨
RAC 10 %

RE, ILE DE Charente Maritime   4A

★★ Hôtel Le Martray
17590 Ars-en-Ré, Ile de Ré
☎ 05 46 29 40 04 Fax 05 46 29 41 19
English spoken

A comfortable, seafront hotel, with a restaurant specialising in seafood, superbly situated opposite the beach on the west side of the island, just before Ars-en-Ré. Some of the bedrooms have a sea view and balcony/verandah. ✓

14 bedrs, all ensuite, ♀ P DB 320-380 B 40 ✕ 130-200 ℂℂ MC Visa Amex ⏚ 8km ⋏ 8km ⋕ ⛨

ROCHEFORT Charente Maritime   4A

★ Hôtel Commerce
Rue Général Bruncher, 17450 Fouras-les-Bains
☎ 05 46 84 22 62 Fax 05 46 84 14 50
Set in the heart of the Fouras-les-Bains peninsula, this peaceful, homely hotel is just 50 m from the main beach. From Rochefort take the N137 towards La Rochelle; about 15 km from Rochefort take a left turn on to D937 to Fouras.

12 bedrs, 7 ensuite, P 500 DB 150-300 B 29 ✕ 90-140 ℂℂ MC Visa ☑ ⋏

★★ Hôtel des Vermandois
33 rue E. Combes, 17300 Rochefort
☎ 05 46 99 62 75 Fax 05 46 99 62 83
English spoken
A peaceful, 17th century, residence situated in the town centre close to Pierre Loti's house. From La Rochelle on the D137, take the D733 and at the roundabout take the 'Boulevard Pouzet'.

10 bedrs, all ensuite, ♀ P DB 190-300 B 30 ℂℂ MC Visa ⏚ ⋏ ⋏
RAC 10 % 1 Nov-28 Feb

LA ROCHELLE Charente Maritime   4A

★★ Hôtel Frantour St-Nicolas
13 rue Sardinerie, 17000 La Rochelle
☎ 05 46 41 71 55 Fax 05 46 41 70 46
English spoken
A charming renovated mansion, with indoor garden, set in the heart of the old town. Conveniently situated for the pedestrian precinct and only a few minutes walk from the ancient harbour. Free undercover parking on presentation of this book, from Oct-May.

79 bedrs, all ensuite, ✦ P 35 DB 320-425 B 49 No restaurant ⒸⒸ MC Visa Amex ▸ 6km 🚗 🖼 6km ⚏ ♪ ♿
RAC **Free indoor parking Oct-May**

★★ Hôtel Trianon et de la Plage
6 rue Monnaie, 17000 La Rochelle
☎ 05 46 41 21 35 Fax 05 46 41 95 78
English spoken
Closed 23 Dec-1 Feb
Formerly a private residence, this hotel, with pretty rooms and elegant furnishings, has been owned by the same family since the 1920s and has all the charm and personal touches of a much-loved home. Situated close to the beaches in old quarter of town.

25 bedrs, all ensuite, ✦ P DB 360-455 B 43 ✕ 95-188 ⒸⒸ MC Visa Amex ▸ 5km 🖼 ⚏

★ Hôtel de Bordeaux
43 rue St-Nicholas, 17000 La Rochelle
☎ 05 46 41 31 22 Fax 05 46 41 24 43
English spoken
A centrally situated hotel, close to the port, in the St-Nicolas quarter where a flea market is held every Thursday and Saturday.

22 bedrs, 12 ensuite, P 200 DB 160-260 B 28-30 ⒸⒸ MC Amex ▸ 2km 🖼

★★★ Hôtel de France & d'Angleterre
20 rue Rambaud, 17000 La Rochelle
☎ 05 46 41 23 99 Fax 05 46 41 15 19
English spoken
A centrally situated former mansion with nice furniture, large gardens and air-conditioning. There are several restaurants at the port - 6 minutes walk.

36 bedrs, all ensuite, ✦ P 4 DB 315-560 B 45 No restaurant ⒸⒸ MC Visa Amex ▸ 🖼 ⚏

★★ Hôtel du Commerce
6 place de Verdun, 17000 La Rochelle
☎ 05 46 41 08 22 Fax 05 46 41 74 85
English spoken
A Logis de France hotel in the centre of the old town opposite the cathedral and a car park.

63 bedrs, 49 ensuite, P DB 165-320 B 32 ✕ 75-102 ⒸⒸ MC Visa Amex ▸ 7km 🖼 ⚏ ♪

ROYAN Charente Maritime   4A

★★★ Family Golf Hôtel
28 bd Garnier, 17200 Royan
☎ 05 46 05 14 66 Fax 05 46 06 52 56
English spoken
This hotel, situated on Royan beach, is close to the yacht and fishing harbour and has a panoramic view over the bay and the port.

33 bedrs, 30 ensuite, ✦ P 6 DB 350-500 B 42 No restaurant ⒸⒸ MC Visa ▸ 5km 🖼 ♪

★★★ Grand Hôtel de Pontaillac
195 av Pontaillac, 17200 Royan
☎ 05 46 39 00 44 Fax 05 46 39 04 05
English spoken
Closed 10 Oct-1 May

A very nice hotel, with individualised, renovated rooms, a garden and car park, pleasantly situated in the centre of the beach, close to the casino.

40 bedrs, all ensuite, ✦ P 20 DB 380-580 B 45 No restaurant ⒸⒸ MC Visa ▸ 4km 🚗 🖼 ♪ ♿
RAC **5 %**

★★ Hôtel Beauséjour
32 av de la Grande Conche, 17200 Royan
☎ 05 46 05 09 40 Fax 05 46 05 39 41
English spoken
Closed 15 Dec-15 Jan
A quiet hotel, 100 m from Royan's main beach, offering quality French cuisine and an outdoor dining area. Access: look near the beach for 'Le Tiki' brasserie, the hotel is 150 m on the opposite side of the street.

14 bedrs, all ensuite, ✦ P DB 250-320 B 32 ✕ 60-120 ⒸⒸ MC Visa ▸ 5km 🚗 🖼 ♪
RAC **10 % except Jul-Aug**

Short Breaks
Many hotels provide special rates for weekend and mid-week breaks - sometimes these are quoted in the hotels entry, otherwise ring direct for the latest offers.

★★★ Hôtel Résidence de Rohan
Parc des Fées, route de St-Palais, 17640 Royan
☎ 05 46 39 00 75 Fax 05 46 38 29 99
English spoken
Closed 15 Nov-31 Mar

An old house with the beach of Vaux-Nauzan at the end of the garden. From the centre of Royan take D25 towards the beach at Pontaillac and St-Palais-sur-Mer.

41 bedrs, all ensuite, **P** 25 **DB** 300-660 **B** 54 No restaurant **CC** MC Visa Amex ⅔ ▸ 4km 🔲 🔲 ⅲ

★★ Hôtel Climat de France
route de Royan, 17100 Saintes
☎ 05 46 97 20 40 Fax 05 46 92 22 54
English spoken
From station or motorway E5 take exit 25 and head towards Royan on the N150. The hotel is about 1 km on from the exit.

36 bedrs, all ensuite, ♄ **P** **DB** 270-282 **B** 49 ✕ 57-85 **CC** MC Visa Amex ⅔ ⅔ ▸ 3km 🔲 🔲 3km ⅲ ⋈ ⅍
RAC 10 % on room rate

★★ Hôtel Ibis
1 rue de la Côte de Beauté, Route de Royan, 17100 Saintes
☎ 05 46 74 36 34 Fax 05 46 93 33 39
English spoken
The hotel has an outdoor pool and 71 rooms, each with TV (Canal + and satellite network) bathroom and telephone. Restaurant offers traditional and regional cuisine.

71 bedrs, all ensuite, **P** 90 **DB** 270-335 **B** 35 ✕ 55-95 **CC** MC Visa Amex ⅔ ▸ 🔲 ⅲ ⅍

★★ Hôtel au Terminus
2 rue J Moulin, 17100 Saintes
☎ 05 46 74 35 03 Fax 05 46 97 24 47
English spoken
Closed 23 Dec-16 Jan
Delightful, traditional and recently renovated 1920s building, opposite the SNCF station, with little or no train noise. Run by an Irish/French couple who give a warm welcome. Member of the Bonjour Scheme.

28 bedrs, all ensuite, ♄ **P** 4 **DB** 200-390 **B** 33 No restaurant **CC** MC Visa Amex ▸ 4km 🔲 ⅲ ⅍
RAC 10 %

★★ Inter Hôtel Au Bleu Nuit
1 rue Pasteur, 17100 Saintes
☎ 05 46 93 01 72 Fax 05 46 74 43 80
English spoken
Take Saintes-Centre exit from A10. The hotel is 30 m before the tourist information office.

35 bedrs, all ensuite, ♄ **P** **DB** 180-340 **B** 30 No restaurant **CC** MC Visa Amex ⅔ ▸ 10km 🔲 🔲 🔲 🔲 ⅍ ⅍

★★ Relais du Château
place des Marronniers, 79100 Oiron
☎ 05 49 96 54 96 Fax 05 49 96 54 45
English spoken
Closed 1-14 Jan
A small, comfortable and friendly Logis de France hotel just 200 m from the Château d'Oiron. Restaurant, with beamed ceiling and open fireplace, offers regional and traditional cuisine. Oiron is on D64, south of the D759 Thouars to Loudun road.

14 bedrs, 10 ensuite, ♄ **P** **DB** 150-230 **B** 30 ✕ 65-225 **CC** MC Visa ▸ 🔲 ⅲ ⅍ ⅍

Burgundy

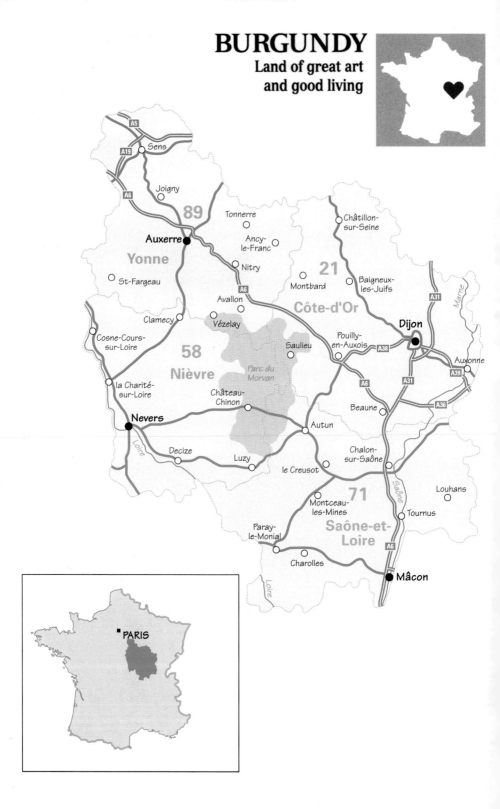

BURGUNDY
Land of great art and good living

In the fifteenth century, Burgundian dukes ruled over an empire which was, at the time, one of the most powerful in Europe. This area of rich and rural nature has always had influence beyond its size. Burgundy is still one of the more prosperous of the French regions, not least because of the wonderful quality of its wine, which appears to be universally enjoyed by the world's wine drinkers.

Dijon, the Burgundian administrative capital, was once ranked as one of the foremost cities of arts and education in Europe. In the heyday of the Burgundian Empire, the ruling dukes, who had immense power across much of the continent, ploughed enormous sums into developing the city.

After 1477, when the area was joined to the French Kingdom by Louis XI, Dijon's status waned. However, the city remained important, and not just to mustard-eaters. For a taste of the old imperial order, visit the Palais des Ducs. Here, Philippe the Bold, Charles the Rash, Jean the Fearless and Philippe the Good plotted their domination of Europe.

Don't miss the delightful Musée des Beaux-Arts, which houses one of the best provincial collections in France (certainly the best collection in Burgundy). Monet, Manet and Rubens are well-represented in this collection.

The Grand Place de la Libération is one of the city's focal points. Dijon history is reflected in its many name changes which have confused the local population at regular intervals over past centuries: Place Royale, Place de la Révolution, Place Impériale and Place d'Armes.

For a taste of Dijon café-culture and, perhaps, a drop of wine, head for the place François-Rude.

To the south, **Beaune** is a major centre of Burgundian wine-making. Beaune is the capital of the Côte d'Or, which is thought by some to be the home of the best wines in the world.

age 175: Burgundy Saône et Loire Roc de Solutre Marconnais Vineyards
bove: Lac de Panneciere at Nievre

Many of the industry's great names have cellars (*caves*) here. You can happily spend hours wandering through the cool cellars and tasting the various tipples on offer. Look carefully at the prices; some of the older vintages can be staggeringly expensive.

To learn more about the art of viticulture, visit the well-presented Musée des Vins. Non-alcoholic attractions include the Hôtel-Dieu, one of the foremost sights in Burgundy. Built by Philippe le Bon's chancellor in 1443, the Hôtel-Dieu was actually a hospital for plague victims. The rather plain exterior gives little warning that, inside, the Hôtel-Dieu is a breathtaking orgy of intricate patterns, painted ceilings and fiddly carvings.

If Beaune leaves you feeling keen to find out more about Burgundy's wines, follow the A6 south towards **Chalon-sur-Saône**, Mâcon and the Beaujolais region.

There is little to hold the traveller's attention in Chalon, but, further south, the roadside view rises into the rolling vineyards of the Mâconnais.

This is where the south makes its first tentative steps into the climate and nature of the north; red roofs and warmer breezes remind you that you're heading for the Mediterranean – albeit a long way off!

Mâcon itself is a pleasant, but hardly captivating, town. It is a prosperous commercial centre thanks to its wonderful wines. Both red and white wines are produced, but the white (made from the Chardonnay grape) is more successful. The Mâconnais vineyards eventually give way to those of the Beaujolais region, whose wines are presently enjoying something of a boom in popularity.

Like so much of France, the beauty of this part of Burgundy is not easily pinpointed. The vineyards are interesting, and towns such as Mâcon are attractive enough. But the real joy of southern Burgundy is the variety of its landscape. The main routes south do not give adequate opportunity to appreciate this diversity, and there is a lot to be said for taking some time to explore the more remote parts of the region.

One convenient base from which to do this

Above: Auxerre is a lovely place in which to wander aimlessly; the river has carved some beautiful bank-side views and the town is a chain of churches, squares and attractive streets

s the ancient Roman town of **Autun**. At its zenith, Autun's population reached 80,000. The town was an important centre of education. Today, the town has fewer than 20,000 inhabitants, and its influence has been in steady decline for two millennia. It is, however, an enjoyable place to spend some time.

The Romans left Autun with several treasures; find the surviving Roman gates and the remains of a Roman theatre. The theatre was the biggest in Gaul – a testament to the town's cultural significance. More impressive is the mighty Cathédrale St-Lazare. The cathedral, begun in 1120, replaced an existing one which was eventually demolished in the eighteenth century. Look for Gislebertus' famous treatment of the Last Judgement in the tympanum.

Voltaire unwittingly saved the masterpiece, when in 1766 he attacked the work as clumsy, and it was subsequently plastered over. That act probably saved it from destruction during the Revolution. Gislebertus' apocalyptic message is clear: be saved or be damned.

If you decide to head north from Autun to Vézalay, stop off at **Saulieu**. This is the best town in Burgundy in which to eat. Saulieu has made a living feeding passing travellers since Roman times.

Vézalay is unmissable – and so fairly crowded. With less than 1,000 Vézeliens, this charming village is utterly overwhelmed by tourism.

Despite the scrum, La Madeleine is still a real 'must see' sight. This foremost romanesque building was a focal point for Christian pilgrimage because Mary Magdalen's remains were thought to be buried here. The Papacy confirmed this theory for over 200 years. Throughout that time, La Madeleine enjoyed unparalleled attention. However, a rival claim came from St-Maxim in Provence, where locals argued that they had found the real remains of Mary. In 1295, a Papal Bull ruled in favour of Provence and La Madeleine was quickly forgotten. However, the building is still one of the most impressive in France. In typically romanesque fashion, the plain exterior (with the exception of the magnificent tympanum) gives no hint at the glory inside. The

ceilings and columns are laboriously detailed with biblical scenes and strangely, astrological symbols.

Nearby **Avallon** is a quieter and less dramatic place. It is though, a seductive town, which comes as a welcome retreat after the crammed streets of Vézalay. Great chunks of medieval fortification have survived and the town is still ringed by its ancient and impressive walls. Go to the Parc des Chaumes for great views across the town and down into the rue de Lormes. North-west Burgundy is dominated by Sens and Auxerre.

Auxerre, a city of spires which straddles the River Yonne, is the capital of the Yonne region of Burgundy. It is also well-placed for visiting the Chablis vineyards. As Chablis can be a bit over-priced in Britain, it is worth stocking up on the gorgeous wine in Auxerre.

Sens, to the north of Auxerre, is a smaller and, arguably, less interesting city. The main attraction is the Cathédrale de St-Etienne which was one of the most influential Gothic cathedrals in France – both religiously and architecturally. In fact, the original plan was Romanesque, but the twelfth-century Gothic style eventually prevailed. It was seen for some time as a blueprint for other Gothic cathedrals across the area.

What to do in Burgundy

- Taste the fine wines of Beaune, Chablis or Mâcon.
- Visit the Musée des Beaux-Arts in Dijon, which houses one of the best provincial collections in France.
- Get off the tourist trail south and explore the quiet villages and country roads of southern Burgundy.
- Don't miss Burgundy's most impressive building: La Madeleine at Vézalay.
- Decode Gislebertus' famous scenes of the Last Judgement, which are carved into the tympanum on the Cathédrale St-Lazare at Autun.
- Take a beautiful Yonne-side walk in Auxerre, or, better still, take a boat trip from Auxerre into the rolling Burgundian countryside.

Festivals in Burgundy

March
- Auxonne Carnival, Auxonne
- Chalon-sur-Saône Carnival, Chalon-sur-Saône

April
- Spring Festival, Châtillon-sur-Seine

May
- National Wine Fair, Mâcon
- Hot Air Balloon Festival, Chalon-sur-Saône

June
- Jazz Festival, Auxerre
- Music Festival, Dijon
- Boating Festival, St-Jean-de-Losne

July
- National Festival of Street Artists, Chalon-sur-Saône
- Festival of Music and Theatre, Ancy-le-Franc
- Music Festival, Ancy-le-Duc

August
- Wine Festival, Chagny
- Flower Festival, St-Honoré-les-Bains
- Wine Festival, Tannay

September
- International Folklore and Wine Festival, Dijon
- Music Festival, Nevers

October
- Photography and Film Festival, Chalon-sur-Saône
- International Gastronomy Festival, Dijon

Below: Celebrations at the wine fair, Dijon, in September

Getting there

By road
The major artery through Burgundy is the fast A6 between Paris and Lyon via Dijon.

By rail
By TGV:
- Paris Gare de Lyon to Montbard takes 1 hour 50 mins
- Paris Gare de Lyon to Beaune takes 2 hours 15 min
- Paris Gare de Lyon to Dijon takes 1 hour 36 mins
- Paris Gare de Lyon to Chalon sur Saône takes 2 hours 19 mins

By air
Dijon-Bourgogne International Airport (◐ 3 80 67 67 67, Fax: 3 80 63 02 99) is 4 miles south-east of Dijon. Get into Dijon by taxi or airport shuttle bus.
For car hire contact:
- Avis ◐ 3 80 43 60 76
- Europcar ◐ 3 80 43 28 44

TOURIST INFORMATION
- **Burgundy Tourist Office**
  Conseul Général, BP 1602,
  21035 Dijon Cedex
  ◐ 3 80 30 59 45

AUTUN Saône et Loire　　3C

★★ Golf Hôtel
Au plan d'eau du Vallon, 71400 Autun
☎ 03 85 52 00 00 Fax 03 85 52 20 20
English spoken

With a large terrace and a splendid view of the town centre and cathedral this hotel is very quiet and close to lake. A 15 minute walk from the town centre. The restaurant speciality is prime cuts of grilled Charollais beef.

43 bedrs, all ensuite, ⊬ P 45 DB 250-278 B 35 ✕ 59-185 ⓒ MC Visa Amex ▸ 1km 🔲 🔲 🔲 ⅲ 🅰 ⅙
RaC **5 % on room rate**

★★ Hôtel Arcades
22 avenue de la République, 71400 Autun
☎ 03 85 52 30 03 Fax 03 85 86 39 09
English spoken

Situated opposite the station and a restaurant in the heart of Autun, this hotel, close to the town's main monuments, offers a warm welcome and guarantees a peaceful, comfortable stay.

32 bedrs, 31 ensuite, ⊬ P DB 275 B 35 No restaurant ⓒ MC Visa Amex ▸ 2km 🔲 🅰
RaC **10 %**

AUXERRE Yonne　　2D

★★ Hôtel Seignelay
2 rue Pont, 89000 Auxerre
☎ 03 86 52 03 48 Fax 03 86 52 32 39
English spoken

A traditional welcome and pretty interior terrace await in this town centre hotel. This hotel is situated 150 km from Paris and 25 km from Chablis.

21 bedrs, 19 ensuite, ⊬ P DB 150-300 B 38 ✕ 78-135 ⓒ MC Visa ▸ 15km 🔲 ⅲ 🅰
RaC

★★ Hôtel Soleil d'Or
N77, 89230 Montigny-la-Resle
☎ 03 86 41 81 21 Fax 03 86 41 86 88
English spoken

Set next to the church in the middle of the village, the hotel is on the N77. Its elegant, bright dining room has lots of flowers and a fountain. Specialities included foie gras with exotic fruits, gently fried in a caramel sauce and fillet of sea bream.

16 bedrs, all ensuite, ⊬ P DB 195-310 B 40 ✕ 98-325 ⓒ MC Visa Amex 🔲 ⅲ 🅰 ⅙
RaC **5 %**

★★ Hôtel de Normandie
41 bd Vauban, 89000 Auxerre
☎ 03 86 52 57 80 Fax 03 86 51 54 33
English spoken

With a charming and warm atmosphere the 47 quiet bedrooms have modern ensuite bathrooms and are equipped with telephones, computer sockets, television (national & foreign channels). The 24 hour room service menu offers a wide selection for all tastes.

47 bedrs, all ensuite, ⊬ P 30 DB 290-370 B 36 ✕ 25-46 (room service) ⓒ MC Visa Amex 🔲 🔲 ▸ 10km 🔲 🔲 ⅲ 🅰 ⅙
RaC **5 %**

BEAUNE Côte d'Or　　3C

★★★ Hôtel Belle Epoque
15 Fg Bretonnière, 21200 Beaune
☎ 03 80 24 66 15 Fax 03 80 24 17 49
English spoken

A local-style, medieval house now modernised. On the N74 going from the town centre towards Autun, close to the famous Hospices de Beaune.

16 bedrs, all ensuite, ⊬ P 18 DB 345-695 B 45 No restaurant ⓒ MC Visa Amex ▸ 5km 🔲 ⅲ 🅰

★★ Hôtel Climat de France
av Charles de Gaulle, Parc Hôtelier, 21200 Beaune
☎ 03 80 22 74 10 Fax 03 80 22 40 45
English spoken

A modern hotel with good facilites including several family rooms and a wine bar. Friendly, efficient service and a modern restaurant offering an hors d'oeuvre menu and an extensive wine list. 500 m from A6-Sud exit towards Beaune.

50 bedrs, all ensuite, **✝ P** 50 **DB** 280-330 **B** 37 **✕** 70-120 **CC** MC Visa Amex 📠 ▸ 2km 🏖 ⚌ ♿
RaC 10 %

★★★★ Hôtel Le Cep
27 rue Maufoux, 21200 Beaune
📞 03 80 22 35 48 **Fax** 03 80 22 76 80
English spoken
A 16th century private residence in the centre of Beaune with stunning décor in traditional French style.

53 bedrs, all ensuite, **✝ P** 30 **DB** 700-1,500 **B** 80 No restaurant **CC** MC Visa Amex ▸ 4km 🏖 ⚌ ♿

★★★ Hôtel Les Paulands
Ladoix-Serrigny, 21550 Beaune
📞 03 80 26 41 05 **Fax** 03 80 26 47 56
English spoken
Burgundian house standing in its own vineyards, the new restaurant with terrace and bar specialises in jambon persillé, boeuf bourguignon and escargots bourguignon. From A6, Nuits-St-George exit, take the N74 towards Aloxe-Corton/Ladoix-Serrigny.

20 bedrs, all ensuite, **✝ P DB** 360-490 **B** 49 **✕** 88-136 **CC** MC Visa ⚡ ▸ 6km 🏖 ⚌

★★★ Hôtel du Château de Challanges
rue des Templiers, 21200 Beaune
📞 03 80 26 32 62 **Fax** 03 80 26 32 52
English spoken
Closed 30 Nov-15 Mar

A small château set in a large park, close to the historic town of Beaune. Exit off A6, follow signs towards Dole-Seurre then turn right into rte de Challanges.

10 bedrs, all ensuite, **✝ P DB** 530-1,150 **B** 60 No restaurant **CC** MC Visa Amex ▸ 2km 🏖 ⚌ ✎

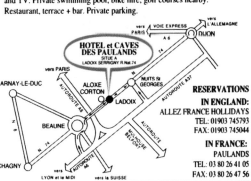

CHAGNY Saône et Loire   3C

★★★ Château de Bellecroix
rte de Chalon, 71150 Chagny
☎ 03 85 87 13 86 Fax 03 85 91 28 62
English spoken
Closed 20 Dec-15 Feb
*A pleasing combination of 12th and 18th century
architecture, once home to a commander of the
Knights of Malta. Set in lovely parkland, the hotel is
beautifully furnished, peaceful and relaxing.*

21 bedrs, all ensuite, ⌕ P DB 600-1,000 B 68 ✗ 260-
360 ℂℂ MC Visa Amex ☇ ⴑ 10km ▣ 5km ⊠ ⠏

CHALON-SUR-SAONE Saône et Loire   3C

★★ Hôtel Relais du Montagny
71390 Buxy *04 94 94*
☎ 03 85 92 19 90 Fax 03 85 92 07 19
English spoken
*From the A6, take Chalon-Sud exit towards Monceau
on the E607/N80. After 200 m turn left onto the D981
and carry on for 13 km. The hotel is on the outskirts
of the village.*

30 bedrs, all ensuite, ⌕ P DB 320-370 B 40 ✗ 75-200
ℂℂ MC Visa Amex ☇ ⴑ 15km ⊠ ▣ ⊠ ⠏ ⌀ ⅃
RaC 5 % on room rate and breakfast

Hôtel St-Georges
32 av Jean Jaurès, 71100 Chalon-sur-Saône
☎ 03 85 48 27 05 Fax 03 85 93 23 88
English spoken

*A very comfortable, traditional hotel. In the warm
atmosphere of the dining room you will discover a
cuisine made with the best products of 'Bourgogne'.*

48 bedrs, all ensuite, ⌕ P 20 DB 380-570 B 55 ✗ 115-
400 ℂℂ MC Visa Amex ⴑ ▣ ⊠ ⠏ ⌀
RaC 5 % on room rate

CHAROLLES Saône et Loire   5B

★★★ Château de Dravert
71220 La Guiche
☎ 03 85 24 67 38 Fax 03 85 24 69 69

*17th century Château de Dravert set in peaceful
private parkland has individually furnished rooms,
each with a private jacuzzi, gourmet cooking
preceeded by wine-tasting from the cellars and an
indoor swimming pool with underwater massage.*

6 bedrs, all ensuite, P 10 DB 690-890 B 60 ✗ 350-450
ℂℂ MC Visa Amex ☇ ⴑ ▣ ⊠ ⌀
RaC

CHATILLON-SUR-SEINE Côte d'Or   3C

★★ Hôtel Le Santenoy
21330 Marcenay-le-Lac
☎ 03 80 81 40 08 Fax 03 80 81 43 05
English spoken
*The hotel is 1 km from the village, on the bank of the
lake. Marcenay-le-Lac is 14 km from Châtillon-sur-
Seine towards Tonnerre. The restaurant serves
Burgundian cuisine and overlooks the lake.*

18 bedrs, 15 ensuite, ⌕ P DB 142-250 B 30-40 ✗ 74-
198 ℂℂ MC Visa ⴑ ▣ ⊠ ⠏ ⌀ ⅃

★★★ Hôtel de la Côte d'Or
Rue Charles Ronot, 21400 Châtillon-sur-Seine
☎ 03 80 91 13 29 Fax 03 80 91 29 15
English spoken

*Built in 1738, an old coaching house that still offers
a warm welcome to weary travellers. Gourmet cuisine
with Burgundian specialities served outside in
summer.*

10 bedrs, all ensuite, ⌕ P DB 320-600 B 38-50 ✗ 95-
185 ℂℂ MC Visa Amex ▣ ⊠

CLAMECY Nièvre   2D

★★★ Hôtel de la Poste
9 place Emile Zola, 58500 Clamecy
☎ 03 86 27 01 55 Fax 03 86 27 05 99
English spoken
A former staging post from the turn of the 7th century. In the centre near the bridge over the Yonne. Towards road D151, 45 km from Auxerre, 65 km from Walard.

15 bedrs, all ensuite, ♀ P DB 245-315 B 35 ✕ 100-200 ₵₵ MC Visa Amex ▸ 🖫 🖾 ⦙⦙⦙ ♪

DIJON Côte d'Or   3C

★★ Hostellerie de Côte
Marsannay-la-Côte, 21160 Dijon
☎ 03 80 51 10 00 Fax 03 80 58 82 97
English spoken
Closed 30 Nov-29 Feb
In the heart of Burgundy, this is a traditional hotel with terraces overlooking vineyards. Well situated for an overnight stay and about 5 km south-west of Dijon, off the N74.

41 bedrs, all ensuite, ♀ P 60 DB 250-290 B 38 ✕ 85-185 ₵₵ MC Visa Amex ▸ 🖫 🖫 🖾 ⦙⦙⦙ ♪ 🕭
RaC 5 %

★★ Hôtel St-Georges
carrefour de l'Europe, 21700 Nuits-St-Georges
☎ 03 80 61 15 00 Fax 03 80 61 23 80
English spoken

A modern hotel just off the Nuits-St-Georges A31 motorway exit towards the town centre. The hotel offers an indoor car park, snooker room, wine bar and sampling menus in the restaurant.

47 bedrs, all ensuite, ♀ P 50 DB 305-345 B 48 ✕ 120-425 ₵₵ MC Visa Amex ⊰ ▸ 15km 🖫 🖫 🖾 ⦙⦙⦙ ♪ 🕭

★★ Hôtel Victor Hugo
23 rue Fleurs, 21000 Dijon
☎ 03 80 43 63 45
English spoken
A friendly hotel in the town centre located in a small and quiet street.

23 bedrs, all ensuite, P 14 DB 230-270 B 29 No restaurant ₵₵ MC Visa ▸ 🖾

★★★ Hôtel Wilson
place Wilson, 21000 Dijon
☎ 03 80 66 82 50 Fax 03 80 36 41 54
English spoken
Closed 31 Dec

A former coaching inn, this 17th century hotel, full of character, is situated south of Dijon just 5 minutes walk from the town centre towards the airport. With a highly-acclaimed restaurant serving truly gourmet cuisine.

27 bedrs, all ensuite, ♀ P 14 DB 350-490 B 57 No restaurant ₵₵ MC Visa Amex ▸ 10km 🖾 ♪ 🕭

★★★ Quality Hôtel du Nord
place Darcy, 21000 Dijon
☎ 03 80 30 58 58 Fax 03 80 30 61 26
English spoken
Closed 23 Dec-6 Jan
The hotel is situated in the centre of Dijon, 5 minutes walk from the station, near the information point. Wine bar.

27 bedrs, all ensuite, P DB 350-430 B 49 ✕ 99-200 ₵₵ MC Visa Amex ▸ ⦙⦙⦙

DONZY Nièvre   2D

★★ Hôtel Le Grand Monarque
Près de l'Eglise, 58220 Donzy
☎ 03 86 39 35 44 Fax 03 86 39 37 09
English spoken
A small hotel with old-world charm. Donzy is south-east of Cosne-Cours sur Loire on D33. The restaurant has fine gourmet cuisine. Specialities include coq au Sancerre rouge, jambon saupiquet, magrets de canard and profiteroles au chocolat.

11 bedrs, all ensuite, P 8 DB 255-295 B 37 ✕ 105-220 ₵₵ MC Visa ▸ 🖫 🖾 ⦙⦙⦙ ♪
RaC 5 %

GEVREY-CHAMBERTIN Côte d'Or 3C

★★★ Hôtel Arts et Terroirs

28 rte de Dijon, 21220 Gevrey-Chambertin
03 80 34 30 76 Fax 03 80 34 11 79
English spoken

In the heart of a wine-producing area, a very comfortable hotel with fine antique furniture, a wine bar and lovely gardens. South-west of Dijon, off A31

16 bedrs, all ensuite, **P** 16 **DB** 330-580 **B** 45 No restaurant **CC** MC Visa Amex 10km
RAC 10 % except weekends

MACON Saône et Loire 5B

★★★ Auberge La Sarrasine

Le Logis-Neuf, Confrançon, 01310 Polliat
04 74 30 25 65 Fax 04 74 25 24 23
English spoken

A beautifully situated hotel offering speciality cuisine including poulet de Bresse, grenouilles and pigeonneau rôti. From Mâcon cross River Saône towards Bourg-en-Bresse. Continue for 18km on the N79 to village of Logis-Neuf. The hotel is just 1 km on.

11 bedrs, all ensuite, **P** 11 **DB** 398-890 **B** 58-68 ✕ 99-290 **CC** MC Visa Amex 10km

★★★ Hostellerie Sarrasine

Route Nationale 79, 01750 Replonges
03 85 31 02 41 Fax 03 85 31 11 74
English spoken
Closed Jan

From Mâcon cross the River Saône towards Bourg-en-Bresse. Continue straight ahead on N79 for 3 km to La Madeleine and this small, luxuriously decorated hotel is 500 m after the second set of traffic lights.

7 bedrs, all ensuite, **P** 7 **DB** 390-790 **B** 58-68 ✕ 99-350 **CC** MC Visa Amex 2km

★★ Hôtel Ibis Mâcon-Sud

Les Bouchardes-Chaintré, 71570 Crêches-sur-Saône
03 85 36 51 60 Fax 03 85 37 42 40
English spoken

A Mâconnais style hotel with 62 renovated rooms, air-conditioned restaurant, 24 hour reception, satellite TV, regional cuisine and wines and a secure car park. Ideal for touring Burgundy. A6 Motorway, Mâcon-Sud.

62 bedrs, all ensuite, **P** 100 **DB** 315 **B** 36 ✕ 55-95 **CC** Visa Amex

MAGNY-COURS Nièvre 2D

★★★ Holiday Inn Nevers

Ferme du Domaine de Bardonnay, 58470 Magny-Cours
03 86 21 22 33 Fax 03 86 21 22 03
English spoken

43 bedrs, all ensuite, ★ P 50 DB 212-384 B 30 ✗ 68-134 ℂℂ MC Visa ⊘ ㋔

MIREBEAU Côte d'Or 3C

★★ Auberge des Marronniers
place Général Viard, 21310 Mirebeau-sur-Bèze
☎ 03 80 36 71 05 Fax 03 80 36 75 92
English spoken
Closed 22 Dec-8 Jan
A peaceful riverside hotel with a restaurant overlooking terraced flower gardens and the river. Tennis, swimming pool, canoeing and kayaking nearby.

16 bedrs, all ensuite, P 10 DB 180-230 B 25 ✗ 61-170 ℂℂ Visa Amex ➤ 20km 🖪 🖾 ⊞ ⊘ ㋔

NEVERS Nièvre 2D

★★★ Hôtel Loire
Quai de Médine, 58000 Nevers
☎ 03 86 61 50 92 Fax 03 86 59 43 29
English spoken
A quiet, riverside hotel offering views of the old bridge and the Loire from most of the bedrooms and the restaurant. About 200 m from the town centre and shopping facilities and 5 minutes drive from the station. Near N7.

58 bedrs, all ensuite, ★ P DB 430-460 B 42-70 ✗ 115-220 ℂℂ MC Visa Amex ➤ 9km 🖪 ⊞

★★ Hôtel Molière
25 rue Molière, 58000 Nevers
☎ 03 86 57 29 96 Fax 03 86 36 00 13
English spoken
Closed 22 Dec-3 Jan
The Hôtel Molière offers a fine breakfast and pleasant rooms (connecting for families), in a quiet, verdant setting. Access via Nevers exit from N7, after the BP station take the first on the right. Free indoor car park for guests.

18 bedrs, 16 ensuite, ★ P 30 DB 260-280 B 33-38 No restaurant ℂℂ MC Visa ➤ 🖾 ⊘

★★★ Hôtel de Diane
38 rue du Midi, 58000 Nevers
☎ 03 86 57 28 10 Fax 03 86 59 45 08
English spoken
A centrally situated hotel, close to the station and the River Loire. From the station's main gate take the ave de Gaulle and then the second right.

30 bedrs, all ensuite, ★ P 12 DB 490-590 B 48 ✗ 79-152 ℂℂ MC Visa Amex ➤ 10km ⊞ ⊘ ㋔
RAC 10 %

Partly converted from an old farmhouse, the hotel is a pleasing blend of old and new. Next to the Magny-Cours car race-track and golf course. Located on N7, 15 km from Nevers. Restaurant speciality is pièce de Charolais.

70 bedrs, all ensuite, ★ P 70 DB 350-460 B 60 ✗ 98-250 ℂℂ MC Visa Amex ⌿ 🖾 ▦ ➤ ▣ ⊞ ⊘ ㋔

MEURSAULT Côte d'Or 3C

★★★ Hôtel Les Magnolias
8 rue P Joigneaux, 21190 Meursault
☎ 03 80 21 23 23 Fax 03 80 21 29 10
English spoken
Closed Dec

A small hotel with courtyard, garden and individually decorated rooms with luxurious ensuite bathrooms, set in a quiet village surrounded by vineyards. Leave A6 at Beaune and then N74, or A6 exit at Chalon-sur-Saône, then N6 and N74. 6 km from Beaune.

12 bedrs, all ensuite, P 12 DB 400-620 B 48 ℂℂ MC Visa Amex ⌿ ➤ 6km 🖾 ⊘ ㋔

★★ Motel au Soleil Levant
rte de Beaune, 21190 Meursault
☎ 03 80 21 23 47 Fax 03 80 21 65 67
English spoken
South-west from Beaune, take a right fork on the D973 towards Meursault. Pass through the vineyards of Pommard and Volnay and on the approach to Meursault turn left and the motel is about 400 m ahead.

POUILLY-EN-AUXOIS Côte d'Or   3C

★★★ Hostellerie du Château de Ste-Sabine
Ste-Sabine, 21320 Pouilly-en-Auxois
☎ 03 80 49 22 01 Fax 03 80 49 20 01
English spoken

A beautiful 18th-century castle, with tastefully decorated rooms and a gourmet restaurant, overlooking the wildlife park. Halfway between Paris and Lyon on the A6, look for the Pouilly-en-Auxois exit. Special half-board tariffs available.

16 bedrs, 12 ensuite, **P** 50 **DB** 300-740 **B** 50 ✕ 150-330
C MC Visa ⟶ ▸ 15km 🖊 🖾 ⚌ ⌀
RAC 8 %

ROMANECHE-THORINS Saône et Loire   5B

★★★ Hôtel Les Maritonnes
route de Fleurie, 71570 Romanèche-Thorins
☎ 03 85 35 51 70 Fax 03 85 35 58 14
English spoken
Closed mid Dec-mid Jan

A charming hotel, offering classic French cuisine, owned by the same family since 1895 and beautifully set in the heart of the Beaujolais region between Lyon and Macon.

20 bedrs, all ensuite, ⊶ **P** 20 **DB** 390-550 **B** 60 ✕ 195-420 **C** MC Visa Amex ⟶ ▸ 15km 🖾 ⚌

ST-FLORENTIN Yonne   3C

★★★ Hôtel La Grande Chaumière
3 rue des Capucins, 89600 St-Florentin
☎ 03 86 35 15 12 Fax 03 86 35 33 14
English spoken
Closed 8 Dec-15 Jan
A charming, comfortable hotel, with lovely gardens and a renowned restaurant, located 25 km north of Auxerre.

10 bedrs, all ensuite, **P** 10 **DB** 350-850 **B** 58 ✕ 215-495
C MC Visa Amex ▸ 🖾

ST-MARTIN-EN-BRESSE Saône et Loire   3C

★★ Hôtel au Puits Enchanté
71620 St-Martin-en-Bresse
☎ 03 85 47 71 96 Fax 03 85 47 74 58
English spoken
Situated in the centre of the little village of St-Martin-en-Bresse, this recently recommended, family-run hotel is surrounded by lovely countryside. Take the D35 from the N73 to St-Martin.

14 bedrs, all ensuite, ⊶ **P** **DB** 200-290 **B** 38 ✕ 98-225
C MC Visa ▸ 5km 🖾 🖊 🖾 ⚌ ⌀

SANTENAY-EN-BOURGOGNE Côte d'Or   3C

★★★★ Le Château de Crée
Les Hauts de Santenay, 21590 Santenay-en-Bourgogne
☎ 03 80 20 62 66 Fax 03 80 20 66 50
English spoken
Closed Jan-Feb

The hotel has four double 'prestige' rooms, 2 with fourposter beds, a 16th century cellar, view of centenary park, vineyard, library, snooker, bars and gourmet cuisine. A6 motorway exits; Beaune/Sud or Chalon-sur-Saône/Nord. Follow Chagny on N74.

4 bedrs, all ensuite, **P** **DB** 650-1,250 **B** included
✕ 300-600 **C** MC Visa ⟶ 🄿 ▸ 🖊 🖾 ⚌
RAC 5 %

★★ Hôtel Relais Arcade
9 Cours de Tarbe, 89100 Sens
☎ 03 86 64 26 99 Fax 03 86 64 46 29
English spoken
Situated in the town centre, this hotel, built in 1989, offers a peaceful atmosphere and a warm welcome.

44 bedrs, all ensuite, ⭐ **P** 22 **DB** 210-400 **B** 36 ✕ 58-127 **CC** MC Visa Amex ▸ 🎲 🖼 ♨ ⌗ ♬ ♿

★★★ Hôtel Le Rempart
2 av Gambetta, 71700 Tournus
☎ 03 85 51 10 56 Fax 03 85 51 77 22
English spoken
This highly recommended hotel, formerly a 15th century guardhouse on the ramparts of the town wall, has been renovated to a high standard and is fully air-conditioned. Take Tournus exit from A6/N6 and head towards town centre.

37 bedrs, all ensuite, ⭐ **P** **DB** 395-795 **B** 50 ✕ 165-420 **CC** MC Visa Amex ▸ 18km 🎲 ⌗ ♿

★★★ Hôtel Le Sauvage
place du Champ de Mars, 71700 Tournus
☎ 03 85 51 14 45 Fax 03 85 32 10 27
English spoken

This hotel has all the charm of the past and all the comfort of the present. Restaurant offers gourmet and regional cuisine and the best Burgundy wines. Leave A6 at Tournus exit, follow signs to town centre and hotel is right opposite the railway line.

30 bedrs, all ensuite, ⭐ **P** 10 **DB** 390-430 **B** 40 ✕ 84-200 **CC** MC Visa Amex ▸ 10km 🎲 🖼 ⌗ ♬ ♿

★★ Hôtel de la Paix
9 rue Jean Jaures, 71700 Tournus
☎ 03 85 51 01 85 Fax 03 85 51 02 30
English spoken
Closed Jan

Just a couple of yards away from the famous St-Philibert abbey, the hotel is quietly and pleasantly situated in the centre of town near the river. Air-conditioned restaurant offers specialities incuding pavé de boeuf. Only three minutes from the motorway.

24 bedrs, all ensuite, ⭐ **P** 20 **DB** 260-323 **B** 38 ✕ 90-200 **CC** MC Visa ▸ 20km 🎲 ⌗ ♬ ♿

★★ Hôtel Le Voutenay
8 route Nationale, 89270 Voutenay-sur-Cure
☎ 03 86 33 51 92 Fax 03 86 33 51 91
English spoken
Closed Jan
An 18th century manor, on the Cure river bank, in a wooded park 10 km from Vézelay and Avallon and 40 km from Auxerre. Exceptional location for short, tourist trips. Easy access: A6 motorway, exit Nitry, then towards Vézelay.

6 bedrs, all ensuite, ⭐ **P** **DB** 250-350 **B** 40 ✕ 105-220 **CC** MC Visa Amex 🎲 ⌗ ♬

Franche
-Comté

Franche-Comté, the 'free country', rises from the thickly-forested flood plains of the Saône into the spectacularly dramatic terrain which typifies the French border with Switzerland. Its tallest peak is the **Mont d'Or** at 1,460 metres. Further east, the mountains reach much higher, but Mont d'Or is still profoundly impressive. At its foot, the River Doubs digs its serpentine route through attractive and diverse countryside.

France has always felt vulnerable to attack from the east and the north. This has happened twice this century. While the mountains of Franche-Comté offer some natural protection, the 20-mile-wide 'gap' between the Vosges and Jura ranges has traditionally been a convenient back door for invading armies. This is why **Belfort** is such a tough-looking town; it was built to plug the gap. The fortress at Belfort is worth exploring. It was started by Vauban in 1675 and is a fascinating example of defensive architecture – not that it helped much! Look out for the Porte de Brisach, a triumphal arch built in honour of the so-called 'Sun King'. This is also an area rich in natural deposits. Indeed, mining and military might are the two most significant forces in Belfort's history.

Belfort is rich in ore, but **Ronchamp** is famous for coal. In its heyday, Ronchamp had the deepest shaft in France – it went down a staggering 1,008 metres. Mining is a dangerous job, a fact well illustrated by the exhibitions at the Maison de la Mine.

More uplifting is the wonderful chapel which was built to commemorate those who were killed in battle here in 1944. It is one of Le Corbusier's best-known and most successful designs. The Chapelle du Notre-Dame-du-Haut is a place of pilgrimage – as much for architecture students as for the relatives of those who died. The chapel's interior is lit by a kaleidoscopic mix of colours streaming through the multi-coloured windows along each wall.

The people of Franche-Comté like nothing more than a good museum. You will find museums that exhibit all manner of things, throughout the area.

Pages 190–191: The Cascades de l'Hérisson in the Jura – an area characterised by rivers that vanish and suddenly reappear out of limestone rock walls and by spectacular caves (notably the Gouffre de Poudrey, the largest in France with stalactites 7 m long)

Above left: The famous lion of Belfort

Above right: The Bienne Valley in the Jura national park

At **Champlitte** there is an engaging Musée d'Arts et Traditions Populaires de Franche-Comté and, more promising, a Musée du Vins. The Musée 1900 is a painstaking reconstruction of a market town of that year. From costumes to cars, every detail is accurate.

Franche-Comté is one of France's main areas of industry. The Peugeot family ran a steel mill in **Montbélliard** before they started experimenting with bizarre machines called automobiles. They set up a factory in nearby **Soshaux**. It is still the company's principal production centre. The Musée Peugeot houses a fantastic collection of old cars. The lion motif on Peugeot grilles is the same as the logo of the Franche-Comté region.

Unless you are utterly mechanically-minded, **Besançon** is a much more interesting town. This area played a particularly gallant role in the underground fight against Nazi Germany and the collaborative Vichy regime. The eye-opening Musée de la Resistance et de la Déportation and the Musée Populaire Comtois give vivid accounts of that secret war.

Besançon was once a Roman town, and evidence of that occupation can be seen in the ruins of a theatre from that time and in a rather unusual Roman nymphaeum, or water cistern.

Of more catholic appeal is the charming town of **Ornans** which was the subject of several paintings by local hero and influential artist Gustave Courbet. His *The Burial at Ornans* from 1850 hangs in the Louvre. Visit the Musée de la Maison Natale Gustave Courbet to find out more about the man and his work.

In fact, Courbet's story is an interesting one. A defender of the 1871 Paris Commune, Courbet was blamed by Bonapartist deputies for the destruction of the Vendome column. This could hardly have been more unfair, since Courbet had not only left the Commune some weeks before the column fell, but had tried hard to save national treasures including Fountainbleu. He was hounded for an enormous fine of 500,000 gold francs, forcing him to flee to Switzerland where he eventually died in 1877.

To the south-west of Besançon, **Arc-de-Senans** attracts visitors to its remarkable *Saline Royale*, a convoluted eighteenth-century system used to process brine which was drawn from huge underground reservoirs. More impressive, perhaps, are the salt workers' socially-responsible living quarters which, at the time, constituted a major step forward in the treatment of workers.

With the exception of **Morans-en-Montagne** and its remarkable toy museum (this is the toy-making capital of France), there is little else in this part of Franche-Comté except wild scenery and fresh mountain air. If you are in need of more focused amusement, however, try the towns of **Dole** and **Arbois**. They are locked in a bitter dispute over which was the true home of the great Louis Pasteur. Pasteur, the father of microbiology, was born in Dole but grew up in Arbois. There are museums in both towns.

Above: A Torpedo Tupe 127 (built in 1912) – just one of the exhibits at the Musée Peugeot at Sochaux

What to see, do and taste in…

The Doubs, Loue and Dessoubre river valleys

To see: The Doubs springs in Villiers-le-Lac and the Montbenoît Abbey.

To do: Climb the Brême cliffs or fly fish in the Dessoubre river.

To taste: The fario trout and the Pontarlier-Anis aniseed aperitif.

The Jura Mountains

To see: Wooden cask- and barrel-making at the Cooper's Museum in Bois d'Amont and the medieval town of Nozeroy.

To do: Visit a cheesemaking dairy, mountain bike down one of the permanent bike tracks or go summer tobogganing at Métabief.

To taste: Jura honey, Morbier soft cheese, Gex blue cheese, the Jésu sausage from Morteau and Michons de Choux sweets.

Bresse and Revermont

To see: The arcades of thermal spa town Lons-le-Saunier and the Wine Institute in the Pécauld Castle at Arbois.

To do: Go hang gliding or paragliding at Mont Poupet or visit Arlay Castle.

To taste: The Rouget de l'Isle cake in Lons-le-Saunier, the straw and yellow wines.

The Lake District

To see: The view of the four lakes from the Pic de L'Aigle (Eagle's Peak), the Vougland Dam and the Langouette gorge.

To taste: Grayling fish and the Chalain pebble chocolates.

The Vosges Mountains

To see: Bartholdi's Lion, the stained glass windows of the Église du Sacré-Coeur in Audincourt, the half-timbered houses in the Sundgau region.

To do: Go walking in the Regional Park of Ballons des Vosges or relax and enjoy the thermal spa at Luxeuil.

To taste: Luxeuil ham, cancoillotte cheese and Belfore cake.

The Saône valley

To see: The Baron Martin Museum in Gray, La Rochère.

To do: Go walking in the Gy hills or take a boat down the Saône river.

To taste: Freshwater crayfish, wine from Champlitte and snails from Marnay.

Getting there

By road

The A36 from Lyon into Germany links Beaune, Dole, Besançon and Montbeliard. The A39 links Dole to Paris via Dijon.

By rail

By TGV:
- Paris Gare de Lyon to Besançon takes 2 hours 40 mins)
- Paris Gare de Lyon to Dole takes 2 hours
- Paris Gare de Lyon to Mouchard takes

2 hours 20 mins
- Paris Gare de Lyon to Neuchâtel takes 3 hours 51 mins
- Paris Gare de Lyon to Pontarlier takes 3 hours 8 mins
- Besançon to Lille takes 3 hours 35 mins

By boat

Boats are for hire on the Saône and the Doubs from:

- Connoisseur Cruisers, Gray
  📞 3 84 64 95 20
- Lacaboat Plaisance, Corre
  📞 3 84 92 59 66
- Loisir Nautic de France, Port-sur-Saône
  📞 3 84 91 59 33

By air

Bâle Mulhouse International Airport (📞 3 89 90 31 11, Fax: 3 89 90 25 11) is around 20 miles south-east of Mulhouse.

For car hire contact:
- Avis 📞 3 89 90 29 39
- Budget 📞 3 89 90 28 21
- Hertz 📞 3 89 67 70 82

TOURIST INFORMATION
- **Franche-Comté Tourist Office**
  28 rue de la République, 25000 Besançon
  📞 03 81 25 08 08

BAUME-LES-DAMES Doubs   3D

★★ Auberge des Moulins
rte Pontarlier, Pont-les-Moulins, 25110 Baume-les-Dames
☎ 03 81 84 09 99 Fax 03 81 84 04 44
English spoken
Closed 19 Dec-26 Jan

Let yourself be seduced by the beauty of the Cusanein valley and receive a 15% discount on accommodation rate (not Jul/Aug). Tasty gourmand cuisine created by the landlord. 30 minutes from Besançon and Montbéliard.

12 bedrs, all ensuite, ⚄ P 35 DB 285 B 30 ✕ 98-155
℅ MC Visa Amex ▸ 15km 🔲 🖼 ⋕ 🏊
RAC **15 % except Jul-Aug**

BESANCON Doubs   3D

★★ Hôtel de Paris
33 rue des Granges, 25000 Besançon
☎ 03 81 81 36 56 Fax 03 81 61 94 90
English spoken
The Hôtel de Paris, situated in the town centre, offers 55 rooms overlooking the garden or courtyard as well as exceptional calm.

55 bedrs, 39 ensuite, ⚄ P 40 DB 240-320 B 38-57 ℅
MC Visa Amex ▸ 10km 🖼 ⋕ 🏊 ♿
RAC **10 %**

CHAMPAGNOLE Jura   3C

★★ Hôtel Ripotot
54 rue Maréchal Foch, 39300 Champagnole
☎ 03 84 52 15 45 Fax 03 84 52 09 11
English spoken
Closed 15 Nov-1 Apr

Situated in the heart of the Jura between the waterfalls, forest and the lakes. Full-board pension and half-board pension possible.

50 bedrs, 35 ensuite, ⚄ P DB 260-320 B 38 ✕ 88-240
℅ MC Visa ▸ 19km 🔲 🔲 🖼 ⋕ 🏊 ♿
RAC **5 %**

★★★ Hôtel du Parc
13 rue Paul Cretin, 39300 Champagnole
☎ 03 84 52 13 20 Fax 03 84 52 27 62
English spoken

A traditional hotel in a quiet position just 5 minutes walk from the town centre. Close to the River Ain and public gardens. Well located for long forest and river walks. On the N5.

20 bedrs, all ensuite, ⚄ P 20 DB 260-320 B 32-35
✕ 75-180 ℅ MC Visa Amex ▸ 🖼 ⋕ 🏊 ♿
RAC **5 %**

COMBEAUFONTAINE Haute Saône   3C

★★ Hôtel Balcon
70120 Combeaufontaine
☎ 03 84 92 11 13 Fax 03 84 92 15 89
English spoken
Closed 26 Dec-12 Jan
A pretty flower-bedecked hotel in a quiet part of France. Comfortable, with a heavy emphasis on the kitchen. Combeaufontaine lies on the N19 between Langres and Vesoul. Has a well-regarded restaurant, specialising in regional France - Comté cuisine.

17 bedrs, 14 ensuite, P 10 DB 250-380 B 40 ✕ 145-320
℅ MC Visa Amex 🔲 7km 🖼 12km ⋕ 🏊

LUXEUIL-LES-BAINS Haute Saône   3D

★★★ Hôtel Beau Site
18 rue Georges Moulimard, 70300 Luxeuil-les-Bains
☎ 03 84 40 14 67 Fax 03 84 40 50 25
English spoken
The hotel, set in a large garden next to thermal baths, lies to the west of the town centre (10 minutes on foot), 50 m from the casino. Follow signs for 'Les Thermes'. Restaurant on the terrace in summer.

33 bedrs, all ensuite, ⚑ **P** **DB** 220-340 **B** 40 ✗ 85-230 ((MC Visa ⫐ ► 10km 🚗 🖼 ⋕ ♫ ♿
RAC 5 %

MONTBELIARD Doubs   3D

★★ Hôtel Bristol
2 rue Velotte, 25200 Montbéliard
📞 03 81 94 43 17 **Fax** 03 81 94 15 29
English spoken
Quiet, traditional, city-centre hotel near the station and pedestrian area.

43 bedrs, 38 ensuite, **P** **DB** 180-425 **B** 34 No restaurant ((MC Visa Amex ► 14km 🚗 🖼 ⋕ ♫
RAC 10 %

★★ Hôtel Joffre
34 bis av Mal Joffre, 25200 Montbéliard
📞 03 81 94 44 64 **Fax** 03 81 94 37 40
English spoken
A comfortable hotel, with private parking, located 400 m from the station and 600 m from the A36 motorway. All rooms have direct telephone lines and TV with Canal +.

62 bedrs, all ensuite, ⚑ **P** 53 **DB** 234-320 **B** 35-43 ✗ 25-60 ((MC Visa Amex ► 🚗 ⋕ ♫ ♿
RAC 10 %

MOREZ Jura   6A

★★ Hôtel de la Poste
1 rue Docteur Regad, 39400 Morez
📞 03 84 33 11 03 **Fax** 03 84 33 09 23
English spoken
A comfortable hotel, close to the ski slopes, with a renowned restaurant offering regional specialties. On the main Paris-Dijon-Genève road.

36 bedrs, 21 ensuite, ⚑ **P** 15 **DB** 160-270 **B** 30-35 ✗ 50-240 ((MC Visa Amex ► 9km 🚗 🖼 ⋕ ♫ ♿
RAC 10 % low season

PONTARLIER Doubs   3D

★★ Hôtel Bon Repos
25160 Les Grangettes
📞 03 81 69 62 95 **Fax** 03 81 69 66 61
English spoken
Closed 20 Oct-21 Dec
A highly recommended comfortable and friendly hotel set in beautiful, quiet countryside close to Lac de St-Point. From Pontarlier, go south on N57 then take D437 towards Lac de St-Point; at the lake drive along the western shore to Les Grangettes.

16 bedrs, 11 ensuite, **P** **DB** 173-244 **B** 30 ✗ 69-169 ((MC Visa Amex

ST-CLAUDE Jura   6A

★★ Hôtel St-Hubert et Restaurant Le Loft
3 Place St-Hubert, 39200 St-Claude
📞 03 84 45 10 70 **Fax** 03 84 45 64 76
English spoken
Closed 21 Dec-2 Jan

A modern hotel, with a restaurant offering regional specialities, situated close to the cathedral. Access: from the cathedral drive 400 m towards Genéve and the hotel is on the left.

30 bedrs, all ensuite, ⚑ **P** 12 **DB** 240-400 **B** 32-34 ✗ 80-162 ((MC Visa ► 4km 🚗 ⋕ ♫
RAC 10 %

SALINS-LES-BAINS Jura   3D

★★ Grand Hôtel des Bains
1 place des Alliés, 39110 Salins-les-Bains
📞 03 84 37 90 50 **Fax** 03 84 37 96 80
English spoken
Closed 6-21 Jan

A hotel with character, located in the heart of a small, charismatic, spa town.

31 bedrs, 30 ensuite, ⚑ **P** **DB** 280-395 **B** 40 ✗ 100-250 ((MC Visa 🔲 ⫐ 🖼 📺 ► 🔲 🚗 🖼 ⋕ ♫

Limousin-
Auvergne

REGION LIMOUSIN

Remote, rural and restful, Limousin-Auvergne is the oldest part of France and the most isolated.

It is also very beautiful; rugged volcanic peaks stand over the lakes, rivers and lush forests which typify the Massif Central.

However, a comparatively insular local population and a perceived inaccessibility have conspired to curb tourism in the area. This is good news for travellers who want to get away from it all – Limousin-Auvergne is the perfect retreat.

Vichy is one of the best-known towns in the Auvergne. Today it is famous for its spas, which may or may not have curative powers. To many people, however, Vichy is inextricably linked to French collaboration during World War II. The 'Vichy Regime', led by Marshal Pétain, was formed through French collusion with Nazi Germany and had the town of Vichy as its capital.

Today, life in Vichy revolves around the spas and the visitors who use them. Various types of sulphurous spa water are on offer at the Halle des Sources. Thousands of people come to drink this rank, but supposedly restorative, water.

Vichy also has some excellent sports facilities. If you aren't in town to improve your well-being, you will find that Vichy is an attractive and elegant place, but one which has little of specific interest to the healthy.

Auvergne's capital is **Clermont-Ferrand**, a vigorous place which draws the region's youth like moths to a light.

Clermont-Ferrand is a convenient base from which to explore Parc des Volcans and Puy de Dôme. It is also an attractive and enjoyable town in its own right.

Like Angers in the Loire, Clermont-Ferrand is built primarily from black stone, which gives the place an unusual – if slightly hard – atmosphere. Lively bars and restaurants add plenty of colour to this inky backdrop.

The two most important and impressive buildings are the Cathédrale de Notre-Dame and the Basilique Notre-Dame du Port.

The former is a dark but fragile-looking cathedral which towers over the city centre, while the latter is an older and perhaps more appealing church from the Romanesque period.

Pages 198–199: The Massif Central in Auvergne, a view of the cable car to the summit of Puy de Sancy
Above: Vichy's Therme du Dome

Just a short drive west of Clermont-Ferrand stands Puy de Dôme, the highest volcanic peak in the area (1,465 metres) and a spectacular vantage point.

From here, the panorama of the Forez peaks and around 80 other volcanoes is unmissable.

Some rather disappointing ruins remain of a Roman temple to Mercury which once stood near the summit. A television mast now stands where Mercury's effigy had surveyed the surrounding pinnacles.

Also in the northern part of the Auvergne, the wonderful Forest of Tronçais extends from industrial **Montluçon**, as though compensating for the city's pollution.

This is one of the most important and beautiful oak forests in Europe. Most watersports are catered for on the forest's lakes and several large herds of deer roam the woods.

Heading south across the Dordogne Valley, the terrain rises and falls with the steep mountains and volcanoes which characterise the Auvergne.

The south east hides the most extraordinary man-made spectacle in the region:– **Le-Puy-en-Velay**. Le Puy was – and, indeed, still is – an important starting point for pilgrims heading south to Santiago de Compostela in Spain.

It is a most bizarre place; two puys stand over the huddled and charming town centre like watchful parents.

One puy is also the town's highest point. On it towers an enormous red statue of Notre-Dame-de-France, which was built from molten gunmetal captured during the Crimean War.

The other puy is steeper – almost vertical. At the sharpened summit stands the impossible-looking church of St-Michel-d'Aiguilhe.

The eleventh-century effort which must have gone into the construction of this church is almost beyond belief. Just climbing to the top, unencumbered by building blocks or tools, is exhausting enough (although the views are a real incentive).

Limousin, to the west of Auvergne, is the other half of the partnership which makes up this region.

Although littered with ancient abbeys and crumbling châteaux, Limousin has few 'must see' sights with which to tempt the traveller.

Above: The distinguishing twin peaks of Puy-en-Velay

That's not to say that Limousin isn't worth visiting; on the contrary, this region is quietly spectacular and is ideal for anyone hoping to enjoy a stress-free break in the country.

Limoges is the capital of Limousin and was once an important Roman town called Augustoritum. It was named after Emperor Augustus, during whose reign the town was founded. Archaeologists are still digging up Roman artefacts and even whole villas.

The middle ages saw the town split into two. One centre, la Cité, developed around the cathedral and bishop's palace, while the other, le Château, grew up around the abbey of Saint-Martial.

Since then, la Cité has provided a cultural hub, while le Château has become a base for industry. Limoges' most successful industry is porcelain.

This long history has left Limoges with a number of fascinating old streets and buildings.

Look out for the Cour du Temple, rue de la Boucherie and the Cathedral of Saint-Etienne.

Closer to the Auvergne border, **Aubusson** sits at the centre of the Creuse Valley. This is the tapestry capital of the world. International master-weaver John Lurçat came to Aubusson in 1937. Here he set about creating tapestries which would later be seen as major works of art. The town itself is visually appealing. Architectural progress in Aubusson appears to have stopped altogether in the Middle Ages. Visit the family house of the Vieux Tapissier which has been the centre of Aubusson weaving since the sixteenth century.

Brive-la-Gaillarde makes a pleasant enough port of call on the journey south. The word 'Brive' strikes fear into rugby clubs across Europe; the town's team is exceptional. This skill might be the result of the town having had to defend itself regularly over the course of its history. During the Middle Ages, Brive was attacked almost on a weekly basis due to its wealth. The town always managed to protect itself, earning it its name.

Among the town's more interesting buildings, the Abbey of Saint-Martin and the Maison des Clarisses stand out as two of the best.

Getting there

By road

The major arteries through Limousin-Auvergne are:

- A71 Clermond-Ferrand to Paris via Riom, Gannat and Bourges
- A75 (toll-free) Clermond-Ferrand to Montpellier (and Spain) via Lempdes, Saint-Flour and Béziers
- A72 Clermond-Ferrand to Lyon via Thiers and Saint-Etienne
- A20 Bessines-sur-Gartempe to Montauban via Limoges.

By rail

Direct TGV services to Clermond-Ferrand from Paris, Besançon, Dijon, Lyon, Marseille, Nimes, Montpellier, Béziers, Toulouse, Bordeaux, Brive, Limoges and Nantes.

By air

Clermont-Ferrand Aulnat Airport (☏ 4 73 62 71 00, Fax: 4 73 62 71 29) is 4 miles east of Clermond-Ferrand.

For car hire contact:

- Avis ☏ 4 73 91 18 08
- Europcar ☏ 4 73 91 18 07
- Hertz ☏ 4 73 62 71 93

TOURIST INFORMATION

- **Limousin Tourist Office**
  Hôtel de Région, 27 bd de la Corderie, 87000 Limoges
  ☏ 5 55 45 18 80
  Fax: 5 55 45 18 18

- **Auvergne Tourist Office**
  23 rue Julien, 63000 Clermont-Ferrand
  ☏ 4 73 29 49 49
  Fax: 4 73 34 11 11

Left: Limousin-Auvergne maintains France's culinary reputation, with specialities including smoked venison, sausage, rustic soups and summerfruits

ARGENTAT Corrèze   5A

★★ Hôtel Le Sablier du Temps
13 rue Vachal, 19400 Argentat
☎ 05 55 28 94 90 Fax 05 55 28 94 99
English spoken
Closed 5-26 Jan & 16-30 Mar
*Opposite the Post Office in the town centre, this hotel
has quiet, spacious and well equipped rooms. Coming
from Tulle towards Argentat, straight ahead at the
traffic light to the Post Office. A very pretty location.*

24 bedrs, all ensuite, ⊶ **P** 13 **DB** 250-350 **B** 30-35
✕ 90-190 **CC** MC Visa Amex ⌇ ▣ ▸ ▨ ▨ ⫟ ⌇ ᴊ
RAC 5 %

★★ Hôtel du Lac
19430 Camps
☎ 05 55 28 51 83 Fax 05 55 28 53 71
English spoken
*A modern good value Logis hotel with nearby chalets
also available. From Argentat go south on the D120,
then right on the D41 to Camps, about 20 km from
Agentat. On the site of Rocher du Peintre.*

11 bedrs, 10 ensuite, ⊶ **P** **DB** 220-260 **B** 28 ✕ 70-210
CC MC Visa ▸ 30km ▨ ▨ ▨ ⫟
RAC 10 % Oct-May

AURILLAC Cantal   5A

★★ Auberge de la Tomette
15220 Vitrac
☎ 04 71 64 70 94 Fax 04 71 64 77 11
English spoken

*A charming, friendly hotel in lovely countryside.
Lying 25 km south of Aurillac, Vitrac is a small
village amongst the hills. From Aurillac take N122
south then left on to D66 to Vitrac.*

15 bedrs, all ensuite, ⊶ **P** **DB** 250-320 **B** 43 ✕ 69-200
CC MC Visa Amex ⌇ ▣ ▸ 14km ▨ ⫟ ᴊ

Don't forget to mention the guide
When booking, please remember to tell the
hotel that you chose it from the
RAC France for the Independent Traveller

AYEN Corrèze   4B

★ La Maison Anglaise
St-Robert, 19310 Ayen
☎ 05 55 25 19 58 Fax 05 55 25 23 00
English spoken
Closed Feb

*Small country hotel on the Dordogne border in one of
the prettiest villages in France, 30 minutes north-west
of Brive. Panoramic views, bar, lounge, open log fires
and traditional cuisine in the elegant restaurant*

6 bedrs, all ensuite, ⊶ **P** 4 **DB** 250-350 **B** 45 ✕ 65-260
CC MC Visa ▣ ⌇ ▸ ▨ ▨ ▨ ⫟
RAC 5 % except May-Sep

BRIVE-LA-GAILLARDE Corrèze   4B

★★★ Soph' Motel
Saint Pardoux l'Ortigier, 19270 Brive
☎ 05 55 84 51 02 Fax 05 55 84 50 14
English spoken
Closed 1 Jan-15 Jan

*Soph' Motel mixes comfort and tradition. Situated on
N20 towards Brive and 8 km after Uzerche (A20, exit
46).*

24 bedrs, all ensuite, ⊶ **P** 50 **DB** 280-950 **B** 38 ✕ 80-
180 **CC** MC Visa Amex ⌇ ▨ ▣ ▸ ▨ ▨ ▨ ⫟ ᴊ ᴊ
RAC 10 %

CHAMPAGNAC Cantal   5A

★★★ Château de Lavendes
Route de Neuvic, 15350 Champagnac
☎ 04 71 69 62 79 Fax 04 71 69 65 33
English spoken
Closed 15 Nov-1 Mar

An elegant château set in parkland. Converted in 1986, the hotel is full of character and dates back to 1323. Located 10 km from Bort-les-Orgues, on D15 to Neuvic.

8 bedrs, all ensuite, **P** 12 **B** 55-65 ✗ 135-198 ₡ MC Visa Amex ⚡ ▶ 10km 🖊 🖻
RAC 10 %

CHATELGUYON Puy de Dôme 5A

★★ Hôtel Bains
12/14 av Baraduc, 63140 Châtelguyon
📞 04 73 86 07 97 Fax 04 73 86 11 56
English spoken
Closed 1 Oct-5 Mar

Town centre hotel with a pretty garden. Châtelguyon is 15 km from Clermont-Ferrand, just off the A71.

37 bedrs, 30 ensuite, ♒ **P** 7 **DB** 200-280 **B** 40 ✗ 90-140 ₡ MC Visa Amex ▶ 5km 🖻
RAC 5 %

★★★ Hôtel Mont Chalusset
rue Punett, 63140 Châtelguyon
📞 04 73 86 00 17 Fax 04 73 86 22 94
English spoken
Closed Oct & Apr

In the heart of the park of Auvergne's volcanos, a rare place to appreciate the sweetness of life with pace, comfort, warm welcome and a flower garden. Traditional reputed cuisine, made from fresh local products and a prestigious cellar.

40 bedrs, all ensuite, ♒ **P** 12 **DB** 290-360 **B** 46 ✗ 100-260 ₡ MC Visa Amex 🗙 📶 ▶ 5km 🖊 🖻 ♨ ⚗ ⚬
RAC 10 % on room rate

★★★ Hôtel Régence
31 av Etats-Unis, 63140 Châtelguyon
📞 04 73 86 02 60 Fax 04 73 86 12 49
English spoken
Closed 15 Apr-25 Dec

Traditional French hotel displaying 18th century antique furniture. In a thermal spa town that can be reached from the Riom-Est exit off A71 or D78 off N9. Special package available including room, dinner and breakfast. Details on request. Free parking.

27 bedrs, all ensuite, **P** 18 **DB** 190-215 **B** 40 ✗ 75-120 ₡ MC Visa ▶ 🖊 ♨

★★★★ Hôtel Splendid
rue Angleterre, 63140 Châtelguyon
📞 04 73 86 04 80 Fax 04 73 86 17 56
English spoken
Closed 15 Oct-15 Apr

19th century hotel in the heart of the Auvergne, surrounded by park. The restaurant offers refined and healthy cuisine or in summer enjoy your meals beside the pool. Fly over the Auvergne volcanos in hot-air balloon or helicopter.

80 bedrs, all ensuite, ♒ **P** **DB** 470-1,400 **B** 59 ✗ 90-170 ₡ MC Visa Amex ⚡ 🗙 ▶ 7km 📶 🖊 🖻 ♨ ⚗
RAC 5 %

CLERMONT-FERRAND Puy de Dôme 5A

★★ Hôtel Athena
2 av Rouzaud, 63130 Royat
04 73 35 80 32 Fax 04 73 35 66 26
English spoken
Cheerful and bright, the hotel offers every comfort. 5 minutes drive from the centre of Clermont-Ferrand on the A71 to Royat. It has a lively brasserie/pub offering a selection of salads and pizzas and a good choice of beers.

24 bedrs, all ensuite, P 5 DB 290 B 30 CC MC Visa Amex 8km
RAC 10 %

★★ Hôtel Relais des Puys
La Baraque, 63870 Orcines
04 73 62 10 51 Fax 04 73 62 22 09
English spoken
Closed 10 Dec-1 Feb
Standing high above Clermont-Ferrand (7 km) at the foot of the mountains, a hotel run with enthusiasm by the Esbelin family for 6 generations. From Clermont-Ferrand follow signs for Limoges/Puy de Dôme via D941A.

25 bedrs, 23 ensuite, P 30 DB 160-310 B 35 ✗ 80-180 CC MC Visa Amex

★★★ Hôtel de Lyon
16 place Jaude, 63000 Clermont-Ferrand
04 73 93 32 55 Fax 04 73 93 54 33
English spoken

Beside Vercingétorix statue, in the heart of Clermont-Ferrand and the Place de Jaude, the hotel has 32 soundproof rooms, ensuite with cable TV. The pub-brasserie offers a continous service between 11 and 1.30, all in a pleasant and warm atmosphere.

32 bedrs, all ensuite, P 30 DB 320-350 B 35-42 CC MC Visa Amex 5km
RAC 15 %

DONZENAC Corrèze 4B

★★ Hôtel de la Maleyrie
La Croix de Maleyrie, 19270 Sadroc
05 55 84 50 67 Fax 05 55 84 20 63
English spoken
Closed Oct
On the N20, 15 km north of Brive and 25 km south of Uzerche: exit junction 47, hotel is 1 km distant. Indoor car park available.

15 bedrs, 13 ensuite, P 30 DB 120-230 B 30 ✗ 70-160 CC MC Visa

GARABIT Cantal 5A

★★ Hôtel Beau Site
Garabit, 15320 Loubaresse
04 71 23 41 46 Fax 04 71 23 46 34
English spoken
Closed winter
The hotel has a relaxing atmosphere, large garden and wonderful views. From the A75, take exit 30 or 31 then the N9. Enjoy fine cuisine and panoramic views of Eiffel's viaduct and Lake Garabit.

16 bedrs, all ensuite, P 20 DB 150-270 B 35 ✗ 71-180 CC MC Visa
RAC 10 % low season

ISSOIRE Puy de Dôme 5A

Hôtel Le Relais
1 av Gare, 63500 Issoire
04 73 89 16 61 Fax 04 73 89 55 62
English spoken
Closed 25 Oct-5 Nov & 1-7 Jul
In the town centre, close to the church and railway station. From Issoire, north on N9 towards Clermont-Ferrand.

6 bedrs, 3 ensuite, P DB 179-265 B 29 ✗ 58-158 CC MC Visa
RAC 5 % except Jul-Sept

LIMOGES Haute Vienne 4B

★★★ Hôtel Jeanne d'Arc
17 av Général de Gaulle, 87000 Limoges
05 55 77 67 77 Fax 05 55 79 86 75
English spoken
Closed 24 Dec-2 Jan
A comfortable, traditional hotel with well-equipped rooms. Follow the signs for Limoges-Centre or Gare des Bénédictins.

50 bedrs, all ensuite, P DB 260-400 B 40 No restaurant CC MC Visa Amex 5km

★★ Hôtel Orléans Lion d'Or
9 cours Jourdan, 87000 Limoges
05 55 77 49 71 Fax 05 55 77 33 41
English spoken
Closed 19 Dec-5 Jan

A charming, town centre hotel with a quiet environment, family furniture, TV, bar and sitting rooms. Follow signs to Limoges-Centre and Gare des Bénédictins.

42 bedrs, 38 ensuite, ♈ P 12 DB 260-290 B 32 ▸ ⊠ ⠇⠇⠇ ♪

MARINGUES Puy de Dôme   5A

★★ Hôtel Clos Fleuri
18 route de Clermont, 63350 Maringues
☎ 04 73 68 70 46 Fax 04 73 68 75 58
English spoken

From motorway A71 take the Riom exit in the direction of Ennezat to Maringues. Motorway A72, junction Thiers-Ouest, direction Pont de Dore to Maringues.

15 bedrs, all ensuite, P 50 DB 200-300 B 32 ✕ 75-220 ℂℂ MC Visa ⋥ ▸ ⊡ ♪ &

MAURS Cantal   5A

★★★ Hôtel La Châtelleraie
15600 St-Etienne-de-Maurs
☎ 04 71 49 09 09 Fax 04 71 49 07 07
English spoken
Closed All Saints Day/Easter

A converted château set in 24 acres of parkland. Maurs is north-east of Figeac on the N122. St-Etienne is just north of Maurs on the same road.

3 bedrs, all ensuite, ♈ P 40 DB 310-420 B 40 ✕ 115-150 ℂℂ MC Visa ⊡ ⋥ ⊠ ▣ ▸ ⊡ ⊠ ⠇⠇⠇ &

MENAT Puy de Dôme   5A

Auberge Maître Henri
63560 Pont-de-Ménat
☎ 04 73 85 50 20 Fax 04 73 85 50 57
English spoken
A family hotel, with a shaded terrace and a play area for children, situated in the Sioule gorge at Pont-de-Ménat.

5 bedrs, all ensuite, ♈ P 20 DB 170 B 34 ✕ 70-160 ℂℂ MC Visa ▧ ▣ ⊠

MONTLUCON Allier   5A

★★ Hôtel Garden
12 av Marx Dormoy, 03310 Neris-les-Bains
☎ 04 70 03 21 16 Fax 04 70 03 10 67
English spoken
Closed 2-25 Jan
A pretty hotel, 3 minutes from the centre of this spa town, offering a good choice of set or à la carte menus in a restaurant with panoramic parkland views. Within the Auvergne/Berry/Creuse triangle, on the A71 10 km south of Montluçon.

19 bedrs, all ensuite, ♈ P 15 DB 240-295 B 32 ✕ 78-195 ℂℂ MC Visa Amex ⋥ ▸ 4km ▣ ⊠ ⠇⠇⠇ ♪
RAC 5 %

MOULINS Allier   5A

★★★ Hôtel de Paris Jacquemart
21 rue Paris, 03000 Moulins
☎ 04 70 44 00 58 Fax 04 70 34 05 39
English spoken
Closed 26 Jan-16 Feb & 20 Jul-3 Aug

This 19th century hotel, situated on the edge of the historic Moulins quarter, offers refined seasonal cuisine, comfortable surroundings and a warm welcome. 5 minutes from station; 45 minutes Vichy airport, 30 minutes N2, exit Montmarault.

27 bedrs, 21 ensuite, ♈ P 15 DB 350-800 B 55 ✕ 150-450 ℂℂ MC Visa Amex ⋥ ▸ 5km ⊠ ⠇⠇⠇ &

PEYRAT-LE-CHÂTEAU Haute Vienne   5A

★★★ Hôtel La Caravelle
Lac de Vassivière, 87470 Peyrat-le-Château
📞 05 55 69 40 97 Fax 05 55 69 49 51
A comfortable hotel with attractive accommodation and a terrace and dining room overlooking Lake Vassivière. Situated 7 km from Peyrat-le-Château on the D13.

21 bedrs, all ensuite, **P** 20 **DB** 310-320 **B** 56 ✕ 120-240 ℂℂ MC Visa ⭐ ▶ 6km 🎱 🖼 ⅲ ⋈

ST-FLOUR Cantal   5A

★★ Auberge La Providence
1 rue Château d'Alleuze, 15100 St-Flour
📞 04 71 60 12 05 Fax 04 71 60 33 94
English spoken
A peaceful old inn, a former staging post completely renovated, with a lovely dining room featuring original Auvergne woodwork. Located on the outskirts of St-Flour, on the pilgrim route to St-Jacques-de-Compostelle and road to Chateau d'Alleuze.

10 bedrs, all ensuite, ⋔ **P** 10 **DB** 350 **B** 33 ✕ 70-130 ℂℂ MC Visa 🎱 🖼 ⅲ ⋈ ♿

★★ Grand Hôtel de Voyageurs
25 rue du Collège, 15100 St-Flour
📞 04 71 60 34 44 Fax 04 71 60 00 21
English spoken
Closed 1 Nov-1 Apr
A relaxing, tranquil hotel, with a pretty flower-filled terrace and a restaurant taking full advantage of fresh local produce, set in the heart of medieval St-Flour.

30 bedrs, 26 ensuite, ⋔ **P** 18 **DB** 150-350 **B** 37 ✕ 88 ℂℂ MC Visa 🖼 ⅲ ⋈

★★ Hôtel Le St-Jacques
8 place de la Liberté, 15106 St-Flour
📞 04 71 60 09 20 Fax 04 71 60 33 81
English spoken
Closed 15 Nov-5 Jan
A characterful hotel, situated at the lower end of the medieval town, with a restaurant offering à la carte menus and grills plus delicious, regional produce to try at your leisure.

28 bedrs, all ensuite, ⋔ **P** 10 **DB** 260-420 **B** 42 ✕ 90-230 ℂℂ MC Visa ⭐ 🎱 🖼 ⅲ ⋈
RAC

★★ Hôtel Les Messageries
23 av Charles de Gaulle, 15100 St-Flour
📞 04 71 60 11 36 Fax 04 71 60 46 79
English spoken
Closed 1 Oct-31 Mar

A very quiet hotel, offering regional cuisine, only 5 minutes from the town centre. St-Flour is situated south of Clermont-Ferrand on A75. The hotel is close to the station in the 'ville basse'.

17 bedrs, all ensuite, ⋔ **P** 30 **DB** 200-600 **B** 45-50 ✕ 80-300 ℂℂ MC Visa ⭐ 🖾 ▶ 🎱 🖼 ⅲ ⋈ ♿
RAC **10 %**

ST-MARTIN-LA-MEANNE Corrèze   5A

★★ Hôtel Voyageurs
place de la Mairie, 19320 St-Martin-la-Meanne
📞 05 55 29 11 53 Fax 05 55 29 27 70
English spoken

A small hotel, with a delightful old traditional dining room, situated near the Dordogne gorges. Comfortable and full of character. On D18, 8 km north of Argentat.

8 bedrs, all ensuite, ⋔ **P** 30 **DB** 235-305 **B** 30-49 ✕ 89-200 ℂℂ MC Visa ▶ 🎱 🖼 ⋈ ♿
RAC **5 %**

SALERS Cantal   5A

★★★ Hostellerie de Maronne
Le Theil, 15140 Salers
📞 04 71 69 20 33 Fax 04 71 69 28 22
English spoken
Closed 5 Nov-20 Mar

6 km away from Salers, in the superb Maronne Valley, a Relais du Silence hotel to relax in. A good base for exploring the Cantal.

21 bedrs, all ensuite, ⼁ P 25 DB 460-700 B 60 ✕ 150-250 ℂℂ MC Visa Amex ⼐ ▸ 25km ⊠ ☑ ✈ ⌗ ⼟ ⼖
RAC

★★ Hôtel Le Bailliage
rue Notre Dame, 15410 Salers
☎ 04 71 40 71 95 Fax 04 71 40 74 90
English spoken
A country style family-hotel surrounded by flower gardens, offering spacious bedrooms and regional cuisine with specialties. On the D680, west of Murat and south-east of Mauriac.

30 bedrs, all ensuite, ⼁ P DB 250-380 B 37 ✕ 68-165 ℂℂ MC Visa Amex ⼐ ▸ 15km ✈ ⌗ ⼟

LE VEURDRE Allier   2D

★★ Hôtel Pont-Neuf
Fg de Lorette, 03320 Le Veurdre
☎ 04 70 66 40 12 Fax 04 70 66 44 15
English spoken
Closed 25-31 Oct & 15 Dec-15 Jan

Recommended as an 'excellent little hotel that is exceptionally good value for money'. An oasis in France, hotel has a private garden, borders the Allier River and is 20 km from the largest oak forest in Europe. N7 then D978 from St-Pierre-le-Moutier.

6 bedrs, all ensuite, ⼁ P 35 DB 235-350 B 40 ✕ 85-25 ℂℂ MC Visa Amex ⼐ ✕ ▣ ▸ 15km ⊠ ☑ ✈ ⌗ ⼟
RAC 15 % on room rate

VICHY Allier   5A

★★ Château de la Rigon
oute de Serbannes, 03700 Bellerive-sur-Allier
☎ 04 70 59 86 46 Fax 04 70 59 94 77
English spoken
Closed Dec-Jan

Set in 8 acres of parkland with century-old trees, this charming 18th century residence is a haven of peace and relaxation, with individually furnished rooms and heated pools under a 19th century glass roof.

9 bedrs, all ensuite, P DB 270-330 B 36 ℂℂ MC Visa ✕ ▸ 2km ☑ ✈ ⼟
RAC 5 %

★★ Hôtel Arcade
16 bis Quai d'Allier, 11 et 13 Av Pierre Cou, 03200 Vichy
☎ 04 70 98 18 48 Fax 04 70 97 72 61
English spoken
Situated on the lake shore, near its source. From Paris take A71 and turn left after the bridge. From Lyon take the A72 and follow the signs for Quartier Thermal.

48 bedrs, all ensuite, ⼁ P 20 DB 220-300 B 35 ✕ 60-250 ℂℂ MC Visa Amex ▣ ▸ ⊠ ☑ ✈ ⌗ ⼟ ⼖
RAC 10 %

VIEILLEVIE Cantal   5C

★★ Hôtel Terrasse
15120 Vieillevie
☎ 04 71 49 94 00 Fax 04 71 49 92 23
English spoken
Closed 15 Nov-1 Apr
A charming hotel set in the heart of the countryside on the banks of the River Lot. Meals can be served on the shady terrace in good weather. The village of Vieillevie is 15 km from Conques.

26 bedrs, 24 ensuite, ⼁ P 15 DB 170-250 B 37 ✕ 58-170 ℂℂ MC Visa ⼐ ⊠ ☑ ✈ ⌗ ⼟ ⼖
RAC 5 %

Rhône-
Alpes

RHÔNE-ALPES

TOURISME

Choisissez vos Couleurs

For everyone except the region's administrators, Rhône-Alpes is two distinct areas: the Rhône Valley and the area which forms the Alpine border with Switzerland and Italy.

The Rhône Valley is famous the world over for the quality of its wine. The best-loved of the Côtes du Rhône wines are the Hermitages and Crozes Hermitage. Most vineyards are based in the Tain l'Hermitage canton (some 45 miles south of Lyon) and many welcome visitors and would-be wine-tasters.

The largest city in the region (and the third-largest in France) is **Lyon**. This city is seen as the gateway to Provence, which is why many visitors, excited by their proximity to the south, are tempted to shoot straight past without stopping. Those who do stop to spend a day or two in Lyon are invariably glad they did.

Lyon is a busy commercial centre, which does not need or seek tourism like many other parts of France.

That said, it is a far more attractive city than many people suppose. Only Paris makes such good use of a river, and few French cities have such a strong and appealing cultural scene. Take a walk alongside the Rhône at night for a wonderful view of the floodlit buildings which line both banks.

The Lyonnais eat very well. This is a city where chefs are idolised. Indeed, many have become TV stars. Old Lyon has the highest concentration of fine restaurants.

If you're not too squeamish, try quenelles, the offal dumplings which are a local speciality. They're tastier than you would think!

More appealing, perhaps, is the gorgeous chocolate for which Bernachon has become world-famous.

Silk is another Lyonnais speciality - although the industry has been in steady decline for years. See the old weaving techniques demonstrated at La Maison des Canuts in La Croix-Rousse district which was once the centre of the silk industry.

The Musée des Beaux-Arts and Musée St-Pierre d'Art Contemporain together form a fairly impressive collection of art from the Middle Ages onwards.

To the east of Lyon lie three cities on more or less the same longitude.

Pages 210–211: Vallée Blanche with a view of Aiguille Midi
Above: The Rhône-Alpes is an area of outstanding natural beauty – Vanoise is popular with walkers out of season

The northernmost and, arguably, the prettiest of these is **Annecy**. The main drag in the old town is the rue St-Claire, which runs close to the imposing Palais de l'Isle. For an insight into the geological history of the Alps, visit the Musée du Château.

Chambéry was the capital of Savoy until Turin took over in the sixteenth century. Visit the fifteenth century castle chapel where, for a time, the Turin Shroud was kept.

Although Chambéry is a pleasant city, occupying an enviable position in the foothills of the Alps, there is little else of any great interest here.

Grenoble, some miles south of Chambéry, is far more exciting.

On two rivers, with the Alps looming large to the east, the French-Alpine capital sits in a suitably delightful location. The citizens of Grenoble played a particularly gallant role in the French Resistance during World War II. That history is presented at the Musée de la Résistance et de la Déportation, which also documents the effect of the Holocaust on the region.

Less sobering is the place Grenette, which is the hub of the city's café-life. This is the perfect place to sit back and watch the Grenoblois go about their business.

A more elevated view of the city can be seen from the Fort de la Bastille which towers over Grenoble from its lofty perch above the banks of the River Isère. You can get to the Fort by téléférique from the Stéphane-Jay pier.

Above: Annecy is situated on the edge of the beautiful Lac d'Annecy and a castle stands over the most attractive stretch of tangled avenues

What to do in Rhône-Alpes

- Taste some of the best food in France in one of Lyon's amazing restaurants.
- Take the téléférique from Grenoble to the Fort de la Bastille and enjoy a great view of the city and the Alps.
- See where the Turin Shroud was kept in Chambéry, the former capital of Savoy.
- Sample some of the finest wines in France in the Côtes du Rhône region.
- Ski!

TOURIST INFORMATION
- **Rhône-Alpes Tourist Office**
  104 route de Paris, 69260
  Charbonniere-les Bains
  ☏ 4 72 59 21 59
  Fax: 4 72 59 21 60

Skiing and snowboarding

The Rhône-Alpes region is heaven for skiers and snowboarders. Resorts have been developing for years. Chamonix, Megeve, Val d'Isère, Tignes, Courchevel, Méribel, Val Thorens, Les Deux-Alpes... the list of top-quality ski centres goes on and on. These same resorts pioneered snowboarding in Europe.

Apart from the fact that French ski resorts often have more than their fair share of good restaurants, hotels and nightlife, there are two things which really set the likes of Val d'Isere and Courchevel apart from other European ski resorts: the extent and efficiency of the ski lift systems, and the high standard of piste grooming. Artificial snow machines make sure that the major resorts have a solid base of snow early on in the season. This usually ensures that the runs remain open for a long time.

On the downside, most French Alpine resorts have been developed with little regard for aesthetics. Gradually, though, the worst of the fifties, sixties and seventies developments are being torn down in favour of buildings which better reflect their beautiful location.

Val Thorens, in the Trois-Vallées, is the highest ski resort in Europe (2,300 metres) and so still has good snow even when other resorts are beginning to fail. Skiing here is best-suited to intermediates, although the snow is normally dry and so accessible to beginners.

The British have long been in love with **Méribel**, which sits at the centre of the Trois Vallées. The resort was founded in 1938 by an enterprising Scotsman called Colonel Peter Lindsay. It is the most attractive purpose-built resort in France. Méribel-Centre is built on a steep slope, which has led to the development of several mini-centres. These are linked to one another by a free shuttle bus. Further up the valley, Méribel-Mottaret is an almost separate section of resort. It is not as attractive as the Méribel-Centre, but has better links to the Trois Vallées circuit. Chalet-style accommodation is at its best here, with many pine-clad cabins offering 'ski-out/ski-in'

Above: Lac de Chevrieres at Tignes

access straight onto the piste. Another gem of the famous Trois Vallées is **Courchevel** 1850 – so-named to avoid confusion with the three other Courchevels of differing altitude. All are inter-linked, but Courchevel 1850 is the highest and by far the most impressive ski centre of the four.

This is an upmarket resort, with nine four-star hotels, some great restaurants and glitzy nightlife. Skiers can slide right up to the front door of most of its hotels.

Hardcore skiers know that **Tignes** offers some of the best off-piste opportunities in the world. Purpose-built and fairly uninspiring, the resort of Tignes could be better. The skiing, however, could not. At 2,100 metres, Tignes is almost guaranteed good snow.

Nearby **Val-d'Isère** is easily reached from Tignes. In fact, skiers of intermediate ability or above can make use of both areas with the help of a joint ski-pass and an extensive system of lifts. Despite giving every indication of being built in hurry, Val-d'Isère is actually an ancient Alpine village. It is gradually being brightened up.

Whatever the place looks like, no-one could deny that its location is magnificent, the skiing is fantastic and – crucially – the ski-lift system is without equal.

To the north, near the Swiss border, sits **Chamonix** – another popular centre for winter sports. Head here for hang-gliding, mountain climbing and, of course, skiing. The really brave could attempt Vallée Blanche, the longest run in Europe.

Chamonix has a much longer pedigree than most of its rivals in the Rhône-Alpes. The town hosted the first Winter Olympics in 1924 – long before anyone had even thought of Méribel or Courchevel or, indeed, most French Alpine ski resorts.

Left: The Chapelle du Praz at Chamonix

When to ski

Dec/Jan	Cold temperatures mean great snow, but the days are short
Feb	Good powder snow, but this is the peak time for European families to take their kids to the slopes. It can be crowded.
March	The combination of sun and snow makes this a great time to go
Apr/May	You might need to head higher to find good snow, but the sunshine is a bonus

Getting there

By road

Major routes through Rhône-Alpes:

* A7 Marseille to Lyon
* A49 Valence to Grenoble
* A51 Marseille to Grenoble
* A41 Grenoble to Annecy
* A48 Lyon to Grenoble
* A43 Lyon to Chambery

By rail

By TGV:

* Paris Gare de Lyon to Lyon takes 2 hours
* Paris Gare de Lyon to Saint Etienne takes 2 hours 50 mins
* Paris Gare de Lyon to Grenoble takes 2 hours 50 mins)
* Paris Gare de Lyon to Annecy takes 3 hours 40 mins
* Paris Gare de Lyon to Valence takes 2 hours 30 mins
* Paris Gare de Lyon to Chambery takes 2 hours 50 mins
* Paris Gare de Lyon to Bourg-en-Bresse takes 2 hours.

By air

Lyon Satolas Airport (☎ 4 72 22 72 21, Fax: 4 72 22 74 71) is 20 miles east of Lyon. Get into to Lyon by taxi (☎ 4 72 22 70 90) or bus (☎ 4 72 22 61 27). For car hire contact:

* ADA ☎ 4 72 22 74 92
* Europcar ☎ 4 72 22 75 27
* Avis ☎ 4 72 22 75 43

Grenoble Saint Geoirs Airport (☎ 4 76 65 48 48, Fax: 4 76 65 57 00) is 30 miles north of Grenoble.

For car hire contact:

* Avis ☎ 4 76 65 41 96
* Europcar ☎ 4 76 93 52 13
* Hertz ☎ 4 76 93 53 13

Below: The Casino Aix Les Bains at Savoie

AIX-LES-BAINS Savoie   6A

★★ Hôtel Davat

Le Grand Port, 73100 Aix-les-Bains
☎ 04 79 63 40 40 Fax 04 79 54 35 68
English spoken
Closed 2 Nov-1 Mar
*Pretty hotel/restaurant, set close to the lake and 2 km
from the town centre. The gourmet restaurant
specialises in fish dishes. Meals can be served on the
terrace overlooking the lovely gardens.*

20 bedrs, all ensuite, ⚡ P 40 DB 230-280 B 35 ✗ 90-
240 ℂℂ MC Visa Amex ▶ 3km ⠇
RaC 10 %

★★★★ Park Hôtel

av Charles de Gaulle, BP 525, 73105 Aix-les-Bains
☎ 04 79 34 19 19 Fax 04 79 88 11 49
English spoken
*Situated in the heart of town and in a large leisure
complex, this hotel is on the shore of Lake Bourget.
This beautiful and relaxing centre is at the
intersection of the Lyon, Genève and Turin
motorways.*

102 bedrs, all ensuite, ⚡ P DB 440-780 B 68 ✗ 74-130
ℂℂ MC Visa Amex ▣ ▨ ▦ ▶ 2km ▨ ▨ ▨ ⠇ ⓱
RaC 15 %

★★★ Résidence Hôtel Les Loges du Park

Rue Jean-Louis Victor Bias, BP 525, 73105 Aix-les-
Bains Cedex
☎ 04 79 35 74 74 Fax 04 79 35 74 00
English spoken

*Set in parkland, accommodation consists of modern,
light and airy apartments and studios, each with its
own terrace and accommodating from 2 to 4 persons.
Excellent facilities.*

71 bedrs, all ensuite, ⚡ P 200 DB 221-480 B 45-61
✗ 80-115 ℂℂ MC Visa Amex ▣ ▨ ▦ ▶ 2km ▨ ⠇ ∅ ⓱
RaC

Don't forget to mention the guide
When booking, please remember to tell the
hotel that you chose it from the
**RAC France for
the Independent Traveller**

L'ALPE-D'HUEZ Isère   6A

★★★ Hôtel au Chamois d'Or

Rond Point des Pistes, 38750 L'Alpe-d'Huez
☎ 04 76 80 31 32 Fax 04 76 80 34 90
English spoken
Closed 25 Apr-15 Dec
*The hotel is set on the ski slopes. Its cuisine, south-
facing terrace and warm atmosphere make for an
excellent holiday. Half board 700 to 970 FF. The
restaurant with terrace serves fresh fish specialities
and traditional cuisine.*

45 bedrs, all ensuite, ⚡ P 26 DB 810-1,350 B 75
✗ 145-250 ℂℂ MC Visa ▣ ▨ ▦ ▨ ⠇ ∅

ANNECY Haute Savoie   6A

★★ Hôtel Arcalod

Doussard, 74210 Bout-du-Lac
☎ 04 50 44 30 22 Fax 04 50 44 85 03
English spoken
Closed Nov-Jan

*A family-run hotel in unspoilt countryside, 1 km from
Lake Annecy. Doussard is on N508 between Annecy
and Albertville. The restaurant's specialities are
terrine de canard, filet de féra and parfait chartreux.*

33 bedrs, all ensuite, ⚡ P DB 250-450 B 35-45 ✗ 75-
150 ℂℂ MC Visa Amex ▣ ⚲ ▦ ▶ 3km ▨ ▨ ▨ ⠇ ∅
⓱

★★★ Hôtel Faisan Doré

34 avenue d' Albigny, 74000 Annecy
☎ 04 50 23 02 46 Fax 04 50 23 11 10
English spoken
Closed 15 Dec-25 Jan

The hotel lies 1 km from the old town of Annecy and 100 m from the lake, casino and beach. From the centre of Annecy follow directions to the 'Impérial' and Thônes. The traditional restaurant offers specialities of fresh lake fish and Savoyard dishes.

40 bedrs, all ensuite, ✝ P 4 DB 320-530 B 45-50 ✗ 100-190 ℂℂ MC Visa ▣ ⁂ ♫

★★ Hôtel Ibis
12 rue de la Gare, 74000 Annecy
☎ 04 50 45 43 21 Fax 04 50 52 81 08
English spoken
In the old town beside the River Thiou which is overlooked by some of the bedrooms' balconies. Take Annecy-Sud Exit from A41, follow signs for the station, then park at the Sainte-Claire Municipal Car Park as hotel is in a pedestrianised area.

85 bedrs, all ensuite, ✝ P DB 340-390 B 35 ✗ 55-95 ℂℂ MC Visa Amex ▶ 15km ▣ ♫

★★★ Hôtel Mercure
rte Aix-les-Bains, 74600 Annecy
☎ 04 50 52 09 66 Fax 04 50 69 29 32
English spoken
This is a comfortable hotel with good facilities and a superb view over the mountains. Leave A41 at Annecy-Sud exit and then go towards Chambéry on the N201.

66 bedrs, all ensuite, ✝ P 80 DB 375-495 B 52 ✗ 69-115 ℂℂ MC Visa Amex ⊰ ▶ 15km ⊠ ▣ ▣ ⁂ ♫ ♿
RAC 10 %

★★ Hôtel du Lac
74410 Duingt
☎ 04 50 68 90 90 Fax 04 50 68 50 18
English spoken
Closed 15 Oct-15 Feb

A fully renovated hotel with its own private beach and pontoon. It has beautiful views of the surrounding lake and countryside. 12 km from Annecy towards Albertville.

23 bedrs, all ensuite, P DB 290-380 B 42 ✗ 135-220 ℂℂ MC Visa ⊰ ▶ 10km ▣ ▣ ⁂ ♫

★★ Hôtel Les Persèdes
Lavilledieu, 07170 Aubenas
☎ 04 75 94 88 08 Fax 04 75 94 29 02
English spoken
Closed 15 Oct-1 Apr

A recently built hotel which is quiet and comfortable. It is close to N102 linking Auvergne to the Rhône Valley. An ideal stopover with closed car park.

24 bedrs, all ensuite, P 40 DB 290-380 B 40-43 ✗ 88-190 ℂℂ MC Visa ⊰ ▶ ▣ ▣ ⁂ ♿
RAC 5 %

★★ Hôtel Mont-Brouilly
69430 Quincie-en-Beaujolais
☎ 04 74 04 33 73 Fax 04 74 69 00 72
English spoken
Closed Feb

In the heart of the Beaujolais region. West of Belleville and A6 on the D37, towards Beaujeu. Hotel is 1 km from the village of Cercié. The air-conditioned restaurant specialities include coq au vin, grenouilles en persillade and escargots de Bourgogne.

29 bedrs, all ensuite, ✝ P 50 DB 280-330 B 35 ✗ 90-230 ℂℂ MC Visa Amex ⊰ ▶ 25km ▣ ⁂ ♫ ♿

BELLEVILLE Rhône   5B

★★★★ Château de Pizay
St-Jean-d'Ardières, Pizay, 69220 Belleville
☎ 04 74 66 51 41 Fax 04 74 69 65 63
English spoken
Closed 24 Dec-2 Jan
*A 14th and 15th century château set in parkland.
Accommodation is in the château itself and also in
the grounds. Leave N6 at St-Jean-d'Ardières and turn
left at the end of the village; Château de Pizay is
straight ahead.*

62 bedrs, all ensuite, **P DB** 575-715 **B** 65 ✕ 200-395
CC MC Visa Amex ⅔ ▸ 20km ▣ ⅲ ⅋
RƎC 5 %

BOURG-EN-BRESSE Ain   5B

★★ Hôtel Ibis
bd Charles de Gaulle, 01000 Bourg-en-Bresse
☎ 04 74 22 52 66 Fax 04 74 23 09 58
English spoken
*The hotel is near Brou church and has a charming
garden and terrace.*

62 bedrs, all ensuite, ⸙ **P DB** 295-325 **B** 36 ✕ 55-95
CC MC Visa Amex ⅲ ⅋ ⅋

★★ Hôtel Le Logis de Brou
132 bd de Brou, 01000 Bourg-en-Bresse
☎ 04 74 22 11 55 Fax 04 74 22 37 30
English spoken
*Soundproof hotel that is close to the magnificent Brou
church. Situated 7 minutes from junction Bourg-Sud
on A40 motorway.*

30 bedrs, all ensuite, **P** 20 **DB** 300-380 **B** 40 No
restaurant **CC** MC Visa Amex ▸ 5km ▣ ⅲ
RƎC 5 %

★★★ Hôtel du Prieuré
49 bd de Brou, 01000 Bourg-en-Bresse
☎ 04 74 22 44 60 Fax 04 74 22 71 07
English spoken
*Set in a quiet position in a park, 200 m from the
Brou church. Rooms are spacious and stylish.*

14 bedrs, all ensuite, ⸙ **P** 15 **DB** 350-550 **B** 50 No
restaurant **CC** MC Visa Amex ▸ 10km ▣ ⅋
RƎC 5 %

BOURG-ST-MAURICE Savoie   6A

★★★ Hôtel L'Autantic
rte d'Hauteville, 73700 Bourg-St-Maurice
☎ 04 79 07 01 70 Fax 04 79 07 51 55
English spoken

*A modern stone and pine chalet-style hotel, set back
from the road at the edge of town. Offers very
comfortable accommodation and excellent facilities.*

23 bedrs, all ensuite, ⸙ **P** 30 **DB** 260-440 **B** 40 No
restaurant **CC** MC Visa Amex ▣ ▸ 18km ▣ ▣ ⅲ ⅋ ⅋
RƎC 8 %

LE BOURGET-DU-LAC Savoie   6A

★★ Hôtel Beaurivage
100 bd du Lac, 73370 Le Bourget-du-Lac
☎ 04 79 25 00 38 Fax 04 79 25 06 49
English spoken
*A small hotel in a quiet lakeside setting at the
southern tip of Lake Bourget. 10 km from either
Chambéry or Aix-les-Baines on the N504 and linked
from Annecy via the main N211.*

7 bedrs, 6 ensuite, **P** 15 **DB** 290-310 **B** 45 ✕ 110-250
CC MC Visa Amex ▸ 8km ▣ ▣ ⅋

★★★ Hôtel Ombremont
Restaurant Le Bateau Ivre, 73370 Le Bourget-du-Lac
☎ 04 79 25 00 23 Fax 04 79 25 25 77
English spoken
Closed Nov-May

*A lovely hotel in a park with century-old trees and an
exceptional view over Lake Bourget features
personalised guest rooms, terraces, gourmet
restaurant, sauna, lounge-bar, French billiards and
a swimming pool.*

17 bedrs, all ensuite, ⸙ **P DB** 810-1,420 **B** included
✕ 195-510 **CC** MC Visa Amex ⅔ ▣ ▸ 9km ▣ ⅲ

★★ Hôtel Otelinn
13 rue du Creuzat, 38080 L'Isle d'Abeau
📞 04 74 27 13 55 Fax 04 74 27 22 21
English spoken
A modern hotel, convenient for both the airport and the motorway. From A43, take exit to l'Isle d'Abeau-East and follow signs to l'Isle d'Abeau village. Located 5 km west of Bourgoin.

45 bedrs, all ensuite, ⚑ P DB 220-288 B 35 ✕ 82-152 ℂℂ MC Visa Amex ▸ 2km 🖼 2km ⁝⁝⁝ ⌀ ♿
RAC 10 %

CERDON Ain 2D

★ Hôtel Carrier
RN 84, 01450 Cerdon
📞 04 74 37 37 05 Fax 04 74 37 36 39
English spoken
Closed Jan
Situated on the N84 between Lyon and Genève, in an area popular with tourists, the hotel offers traditional cuisine, full board and a pleasant setting.

12 bedrs, 6 ensuite, ⚑ P DB 175-230 B 30 ✕ 70-230 ℂℂ MC Visa Amex 🖼
RAC 5 %

CHAMONIX-MONT-BLANC Haute Savoie 6A

★★★★ Hôtel Albert 1er
119 impasse du Montenvers, BP 55, 74400 Chamonix-Mont-Blanc
📞 04 50 53 05 09 Fax 04 50 55 95 48
English spoken
Closed 3-10 May & 24 Oct-1 Dec

Beautiful hotel, only a stone's throw from the centre of town, with a backdrop of mountains and lakes. The highly acclaimed restaurant offers fine, inventive cuisine and regional specialities. Just to the south of the N506.

32 bedrs, all ensuite, ⚑ P DB 690-2,800 B 75 ✕ 195-470 ℂℂ MC Visa Amex 🖼 ⌇ 🖼 🖼 ▸ 2km 🖼 ⁝⁝⁝ ♿

★★★ Hôtel Grands Montets
340 chemin des Arbérons, Argentière, 74400 Chamonix-Mont-Blanc
📞 04 50 54 06 66 Fax 04 50 54 05 42
English spoken
Closed 1 May-20 Jun

Located close to cable car for the Grand Montets, this Savoyard cottage is full of green in summertime and offers regional and traditional cuisine.

40 bedrs, all ensuite, ⚑ P 40 DB 450-654 B 40 ✕ 98-135 ℂℂ MC Visa Amex ▸ 6km 🖼 ⁝⁝⁝ ⌀
RAC 5 %

★★★ Hôtel La Vallée Blanche
36 rue du Lyret, 74400 Chamonix-Mont-Blanc
☎ 04 50 53 04 50 Fax 04 50 55 97 85
English spoken

A charming hotel, cosy and comfortable with hand-painted furniture. Piano bar and riverside terrace. Five minutes walk from the cable cars and all facilities. From the motorway take the first Chamonix-Sud exit, then follow signs to the town centre.

24 bedrs, all ensuite, ✹ **P DB** 416-700 **B** 44 ✗ 85-190
((MC Visa Amex ↑ 3km 🔲 ᕒ
RAC 5 %

★★★ Hôtel Montana
74400 Argentière
☎ 04 50 54 14 99 Fax 04 50 54 03 40
English spoken
Closed 15 May-15 Oct
Picture-postcard alpine chalet facing the Aiguilles Verte. Stunning views all around of the Chamonix valley and Mont Blanc beyond. Artenière is 7 km north of Chamonix on N205. It has its own lifts but connects to the Chamonix-Mont Blanc circuit.

24 bedrs, all ensuite, ✹ **P** 20 **DB** 470-510 **B** 50 ✗ 110-150 ((MC Visa 🔲 ↑ 🔲 ▦ ᕒ

★★ Hôtel Richemond
228 rue Dr Paccard, 74400 Chamonix-Mont-Blanc
☎ 04 50 53 08 85 Fax 04 50 55 91 69
English spoken
Closed 20 Apr-15 Jun & 15 Sep-20 Dec
A traditional hotel in the town centre close to the cable car and bus stations. Rear entrance on allée Recteur Payot.

Facilities for the Disabled

Hotels do their best to cater for disabled visitors. However, it is advisable to contact the hotel direct to ensure it can provide for a particular requirement.

53 bedrs, all ensuite, ✹ **P** 30 **DB** 380-458 **B** 38 ✗ 85
((MC Visa Amex ↑ 2km
RAC 8 %

★★ Hôtel Christin
Chamoux, 73390 Chamousset
☎ 04 79 36 42 06 Fax 04 79 36 45 43
English spoken
From Albertville (20 km) take N90 towards Chambery, at the Royal Bridge turn as if going to Italy and follow Hôtel Christin signs.

18 bedrs, 9 ensuite, **P DB** 200-300 **B** 26-38 ✗ 70-150
((MC Visa 🔲 ▦ ᕒ

★★ Hôtel L'Ancolie
73350 Champagny-en-Vanoise
☎ 04 79 55 05 00 Fax 04 79 55 04 42
English spoken
Situated in an old Savoyard village in the La Plagne area, 33 km from Albertville. (Prices quoted are for half board.)
31 bedrs, all ensuite, ✹ **P** 30 **DB** 305-640 **B** 50 ✗ 95-115 ((MC Visa ᕒ 🔲 🔲 🔲 ▦ ᕒ ᕒ
RAC 5 %

★★ Hôtel Le Veymont
26420 St-Agnan-en-Vercors
☎ 04 75 48 20 19 Fax 04 75 48 10 34
English spoken
Closed 15 Nov-20 Dec

This friendly English run hotel is situated in a small village in the breathtaking Vercors mountain range in the French Alps.

17 bedrs, all ensuite, ✹ **P DB** 235-250 **B** 35 ✗ 90-110
((MC Visa 🔲 ↑ 2km 🔲 🔲 🔲 ▦
RAC

LA COMBE AIGUEBELETT Savoie — 5B

★★ Hôtel de la Combe Chez Michelon
La Combe, 73610 Aiguebelette-le-Lac
☎ 04 79 36 05 02 Fax 04 79 44 11 93
English spoken
Closed 13 Nov-20 Dec

Warm, welcoming, comfortable hotel, offering gourmet cuisine and excellent service in an exceptional location overlooking the lake. Established for 5 generations. From motorway, follow the east bank of the lake along the mountain side.

9 bedrms, all ensuite, **P** 4 **DB** 206-358 **B** 39 ✕ 145-230
℃ MC Visa ▸ 🗹 🗷 ░ 🕭

RAC Free drinks offered

CONDRIEU Rhône — 5B

★★★★ Hôtel Beau Rivage
2 rue du Beau Rivage, 69420 Condrieu
☎ 04 74 59 52 24 Fax 04 74 59 59 36
English spoken

former fisherman's home beautifully renovated and situated between the Rhône and the hills. This hotel has comfortable, individually decorated rooms, lovely gardens and a very warm welcome.

5 bedrs, all ensuite, ⊁ **P** **DB** 550-850 **B** 65 ✕ 195-610
MC Visa Amex ▸ 20km 🗹 ░ ₰ 🕭

CORPS Isère — 6A

★★ Boustigue Hôtel
rte La Salette, 38970 Corps
☎ 04 76 30 01 03 Fax 04 76 30 04 04
English spoken
A most attractive, family-run hotel set in lovely natural parkland. It offers relaxation, a warm and cosy atmosphere and wonderful views. From Corps take the La Salette road and hotel is signposted along this road.

30 bedrs, all ensuite, ⊁ **P** 50 **DB** 260-360 **B** 38 ✕ 92-160 ℃ MC Visa ⊰ 🗷 ▣ ▸ ▸ 20km 🗷 🗹 5km ░ ₰
RAC 10 % on room rate

COURS-LA-VILLE Rhône — 5B

★★ Hôtel Le Pavillon
Col du Pavillon, 69470 Cours-la-Ville
☎ 04 74 89 83 55 Fax 04 74 64 70 26
English spoken

Family-run hotel set in lovely countryside at a height of 755 m. Comfortable, light and airy accommodation. A welcoming apértif is offered on arrival. The French cuisine includes regional specialities.

21 bedrs, all ensuite, ⊁ **P** **DB** 330-370 **B** 38 ✕ 78-270
℃ MC Visa 🗹 🗷 ░ ₰ 🕭
RAC Complimentary apértif

CREST Drôme — 5B

★★ Grand Hôtel
60 rue Hôtel de Ville, 26400 Crest
☎ 04 75 25 08 17 Fax 04 75 25 46 42
English spoken
A quiet, comfortable 19th century hotel offering traditional regional cuisine. Crest is between Loriol and Valence.

20 bedrs, 9 ensuite, ⊁ **P** 6 **DB** 140-330 **B** 33 ✕ 80-200
℃ MC Visa ▸ 15km 🗹 🗷 ░

LES ECHELLES Savoie   5B

★ Auberge du Morge
Gorges de Chailles, 73360 Les Echelles
☎ 04 79 36 62 76 Fax 04 79 36 51 65
English spoken
Closed 1 Dec-20 Jan
*An inn in the Gorges de Chailles, near a trout stream.
Located 3 km north of Les Echelles, access from N6.*

7 bedrs, 5 ensuite, **P** 25 **DB** 160-220 **B** 28 ✕ 80-250 **CC**
MC Visa ◫ ▣

EVIAN-LES-BAINS Haute Savoie   6A

★★ Hôtel Bois Joli
La Beunaz, St-Paul-en-Chablais, 74500 Evian-les-Bains
☎ 04 50 73 60 11 Fax 04 50 73 65 28
English spoken

*In a valley overlooked by mountains, this pretty Relais
du Silence hotel offers some spectacular views and a
restful stay near Lake Léman. 13 km from Thonon-
les-Bains on the N5 heading east to Evian, take the
D21 towards St-Paul-en-Chablais and Bernex.*

24 bedrs, all ensuite, ✝ **P** 30 **DB** 290-360 **B** 40 ✕ 98-
230 **CC** MC Visa Amex ⌇ ▣ ▸ 8km ▢ ◫ ▣ ⅲ ₺
RAC 10 % on room rate

★★ Hôtel Chez Tante Marie
BP3, 74500 Bernex
☎ 04 50 73 60 35 Fax 04 50 73 61 73
English spoken
Closed 15 Oct-15 Dec

*A very cosy chalet close to Lac Léman and 12 km
from Evian, in a pretty alpine village in lovely
surroundings. From Evian D21 to St-Paul and on to
Bernex. The restaurant serves traditional and local
specialities using fresh local produce.*

27 bedrs, all ensuite, **P** 35 **CC** MC Visa ▸ 72km ▣ ⅲ
RAC 5 %

★★ Hôtel Panorama
Grand-Rive, 74500 Evian-les-Bains
☎ 04 50 75 14 50 Fax 04 50 75 59 12
English spoken
Closed 1 Oct-30 May

*On the Montreux side of Evian, the hotel looks across
Lac Léman to Lausanne. Enjoy excellent fresh fish
from the lake.*

29 bedrs, all ensuite, ✝ **P** 6 **DB** 280-340 **B** 35 ✕ 75-180
CC MC Visa Amex ▸ 3km ▣ ▣

FERNEY-VOLTAIRE Ain   6A

★★ Hôtel de France
1 rue Genève, 01210 Ferney-Voltaire
☎ 04 50 40 63 87 Fax 04 50 40 47 27
English spoken

*Just 1 km from the airport, this small, comfortable
and very quiet establishment is the closest French
hotel to Genève. Restaurant offers traditional French
cuisine, excellent meat and fish dishes. (Half board
available from 385 FF per night).*

14 bedrs, all ensuite, ✝ **P** **DB** 295-350 **B** 40 ✕ 115-25
CC MC Visa Amex ▸ 5km ▣ ⅲ ⌀ ₺
RAC 10 %

GRENOBLE Isère   6A

★★ Comfort Inn Primevère
2 rue de l'Europe, 38640 Claix
☎ 04 76 98 84 54 Fax 04 76 98 66 22
English spoken

A small hotel with air-conditioned rooms and a large terrace. Enjoy the restaurant's charming atmosphere while tasting the traditional, quality cooking featured in the various menus. 8 km south of Grenoble centre.

45 bedrs, all ensuite, **P** 70 **DB** 290-296 **B** 36 ✕ 85-186 **CC** MC Visa Amex ⅔ ► 5km 🖼 ⅲ ✍ ♿

★★ Hôtel Campanile
4 rue Jean Moulin, Rondeau Rive Gauche, 38180 Seyssins
☎ 04 76 49 00 41
English spoken
Open 7 days a week, this hotel has a 24 hour automatic key machine (with bank card), which takes over from reception after 11 pm for advanced booking purpose.

47 bedrs, all ensuite, ☇ **P** **DB** 278-298 ✕ 66-107 **CC** MC Visa Amex 🖼 ► 🖳 🖼 ⅲ ✍ ♿
RaC 8 %

★★★ Château de la Commanderie
17 avenue Echirolles, 38320 Eybens
☎ 04 76 25 34 58 Fax 04 76 24 07 31
English spoken

A comfortable 18th century château set in parkland. Restaurant offers refined, classic cuisine served in either the dining room or on the terrace. From Grenoble, follow Rocade-Sud signs, take exit 6 (Eybens/Bresson) and follow signs.

25 bedrs, all ensuite, ☇ **P** **DB** 465-695 **B** 60-70 ✕ 165-265 **CC** MC Visa Amex ⅔ ► 3km 🖼 ⅲ ✍
RaC 5 %

★★★ Hôtel Terminus
10 place de la Gare, 38000 Grenoble
☎ 04 76 87 24 33 Fax 04 76 50 38 28
English spoken
From motorway, exit towards Bastille and follow Gare signs. Renovated hotel, air-conditioned and soundproof, in the town centre opposite SNCF train station and close to a pedestrian only street with shops and gourmet restaurant.

30 bedrs, all ensuite, ☇ **P** 6 **DB** 300-500 **B** 38 ✕ 80 **CC** MC Visa Amex ► 🖼 ⅲ
RaC 10 %

★★★ Hôtel d'Angleterre
5 pl V-Hugo, 38000 Grenoble
☎ 04 76 87 37 21 Fax 04 76 50 94 10
English spoken
In the heart of the city, this hotel has 66 sound-proof, air-conditioned rooms. It has cable TV (24 channels), room service and 24 rooms have a jacuzzi. Take Grenoble-Centre exit from A48, then signs to the town centre.

66 bedrs, all ensuite, ☇ **P** **DB** 390-690 **B** 55 No restaurant **CC** MC Visa Amex
RaC 10 %

GRESY-SUR-ISERE Savoie   6A

★★ Hôtel La Tour de Pacoret
73740 Grésy-sur-Isère
☎ 04 79 37 91 59 Fax 04 79 37 93 84
English spoken

In a charming countryside site, a beautiful and original 14th century watchtower transformed into an intimate and fine hotel-restaurant. With panoramic views of the Combe-de-Savoie and the Alps. Ideal place to visit the Savoyard countryside and its lakes.

9 bedrs, all ensuite, ☇ **P** **DB** 320-435 **B** 50 ✕ 90-245 **CC** MC Visa ⅔ ► 🖳 🖼 ✍

GRIGNAN Drôme   5D

★★★★ Manoir de la Roseraie
route de Valréas, 26230 Grignan
☎ 04 75 46 58 15 Fax 04 75 46 91 55
English spoken
Closed 4 Jan-15 Feb

*A deluxe 19th century manor house in a 5 acre park,
set at the foot of Madame de Sevigne's château. Enjoy
the culinary delights of regional cooking together with
the great wines of the Côtes du Rhône.*

15 bedrs, all ensuite, ⚹ P 20 DB 690-1,680 B 90
✕ 195-250 ℂℂ MC Visa Amex ⋛ ⊦ 8km ⊠ ▨ ▨ ⊞ ∅
&

JULIENAS Rhône   5B

★★ Hôtel des Vignes
rte St-Amour, 69840 Julienas
☎ 04 74 04 43 70 Fax 04 74 04 41 95
English spoken
*The hotel is set in its own grounds in the middle of a
vineyard, half a mile from the village. South-west of
Mâcon, motorway A6.*

22 bedrs, all ensuite, ⚹ P 22 DB 255-280 B 36 No
restaurant ℂℂ MC Visa ⊞ &

LAMASTRE Ardèche   5B

★★★ Château d'Urbilhac
route de Vernoux, 07270 Lamastre
☎ 04 75 06 42 11 Fax 04 75 06 52 75
English spoken

*A château in exceptionally beautiful, forested
countryside. Elegant, comfortable rooms with
panoramic views across a 65 hectare park. It has a
sun terrace above the pool on the château ramparts
and is quiet and very relaxing.*

13 bedrs, all ensuite, ⚹ P 13 DB 550-700 B 65 ✕ 230
ℂℂ MC Visa Amex ⋛ ⊦ ⊠ ▨ ▨ &
ЯᗋＣ **Champagne offered**

LANSLEBOURG Savoie   6A

★★★ Hôtel Alpazur
73480 Val-Cenis
☎ 04 79 05 93 69 Fax 04 79 05 81 96
English spoken
*A comfortable, chalet-style hotel, situated at the foot
of the slopes. Rooms with a balcony overlook the
mountain. Restaurant serves specialities based on
dishes served at the court of the dukes of Savoy.
Access from N6.*

24 bedrs, all ensuite, ⚹ P 10 DB 290-400 B 40 ✕ 100-
260 ℂℂ MC Visa Amex ▨ ⊠ ⊞ ∅
ЯᗋＣ **5 %**

LYON Rhône   5B

★★★★ Grand Hôtel Château Perrache
12 cours de Verdun, Rambaud et Espanade de, 69002
Lyon
☎ 04 72 77 15 00 Fax 04 78 37 06 56
English spoken
*A historic graded building, in the heart of the
peninsula, close to the station, and walking distance
from the traditional Lyon's 'Bouchons'. Restaurant
with a very comfortable dining room and fine
cuisine. Centrally located, exit Centre Ville-Perrache.*

121 bedrs, all ensuite, ⚹ P 50 DB 515-870 B 70 ✕ 137-
177 ℂℂ MC Visa Amex ⊦ 10km ⊞ &
ЯᗋＣ **10 %**

★★★★ Grand Hôtel Concorde
11 rue Grolée, 69002 Lyon
☎ 04 72 40 45 45 Fax 04 78 37 52 55
English spoken
*This 19th century hotel, in the centre of Lyon on the
banks of the Rhône, has been completely redecorated
to combine old world and elegance with traditional
charm and contemporary comfort. Follow the River
Rhône up to the Wilson Bridge.*

143 bedrs, all ensuite, ⚹ P DB 720-990 B 75 ✕ 85
(plus à la carte) ℂℂ MC Visa Amex ⊞ ∅
ЯᗋＣ **15 %**

★★★★ Hôtel Cour des Loges
6 rue Boeuf, Vieux-Lyon, 69005 Lyon
☎ 04 72 77 44 44 Fax 04 72 40 93 61
English spoken

A fine hotel comprising four Renaissance houses dating from the 14th, 16th and 17th centuries, blended with contemporary artists' furnishings and art work. Restaurant offers gourmet cuisine in an informal setting. English, Spanish and German spoken

63 bedrs, all ensuite, ✦ P DB 1,200-1,800 B 120 (plus à la carte) CC MC Visa Amex 🔲 🔲 ▸ ⛶ ⅲ ⌀ ⅋
RAC

★★★★ Hôtel La Tour Rose
22 rue du Boeuf, 69005 Lyon
📞 04 78 37 25 90 Fax 04 78 42 26 02
English spoken

The hotel, in three buildings dating from the 15th and 18th centuries, is a haven of comfort and conviviality. Courtyards and gardens lead to bar, bedrooms are individually decorated to represent different periods in the history of Lyon's silk industry.

12 bedrs, all ensuite, ✦ P DB 950 2,800 B 95 ✕ 295-595 CC MC Visa Amex ▸ ⛶ ⅲ ⌀ ⅋
RAC 20 % on lunch

★★ Hôtel Paris
16 rue Platière, Centre-ville, 69001 Lyon
📞 04 78 28 00 95 Fax 04 78 39 57 64
English spoken
A charming, traditional, centrally located hotel offering a warm welcome and the chance to appreciate the well decorated rooms. Access via Quai de Saône or Rue Paul, then Navard.

30 bedrs, all ensuite, ✦ P DB 250-295 B 35 CC MC Visa Amex ⌀

★★★★ Hôtel Royal
20 pl Bellecour, 69000 Lyon
📞 04 78 37 57 31 Fax 04 78 37 01 36
English spoken

Centrally situated, between the Rhône and the Saône rivers, the hotel overlooks a beautiful square and is close to the shops. The 'Petit Prince' restaurant is known for its fine food. From motorway, exit Centre Ville-Bellecour.

80 bedrs, all ensuite, P DB 720-950 B 72 ✕ 72-142 CC MC Visa Amex ⅲ

★★★★ Hôtel de Lyon Métropole
85 quai Joseph Gillet, 69004 Lyon
📞 04 72 10 44 44 Fax 04 78 39 99 20
English spoken

A 4 star hotel, located on the banks of the River Sâone, 5 minutes from the city centre, supervised underground car park. 2 restaurants, exceptional sport complex.

118 bedrs, all ensuite, ✦ P DB 590-850 B 80 ✕ 150-300 CC MC Visa Amex 🔲 ▸ ⛶ ⛶ ⛶ ⅲ ⌀ ⅋
RAC 15 %

★★ Hôtel de Normandie
3 rue du Bélier, 69002 Lyon
☎ 04 78 37 31 36 Fax 04 72 40 98 56
English spoken

This hotel, situated in the heart of the peninsula, on the edge of the motorway interchange of Lyon Perrache is conveniently placed for access to all the main roads and railways.

39 bedrs, 21 ensuite, ⚑ **P** 2 **DB** 160-274 **B** 29 No restaurant **CC** MC Visa Amex
RƎC **10 %**

MEGEVE Savoie   6A

★★★ Hôtel L'Igloo
au sommet du Mont d'Arbois, 74170 Megève
☎ 04 50 93 05 84 Fax 04 50 21 02 74
English spoken
Closed 20 Sep-15 Dec & 20 Apr-15 Jun
Only accessible by cable car Mont Arbois from Megève, L'Igloo is set in the wilds and offers chalet-style accommodation with exceptional views of Mont Blanc. A warm, welcoming hotel with a gourmet restaurant offering Savoyard specialities.

11 bedrs, all ensuite, ⚑ **P** **DB** 600-950 ✕ 150-300 **CC** MC Visa Amex ⌂ 🖾 ▸ 1km 🖾 ⅲ ♫
RƎC **10 %**

★★ Hôtel Le Tetras
rte Saises, 73590 Notre-Dame-de-Bellecombe
☎ 04 79 31 61 70 Fax 04 79 31 77 31
English spoken
Closed 20 Apr-15 May & 1 Nov-12 Dec

A comfortable hotel-cottage with 23 rooms, heated swimming pool, sauna, jacuzzi and mini-golf. Open from 15 May to 1 Nov. A 15% discount is offered with RAC handbook. Access through Albertville or Sallanches motorway.

23 bedrs, all ensuite, **P** **DB** 260-360 **B** 45 ✕ 80-160 **CC** MC Visa Amex ⌂ ▸ 15km 🖾 🖾 ⅲ ⅟
RƎC **15 % 25% on suites and apartments**

★★ Hôtel Week End
route Rochebrune, 74120 Megève
☎ 04 50 21 26 49 Fax 04 50 21 26 51
English spoken
Quiet, cosy and comfortable chalet hotel, with lovely views over the village, 5 minutes from the town centre and close to the ski lift and téléphérique.

16 bedrs, all ensuite, ⚑ **P** 8 **DB** 480-580 **B** included **B** 35 No restaurant **CC** MC Visa ▸ 2km 🖾 1km ♫
RƎC **8 %**

LES MENUIRES Savoie   6A

★★★ Hôtel L'Ours Blanc
Reberty 2000, 73440 Les Menuires
☎ 04 79 00 61 66 Fax 04 79 00 63 67
English spoken
Closed 14 Dec-25 Apr

Set at an altitude of 2000 m, a chalet-style hotel with gourmet restaurant, in the 'Trois Vallées' skiing area. Take D915 from Moutiers to the resort of Les Menuires, follow the road to the left and the hotel is 1.5 km further along in Reberty 2000.

49 bedrs, all ensuite, ⚑ **P** **DB** 380-620 **B** 50 ✕ 150-260 **CC** MC Visa Amex 🖾 🖾 ⅲ ♫ ⅟
RƎC **8 %**

MERIBEL-LES-ALLUES Savoie   6A

★★★ Hôtel Alba
route du Belvédère, 73550 Méribel-les-Allues
☎ 04 79 08 55 55 Fax 04 79 00 55 63
English spoken

The hotel offers charming, comfortable rooms and gastronomic delights. Situated at the foot of the slopes in the heart of skiing activities, close to the ski school and the chairlift.

20 bedrs, all ensuite, ✦ P DB 680-890 B 70-90 ✕ 68-245 ₡₡ MC Visa 🖥 ⠿ ⌗ ⌀ ⚲
RAC 5 %

★★★ Hôtel Les Arolles
Méribel-Mottaret, 73550 Méribel-les-Allues
☎ 04 79 00 40 40 Fax 04 79 00 45 50
English spoken
Closed 15 Dec-2 May

The hotel, situated on the main ski run, has a large south facing terrace and excellent facilities. 4 km above Méribel; turn right over river on entering Méribel-Mottaret and go to the top of the resort.

60 bedrs, all ensuite, ✦ P DB 800-1,200 B included ✕ 120-180 ₡₡ MC Visa 🖥 ⊞ 🖥 ⌗ ⚲
RAC

★★ Hôtel au Sans Souci
à St-Paul-lès-Monestier, 38650 Monestier-de-Clermont
☎ 04 76 34 03 60 Fax 04 76 34 17 38
English spoken
Closed Jan

This family-run hotel, in a parkland setting, has a country-style, terraced restaurant offering regional cuisine prepared with local ingredients and free range poultry. 2 km from Monestier-de-Clermont towards Gresse-en-Vercours.

11 bedrs, all ensuite, ✦ P 30 DB 260-300 B 37 ✕ 92-230 ₡₡ MC Visa 🖥 ⌗ ⠿ ⌀ ⊞ ⌗
RAC 5 %

★★★ Hôtel Domaine du Colombier
Route de Donzère, 26780 Malataverne
☎ 04 75 90 86 86 Fax 04 75 90 79 40
English spoken

A 13th-century country house with comfortable, individualised rooms and vaulted dining-room, set in a 4 acre park in Provençal Drôme. From A7 take exit Montélimar-Sud: Malataverne is 4 km on.

25 bedrs, all ensuite, ✦ P DB 450-1,200 B 70-77 ✕ 150-360 ₡₡ MC Visa Amex 🖥 ⌗ ⊞ ⌗ ⚲
RAC 5 % on room rate

★★★ Hôtel de France
44 rue du Docteur Mercier, 01130 Nantua
☎ 04 74 75 00 55 Fax 04 74 75 26 22
English spoken
Closed 1 Nov-20 Dec
An old coaching-inn offering a warm welcome, individually furnished, soundproofed bedrooms and a restaurant with speciality cuisine including gratin de queues d'écrevisses, poulet aux morilles à la crème. On A40 from Paris take exit 8, from Genève exit 9.

16 bedrs, all ensuite, ✦ P 18 B 35 ✕ 130-198 ₡₡ MC Visa Amex ⠿ ⌗ ⚲

NYONS Drôme 5D

★★★ Auberge du Vieux Village

Route de Gap, Aubres, 26110 Nyons
☎ 04 75 26 12 89 Fax 04 75 26 38 10
English spoken
Built on the former site of the medieval château of Aubres, the hotel offers wonderful views over the hills. Most of the rooms have their own terrace. Restaurant offers carefully prepared dishes using free-range produce.

23 bedrs, all ensuite, ⚓ P DB 300-780 B 52 ✕ 80-240
((MC Amex ⟳ ☒ ▦ ▸ 18km ☒ ☑ ☒ 1km ⠇⠇ ⌀ ⚿
RAC 10 %

PRIVAS Ardèche 5B

★★ Hôtel Le Panoramic Escrinet

07000 Privas
☎ 04 75 87 10 11 Fax 04 75 87 10 34
English spoken
Closed 16 Nov-15 Mar

A small, family hotel and restaurant, offering gourmet Ardéchoise cuisine, in a lovely garden-park setting with wonderful views over the valley and Cévennes. Located at Col de l'Escrinet, between Privas and Aubenas on N104.

20 bedrs, all ensuite, ⚓ P 20 DB 270-500 B 38 ✕ 135-300 ((MC Visa Amex ⟳ ☒ ⠇⠇
RAC 10 % on room rate

ROANNE Loire 5B

★★ Hôtel Ibis

53 bd Charles de Gaulle, au Côteau, 42120 Roanne
☎ 04 77 68 36 22 Fax 04 77 71 24 99
English spoken
A 2 star hotel with an air-conditioned restaurant. Situated south of Roanne, towards Lyon and St-Etienne.

67 bedrs, all ensuite, ⚓ P DB 295-320 B 37 ✕ 60-110
((MC Visa Amex ⟳ ▸ 6km ☒ ⠇⠇ ⌀ ⚿
RAC 5 %

★★ Hôtel Relais de Roanne

Route de St-Germain, 42640 Roanne
☎ 04 77 71 97 35 Fax 04 77 70 88 15
English spoken
Situated on the outskirts of the city, in 5 acres of land, this hotel has well equipped bedrooms and a comfortable restaurant offering traditional cuisine. Open everyday of the year.

30 bedrs, all ensuite, ⚓ P 50 DB 230-315 B 35 ✕ 85-290 ((MC Visa Amex ☑ ☒ ⠇⠇ ⌀ ⚿
RAC 10 %

ROMANS-SUR-ISERE Drôme 5B

★★ Karene Hôtel

Quartier St-Vérand, RN 92, 26750 Romans-sur-Isère
☎ 04 75 05 12 50 Fax 04 75 05 25 17
English spoken
Closed 20 Dec-6 Jan
A modern, comfortable hotel, with bar, restaurant, swimming pool and view of the Vercors region, situated in a pretty wooded park. A nice place to enjoy sunny days in the countryside.

23 bedrs, all ensuite, ⚓ P 15 DB 290-330 B 45 ✕ 100-130 ((MC Visa Amex ⟳ ▸ ☒ ⠇⠇ ⌀ ⚿

ROUSSILLON Isère 5B

★★ Hôtel Le Médicis

rue F Léger, 38150 Roussillon
☎ 04 74 86 22 47 Fax 04 74 86 48 05
English spoken

A modern, elegant, family-run hotel, with 15 individualised rooms, quietly situated in the verdant Rhône Valley. Travel 50 km south of Lyon on N86; exit junction Vienne and head for Roussillon.

15 bedrs, all ensuite, ⚓ P 15 DB 260-320 B 35-45 No restaurant ((MC Visa ▸ ☒ ⠇⠇ ⌀ ⚿
RAC 10 % except Jul & August

ST-PAUL-TROIS-CHATEAUX Drôme 5D

★★★ Auberge des Quatre-Saisons

26130 St-Restitut
☎ 04 75 04 71 88 Fax 04 75 04 70 88
Closed 30 Dec-2 Feb

A7 *motorway, exit Bollene, 7 km on D59. Situated in the heart of a 12th century village in romanesque houses with all modern comforts.*

4 bedrs, all ensuite, 🛏 **P** **DB** 380-450 **B** 50 ✕ 185-350
℀ MC Visa Amex
ⱤⱭⵌ 10 %

★★★ Hôtel L'Esplan
Place Médiéval de l'Esplan, 26130 St-Paul-Trois-
Châteaux
📞 04 75 96 64 64 **Fax** 04 75 04 92 36
English spoken
Closed 20 Dec-6 Jan

A restored 16th century mansion combining traditional and contemporary architecture. Modern, air-conditioned rooms and a garden terrace. Going south on A7, take Montelimar-Sud exit: toward Avignon, after 4km, see signs to Château.

36 bedrs, all ensuite, 🛏 **P** **DB** 360-490 **B** 40 ✕ 98-350
℀ MC Visa Amex ✦ 4km ⛳ ♨

SERRIERES Ardèche   5B

★★ Hôtel Schaeffer
N86, 07340 Serrières
📞 04 75 34 00 07 **Fax** 04 75 34 08 79
English spoken
Closed Jan

A small, village hotel, on the banks of the Rhône, with a modern, stylish restaurant using fresh local produce. Take the Chanas exit from A7 north of Valence and Serrières is on the N82. Free garage available.

11 bedrs, all ensuite, 🛏 **P** 11 **DB** 295-340 **B** 45 ✕ 130-460 ℀ MC Visa Amex ✦ 12km ⛳ ♨

HÔTEL SCHAEFFER

Situated in the heart of the 'Côtes du Rhône' vineyards, small hotel in the village, on the Rhône river bank.
Creative and delicate cuisine, game in season.
Exit 3 km from A7 motorway, exit Chanas 50 km from Lyon on N86

- ● *Cellar tour and sampling possible*
- ● *5 km from animal park 'Peaugres'*
- ● *'Alambic' museum 3 km*

HÔTEL SCHAEFFER, N86
07340 SERRIÈRES, FRANCE
TEL: 04 75 34 00 07 FAX: 04 75 34 08 79

SEYSSEL Haute Savoie   5B

★★ Hôtel du Rhône
Rive droite, 01420 Seyssel
📞 04 50 59 20 30 **Fax** 04 50 56 10 12
English spoken

A very comfortable family-run hotel delightfully situated on the banks of the Rhône. Highly recommended. From A40 motorway, go south on the D991 to Seyssel.

12 bedrs, 7 ensuite, 🛏 **P** **DB** 130-260 **B** 30 ✕ 95-155
℀ MC Visa ⅔ ✦ 15km ⛳ ⛳ ♨ ✐

TALLOIRES Haute Savoie   6A

★★★ Hôtel Beau Site
74290 Talloires
☎ 04 50 60 71 04 Fax 04 50 60 79 22
English spoken

*An excellently appointed hotel, with superb views of
the lake and mountains, quietly situated in a
peaceful park adjacent to the eastern shore of Lake
Annecy. Restaurant offers gourmet cuisine. Off
D509A.*

29 bedrs, all ensuite, ♀ P DB 450-1,000 B 60 ✕ 175-
300 ℂℂ MC Visa Amex ▸ 3km 🔲 🔲 🔲 ⠶

★★ Hôtel La Charpenterie
74290 Talloires
☎ 04 50 60 70 47 Fax 04 50 60 79 07
English spoken
Closed 4-29 Jan

*A warm, welcoming chalet-style hotel with lovely
views. Accommodation to suit couples or families,
each room has its own private balcony. On the
eastern shore of the lake, 10 km from Annecy.
Restaurant offers fresh fish specialities.*

18 bedrs, all ensuite, ♀ P 11 DB 240-390 B 45 ✕ 100-
165 ℂℂ MC Visa Amex ▸ 3km 🔲 🔲 ⠶ ⠶
RAC 10 %

★★★★ Hôtel Le Cottage Fernand Bise
Route du port, 74290 Talloires
☎ 04 50 60 71 10 Fax 04 50 60 77 51
English spoken
Closed Oct-Apr

*Completely renovated in 1996, the hotel and its large
flower garden face Lake Annecy. Most of the rooms
have a lake view and a balcony. Gourmet restaurant
offers fresh fish specialities; in summer meals are
served on the large terrace.*

35 bedrs, all ensuite, ♀ P DB 450-1,100 B 65 ✕ 140-
270 ℂℂ MC Visa Amex ⤴ 🅿 ▸ 2km 🔲 🔲 🔲 ⠶ ⠶ ⠶

TOURNON Ardèche   5B

★★★ Hôtel du Château
12 Quai Marc Seguin, 07300 Tournon-sur-Rhône
☎ 04 75 08 60 22 Fax 04 75 07 02 95
English spoken

*A comfortable hotel on the banks of the River Rhône,
2 km from the motorway exit. Rooms have TV with
some English channels, Sky News, Eurosport and CNN
(USA).*

**When parking your car ensure you are not
facing oncoming traffic. This will help
you when you return to your car.**

14 bedrs, all ensuite, ♀ P 11 DB 330-370 B 40 ✕ 100-
295 ℂℂ MC Visa Amex ▸ 15km 🔲 ⠶ ⠶ ⠶

VALENCE Drôme   5B

★★ Hôtel Les Négociants
27 avenue Pierre Sémard, 26000 Valence
☎ 04 75 44 01 86 Fax 04 75 44 77 57
English spoken
Closed 22 Dec-5 Jan

*Welcoming, town centre hotel with pleasant,
soundproofed rooms and quality restaurant cuisine
utilising fresh products from the market. Towards
Valence-Sud, then Valence-Centre towards SNCF
station. A member of the Bonjour scheme.*

36 bedrs, all ensuite, ♀ P 10 DB 240-360 B 28-40
✕ 78-180 ℂℂ MC Visa Amex ▸ 🔲 ⠶
RAC 10 %

VALLON-PONT-D'ARC Ardèche   5D

★★ Hôtel du Tourisme
6 rue du Miarou, 07150 Vallon-Pont-d'Arc
☎ 04 75 88 02 12 Fax 04 75 88 12 90
English spoken

*Family owned (since 1937) and run hotel with
friendly atmosphere, situated in the village centre just
100 m from open countryside. Cosy restaurant offers
many specialities including charcuteries maison and
omelette aux truffles.*

29 bedrs, all ensuite, ♀ P 14 DB 260-405 B 33 ✕ 90-
170 ℂℂ MC Visa ▸ 4km 🔲 1km 🔲 ⠶

VILLARS-LES-DOMBES Ain   5B

★★ Hôtel Ribotel
route Lyon, 01330 Villars-les-Dombes
☎ 04 74 98 08 03 Fax 04 74 98 29 55
English spoken

*The Ribotel is a warm, welcoming hotel with a quiet
country atmosphere. Ideal for a stopover or a longer
stay.*

47 bedrs, all ensuite, ★ **P** 50 **DB** 250-300 **B** 35-40 **CC**
MC Visa Amex ⚡ ▸ ▨ ▣ ▨ ⧟ ♪ ⚐
RAC 5 % on room rate

★★★ Hôtel Plaisance
96 av de la Libération, 69652 Villefranche-sur-Saône
☎ **04 74 65 33 52 Fax 04 74 62 02 89**
English spoken
Closed 24 Dec-1 Jan
*The hotel faces a square in the town centre; a
gourmet restaurant, La Fontaine Bleue, is opposite.
Villefranche is the capital of the Beaujolais area, a
good starting point for excusions into the Beaujolais
vineyards.*

68 bedrs, all ensuite, ★ **P** 20 **DB** 359-476 **B** 39-50
✗ 120-200 **CC** MC Visa Amex ▸ 8km ▣ ▨ ⧟ ♪
RAC Free parking (instead of 541 FF)

Aquitaine

Since the 1850s, when Napoleon III and his wife, Empress Eugénie, popularised the resort of Biarritz, Aquitaine has been assured of its place as a major centre for tourism. The area has a lot to offer, framed as it is by the Basques Pyrénées to the south and a beautiful stretch of lush Atlantic coast to the west.

It's easy to see why over four million visitors descend on the region every year.

On first impressions, **Bordeaux** appears to have changed somewhat since Victor Hugo stated, 'take Versailles, add Antwerp, and the result is Bordeaux'.

The extraordinary elegance and obvious opulence that led Hugo to make that remark have now been diluted by the city's increased size and by some poor planning. However, if you look, you will find that Bordeaux still has a good deal of charm with which to tempt the traveller.

Bordeaux is surrounded by the largest wine-making area in the world. This Eden of French viticulture produces a staggering range of wines, and in enormous quantities. Red Bordeaux (often called Claret) is highly popular with the British.

Vineyards extend from the city in every direction, and many conduct tours and allow tastings.

The city itself is most attractive around its eighteenth-century centre.

Although the grandeur that caused writers such as Hugo to gush has now faded somewhat, intricate architecture and a monumental city plan still make an impression on visitors.

There are a number of pleasant squares and boulevards in which to relax. Look out for some real gems of classical design, such as the Place de la Bourse, with its old riverside stock exchange, and the Esplanade des Quinconces, which is thought to be the largest public square in Europe.

The Musée des Beaux-Arts houses an enjoyable collection, which includes works by Rubens and the ever-popular Matisse.

Dining is one of the greatest pleasures in Bordeaux and good restaurants are easy to find.

Enjoy a drop of decent Claret with your meal; look for wine which is marked 'appellation controlée'. This label is given only to the best wine in a particular area.

The Bassin d'Arcachon, to the west of Bordeaux and at the head of the Côte d'Argent, is a pleasant natural bay which boasts 50 miles of beaches.

Most Bordelais head for **Arcachon** itself, which has been a booming seaside resort since the nineteenth century. You'll find some lovely beaches here (although, in the summer, they can get over-crowded) and a lively town.

To the north, **Périgueux** makes a convenient and enjoyable headquarters from which to explore the Dordogne region of Aquitaine. Périgueux is 2,000 years old – a fact which is reflected in the city's rather unimpressive Roman ruins. The neo-Byzantine Cathédral de St-Front is more exciting. It is one of the most interesting Romanesque churches in Aquitaine, if not in France.

Most visitors to Périgueux come in search of history, which pre-dates the Romanesque or, indeed, the Roman.

Evidence of Stone Age man can be found in the amazing cave paintings of the nearby Vézère Valley. No-one knows exactly how the caves were used by prehistoric man. It's possible that these were places of some sort of religious or sacred significance. Whatever

Pages 234–235: Le Puy en Velay
Above: Bordeaux's Place de la Borse

their role, the caves and their incredible wall paintings together constitute one of the most important prehistoric finds anywhere in the world.

A more convenient but less entertaining, base from which to explore the Vézère Valley is **Les Eyzies-de-Tayac**.

Further south, at the point at which the Atlantic coast begins to rise to the Pyrénées, **Biarritz** adds a dose of aristo-glamour to Bayonne's more simple charms.

The former has been a favourite retreat for royalty and the rich, but is now past its best. Those days of Napoleonic blessing have bequeathed the town a slightly overbearing air of self-importance. The beaches are great, though, and the surf is fantastic. Many visitors quite enjoy the old world comfort of the grander hotels.

There are also a couple of suitably plush casinos for those in search of the excitement of the tables.

Bayonne is almost an extension of Biarritz, yet, set some miles inland, it is entirely different in character from it.

Bayonne is more obviously Basque – look out for typically Basque half-timbered houses. It is also cleaner and more 'real'

than its ostentatious neighbour.

Visit the Musée Basque to find out more about the fascinating culture and politics of the region.

With considerably less tourism than it deserves, Bayonne is the perfect place to spend a day or two before tackling the coast or the vast Pyrénées.

Just a few miles south of Biarritz lies **Saint-Jean de Luz**, a lovely fishing port turned beach resort, which is both prettier and friendlier than Biarritz.

With smart shops, neat hotels and a gorgeous beach, the town is often compared to St-Tropez. Unlike St-Tropez, however, you will see fishing boats not bankers' yachts in the harbour at Saint-Jean-de-Luz.

Louis XIV chose to marry the Spanish Infanta Maria Theresa at Saint-Jean de Luz. The extravagant royal wedding took place at the church of Saint-Jean-Baptiste. That event has left a lasting impression on the locals, who still boast of the occasion.

Other royal wedding landmarks include the house in which the King slept the night before the wedding and the house where his bride prepared for the big day.

Above: St-Jean-de-Luz has remained an active port (the town still holds annual festivals of tuna and sardine)

Pau, the capital of the Béarn Province, also claims an impressive royal connection. King Henri IV was born in Pau's château. Despite subsequent adjustments by Louis-Philippe and, later, Napoleon III, the castle is only really worth visiting for the two interesting museums which are located there.
The Musée Béarnais is a surprisingly complete introduction to the local area, while the Musée National painstakingly points out Pau's regal past. Pau is probably the most convenient gateway to the higher Pyrénées – wonderful for walking and – in season – skiing.
The striking landscape is made all the more enjoyable by its relative peace; the Pyrénées aren't as crowded as the Alps. No doubt it was these qualities which caused Pau to become such a fashionable holiday spot for the British gentry in the nineteenth century.

Festivals in Aquitaine

February
*   Antiques Festival, Bordeaux

April
*   Music Festival, Biarritz
*   Ravel Music Festival, St-Jean-de-Luz

May
*   Spring Opera Season, Biarritz

June
*   Jazz, Theatre and Ballet Festival, Gironde
*   Saint-Jean Festival, Saint-Jean-de-Luz

July
*   Jazz Festival, Andernos
*   Dourdogne Music Festival, St-Amand-de-Coly and St-Léon-sur-Vézère
*   Medieval Festival, Eymet
*   Festival of the Theatre, Sarlat
*   Jazz Festival, Villeneuve-sur-Lot
*   Flamenco Festival, Mont-de-Marsan
*   Tuna Festival, Saint-Jean-de-Luz

August
*   Mime Festival, Périgueux
*   Theatre Festival, Citadelle de Blaye
*   Bayonne Festival, Bayonne
*   Ocean Festival, Arcachon

September
*   Music Festival, St Jean de Luz

What to do in Aquitaine
*   Taste Claret in the vineyards of Bordeaux.
*   Laze on golden beaches in the Bassin d'Arcachon.
*   See prehistoric cave paintings, the most impressive in the world, in the Vézère Valley.
*   Eat freshly caught seafood in the pretty resort of Saint-Jean-de-Luz.
*   Break the bank at Biarritz.

Getting there

By road
Major arteries through Aquitaine:
*   A10 Bordeaux to Paris via Poitiers
*   A62 Bordeaux to Toulouse via Agen and Montauban
*   A63/N10 Bordeaux to Biarritz via Bayonne
*   A64 Biarritz to Tarbes via Bayonne and Pau
Coach operators include:
*   Limtour Voyages ☏ 5 53 53 31 03
*   Citram Aquitaine ☏ 5 56 48 10 10
*   RDTL ☏ 5 58 05 66 06
*   Pascale Voyages ☏ 5 59 59 71 55
*   Voyage Ocean Pyrennees ☏ 5 59 23 43 27

By rail
By TGV:
*   Paris Gare Montparnasse to Agen takes 3 hours 50 mins
*   Paris Gare Montparnasse to Dax takes 4 hours
*   Paris Gare Montparnasse to Pau takes 4 hours 50 mins
*   Paris Gare Montparnasse to Bayonne takes 4 hours 35 mins
*   Bayonne to Lille takes 6 hours 50 mins.

By air
Bordeaux International Airport (☏ 5 56 34 50 00, fax 5 56 34 23 01) is 8 miles west of Bordeaux. For car hire contact:
*   Ada ☏ 5 56 34 67 67
*   Europcar ☏ 5 56 34 59 59
*   Hertz ☏ 5 56 34 18 87
Biarritz Anglet Bayonne Airport (☏ 5 59 43 83 83, Fax: 5 59 43 83 86) is about a mile south-east of Biarritz. For car hire try:
*   Avis ☏ 5 59 23 67 92
*   Budget ☏ 5 59 23 58 62

TOURIST INFORMATION
*   **Aquitaine Tourist Office**
    Parvis de Chartron, 33000 Bordeaux ☏ 5 56 01 70 00

AIGUILLON Lot et Garonne   4D

★ Hôtel La Terrasse de l'Etoile
cours A Lorraine, 47190 Aiguillon
☎ 05 53 79 64 64 Fax 05 53 79 46 48
English spoken

An 18th century building, with exposed stone walls, decorated in 1930s style and set in the town centre. Family atmosphere.

17 bedrs, all ensuite, ⚡ P DB 250 B 28 ✕ 75-200 CC
MC Visa Amex ⊰ ▸ 4km 🎮 📺 ⊞ ⌂ ⚘ ㋡
RAC 5 %

★★ Hôtel Le Jardin des Cygnes
route de Villeneuve, 47190 Aiguillon
☎ 05 53 79 60 02 Fax 05 53 88 10 22
English spoken
A most attractive hotel in this small, quiet town by the River Lot. Lovely gardens and swimming pool. From A61, take the exit for Aiguillon. (Half-board from 190 FF to 292 FF).

24 bedrs, all ensuite, ⚡ P 24 DB 195-295 B 12-32
✕ 75-158 CC MC Visa Amex ⊰ 🎮 ⊞ ⚘ ㋡
RAC 10 % on room only, low season.

BAYONNE Pyrénées Atlantiques   4C

★★★ Le Grand Hôtel
21 rue Thiers, 64100 Bayonne
☎ 05 59 59 14 61 Fax 05 59 25 61 70
English spoken
In the heart of the business and shopping area, the hotel lies between the cathedral and the theatre and offers large recently renovated rooms. Situated 5 km from Atlantic Ocean beaches, surfing, fishing, 7 golf courses within 20 km and English spoken.

54 bedrs, all ensuite, ⚡ P 10 DB 410-650 B 45 ✕ 95-135 CC MC Visa Amex ▸ 5km 📺 ⊞ ㋡
RAC 10 % on room rate

BERGERAC Dordogne   4B

★★★ Hôtel au Windsor
Domaine de Lespinassat, rte d'Agen, 24100 Bergerac
☎ 05 53 24 89 76 Fax 05 53 57 72 24
English spoken

In a calm and pleasant setting, the hotel offers air-conditioned rooms, meeting rooms, garden, swimming pool, sauna and a friendly restaurant. Situated close to the airport on the Agen road. Comfort in a modern and sophisticated setting.

50 bedrs, all ensuite, ⚡ P 300 DB 280-320 B 40-50
✕ 90-150 CC MC Visa ⊰ 🗶 📺 ⊞ ⚘ ㋡
RAC 5 %

★★★ Hôtel de Bordeaux
38 place Gambetta, 24100 Bergerac
☎ 05 53 57 12 83 Fax 05 53 57 72 14
English spoken
Closed Jan
The Maury family has been welcoming guests to the hotel since 1855. All modern facilities are offered, including lifts, with a garden around the swimming pool. The meals are beautifully presented in a comfortable and friendly restaurant or on the terrace.

40 bedrs, all ensuite, ⚡ P DB 290-420 B 46 ✕ 100-240
CC MC Visa Amex ⊰ ▸ 15km ⊞ ㋡
RAC 10 % except Jul & Aug

BEYNAC Dordogne   4B

★★ Hôtel Bonnet
24220 Beynac
☎ 05 53 29 50 01 Fax 05 53 29 83 74
English spoken
Traditional Périgord hotel with lovely views over river and garden. From Sarlat (10 km), first hotel on right as you enter Beynac. A rustic-style dining room with open fireplace, serving Périgord cuisine.

22 bedrs, 20 ensuite, ⚡ P 50 DB 230-290 B 35 ✕ 85-250 CC MC Visa Amex ▸ 10km 🎮 📺 ⊞ ⚘

BIARRITZ Pyrénées Atlantiques   4C

★★★★ **Hôtel Miramar**
Avenue de l'Impératrice, 64200 Biarritz
☎ **05 59 41 30 00 Fax 05 59 24 77 20**
English spoken

A very modern hotel of great comfort, facing the ocean with its own private beach and located close to the town centre. Worldwide reputation for its thalassotherapy (spa) centre.

126 bedrs, all ensuite, ⚡ **P** 40 **DB** 960-2,700 **B** 100
✕ 290 (plus à la carte) **CC** MC Visa Amex 🎾 🏊 🎣 💻
▸ 📻 🎿 ⅲ ♬ ♿
RAC 10 % on room rate

★★★★ **Hôtel du Palais**
1 avenue de l'Impératrice, 64200 Biarritz
☎ **05 59 41 64 00 Fax 05 59 41 67 99**
English spoken
Closed Feb

Formerly an imperial palace, the hotel is in the heart of the city and overlooks the fine beaches of Biarritz. Fully renovated with a worldwide reputation for luxury.

156 bedrs, all ensuite, ⚡ **P** 150 **DB** 1,500-2,850 **B** 130
✕ 290-395 🏊 🎣 📺 📻 ▸ 1km 📻 🎿 ⅲ ♬ ♿
RAC 10 %

BISCARROSSE Landes   4C

★★ **Hôtel Atlantide**
place Marsan, 40600 Biscarrosse
☎ **05 58 78 08 86 Fax 05 58 78 75 98**
English spoken

Modern and comfortable, the hotel is in a quiet, town centre position near beaches and lakes.

33 bedrs, all ensuite, ⚡ **P** 40 No restaurant **CC** MC
Visa Amex ▸ 5km 🎾 📻 🎣 ⅲ ♬ ♿

★★ **Hôtel St-Hubert**
588 avenue G. Latécoère, Biscarrosse-Bourg, 40600 Biscarrosse
☎ **05 58 78 09 99 Fax 05 58 78 79 37**
English spoken

Hotel with a large garden, set in a quiet area close to restaurants. Located 600 m from the church, in the direction of Lake Latécoère. Very helpful English-French owners.

16 bedrs, all ensuite, ⚡ **P** 18 **DB** 235-370 **B** 36 No
restaurant **CC** MC Visa ▸ 📻 🎣 ♿
RAC 5 % off season

BORDEAUX Gironde   4B

★★ **Hôtel des 4 Soeurs**
6 cours 30-Juillet, 33000 Bordeaux
☎ **05 57 81 19 20 Fax 05 56 01 04 28**
English spoken
Closed 20 Dec-5 Jan

A renovated hotel in quiet, town centre location. The restaurant is a Napoléon III-style brasserie.

34 bedrs, all ensuite, ⚡ **P** **DB** 350-500 **B** 40 **CC** MC
Visa Amex ▸ 🎣
RAC 30 % at weekends

BRANTOME Dordogne 4B

★★★ Château de la Côte
Biras-Bourdeilles, 24310 Brantôme
☎ 05 53 03 70 11 Fax 05 53 03 42 84
English spoken
Closed 5 Nov-5 Mar except Christmas

Discover the charm of bygone days in one of the nicest 15th century châteaux-hotels of the Périgueux. A refined hotel with splendid architecture, decor and gastronomy and featuring dinner on the terrace, a park, swimming and snooker.

14 bedrs, all ensuite, ⊨ P 100 DB 400-750 B 50-65 ✕ 140-300 ₵₵ MC Visa Amex ⊰ ┝ 15km 🔲 🔲 🔲 Ⅲ ✎
RAC 7 %

★★★ Domaine de la Roseraie
Route d'Angoulème, 24310 Brantôme
☎ 05 53 05 84 74 Fax 05 53 05 77 94
English spoken
Closed 15 Nov-15 Mar

A charming small Relais du Silence hotel set in 4 hectares in a park with fully equipped rooms, gourmet cuisine and regional menu. On the D939 Périgueux to Angoulème road.

7 bedrs, all ensuite, ⊨ P 30 DB 400-750 B 50-70 ✕ 145-225 ₵₵ MC Visa Amex ⊰ ┝ 🔲 🔲 Ⅲ ✎ ☖
RAC 10 % on rooms for 3 nights with breakfast

★★★★ Hôtel Le Moulin du Roc
24530 Champagnac-de-Belair
☎ 05 53 02 86 00 Fax 05 53 54 21 31
English spoken
Closed 1 Jan-7 Mar

On the banks of the River Drôme, a former 17th century mill transformed into a luxury hotel with lovely gardens. Very comfortable rooms with period furnishings.

14 bedrs, all ensuite, ⊨ P DB 410-720 B 30-65 ✕ 160-290 ₵₵ MC Visa Amex 🔲 ⊰ ┝ 20km 🔲 🔲 🔲
RAC 8 % on room rate

LE BUGUE Dordogne 4B

★★★ Manoir de Bellerive
route de Siorac, 24480 Le Buisson-de-Cadouin
☎ 05 53 27 16 19 Fax 05 53 22 09 05
English spoken
Small Relais du Silence château in a 3 hectare park on the edge of the Dordogne. Peaceful setting near Lascaux and Les Eyzies.

23 bedrs, all ensuite, ⊨ P 25 DB 450-850 B 50-70 ✕ 95-280 ₵₵ MC Visa Amex ⊰ 🔲 🔲 ┝ 🔲 🔲 🔲 Ⅲ ✎ ☖
RAC 5 %

CASTELJALOUX Lot et Garonne 4D

★★★ Château de Ruffiac
Ruffiac, 47700 Casteljaloux
☎ 05 53 93 18 63 Fax 05 53 89 67 93
English spoken
A vast 14th century vicarage, next to the church, with views of both mountains and valleys. Comfortable rooms with good facilities. From Casteljaloux, north-west on D655 for 8 km.

20 bedrs, all ensuite, ⊨ P DB 380-480 B 40-50 ✕ 150-190 ₵₵ MC Visa ⊰ ┝ 8km 🔲 🔲 Ⅲ ☖
RAC 10 %

COLY Dordogne 4B

★★★ Manoir d'Hautegente
24120 Coly
☎ 05 53 51 68 03 Fax 05 53 50 38 52
English spoken

Set in the heart of the Périgord and Richard Coeur de Lion country, this small 18th century hotel, with sunny terrace and peaceful atmosphere, stands at the foot of the castle. Restaurant with cosy dining room offers fresh, local dishes.

A former forge and mill of the St-Armand-de-Coly abbey and owned by the family for generations. This elegant residence, situated in the heart of the golden triangle in the Périgord black zone, is close to several famous places.

11 bedrs, 8 ensuite, **P DB** 185-225 **B** 30-35 ✗ 75-175 **CC** MC Visa
RaC

14 bedrs, all ensuite, ⊶ **P DB** 570-970 **B** 65 ✗ 210-380 **CC** MC Visa Amex ⫟ ↑ 20km 🖊 ☒ ⊞ ⌀ ⅍
RaC **10 %**

LES EYZIES-DE-TAYAC Dordogne   4B

COUTRAS Gironde   4B

★★ Hôtel Les Roches
rte de Sarlat, 24620 Les Eyzies-de-Tayac
📞 05 53 06 96 59 **Fax** 05 53 06 95 54
English spoken

★★ Hôtel Henri IV
Place du 8 Mai, 33230 Coutras
📞 05 57 49 34 34 **Fax** 05 57 49 20 72
English spoken

Situated on the outskirts of the famous village of Les Eyzies-de-Tayac, in the heart of the Dordogne, the hotel has a bar and garden.

Close to St-Emilion vineyards, a very comfortable charming hotel with a warm welcome, 50 km east of Bordeaux on the Angoulême road. There is a forest, lake, fishing and hiking available.

41 bedrs, all ensuite, **P** 41 **DB** 280-350 **B** 38 No restaurant **CC** MC Visa ⫟ 🖊 ☒ ⊞ ⅍

14 bedrs, all ensuite, ⊶ **P** 14 **DB** 250-270 **B** 37 No restaurant **CC** MC Visa Amex 🖊 ☒ ⌀
RaC **5 %**

HAGETMAU Landes   4D

EXCIDEUIL Dordogne   4B

Hôtel Le Jambon
rue Carnot, 40700 Hagetmau
📞 05 58 79 32 02
English spoken
In the heart of the Chalosse and close to the European capital of chair production, near to sea and mountains, the 7-room hotel-restaurant is entirely redecorated. A calm, comfortable stay with famous table specialities from the Landes.

★★ Hôtel du Fin Chapon
24160 Excideuil
📞 05 53 62 42 38 **Fax** 05 53 52 39 60
English spoken
Closed 1-15 Feb

7 bedrs, all ensuite, ⊶ **P** 10 **DB** 250-400 **B** 35 ✗ 85-230 **CC** MC Visa ⫟ ⊞

HOSSEGOR Landes   4C

★★★ Hôtel Beauséjour
40150 Hossegor
☎ 05 58 43 51 07 Fax 05 58 43 70 13
English spoken
Closed 15 Oct-28 Apr

1930's building situated in the countryside near lake and sea in an area well known for its golf courses.From the town centre take directions for the seafront, after the bridge on the canal turn right and follow the Tour du Lac road for the hotel (400 m).

45 bedrs, all ensuite, ✝ P 20 DB 300-700 B 65 ✕ 140-300 ℂℂ MC Visa Amex ⊰ ► 1km 🔲 🔳 🔲 ⊞ ✐ ⅃

LACANAU-OCEAN Gironde   4A

★★★ Hôtel Golf
Domaine de l'Ardilouse, 33680 Lacanau-Océan
☎ 05 56 03 92 92 Fax 05 56 26 30 57
English spoken

A 'tonic' holiday, 4 km from a sandy beach and close to a pond for model boats. The hotel and its rooms are in the heart of the international 18 hole golf course. 50 rooms with modern comfort open onto the swimming pool. Self-catering rooms available.

50 bedrs, all ensuite, P 50 DB 300-600 B 35-50 ✕ 65-150 ℂℂ MC Visa Amex ⊰ 🄿 🔳 ⊞ ✐ ⅃
RAC 5 %

LALINDE Dordogne   4B

★★★ Hôtel Château
24150 Lalinde
☎ 05 53 61 01 82 Fax 05 53 24 74 60
English spoken
Closed Jan/3rd week Sep

Between the black and purple zones of the Périgord, the château is of 13th and 18 century architecture and juts out over the River Dordogne. Close to the town centre, but very peaceful with a shaded terrace and pool area.

7 bedrs, all ensuite, ✝ P DB 270-870 B 65 ✕ 110-295 ℂℂ MC Visa Amex ⊰ ► 10km 🔲
RAC **10 % discount if eating at restaurant**

MARMANDE Lot et Garonne   4D

★★ Hôtel Le Capricorne
Route d'Agen, R.N.113, 47200 Marmande
☎ 05 53 64 16 14 Fax 05 53 20 80 18
English spoken
Closed 18 Dec-3 Mar

A modern, quiet, air-conditioned hotel in landscaped grounds, on the southern outskirts of Marmande and close to the Agen road. The restaurant (closed Sat lunch & Sun.) offers local speciality cuisine prepared by chef, Thierry Arbeau.

34 bedrs, all ensuite, ✝ P 34 DB 280 B 36 ✕ 78-220 ℂℂ MC Visa Amex ⊰ ► 3km ⊞ ✐ ⅃

Time
French Summer Time starts at 2am on the last Sunday of March and ends at 3am on the last Sunday of October.
France is, therefore, always one hour ahead of Britain.

MESSANGES Landes   4C

Résidence Arts et Vie Messanges
Quatier Nature, 40660 Messanges
☎ **05 58 48 96 00 Fax 05 58 48 97 09**
English spoken
Closed Nov-Mar

On the Aquitaine coast, the Arts et Vie holiday complex of Messanges boasts tennis courts, pool and billiards. (Prices quoted are per week for 2 room apartment suitable for 4 people).

100 bedrs, all ensuite, **P** 150 **DB** 1,000-1,900 **B** 400 ☒ ▸
▣ ☑ ♫ ♿

NONTRON Dordogne   4B

★★ Hôtel Pelisson
place A Agard, 24300 Nontron
☎ **05 53 56 11 22 Fax 05 53 56 59 94**
English spoken

A former staging post and convent, this family-run hotel is situated in the centre of town. The restaurant offers traditional cuisine and specialities from the Périgord: foie gras, confits, magrets and homemade pastries.

25 bedrs, 18 ensuite, ♚ **P** 30 **DB** 200-300 **B** 34 ✕ 82-250 **CC** MC Visa ⚖ ▸ 30km ▣ ☒ ♨ ♫ ♿

OLORON-STE-MARIE Pyrénées Atlantiques   4C

★★ Hôtel Relais Aspois
route du Col du Somport, Gurmençon-village, 64400 Oloron-Ste-Marie
☎ **05 59 39 09 50 Fax 05 59 39 02 33**
English spoken
A chalet-style hotel with warm, comfortable accommodation, a family atmosphere and a restaurant specialising in Basque cuisine. Gurmençon is 4 km south of Oloron on the N134.

25 bedrs, 20 ensuite, **P** 25 **DB** 160-280 **B** 30 ✕ 55-150 **CC** MC Visa Amex ▸ ▣ ☒ ♨
RAC 1 week inc breakfast for 2 = 3000 FF

PAU Pyrénées Atlantiques   4D

★★ Hôtel Les Bains de Secours
64260 Sévignacq-Meyracq
☎ **05 59 05 62 11 Fax 05 59 05 76 56**
English spoken
An attractively renovated farm, with a restaurant renowned for its fine regional cuisine, situated in the Béarn hills. From Pau, take N134 south, then D934; the hotel is just south of Rébénacq.

7 bedrs, all ensuite, **P** **DB** 270-350 **B** 36 ✕ 80-250 **CC** MC Visa Amex ☒

PERIGUEUX Dordogne   4B

★★★ Hôtel Chandelles
Antonne-et-Trigonant, 24420 Périgueux
📞 05 53 06 05 10 Fax 05 53 06 07 33
English spoken
Closed Jan & Feb
A small hotel, converted from an old farm building, with a restaurant offering classic and regional cuisine prepared with market-fresh produce. Situated 9 km from Périgueux on the way to Limoges.

7 bedrs, all ensuite, ⊁ P 50 DB 200-320 B 40 ✕ 95-390 ℂℂ MC Visa Amex ⤳ ⏵ 9km 🔲 📖 🖼 ⠇
RAC **15 % on room rate**

RIBERAC Dordogne   4B

★★ Hôtel de France
Rue M Dufraisse, 24600 Ribérac
📞 05 53 90 00 61 Fax 05 53 91 06 05
English spoken

An old post house converted into a comfortable, cosy hotel with a pretty flower garden and imaginative cuisine made with fresh Périgord products. A memorable stay is guaranteed.

17 bedrs, 15 ensuite, P DB 140-230 B 35-50 ✕ 70-200 ℂℂ MC Visa ⏵ 📖 🖼 ⠇ ✑
RAC **5 %**

LA ROQUE-GAGEAC Dordogne   4B

★★ Hôtel Gardette
24250 La Roque-Gageac
📞 05 53 29 51 58 Fax 05 53 31 19 32
English spoken
A unique hideaway, in one of the nicest Périgord villages, with regional cuisine and shaded terraces overlooking the Dordogne. 10 km from Sarlat

15 bedrs, all ensuite, ⊁ P 15 DB 200-300 B 32 ✕ 115-245 ℂℂ MC Visa ⏵ 📖 🖼

ST-EMILION Gironde   4B

★★ Hôtel Aub de la Commanderie
rue Cordeliers, 33330 St-Emilion
📞 05 57 24 70 19 Fax 05 57 74 44 53
English spoken
Closed 15 Jan-15 Feb
The Auberge de la Commanderie stands on one of several historic sites in the heart of this medieval town. The main part of the building is of Templar origin and the annex was used as the last hiding place by the counter-revolutionary Girondin deputies.

18 bedrs, all ensuite, P DB 280-550 B 38-48 No restaurant ℂℂ MC Visa ⏵ 📖 🖼 ⠇

★★★ Hôtel Logis des Remparts
18 rue Guadet, 33330 St-Emilion
📞 05 57 24 70 43 Fax 05 57 74 47 44
English spoken
Set in the heart of the medieval city, with views of the vineyards, walls and old town, this charming, refurbished hotel, has a warm atmosphere plus gardens, shaded terraces, private sitting rooms, bar, air-conditioned rooms and private parking.

17 bedrs, all ensuite, P 17 DB 350-650 B 50 No restaurant ℂℂ MC Visa ⤳ ⏵ 🖼 ⠇

ST-JEAN-DE-LUZ Pyrénées Atlantiques   4C

★★ Hôtel Agur
96 rue Gambetta, 64500 St-Jean-de-Luz
📞 05 59 51 91 11 Fax 05 59 51 91 21
English spoken
Closed 15 Nov-1 Mar
Situated in the town centre, 200 m from the beach, the hotel offers comfortable rooms or self catering flats. Contact Jacqui or Alasdair Semple for details.

14 bedrs, all ensuite, P 4 DB 295-395 B 37 No restaurant ℂℂ MC Visa Amex ⏵ 2km 🖼 ✑

★★★ Hôtel Continental
15 avenue de Verdun, 64500 St-Jean-de-Luz
📞 05 59 26 01 23 Fax 05 59 51 17 63
English spoken
A centrally located hotel, 300 m from the beach, close to the port, the station and two 18 hole golf courses. Excellent value for money.

21 bedrs, all ensuite, ⊁ P DB 260-400 B 38 No restaurant ℂℂ MC Visa Amex ⏵

★★★ Hôtel La Réserve
Rondpoint de St-Barbe, 64500 St-Jean-de-Luz
📞 **05 59 26 04 24** Fax **05 59 26 11 74**
English spoken
Closed 15 Nov-20 Mar

*Comfortable hotel with large gardens, directly on the
ocean. Short, pretty walk to town centre and main
beach. 2 km from the motorway A10, exit St-Jean-de-
Luz-Nord. 36 studios and apartments are now
available with complete hotel services.*

76 bedrs, all ensuite, ⊬ P DB 400-800 B 55 ✕ 160-280
℃ MC Visa Amex ⊰ 🄿 ▶ 2km 🔲🔲🔲 ⚒ ♗ &
RAC **10 % except Jul/Aug**

★★★ Hôtel Madison
25 bd Thiers, 64500 St-Jean-de-Luz
📞 **05 59 26 35 02** Fax **05 59 51 14 76**
English spoken

*100 m from the beach and town centre. From St-
Jean-de-Luz, take the A63 towards Biarritz and
follow signs to the centre and beach for 2 km*

25 bedrs, all ensuite, ⊬ P DB 250-460 B 39 No
restaurant ℃ MC Visa Amex 🄵🄴 ▶ 2km ⚒ ♗

★★★★ Hôtel Parc Victoria
5 rue Cepé, 64500 St-Jean-de-Luz
📞 **05 59 26 78 78** Fax **05 59 26 78 08**
English spoken
Closed 15 Nov-15 Mar

*Only a few steps away from the bay and beach of St-
Jean-de-Luz, this beautiful hotel is surrounded by
trees and flower-filled gardens. Each room has
antique furniture and marble bathroom.*

12 bedrs, all ensuite, ⊬ P 14 DB 800-1,300 B 80
✕ 210-350 ℃ MC Visa Amex ▶ 3km 🄴 ⚒ &

ST-PEE-SUR-NIVELLE Pyrénées Atlantiques   4C

★★ Hôtel Restaurant Nivelle
64310 St-Pée-sur-Nivelle
📞 **05 59 54 10 27** Fax **05 59 54 19 82**
English spoken
*Family-run Logis de France hotel, in the centre of this
pretty, rural village, just 5 minutes from the lake.
Take St-Jean-de-Luz exit from N10.*

30 bedrs, all ensuite, P 60 DB 220-360 B 35-55 ✕ 85-
160 ℃ MC Visa Amex ▶ 8km 🔲🄴 ⚒
RAC **5 %**

STE-FOY-LA-GRANDE Gironde   4B

★★ Hôtel La Boule d'Or
Place Jean Jaurès, 33220 Ste-Foy-la-Grande
📞 **05 57 46 00 76** Fax **05 57 46 12 16**
English spoken
*The Hôtel Boule d'Or is a 13th century country-house
located between Bordeaux and Bergerac. You will
find a warm welcome in the heart of Ste-Foy-la-
Grande and its AOC Ste-Foy-Bordeaux vineyard.*

25 bedrs, 21 ensuite, ⊬ P 30 DB 190-260 B 35 ✕ 75-
260 ℃ MC Visa Amex ▶ 🔲🄴 ⚒ ♗
RAC **12 %**

SALIES-DE-BEARN Pyrénées Atlantiques   4C

★★ Hôtel du Golf
64270 Salies-de-Béarn
📞 **05 59 65 02 10** Fax **05 59 38 05 84**
English spoken
*The hotel can be accessed via D30, which runs south
from junction 3 of the A64 towards Salies.*

33 bedrs, all ensuite, ⊬ P 35 DB 250-310 B 30 ✕ 80-
135 ℃ MC Visa ⊰ 🄿 ▶ 🔲🔲🄴 ⚒ &

SALIGNAC Dordogne   4B

★★ Hôtel La Terrasse
24590 Salignac-Eyvigues
📞 05 53 28 80 38 Fax 05 53 28 99 67
English spoken
Closed end of Oct & Easter

Hotel with heated swimming pool, volley ball, table tennis, mountain bikes and one day trips: Restaurant offers foie gras specialities. Situated close to Rocamadour, Lascaux, Sarvat.

13 bedrs, all ensuite, ⋔ P 20 **DB** 250-350 **B** 44 ✕ 88-210 **CC** MC Visa ⇶ 🖼 5km
RƎC Apr-Jun & Oct, 5 nights for 4

SALLES Gironde   4C

★★★★ Résidence du Château de Salles
25 route de Béguey, 33700 Salles
📞 05 57 71 91 00 Fax 05 57 71 92 99
English spoken
100 villas, and a restaurant, with all the comfort you need, set in a 50 hectare private park. Close to the Arcachon beaches, 30 minutes from Bordeaux: take A63 toward Bayonne, then exit 21 Salles/Belin-Belier.

222 bedrs, 138 ensuite, ⋔ P 200 **DB** 90-406 **B** 40-60 ✕ 70-250 **CC** MC Visa Amex ⇶ 🖾 ▸ 🖾 🖾 ♫ 🖾 ⵗ ✍ ♿
RƎC 5 %

SARLAT-LA-CANEDA Dordogne   4B

★★★ Hostellerie de Meysset
Lieu-dit Argentuleau, 24200 Sarlat
📞 05 53 59 08 29 Fax 05 53 28 47 61
English spoken
Closed 10 Oct-11 Apr
Hostellerie, with restaurant, set in parkland 2 km north of Sarlat. Take D47 towards Périguex.

26 bedrs, all ensuite, ⋔ P 35 **DB** 320-490 **B** 50 ✕ 98-250 **CC** MC Visa Amex ▸ ♫ 🖾 ⵗ
RƎC 10 %

★★★ Hôtel Edward 1er
5 rue St-Pierre, 24540 Monpazier
📞 05 53 22 44 00 Fax 05 53 22 53 99
English spoken
Closed 1 Nov-31 Mar

Situated in the heart of Monpazier, one of Europe's oldest walled towns, this restored château offers all modern comforts and lots of character. Set in a region steeped in history.

13 bedrs, all ensuite, ⋔ P 10 **DB** 500-1,000 **B** 65 **CC** MC Visa Amex ⇶ ▸ 20km 🖾 🖾 ✍ ♿
RƎC 10 %

★★★ Hôtel La Madeleine
1 place Petite Rigaudie, 24200 Sarlat-la-Canéda
📞 05 53 59 10 41 Fax 05 53 31 03 62
English spoken
Closed 1 Jan-15 Feb
La Madeleine is situated on the edge of the medieval city. Built in 1840, it is the oldest one in Sarlat but also the best equiped. Entirely refurbished in 1997.

29 bedrs, all ensuite, ⋔ P **DB** 350-405 **B** 46 ✕ 105-195 **CC** MC Visa Amex ▸ 8km ♫ 🖾 ⵗ ✍ ♿

★★★ Hôtel de Selves
93 av de Selves, 24200 Sarlat-la-Canéda
📞 05 53 31 50 00 Fax 05 53 31 23 52
English spoken
Closed 4 Jan-5 Feb
A very comfortable, modern hotel with a lovely garden, satellite television, air-conditioning and sauna. Only 200 m from the old town.

40 bedrs, all ensuite, ⋔ P 15 **DB** 450-570 **B** 50 No restaurant **CC** MC Visa Amex 🖾 ⇶ 🖾 ▸ 6km 🖾 ⵗ ✍ ♿
RƎC 10 %

SORGES Dordogne   4B

★★★ **Hôtel de la Mairie**
Auberge de la Truffe, 24420 Sorges
☎ 05 53 05 02 05 Fax 05 53 05 39 27
English spoken

*This family-run hotel, with a comfortable restaurant
offering local specialities plus classic and modern
cuisine, is on the N21 between Périgueux and
Thiviers. Sorges is in the centre of the foie gras and
truffles area.*

26 bedrs, all ensuite, **P** **DB** 240-300 **B** 35 ✗ 80-260 **CC**
MC Visa Amex ⃛ ► 20km 🖬 ⊠ ⅲ ⅋
RAC **10 %**

VERTEILLAC Dordogne   4B

★★★ **Hostellerie Le Aiguillons**
St-Martial-Viveyrols, 24320 Verteillac
☎ 05 53 91 07 55 Fax 05 53 90 40 97
English spoken
Closed 15 Dec-1 Feb

*A small, family-run hotel offering luxurious
accommodation and an elegant restaurant with
seasonal menus; meals can be served on the terrace
in fine weather.* ✓

8 bedrs, all ensuite, ⊬ **P** 20 **DB** 275-450 **B** 45 ✗ 120-
250 **CC** MC Visa ⃛ ► ⊠ 🖬 ⊠ ⅲ ⅋
RAC **10 %**

VIEUX-MAREUIL Dordogne   4B

★★★ **Hôtel L'Etang Bleu**
24340 Vieux-Mareuil
☎ 05 53 60 92 63 Fax 05 53 56 33 20
English spoken
*A lakeside hotel, offering traditional rustic French
furnishings and regional cuisine, set in extensive
wooded grounds. On the D93, 2 km away from
Vieux-Mareuil.*

11 bedrs, all ensuite, ⊬ **P** **DB** 250-320 **B** 40 ✗ 90-170
CC MC Visa ► 🖬 ⊠ ⅲ
RAC **10 %**

VILLENEUVE-SUR-LOT Lot et Garonne   4D

★★ **Hôtel La Résidence**
17 av Lazare Carnot, 47300 Villeneuve-sur-Lot
☎ 05 53 40 17 03 Fax 05 53 01 57 34
English spoken
Closed 27 Dec-5 Jan
*A quiet, comfortable hotel, with a nice patio and a
lovely garden, close to the town centre.*

18 bedrs, 13 ensuite, ⊬ **P** 10 **DB** 125-285 **B** 28 No
restaurant **CC** MC Visa ► 10km 🖬 ⊠ ⅋

★★★ **Hôtel du Golf**
à Castelnaud-de-Gratecambe, 47290 Villeneuve-sur-
Lot
☎ 05 53 01 60 19 Fax 05 53 01 78 99
English spoken

*The hotel is surrounded by a 75 hectare park. 12 km
north of Villeneuve-sur-Lot towards Bergerac.
Restaurant La Menuisiée offers good quality food.*

38 bedrs, all ensuite, ⊬ **P** 200 **DB** 380-470 **B** 45 ✗ 95-
150 **CC** MC Visa Amex ⃛ ⊡ ► ⊠ 🖬 ⊠ ⅲ ⅋
RAC **10 %**
See advert on next page

VILLEREAL Lot et Garonne   4D

★★ Hôtel du Lac
Route de Bergerac, 47210 Villeréal
☎ **05 53 36 01 39 Fax 05 53 36 36 94**
English spoken
Closed 5 Jan-5 Feb

*A nice, quiet hotel, offering comfortable ensuite
rooms, situated between 13th century farm houses.
Splendid location for walking and cycling tours.*

28 bedrs, all ensuite, ⊮ **P** 30 **DB** 260 **B** 35 ✕ 60 **CC**
MC Visa ⅔ ▸ ▨ ▨ ▨ ⇪ ⌀
RAC 10 % except May-Sept

Midi-Pyrénées

Rocamadour

Gourdon

46
Lot

Figeac

Espalion

Sévérac-
le-Château

12

Cahors

Villefranche-
de-Rouergue

Rodez

Aveyron

Caussade

Millau

Moissac

82

Laguépie

Parc des
Grands-Causses

A75

Condom

Castelsarrasin

Montauban

Albi

St-Affrique

Lectoure

Tarn-et-
Garonne

Gaillac

A62

32

A68

81

Réalmont

Aire-sur-l'Adour

Gers

Auch

l'Isle-
Jourdain

Graulhet

Tarn

Castres

Parc du
Haut Languedoc

Toulouse

Mazamet

Muret

A61

31

Carbonne

Haut-Garonne

Tarbes

Lannemezan

Pamiers

Lourdes

65

A64

St-
Gaudens

09

Argelès-
Gazost

Bagnères-
de-Bigorre

St-Girons

Foix

Hautes-
Pyrénées

Ariège

Cauterets Parc des Pyrénées
Occidentales

Bagnères-
de-Luchon

Ax-les-Thermes

PARIS

TOULOUSE
MIDI
PYRENEES
C O M I T E
REGIONAL
DU TOURISME

Midi-Pyrénées is appropriately named after the midday sun and the mountains which distinguish the region.

Stretching from the Spanish border to the Dordogne and Corrèze, Midi-Pyrénées is both enormous and enormously varied.

All roads will eventually lead to **Toulouse**, the capital of Midi-Pyrénées and France's fourth largest city.

A university with 100,000 students and a reputation for being one of the foremost centres of high-technology industry in Europe have given Toulouse a cutting edge and an appealing cultural vigour.

The most obvious example of that hi-tech industry is Aerospatiale and the Clement Ader Factory. Here, in the largest production space in Europe, the highly successful Airbus A330 and A340 aircraft are manufactured. Airbus has become the world's second most successful manufacturer of civil aircraft.

Toulouse is also a centre for European space research. Visit the fascinating Space City (Cité de l'Espace) which features: a full-scale model of the Arianne V launcher; a planetarium; a massive and fully interactive space exhibition; simulators and various items which have actually been brought back to Earth from space. The monumental Capitole (now the City Hall) is the central feature of Toulouse. Head here for the cultural and political heart of the city. A short walk from the Capitole in any direction will take you to great restaurants, lively cafés and great boutiques.

North east of Toulouse lies **Albi**, a town which has been made famous by Catharism, an extraordinary cathedral and Toulouse-Lautrec.

The Sainte-Cécile Cathedral is, to some, a masterpiece of Gothic giganticism. Certainly it is enormous – it is visible for miles around. Some would say that it is also fortress-like and forbidding. From a distance, the great cathedral looks more like a power station than a place of worship.

Albi's most famous son is the painter Toulouse-Lautrec. He has been well-remembered by his home town; the Palais de la Berbie now hosts the world's largest collection of the man's work.

Page 251: View over the town of Rocamadour
Above: The Pont de St Pierre at Toulouse

Continuing north east towards the Auvergne, one reaches **Rodez** – capital of the Aveyron département. A thirteenth century sandstone cathedral dominates the town, which sits balanced on a hilltop. The views from here are lovely, as lush forest blankets the surrounding peaks.

Despite having a population of 50,000, Rodez has managed to maintain its old world charm. This is thanks largely to an ambitious scheme of pedestrianisation in the Vieille Ville.

West of Rodez, on the Aquitaine side of Midi-Pyrénées, **Cahors** attracts travellers to its impressive architectural inheritance. The star of the show is the Pont Valentré, a fourteenth-century fortified bridge, which is one of the finest bridges in Europe.

Other architectural treats include: the Tower of Pope John XXII (who was born here); the Arc de Diane, which is all that remains of a Gallo-Roman thermal complex; and Saint-Etienne Cathedral.

The area around Cahors is well-known for wine-making. Some vineyards will allow visitors and even offer wine tastings. Try to talk your way into a smaller establishment to increase your chances of some quality time with the wine-makers themselves.

Montauban, south of Cahors, is another attractive medieval stronghold. The whole town enjoys a sort of permanent glow, created by a combination of the seemingly endless sunshine and the fact that the local stone is a reddish colour.

Visit the well-presented Musée Ingres, which is housed in the seventeenth-century former Bishop's Palace, and the medieval Saint-Jacques bell tower.

The Montauban area is perhaps best known for the ingenious Pente d'Eau 'water slope' at nearby **Montech**. This remarkable device allows boats to bypass five locks on the Canal Latéral.

Between Montauban and Lourdes, **Auch** (pronounced 'osh' rather than 'ouch') still draws visitors on the tenuous grounds that it was the home town of d'Artagnan, the legendary musketeer.

The locals have little to show for their hero's exploits – except a triumphant statue of the man. Auch is a pleasant town anyway, and you don't really need an excuse to spend some time wandering among the old streets and buildings.

There is, however, one problem: 370 steps stand between the lower and the upper town. They can be quite tiring!

Lourdes could easily have been a similarly attractive, but unexceptional, town, but it isn't. In 1858, a 14-year-old girl, Bernadette Soubirous, claimed to have seen a vision of the Virgin Mary – the first of eighteen such encounters.

Now some six million Catholics make the pilgrimage to Lourdes every year.

Most visitors head either for the grotto where Bernadette saw Mary, or to the church above it. Lourdes is believed by many pilgrims to possess a curative power, and you will see people leaving gifts in the hope of divine treatment for their particular ailment.

There is little to see or do here that does not involve religion. The Musée Pyrénéen, located in an interesting old château, is the only diversion on offer.

A better castle can be found at **Foix** in south-east Midi-Pyrénées. Built from the eleventh to the fifteenth centuries, the castle of the famous Counts of Foix has no uniform style, but is consistently attractive.

Above: Lourdes is utterly devoted to the miracle 'industry'

From here, the Counts of Foix ruled over a Pyrénéen mini-state until one of them became Henri IV of France. In 1609, Henri annexed the château to the crown.

Foix is strongly medieval and in parts of the town one could quite easily believe the place hasn't changed at all since the sixteenth century. This is especially true during the Medieval Festival, which is held once a year and which sees the entire town step back in time.

Not far from Foix, the pretty Pyrénéen town of **Tarascon-sur-Ariège** serves as a delightful base from which to explore the remarkable prehistoric cave paintings which have been discovered all around this area. Another nearby treat is the castle at **Montségur**. This is a magnificent spectacle, almost – but not quite – a European Machu Picchu, but it has a terrible history. It became the symbol of the southern French Counts' resistance against the northern French army which was led by Simon de Montfort. After a 10-month siege, the castle fell to Montfort. Some 200 Cathars, who refused to renounce their religion, were burnt to death here.

Above: Jacobin – a church with museum

What to do in Midi-Pyrénées

- Get 'hands on' at the amazing exhibition in Space City, Toulouse.
- See the world's largest collection of Toulouse-Lautrec's paintings in the artist's home town of Albi.
- Traverse the magnificent Pont Valentré in Cahors – Europe's best example of a fortified medieval bridge.
- Enjoy the medieval splendour of Foix, once the capital of a Pyrénéen mini-state.

Getting there

By road

Main routes through Midi Pyrénées:
- A64 to Tarbes and Bayonne
- A61 to Lyon and Montpellier
- A68 to Albi and Rodez
- A62 to Paris and Bordeaux

By rail

By TGV:
- Paris Gare Montparnasse to Toulouse takes 5 hours
- Paris Gare Montparnasse to Tarbes takes 5 hours 50 mins
- Paris Gare Montparnasse to Montauban takes 4 hours 35 mins
- Paris Gare Montparnasse to Lourdes takes 5 hours 22 mins

By air

Toulouse-Blagnac International Airport (☎ 5 61 42 44 00, Fax: 5 61 42 45 20) is 6 miles north-west of Toulouse. Get into Toulouse by taxi (☎ 5 61 30 02 54) or bus (☎ 5 61 30 04 89). For car hire try:
- Ada ☎ 5 61 30 00 33
- Avis ☎ 5 61 30 04 94
- Budget ☎ 5 61 71 85 80

TOURIST INFORMATION

- **Midi-Pyrénées Tourist Office**
  54 boulevard de l'Embouchure
  BP 2166, 31022 Toulouse
  ☎ 5 61 13 55 55

AGUESSAC Aveyron   5C

★★ Hôtel Le Rascalat
RN 9, 12520 Aguessac
☎ 05 65 59 80 43 Fax 05 65 59 73 90
English spoken
Closed 25 Dec-15 Mar

Situated at the gateway to the Tarn Gorges, this hotel-restaurant is set back from N9.

18 bedrs, 16 ensuite, ⚓ P 40 DB 190-350 B 35 ✕ 98-160 ℂℂ MC Visa ⤳ 🖪 🖾 ♫

ALBI Tarn   5C

★★ Hôtel Lapérouse
21 place de la Lapérouse, 81000 Albi
☎ 05 63 54 69 22 Fax 05 63 38 03 69
English spoken
A characteristic family hotel with garden, close to the old quarter and cathedral in the heart of Albi.

24 bedrs, 22 ensuite, ⚓ P DB 200-320 B 30 ℂℂ MC Visa Amex ⤳ ► 2km 🖾

★★★ Hôtel Mercure Albi Bastides
41 rue Porta, 81000 Albi
☎ 05 63 47 66 66 Fax 05 63 46 18 40
English spoken

In the listed walls of a 1770 mill, and on the banks of the River Tarn, this hotel faces the Sainte-Cécile cathedral and the Toulouse-Lautrec museum. The restaurant specialises in regional dishes and has a terrace.

56 bedrs, all ensuite, ⚓ P 40 DB 350-530 B 55 ✕ 100-150 ℂℂ MC Visa Amex ► 2km 🖪 🖾 ⚎ ♫ ♿

ARGELES-GAZOST Hautes Pyrénées   4D

★★ Au Primerose Hôtel-Restaurant
23 rue de l'Yser, 65400 Argelès-Gazost
☎ 05 62 97 06 72 Fax 05 62 97 23 08
English spoken
Closed 15 Apr-15 Oct

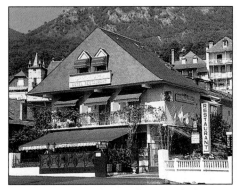

A logis de France hotel situated opposite the large Casino d'Argelès Park, it is located between Lourdes and Gavarnie on the 'Route des Grands Cols du Tour de France'.

26 bedrs, all ensuite, ⚓ P DB 260-300 B 30 ✕ 80-150 ℂℂ MC Visa ► 🖪 🖾 ⚎
RAC 10 % on room rate except in Aug

ARREAU Hautes Pyrénées   4D

★★ Hôtel d'Angleterre
rte Luchon, 65240 Arreau
☎ 05 62 98 63 30 Fax 05 62 98 69 66
English spoken
In the heart of the Aure and Louron valleys, the pretty village of Arreau is full of character. This Logis de France hotel is a former staging post and offers charm and comfort. Take D618 towards the Col de Peyresourde-Aspin.

24 bedrs, all ensuite, P DB 260-350 B 38 ✕ 78-195 ℂℂ MC Visa ► 25km 🖪 🖾 ⚎ ♫

BAGNERES-DE-BIGORRE Hautes Pyrénées   4D

★★ Hostellerie d'Asté
D935, Asté, 65200 Bagnères-de-Bigorre
☎ 05 62 91 74 27 Fax 05 62 91 76 74
English spoken
Closed 12 Nov-15 Dec
The hotel has a large garden and stands on a riverbank, 3 km from Bagnères-de-Bigorre towards the Col de Tourmalet. Free shuttle service to/from ski station.

22 bedrs, 17 ensuite, P 50 DB 198-460 B 37 ✕ 79-199 ℂℂ MC Visa Amex ► 6km 🖾 🖪 🖾 ⚎ ♫

★★ Le Chalet-Hôtel
65710 Ste-Marie-de-Campan
☎ 05 62 91 85 64 Fax 05 62 91 86 17
English spoken
Closed Nov

Super location beside the Aspin and Tourmalet passes, at the foot of the Pic du Midi de Bigorre. Very comfortable with excellent facilities. (Flats and bungalows are also available). Ste-Marie is 10 km south of Bagnères-de-Bigorre, in the Vallée de Campan.

24 bedrs, 17 ensuite, ♂ P DB 200-280 B 30 ✕ 65-130 ⚄ MC Visa Amex ▣ ♗ ⊞ ▸ 10km ▨ ▣ ▨ ⊞ ♪ ♿
RAC 2 %

BAGNERES-DE-LUCHON Haute Garonne   4D

Hôtel Jardin des Cascades
Montauban-de-Luchon, 31110 Luchon
☎ 05 61 79 83 09 Fax 05 61 79 83 09
A hotel restaurant with panoramic views plus traditional and gourmet cuisine. 1.5 km from Luchon. After the archway, walk 200 m.

10 bedrs, 6 ensuite, P DB 190-220 B 35 ✕ 120-160 ▸ ▨

BARBOTAN-LES-THERMES Gers   4D

★★ Hôtel Cante Grit
32150 Barbotan-les-Thermes
☎ 05 62 69 52 12 Fax 05 62 69 53 98
Closed 1 Nov-5 Apr

Opposite the thermal park, a charming country house with a large terrace overlooking a fine garden. A quiet location away from traffic but only 100 m from

the village centre. Traditional and regional cuisine includes foie gras, magret de canard.

21 bedrs, 16 ensuite, ♂ P 20 DB 260-300 B 35 ✕ 85-100 ⚄ MC Visa Amex ▸ 15km ▣ ▨

BROUSSE-LE-CHATEAU Aveyron   5C

★★ Le Relays du Chasteau
12480 Brousse-le-Château
☎ 05 65 99 40 15 Fax 05 65 99 40 15
English spoken
Closed 20 Dec-20 Jan
In one of the nicest villages of France, with a fortified castle, angling, swimming and hiking in the Tarn Valley. D902 between Albi and Millau. Restaurant specialities include truite, foie gras and magret.

12 bedrs, all ensuite, ♂ P 10 DB 210-270 B 30 ✕ 78-185 ⚄ MC Visa ▣ ▨ ♪

CABRERETS Lot   5C

★★ Hôtel Les Falaises
Bouziès, 46330 Cabrerets
☎ 05 65 31 26 83 Fax 05 65 30 23 87
English spoken
Bouziès is a small village on the banks of the River Lot, 27 km from historic Cahors. The restaurant offers regional dishes and good wines.

39 bedrs, all ensuite, P DB 255-355 B 42 ✕ 82-230 ⚄ MC Visa Amex ♗ ▸ ▣ ▨ ⊞
RAC 10 % on room rate

CAHORS Lot   4D

★★★ Hôtel Terminus
5 av Charles de Freycinet, 46000 Cahors
☎ 05 65 35 24 50 Fax 05 65 22 06 40
English spoken

A 1925 hotel, close to the station and town centre. Entirely renovated, it offers comfortable rooms that are individually decorated and a gourmet restaurant.

22 bedrs, all ensuite, P 12 DB 300-900 B 40-60 ✕ 150-340 ⚄ MC Visa Amex ▸ 20km ▨ ▣ ⊞ ♪
RAC 5 %

CARENNAC Lot   5A7

★★ Hôtel Fenelon
46110 Carennac
☎ 05 65 10 96 46 Fax 05 65 10 94 86
Closed 8 Jan-10 Mar

A charming, comfortable hostelry located in the centre of picturesque Carennac, overlooking the River Dordogne. Carennac is about 15 km east of St-Céré, on the D30.

15 bedrs, all ensuite, ⅓ P 15 DB 260-340 B 45 ✕ 95-280 ⅓ ▣

CASTERA-VERDUZAN Gers   4D

★★ Hôtel Tenarèze
32140 Castera-Verduzan
☎ 05 62 68 10 22 Fax 05 62 68 14 69
English spoken
Closed 1 Nov-31 Mar
Set 300 m from a lake with lifeguards, this hotel is the starting point for several day trips. There are two restaurants in town. On D930 halfway between Auch and Condom.

24 bedrs, all ensuite, ⅓ P 12 ℂℂ MC Visa Amex ▣ ▣ ▦ ♫
RAC 5 %

CASTILLON-EN-COUSERANS Ariège   4D

★ Auberge d'Audressein
route Luchon, 09800 Castillon-en-Couserans
☎ 05 61 96 11 80 Fax 05 61 96 82 96
English spoken
Closed 15 Nov-15 Feb
A country inn where you will find regional and gourmet cuisine, a warm, friendly atmosphere and modest rooms with modern comfort.

9 bedrs, 6 ensuite, ⅓ P 6 DB 110-240 B 35 ✕ 80-250 ℂℂ MC Visa ▣ ▣ ▦ ♿

CORDES Tarn   5C

★★ Hostellerie du Parc
rte de Caussade, Les Cabannes, 81170 Cordes
☎ 05 63 56 02 59 Fax 05 63 56 18 03

English spoken
The hostellerie consists of 17 rooms on an island of charm and greenery. Claude Izar offers you delicious south-west dishes. There is a terrace and shaded park available.

17 bedrs, all ensuite, ⅓ P 10 DB 290-440 B 35 ✕ 130-220 ℂℂ MC Visa ⅓ ▣ ▣ ▦
RAC 10 %

EAUZE Gers   4D

Auberge de Guinlet
32800 Eauze
☎ 05 62 09 85 99 Fax 05 62 09 84 50
English spoken
The accommodation consists of bungalows sleeping 4-5 people costing at 1000FF to 2100FF per week depending on the season. Special price 'Green Fees' are available for hotel and bungalow residents. From Eauze take D43, signposted itinerary.

7 bedrs, all ensuite, P 80 DB 240 B 27 ✕ 60-145 ℂℂ MC Visa ⅓ ▣ ▣ ▣ ▣ ♫ ♿

ENTRAYGUES-SUR-TRUYERE Aveyron   5C

★★ Hôtel des Deux Vallées
Avenue du Pont de Truyère, 12140 Entraygues-sur-Truyère
☎ 05 65 44 52 15
Closed Feb
Set in restful surroundings in the Rouergue region with the wild valleys of the Lot and Truyère rivers. From Aurillac, south on the D920 to Entraygues (50 km). Good traditional cuisine is served in a rustic dining room.

16 bedrs, all ensuite, P DB 180-200 B 30 ✕ 70-150

FIGEAC Lot   5C

★★★★ Château du Viguier du Roy
52 rue Droite, 46100 Figeac
☎ 05 65 50 05 05 Fax 05 65 50 06 06
English spoken
Closed 15 Nov-27 Mar

In the heart of the medieval city, a 12-13th century prestigious historic building with original wall panelling, stylish furniture, jacuzzi, tea room, bar, gastronomic restaurant, cloisters and gardens in which to enjoy the calm.

16 bedrs, all ensuite, **↑ P** 20 **DB** 580-1,250 **B** 75 **✕** 130-195 **CC** MC Visa Amex ⨶ ▸ 39km ▦ ▨ ▨ 1km ▥ ✿ ♿

GAVARNIE Hautes Pyrénées   4D

★★ Hôtel Le Marboré
65120 Gavarnie
☎ 05 62 92 40 40 Fax 05 62 92 40 30
English spoken

'n the heart of the Pyrénées National Park, a quiet, Logis de France hotel near the ski slopes. Group discounts for parties of 6 or more. Gavarnie is on D921 south of Gedre. Also a member of the Association of People who like Food in the Pyrénées.

?4 bedrs, all ensuite, **↑ P DB** 260-275 **B** 32 **✕** 96-190 **✕C** MC Visa Amex ⨶ ▨ ▨ ▨ ▨ ▥ ✿ ♿

★★★ Hôtel Vignemale
BP 2, 65120 Gavarnie
☎ 05 62 92 40 00 Fax 05 62 92 40 08
English spoken
Closed 1 Nov-1 Apr
An impressive, newly restored, stone-built hotel in the heart of the Pyrénées National Park. Restaurant offers speciality cuisine. River and pine forest nearby. Close to the Spanish border, 49 km south of Lourdes.
?4 bedrs, all ensuite, **P DB** 490-1,200 **B** 48-58 **✕** 130-50 **CC** MC Visa Amex ▨ ▨ ▨ ▥ ✿ ♿
RAC 10 %

GRAMAT Lot   5A

★★★ Hôtel Le Lion d'Or
place de la République, 46500 Gramat
☎ 05 65 38 73 18 Fax 05 65 38 84 50
English spoken
Closed 16 Dec-15 Jan
This characteristic, ancient residence has a facade of local stone and the interior, featuring a 15th century fireplace, has been updated to provide modern,

functional accommodation. Set back from the main square with a shady terrace and lots of parking.

15 bedrs, all ensuite, **↑ P DB** 330-420 **B** 50 **✕** 100-300 **CC** MC Visa Amex ▸ 20km ▨ ▥ ▥ ✿

★★ Hôtel Le Relais des Gourmands
Avenue de la Gare, 46500 Gramat
☎ 05 65 38 83 92 Fax 05 65 38 70 99
English spoken
A pleasant hotel complex, slightly off the beaten track. Light, comfortable rooms with some lovely views over the gardens and pool area. Refined, imaginative and regional cuisine and an excellent cellar. Gramat is on A140.

16 bedrs, all ensuite, **↑ P** 15 **DB** 280-350 **B** 45 **✕** 85-225 **CC** MC Visa ⨶ ▸ 20km ▨ ▥ ▥ ✿

LABASTIDE-MURAT Lot   4D

★★ Hôtel Climat de France
place de la Mairie, 46240 Labastide-Murat
☎ 05 65 21 18 80 Fax 05 65 21 10 97
English spoken
Closed 15 Jan-15 Dec
An old castle built in 1261, now completely renovated but still retaining its special charm. From the N20 take the D667 to Labastide-Murat. The restaurant offers regional specialities and buffet.

20 bedrs, all ensuite, **↑ P** 100 **DB** 305-340 **B** 35 **✕** 65-135 **CC** MC Visa Amex ▸ 3km ▦ ▨ ▥ ▥ ✿ ♿
RAC 10 % on room rate

LACAUNE Tarn   5C

★★★ Hôtel Fusiès
Rue de la République, 81230 Lacaune-les-Bains
☎ 05 63 37 02 03 Fax 05 63 37 10 98
An old house with modern comfort, 50 rooms, swimming pool, tennis court. 400 m from the casino (slot machines, discotheque, karaoke). Set in a tourist region with lakes and forests.

52 bedrs, all ensuite, **↑ P** 20 **DB** 250-320 **B** 45 **✕** 80-350 **CC** MC Visa Amex ▸ 45km ▨ ▥ ▥ ✿ ♿
RAC 10 %

Time
French Summer Time starts at 2am on the last Sunday of March and ends at 3am on the last Sunday of October.
France is, therefore, always one hour ahead of Britain.

LAVAUR Tarn　　　　　　　　　5C

Hôtel L'Echauguette
81500 Giroussens
☏ 05 63 41 63 65 Fax 05 63 41 63 13
English spoken
A recommended hotel, with a typical country restaurant with fine views, set in a charming village 10 km north of Lavaur. Take the D87, then left onto the D631. Or from A68 motorway between Albi and Toulouse, exit 7 and turn south.

5 bedrs, 3 ensuite, ⚡ P DB 160-270 B 27 ✗ 120-270
CC MC Visa Amex ▸ 10km ▣ ▣
RAC 5 %

LOURDES Hautes Pyrénées　　　　4D

★★★ Hôtel Beauséjour
16 av de la Gare, 65100 Lourdes
☏ 05 62 94 38 18 Fax 05 62 94 96 20
English spoken

A charming, town centre, hotel with a superb view of the Pyrénées, completely refurbished in 1997 to a high standard of comfort. 10 minutes walk from the sanctuaries. Shaded park. Free private parking.

42 bedrs, all ensuite, ⚡ P 25 DB 248-418 B 32 ✗ 55-120 CC MC Visa Amex ▸ ▣ ▣ ⋕ ♪ ♿
RAC 5 % except Aug-Sep

★★★ Hôtel Christina
42 av Peyramale, 65100 Lourdes
☏ 05 62 94 26 11 Fax 05 62 94 97 09
English spoken
Closed 15 Nov-24 Mar
Large, modern hotel only 5 minutes walk from the sanctuaries. All soundproofed rooms with TV and a view of Japanese garden or the mountain. 2 restaurants with good choice of menus and à la carte, plus terrace, boutiques and a play room for children.

210 bedrs, all ensuite, ⚡ P 40 DB 390-420 B included ✗ 110-130 CC MC Visa Amex ▣ ▣ ▸ 3km ▣ ▣ ▣
⋕ ♪ ♿
RAC 5 % with 3 nights stay

★★ Hôtel Le Miramont
Route de Lourdes, 65380 Orincles
☏ 05 62 45 41 02 Fax 05 62 45 47 25
English spoken

Small hotel set in attractive grounds. Go east on D937, then 8 km from Lourdes turn left onto D7 to Orincles.

10 bedrs, 9 ensuite, ⚡ P 15 DB 220-245 B 29 CC MC Visa ⌇ ▸ 8km ▣ ▣ ⋕ ♪
RAC 10 %

★★★ Hôtel Le Relais de Saux
Saux, 65100 Lourdes
☏ 05 62 94 29 61 Fax 05 62 42 12 64
English spoken
A quiet, charming hotel, with a shaded terrace, a park facing the Pyrénées and a highly recommended restaurant using the freshest produce from the local market. North east of Lourdes on the N21 towards Tarbes.

7 bedrs, all ensuite, P DB 350-590 B 45 ✗ 140-310 CC MC Visa Amex ▸ 3km ▣
RAC 5 %

MARTEL Lot　　　　　　　　　5A

★ Hôtel de la Bonne Famille
Sarrazac, 46600 Martel
☏ 05 65 37 70 38 Fax 05 65 37 74 01
English spoken
Run by the same family for three generations, this simple, unpretentious hotel is located in a small countryside village with several interesting sights. The pretty restaurant offers a range of good food including local specialities.

24 bedrs, 6 ensuite, ⚡ P DB 145-245 B 35 ✗ 75-165 CC MC Visa ⌇ ▸ 20km ▣ ▣ ▣ ♪

MILLAU Aveyron　　　　　　　5C

★★★ Grand Hôtel de la Muse et du Rozier
12720 Peyreleau
☏ 05 65 62 60 01 Fax 05 65 62 63 88
English spoken
Closed 5 Nov-15 Mar

A hotel with dreamlike architecture, situated in the heart of the Gorges du Tarn, offers swimming, canoeing and a garden on the Tarn river bank. Take D907 north from Millau and turn off at Rozier.

38 bedrs, all ensuite, ♂ **P** 40 **DB** 410-650 **B** 65 ✕ 95-220 **((** MC Visa Amex ⊰ ⊦ ▣ ▣ ▣ ⊞ ⋒

★★ Hôtel Cévenol
115 rue du Rajol, 12100 Millau
☎ **05 65 60 74 44 Fax 05 65 60 85 99**
English spoken
Closed Dec-Feb

A highly recommended, modern hotel with a warm atmosphere, lovely views and a restaurant with speciality cuisine and a most attractive dining room. 500 m from the town centre towards Montpellier-le-Vieux.

42 bedrs, all ensuite, ♂ **P** 42 **DB** 299-320 **B** 37-52 ✕ 97-139 **((** MC Visa ⊰ ⊦ 40km ▣ ▣ ⊞ ⅋

MONTAUBAN Tarn et Garonne 4D

★ Hôtel du Commerce
9 place Franklin Roosevelt, 82000 Montauban
☎ **05 63 66 31 32 Fax 05 63 03 18 46**
English spoken

A quiet, comfortable, period hotel opposite the cathedral in the heart of the pinkest of the three 'pink' towns. A warm 'midi' welcome, modern comfort and all the charm (and prices) of bygone days await you in this oasis of calm.

28 bedrs, 16 ensuite, ♂ **P** 60 **DB** 140-310 **B** 25-35 No restaurant **((** MC Visa Amex ⊦ 10km ▣ ▣ ⊞ ⅋
RAC 10 % on room rate

MUR-DE-BARREZ Aveyron 5A

★★ Auberge de Barrez
av du Carladez, 12600 Mur-de-Barrez
☎ **05 65 66 00 76 Fax 05 65 66 07 98**
English spoken
Closed Jan

A modern, fully facilitated hotel, with a garden and a restaurant offering local specialities, set amidst rugged scenery close to the Barrage de Sarrans.

18 bedrs, all ensuite, ♂ **P** 25 **DB** 240-480 **B** 37 ✕ 65-195 **((** MC Visa Amex ⊦ 25km ▣ ▣ ⊞ ⅋ ⅋
RAC 5 % except Jul-Aug

NAJAC Aveyron 5C

★★ Hôtel L'Oustal del Barry
Place du Bourg, 12270 Najac
☎ **05 65 29 74 32 Fax 05 65 29 75 32**
English spoken
Closed Nov-Mar

A country house-hotel near Rouergue, with creative and country inspired cuisine, situated in one of the nicest French villages. Leisure activities organised by the hotel include mountain biking, a guided tour of the chateau, swimming and tennis.

20 bedrs, 17 ensuite, ♂ **P** 12 **DB** 300-370 **B** 48 ✕ 95-250 **((** MC Visa Amex ▣ ▣ ▣ ⊞ ⅋ ⅋
RAC 5 %

★★ Hôtel Le Belle Rive
Le Roc du Pont, 12270 Najac-en-Rouergue
☎ **05 65 29 73 90 Fax 05 65 29 76 88**
English spoken
Closed 2 Nov-3 April

A delightful, comfortable hotel, with a light and airy gourmet restaurant, in a beautiful setting on the River Aveyron. Rouergue is a small town overlooked by a castle, 2 km from Najac on the D139.

35 bedrs, all ensuite, ♂ **P** 19 **DB** 245-280 **B** 45 ✕ 85-200 **((** MC Visa ⊰ ▣ ▣ ▣
RAC 10 % with stay of 2 nights

NAUCELLE Aveyron 5C

★★ Hôtel du Château
Castelpers, Lédergues, 12170 Requista
☎ 05 65 69 22 61 Fax 05 65 69 25 31
Closed Oct-Apr

An attractive château, with beautiful views and grounds bordered by trout rivers, conveniently situated for forest walks and other attractions such as village festivals. 12 km from Naucelle station, on N88.

8 bedrs, 7 ensuite, ⚲ P 40 DB 300-490 B 45-48 ✕ 145 ₵ MC Visa Amex 🗐 ⊠ ₺
RAC 10 %

PAYRAC Lot 4B

★★ Hôtel Petit Relais
Calès, 46350 Payrac
☎ 05 65 37 96 09 Fax 05 65 37 95 93
English spoken
A small hotel, with a shaded terrace and a modern restaurant, situated in the attractive village of Calès, close to several popular tourist sites including Rocamadour and Sarlat.

15 bedrs, all ensuite, ⚲ P 20 DB 190-340 B 36 ✕ 75-198 ₵ MC Visa ⋛ ▸ 🗐 ⊠ ₺
RAC 5 %

★★ Hôtel de la Paix
N20, 46350 Payrac
☎ 05 65 37 95 15 Fax 05 65 37 90 37
English spoken
Closed 1 Jan-5 Feb

A characterful former staging post completely renovated and comfortably furnished. Almost all the peaceful rooms are situated at the rear of the building. Payrac is 15 km south of Souillac on the N20; hotel is in the centre of the village.

50 bedrs, all ensuite, ⚲ P 25 DB 250-340 B 32 ✕ 75-160 ₵ MC Visa Amex ⋛ 🖾 ▸ 🗟 🗐 ⊠ ▥ ₺

PUY-L'EVEQUE Lot 4D

★★ Hôtel Le Vert
Mauroux, 46700 Puy-l'Evêque
☎ 05 65 36 51 36 Fax 05 65 36 56 84
English spoken
Closed 12 Nov-14 Feb   •
A warm, welcoming hotel, with carefully designed and individually decorated rooms, in a charming 400 years old farmhouse. The village is south of Puy amongst the Cahors vineyards, close to the River Lot.

7 bedrs, all ensuite, ⚲ P 30 DB 290-390 B 38 ✕ 100-165 ₵ MC Visa Amex ⋛ ▸ 15km ⊠

ROCAMADOUR Lot 5A

★★ Hôtel Le Pagès
Route de Payrac, 46350 Calés
☎ 05 65 37 95 87 Fax 05 65 37 91 57
English spoken

A quiet, relaxing, recently renovated hotel, with a restaurant offering regional specialities, situated in the countryside on the outskirts of Calés. Take D673, route de Payrac.

20 bedrs, all ensuite, ⚲ P 25 DB 180-600 B 35-45 ✕ 75-280 ₵ MC Visa ⋛ ▸ 18km 🗐 ⊠ ♪
RAC 10 %

★★ Hôtel Lion d'Or
46500 Rocamadour
☎ 05 65 33 62 04 Fax 05 65 33 72 54
English spoken
Closed 2 Nov-4 Apr

An old building, situated in the heart of this medieval city, with modern amenities and fine views across the canyon. The restaurant offers speciality cuisine including foie gras and confits canard et oie.

35 bedrs, all ensuite, **P** 30 **B** 35 ✕ 60-220 **CC** MC Visa ▸ 20km 🖬 🖾

★★ Hôtel Panoramic
46500 Rocamadour
📞 **05 65 33 63 06 Fax 05 65 33 69 26**
English spoken
Closed 16 Feb-14 Nov
A traditional hotel with wonderful views of historic Rocamandour, and a large, sunny terrace facing the Causses mountains. The restaurant offers speciality cuisine including foie gras, truite and escargots.

20 bedrs, all ensuite, ✝ **P** 30 **DB** 230-290 **B** 37 ✕ 73-250 **CC** MC Visa Amex 🖾 ▸ 🖾 🖾 ⋕ ♿

★★★ Hostellerie de Cèdres
à Villeneuve-des-Rivière, 31800 St-Gaudens
📞 **05 61 89 36 00 Fax 05 61 88 31 04**
English spoken
Closed Dec

A 17th century manor house, with lovely gardens, surrounded by woodland. Just 1 hour from Toulouse and 30 minutes drive from the Spanish border on the N117.

24 bedrs, all ensuite, ✝ **P** 30 **DB** 380-690 **B** 59 ✕ 155-260 **CC** MC Visa Amex ▵ 🖾 ▸ 9km 🖾 🖾 🖾 ⋕
RAC 10 %

★★ Hôtel de la Poste
3 place Charles de Gaulle, 12130 St-Geniez-d'Olt
📞 **05 65 47 43 30 Fax 05 65 47 42 75**
English spoken
A quiet hotel, with a garden-side restaurant offering regional specialities, set in attractive gardens. From Rodez take N88 to Laissac and then D45 to St-Geniez-d'Olt.

50 bedrs, all ensuite, ✝ **P** **DB** 215-285 **B** 35-39 ✕ 62-138 **CC** MC Visa Amex ▵ ▸ 🖾 🖾 🖾 ⋕ ♪
RAC 10 %

★★ Hôtel de la Neste
65170 St-Lary-Soulan
📞 **05 62 39 42 79 Fax 05 62 39 58 77**
English spoken
Closed May, Oct, Nov.
On the banks of the Neste d'Aure river, in this well known winter sports resort. In the Aure valley, at the gateway to Aragon, Spain and the Pyrénées National Park. Opposite the Spa, with a 'Get in shape' package available.

21 bedrs, all ensuite, **P** 24 **DB** 250-340 **B** 37 ✕ 70-160 **CC** MC Visa ▵ ▸ 28km 🖾 🖾 ⋕ ♪ ♿
RAC 5 %

★★★ Hôtel La Vieille Auberge
rue de la Recège, 46200 Souillac
📞 **05 65 32 79 43 Fax 05 65 32 65 19**
English spoken
A comfortable, well-equipped, hotel near a small river. Ideal for individual travellers and popular with groups (some rooms are for groups only). From the N20, take the avenue Jean-Jaurès towards the railway station and turn first left.

19 bedrs, all ensuite, ✝ **P** 12 **DB** 360 **B** 40 ✕ 100-330 **CC** MC Visa Amex 🖾 ▵ 🖾 🖾 ▸ 10km 🖾 🖾 ⋕ ♪

★★ Inter-Hôtel Le Quercy
rue de la Recège, 46200 Souillac
📞 **05 65 37 83 56 Fax 05 65 37 07 22**
English spoken
Closed Jan
A modern B&B hotel, close to town centre with good restaurant next door. Most rooms have balconies. Good base for exploring the region. 35 km from Brive, 70 km from Cahors.

25 bedrs, all ensuite, ✝ **P** 10 **DB** 250-300 **B** 35 No restaurant **CC** MC Visa ▵ ▸ 20km 🖾 🖾
RAC 10 %

TOULOUSE Haute Garonne   4D

★★ Hôtel Albion
28 rue Bachelier, 31000 Toulouse
☎ 05 61 63 60 36 Fax 05 61 62 66 95
English spoken
*A peaceful, modern hotel in the centre of town: 5
minutes from the station and close to the airport
shuttle.*

27 bedrs, all ensuite, ♀ P DB 260-280 B 35 No
restaurant ((MC Visa Amex ⋕ ⋒ &
RAC 10 %

VILLEFRANCHE-DE-LAURAGAIS Haute Garonne

★★ Hôtel de France
106 rue de la République, 31290 Villefranche-de-
Lauragais
☎ 05 61 81 62 17 Fax 05 61 81 66 04
English spoken
Closed 15 Jan-2 Feb & 4-25 Jul
*A 19th century inn with rustic restaurant serving
traditional and regional cuisine; specialities include
cassoulet, confit and foie gras. Easy access to the A61
for Toulouse.*

18 bedrs, 10 ensuite, ♀ P DB 165-185 B 22 ✕ 67-155
((MC Visa Amex 🅺 🖊 🖻 ⋕
RAC 10 %

VILLEFRANCHE-DE-ROUERGUE Aveyron   5C

★★★ Hôtel Relais de Farrou
au Farrou, 12200 Villefranche-de-Rouergue
☎ 05 65 45 18 11 Fax 05 65 45 32 59
English spoken
Closed 23 Oct-3 Nov & 23 Feb-9 Mar

*Formerly a posthouse this, verdantly situated, leisure
hotel is a gourmet stopover with indoor parking and
its own heli-pad. 3 minutes from Villefranche-de-
Rouergue, south of Figéac on D922.*

26 bedrs, all ensuite, ♀ P 35 DB 320-450 B 45 ✕ 85-
222 ((MC Visa ⚡ 🖻 🅱 ▶ ⬛ 🅺 🖊 🖻 ⋕ ⋒ &
RAC 5 %

Languedoc-Roussillon

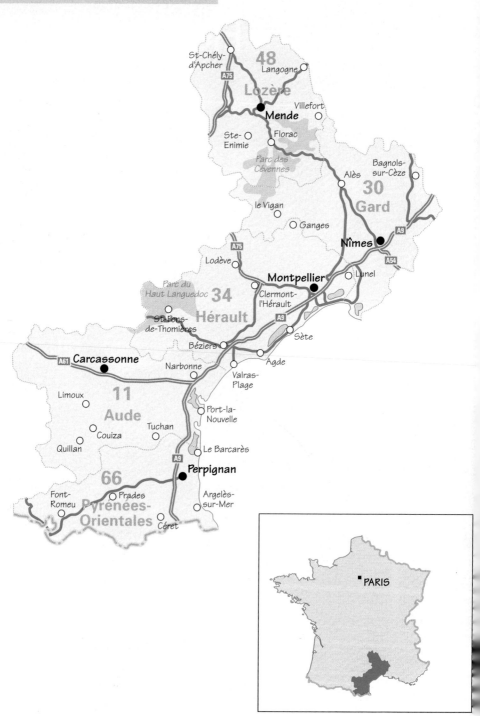

The area where the langue d'Oc (or Occitan language) was once spoken now marks the Languedoc region; albeit much smaller than the original Occitania.

A strong regional identity still persists. The southerly Roussillon area is Catalan, and the locals are keen to highlight their heritage. This is a scenic and sunny part of France, bound by language and framed by the Mediterranean and the Pyrénées.

New arrivals often find themselves in **Nîmes**, the 'Rome of France'. The Romans founded Nemausus on the site of present-day Nîmes, and several buildings from that time remain. The most impressive of these is the Roman arena – one of the best-preserved in the world. It is a versatile building, which has been a theatre for gladiatorial combat, a fort and a poor-house. Now it has reverted to its theatrical role, hosting concerts and bullfights under a new retractable roof.

The Maison Carré is another remarkable Roman legacy. In fact, the 'Maison Carré' is something of a misnomer; it is neither a house nor a square. It is a rectangular temple built in about 20 BC. There are few more impressive temples left from this period, either Roman or Greek, and you would never guess its multifarious past. It has been used for just about every civic function imaginable, from a stable to a town hall. A Roman tower, the Tour Magne, in the immaculate Jardin de la Fontaine offers a stunning vantage point.

Parts of 'old' Nîmes have thankfully now been closed to traffic. One could happily spend hours wandering these archaic and delightful streets.

A rough cotton product called de Nîmes was invented here and sold to the United States, where its name was shortened to 'denim'. The material was first used to clothe slaves but now, of course, it is used to cover the lower extremities of most of the Western World.

Nîmes regularly surprises returning visitors with its rapid pace of change. It has become a fiercely progressive place, which is keen to compete with Montpellier and other commercial centres. For years, the city was held back by a Communist council, which

Page 265: Fortified France – the medieval fortified walls of Carcassonne
Above: Nîmes' first century Roman Ampitheatre

proved inefficient and reactionary. That all changed in 1983, when a new mayor injected some much-needed verve into the city's management.

Uzès makes a great excursion from Nîmes. This elegant town is home to the 'premier duchy in France', the House of Uzès, which still occupies the town's picture-book castle. Heading south, one soon arrives in **Montpellier**, capital of Languedoc-Roussillon and one of the fastest-growing cities in France.

Exciting and vibrant, Montpellier is much more than just a stylish coastal city. Montpellier University is one of the oldest and most respected in Europe. A long list of distinguished alumni includes Nostradamus. Michel de Nostre-Damus studied medicine here in the sixteenth century.

Before penning his own brand of confused, long-winded and – arguably – prophetic poetry, Nostradamus had been one of the most brilliant physicians of his time.

Huge numbers of students still swell the city's population and their effect is as obvious as it is welcome.

Terrace bars, cafés and bistros provide a focus for a rich and youthful cultural scene. This café culture is centred on the wonderful Vieille Ville area.

More stately are the monumental Place de la Comédie and the Opéra, a towering nineteenth century theatre.

The green-fingered might enjoy the Jardin des Plantes, the oldest botanical garden in France.

Beyond Montpellier, a series of resorts capitalises on the expansive sandy beaches which distinguish the Languedoc coast. Not everyone will find this stretch of coast attractive; it is flat and lacks the drama of the Riviera.

Aigues-Mortes is an interesting medieval town which presents quite a sight on the approach. Walled and heavily fortified, the town looks impenetrable.

Above: The place de la Comédie, Montpellier

Louis IX launched his Seventh and Eighth Crusades from here. He died on the Eighth and was later canonised. St Louis' is a much-revered figure in Aigues-Mortes.

Take in the view from the top of the tower on the town's ramparts.

Developers have been hard at work in Languedoc and there are several entirely modern resorts dotted along this westerly expanse of the Mediterranean coast. They include **Port Camargue**, **La Grande-Motte** and **Cap d'Agde**. Each is different in size and style, but they are all purpose-built seaside resorts which, inevitably, lack the authenticity which distinguishes towns such as Aigues-Mortes or Sète.

Sète is a major port – the third largest on the south coast of France – and a centre for commerce. Fishing is a key industry, and this is the main port through which Italian wines are imported into France (to the thinly-disguised chagrin of local wine-makers).

Despite such industrial successes, Sète is the best base from which to explore the surrounding coast and is, in itself, a great place to visit.

The most immediately striking thing about the town is its network of canals, which create a distinctly Venetian feel.

Specific attractions are rather thin on the ground, but the Musée Paul Valéry is worth visiting. The poet was born in Sète and is now buried in the cemetery which inspired his most famous work, *Le Cimetière Marin* (the Cemetery by the Sea).

The view from the cemetery is lovely, and, if you are familiar with the poem, it provides the perfect place to ponder Valéry's musings.

After Sète comes **Béziers**, a town where rugby is the weekly highlight and whose past glories have faded almost completely. The Vieille Ville is attractive, and it makes a spectacular sight from a distance, but there is little reason to spend anymore than a day or even an afternoon here.

Above: Perpignan, an aerial view of the city centre

Likewise, **Narbonne** is attractive enough, but not really a major draw. The wine trade is paramount, and the once proud port has now silted up. The Gothic Cathédrale de St-Just et St-Sauveur is an interesting distraction, as is the horreum (a sort of Roman shopping centre), but there is little else to divert the traveller for long.

A better idea is to move on to **Carcassonne**, one of the most appealing towns in the region due almost entirely to La Cité, the largest medieval fortress in Europe, which towers over the River Aude and the Ville Basse below. At night, when the citadel is floodlit, the effect is quite stunning. This is also a good spot from which to explore the many small, but little-visited, villages which are dotted across the Corbières hills.

The last major town in Roussillon before the Pyrénées is **Perpignan**, the capital of French Catalonia. This city hides a surprising number of interesting buildings and sights within its rather confused and often overlooked mass. The centre of Perpignan is particularly seductive. Here, sophisticated cafés line grand boulevards around place Arago. Perpigan's architecture betrays its past and its proximity to Spain; look out for Spanish details thrown into French designs.

What to do in Languedoc-Roussillon

- Watch opera or a bullfight in the Roman arena in Nîmes – one of the best-preserved in the world.
- Hang out with the lively student population in Montpellier and feel the buzz of this vibrant city.
- Relax in 'Venetian' Sete or visit the cemetery which inspired poet Paul Valéry and where he is now buried.
- Watch the famous Béziers rugby team in action.
- Don't miss the magnificent sight of La Cité at Carcassonne, which is floodlit to stunning effect at night.
- Get lost in the beautiful Corbières hills, where idyllic villages are hidden from the gaze of most visitors.
- Enjoy the beaches at Port Camargue, La Grande-Motte and Cap d'Agde.

Above: From the stylish bistros of Montpellier to the excellent fish restaurants of Sete and the Spanish influence of Perpignan, Languedoc-Roussillon has much to offer food lovers

Festivals in Languedoc-Roussillon

April
- Spring Jazz Festival, Nîmes
- Festival of the Sea, Port Bacarès

June
- Carcassonne Festival, Carcassonne
- Music/Comedy/Dance Festivals, Montpellier

July
- Theatre Festival, Narbonne
- Operetta Festival, Lamalou les Bains
- World Music Festival, La Grande Motte
- Jazz and Comic Book Festival, Chanac

August
- Mediterranean Festival, Hérault
- Folklore Festival, Amélie les Bains

September
- Festival of Photo Journalism, Perpignan

October
- Jazz Festival, Perpignan

TOURIST INFORMATION
- **Languedoc-Roussillon Tourist Office**
  20 rue de la Republique, 34000 Montpellier
  📞 4 67 22 81 00
  Fax: 4 67 58 06 10

Getting there

By road
- A9 Nimes to Perpignan (and Spain) via Narbonne and Montpellier
- A75 Béziers to Clermond-Ferrand via Mende
- A61 Toulouse to Narbonne via Carcassonne

By rail
BY TGV:
- Paris Gare de Lyon to Perpignan takes 5 hours 50 mins
- Paris Gare de Lyon to Nimes takes 3 hours 45 mins
- Paris Gare de Lyon to Narbonne takes 5 hours 20 mins
- Paris Gare de Lyon to Montpellier takes 4 hours 15 mins
- Paris Gare de Lyon to Arles takes 3 hours 45 mins
- Lyon to Montpellier takes 2 hours 35 mins

By air
Montpellier-Méditerranée Airport (📞 4 67 20 85 00, Fax: 4 67 20 03 72) is 4 miles southeast of Montpellier. Get into Montpellier by taxi or 'Les Courriers du Midi' bus. For car hire contact:
- Ada 📞 4 67 20 02 12
- Avis 📞 4 67 20 14 95
- Europcar 📞 4 67 99 82 00

Perpignan-Rivesaltes International Airport (📞 4 68 52 60 70, Fax: 4 68 52 31 03) is 2 miles north of Perpignan. For car hire:
- Ada 📞 4 68 35 69 80
- Europcar 📞 4 68 34 65 03
- Hertz 📞 4 68 51 37 40

AGDE Hérault   5C

★★ Hôtel Azur
18 av Illes d'Amérique, Le Cap d'Agde, 34305 Agde
☎ 04 67 26 98 22 Fax 04 67 26 48 14
English spoken

The hotel is at Cap d'Agde just 400 m from Plage Richelieu, 50 m from the marina and 100 m from the golf course. The restaurant is 50 m from the hotel. Special group discounts available. English satellite television in all rooms. Free private parking.

34 bedrs, all ensuite, ⌖ P DB 250-400 B 35 No restaurant ⅌ MC Visa Amex ⌇ ▣ ▸ ▨ ▣ ⅲ ∅ &

★★★ Hôtel La Tamarissière
lieu-dit La Tamarissière, 34300 Agde
☎ 04 67 94 20 87 Fax 04 67 21 38 40
English spoken
Closed 2 Nov-15 Mar
The hotel overlooks the Hérault estuary and a tiny fishing port. It has pretty bedrooms with balconies and a pretty garden.

27 bedrs, all ensuite, ⌖ P DB 350-610 B 65 ✕ 155-360 ⅌ MC Visa Amex ⌇ ▸ 8km ▨ ▣ 2km ⅲ ∅

AIGUES-MORTES Gard   5D

★★ Hôtel des Croisades
2 rue du Port, 30220 Aigues-Mortes
☎ 04 66 53 67 85 Fax 04 66 53 72 95
English spoken
Closed 15 Nov-15 Dec
The hotel overlooks the fortified town and the port of Aigues-Mortes, with tennis, horse riding and water sports nearby.

14 bedrs, all ensuite, P DB 240-260 B 31-36 No restaurant ⅌ MC Visa ▸ 6km ▨ &

Telephoning the United Kingdom
When telephoning the United Kingdom from France dial 00 44 and omit the initial 0 of the United Kingdom code.

ANIANE Hérault   5C

★★ Hôtel St-Benoit
rte St-Guilhem, 34150 Aniane
☎ 04 67 57 71 63 Fax 04 67 57 47 10
English spoken
Closed 20 Dec-16 Feb

A comfortable hotel set around a large swimming pool, close to the River Hérault. The restaurant specialises in truite, écrevisses and magret de canard.

30 bedrs, all ensuite, ⌖ P 50 DB 275-320 B 35 ✕ 99-170 ⅌ MC Visa ⌇ ▸ 15km ▨ ▣ ⅲ &

ARGELES-SUR-MER Pyrénées Orientales   5C

★★★ Hôtel La Belle Demeure
chemin du Roua, 66700 Argelès-sur-Mer
☎ 04 68 95 85 85 Fax 04 68 95 83 50
English spoken
Closed Nov-Feb

A tastefully restored 17th century mill, between mountains and sea in luxuriant wine country of the Langeudoc-Rousillon. Air-conditioned rooms a lovely mountain view, the vineyards and the gardens. 2 km from the sea. Towards the station with Argelès.

10 bedrs, all ensuite, ⌖ P DB 270-600 B 50 ✕ 120-24 ⅌ MC Visa Amex ⌇ ▣ ▸ 7km ▣ ⅲ &
RAC

BAGNOLS-SUR-CEZE Gard   5D

★★★★ Château de Montcaud

route d'Alès, 30200 Bagnols-sur-Cèze
☎ 04 66 89 60 60 Fax 04 66 89 45 04
English spoken
Closed Jan

Peace and tranquillity characterise this magnificent château, with air-conditioned rooms, set in the heart of a 5 hectare park. An ideal base from which to visit Provence. From Bagnols go towards Alès for 4 km then right towards Donnat.

32 bedrs, all ensuite, ⊨ P DB 790-2,900 B 100 ✕ 145-420 ℂℂ MC Visa Amex ⚑ 🎏 🖾 ▸ 22km 🖾 🖾 🖾 ⋕ ⌀ ⅋
RAC **Upgrading if possible**

Former doctrinaire college, the hotel is a 17th century building in Beaucaire town centre. In the heart of Provence, it is situated 20 km from Nîmes, Avignon, Arles, St-Rémy-de-Provence and Les Baux-de-Provence and 50 km from Saintes-Marie-de-la-Mer.

34 bedrs, all ensuite, ⊨ P DB 330-450 B 40-50 ✕ 98-230 ℂℂ MC Visa ▸ 🖾 🖾 ⋕ ⌀ ⅋

★★★ Hôtel Valaurie

rte de Pont-St-Esprit, 30200 Bagnols-sur-Cèze
☎ 04 66 89 66 22 Fax 04 66 89 55 80
English spoken

CANET-EN-ROUSSILLON Pyrénées Orientales 5C

★★ Hôtel Europa

Avenue des Hauts de Canet, 66140 Canet-en-Roussillon
☎ 04 68 80 51 80 Fax 04 68 80 56 33
English spoken
Closed Christmas

The hotel is situated in a quiet pine forest and offers air-conditioned rooms, bathroom-WC, TV, garage, car park and garden, as well as a terrace with a panoramic view.

22 bedrs, all ensuite, ⊨ P 40 DB 290-310 B 35 (plus à la carte) No restaurant ▸ 🖾 ⅋

BEAUCAIRE Gard   5D

★★★ Hôtel Les Doctrinaires

Quai Général de Gaulle, Angle rue Rabelais, 30300 Beaucaire
☎ 04 66 59 23 70 Fax 04 66 59 22 26
English spoken

Entering Canet Plage beach resort, the Hotel Europa complex welcomes you for a relaxing family holiday. Around its garden and swimming pool, the 76 modern, comfortable, air-conditioned rooms have bath or shower, toilets and colour TV

76 bedrs, all ensuite, ⊨ P 10 DB 270-330 B 45 ✕ 40-150 ℂℂ MC Visa Amex ⚑ ▸ 6km 🖾 🖾 🖾 2km ⋕ ⌀ ⅋
RAC **10 %**
See advert on next page

HOTEL EUROPA

At the entrance of Canet-Plage beach resort, the Hotel Europa complex welcomes you for a relaxing family holiday. Around its gardens and swimming pool, the 76 modern, comfortable, air-conditioned rooms, with bath or shower, WC and colour TV, guarantee you a lazy holiday under the Mediterranean sun. The complex Europa is open all year round. 10 km from Perpignan, 30 km from the Spanish border; at the foot of the Pyrenees and close to the Mediterranean sea.

**RESIDENCE JAMAICA
AVENUE DES HAUTS DE CANET
66141 CANET EN ROUSSILLON
TEL: 04 68 80 51 80
FAX: 04 68 80 56 33**

CARCASSONNE Aude   5C

★★★ Hôtel Donjon
2 rue Comte Roger, Cité Médiévale, 11000 Carcassonne
☎ 04 68 71 08 80 Fax 04 68 25 06 60
English spoken
In the middle of the medieval city, the hotel dates back to the Middle Ages but now provides modern comforts, tranquillity and a warm welcome. From the motorway A61, exit at Carcassonne-Est towards Cité.

37 bedrs, all ensuite, ⊬ P 37 DB 390-855 B 53 ✕ 72-140 ⟪ MC Visa Amex ▶ 3km 🖵 🖾 ⠇
RAC 10 %

★★ Hôtel La Gentilhommière
11800 Carcassonne
☎ 04 68 78 74 74 Fax 04 68 78 65 80
English spoken

Very comfortable hotel typical local architecture. Countryside location with light, airy rooms and only 2 km from the old city of Carcassonne. Motorway A61, exit Carcassonne-Est.

31 bedrs, all ensuite, ⊬ P 31 DB 250-320 B 35-37 ✕ 85-180 ⟪ MC Visa Amex ⤚ ▶ 5km 🖵 🖾 ⠇ ♠ ♿
RAC 5 %

★★★ Hôtel Mercure La Viconte
18 rue Camille Saint-Saëns, 11000 Carcassonne
☎ 04 68 71 45 45 Fax 04 68 71 11 45
English spoken
Just outside the walls of the medieval fortified town, with views of the ramparts. Terraced restaurant with regional specialities and a summertime bar/restaurant beside the pool.

61 bedrs, all ensuite, ⊬ P DB 460-490 B 53 ✕ 75-130 ⟪ MC Visa Amex ⤚ ▶ 4km 🖾 ⠇ ♠ ♿

★★★ Hôtel Montségur et Restaurant Le Langued
27 allée Léna, 11000 Carcassonne
☎ 04 68 25 31 41 Fax 04 68 47 13 22
English spoken
Closed 24 Dec-14 Jan
An elegant and spacious 19th century manor house in the centre of town. The restaurant (opposite the hotel) is run by the same family and serves good, regional food.

21 bedrs, all ensuite, ⊬ P 15 DB 320-490 B 48 ✕ 130-260 ⟪ MC Visa Amex ▶ 2km 🖵 🖾 ⠇

★★ Hôtel des Remparts
3 place du Grand Puits, Cité Médiévale, 11000 Carcassonne
☎ 04 68 71 27 72 Fax 04 68 72 73 26
English spoken
The hotel is converted from an old house within the walls of the medieval city of Carcassonne. From A61 exit at Carcassonne-Est and follow 'Cité Médiévale' signs.

18 bedrs, all ensuite, ⊬ P 18 DB 300-330 B 35 No restaurant ⟪ MC Visa Amex ▶ 2km ♠ ♿

COLLIOURE Pyrénées Orientales   5C

★★★ Hôtel Madeloc
Rue Romain Rolland, 66190 Collioure
☎ 04 68 82 07 56 Fax 04 68 82 55 09
English spoken
Closed Nov-Feb
This hotel has pleasant rooms with individual equipped terraces overlooking either the garden or th swimming pool.

22 bedrs, all ensuite, ⊬ P 22 DB 290-430 B 40 No restaurant ⟪ MC Visa Amex ⤚ ▶ 15km 🖾 ⠇ ♠
RAC 5 % on room rate

FLORAC Lozère　　　　　5C

★★★ Grand Hôtel du Parc
47 av Jean Monestier, 48400 Florac
☎ 04 66 45 03 05 Fax 04 66 45 11 81
English spoken
Closed 1 Jan-15 Mar
Situated 50 m from the town centre, this is a quiet hotel shaded by century-old trees. 19th century building, with a fine staircase, offering traditional cuisine prepared by the hotel's proprietors.

60 bedrs, 54 ensuite, **P** 40 **DB** 260-330 **B** 36 ✖ 92-185 ℂℂ MC Visa Amex ⤢ 🖭 🖼 ⊞

FONT-ROMEU Pyrénées Orientales　　5C

★★★ Hôtel Le Grand-Tetras
Avenue de Brousse, 66120 Font-Romeu
☎ 04 68 30 01 20 Fax 04 68 30 35 67
English spoken
Located in the heart of the ski resort station, in a setting of great comfort and quality. Nice sun terrace with a view of the Pyrénées.

36 bedrs, all ensuite, ⊁ **P** 12 **DB** 260-355 **B** 39-49 ✖ 85-165 ℂℂ MC Visa Amex 🗊 🖾 🖳 ▸ 🖭 🖼 ⊞ ⌀ ⅄ 10 ☙

MEYRUEIS Lozère　　　　5C

★★★ Château d'Ayres
48150 Meyrueis
☎ 04 66 45 60 10 Fax 04 66 45 62 26
English spoken
Closed 30 Nov-27 Mar

A very warm welcome and inspired, creative cuisine are assured at this former 12th century monastery converted into a lovely hotel. Meyrueis is in the heart of the Cevennes National Park where wild horses and bison roam freely.

27 bedrs, all ensuite, **P** 30 **DB** 350-830 **B** 65 ✖ 110-255 ℂℂ MC Visa Amex ⤢ 🖭 🖼 ⊞ ⌀

MONTPELLIER Hérault　　　5C

★★ Hôtel du Parc
8 rue A Bège, 34000 Montpellier
☎ 04 67 41 16 49 Fax 04 67 54 10 05
English spoken
A centrally located Languedocian residence, with garden and flowery breakfast terrace, built in the 18th century and now completely renovated.

19 bedrs, 17 ensuite, ⊁ **P** 12 **DB** 295-360 **B** 40 No restaurant ℂℂ MC Visa Amex ▸ 4km 🖭 🖼 ⌀ ⅄

NARBONNE Aude　　　　　5C

★★★ Hôtel Languedoc
22 bd Gambetta, 11100 Narbonne
☎ 04 68 65 14 74 Fax 04 68 65 81 48
English spoken
An elegant hotel, just 200 m from the cathedral, in the heart of the historic town of Narbonne. Situated opposite the Post Office a few minutes from the station and the Narbonne-Est motorway exit.

40 bedrs, all ensuite, ⊁ **P** 12 **DB** 250-500 **B** 38 ✖ 65-105 ℂℂ MC Visa Amex ▸ 🖼 ⊞ ⌀ ⅄
RAC 10 %

★★★ Hôtel Relais du Val d'Orbieu
11200 Ornaisons
☎ 04 68 27 10 27 Fax 04 68 27 52 44
English spoken
Closed Dec-Jan

This charming hotel, renowned for its fine food and pleasantly situated in a wooded garden, is a renovated mill combining luxury and comfort. Only 15 minutes from Narbonne town centre. Take A9 and exit Narbonne-Sud or the A61 and exit Lezignan-Corbières.

20 bedrs, all ensuite, ⊁ **P** 35 **DB** 390-720 **B** 70 ✖ 125-295 ℂℂ MC Visa Amex ⤢ ▸ 15km 🖾 🖼 ⊞ ⅄
RAC 10 %

★★ Hôtel de la Clape
rue des Flots Bleus, Narbonne Plage, 11100
Narbonne
☎ 04 68 49 80 15 Fax 04 68 75 05 05
English spoken
Closed 31 Oct-31 March
A comfortable family hotel, with a bar specialising in non-alcoholic beverages. From A40 exit Narbonne-Est and take the D168.

15 bedrs, 6 ensuite, ♩ P 29 DB 220-345 B 6-30 CC MC
Visa Amex 🕮 ▸ 🔲 🔲 🖾 ♯ ✐ ♿
RAC 15-30%, depending on season

NIMES Gard   5D

★★★ Hôtel L'Hacienda
Mas de Brignon, 30320 Marguerittes
☎ 04 66 75 02 25 Fax 04 66 75 45 58
English spoken

Set in the sunniest region of France, in the town known as the 'French Rome', this large, peaceful Provençal farm house combines elegance and good taste with a warm welcome and fine cuisine. Exit Nîmes from A9; take N86 to Marguerittes, then follow signs.

12 bedrs, all ensuite, ♩ P 12 DB 350-600 B 65-85
✗ 140-340 CC MC Visa ॐ 🖳 ▸ 10km 🔲 12km 🖾 ♯ ✐

★★ Hôtel Majestic
10 rue Pradier, 30000 Nîmes
☎ 04 66 29 24 14 Fax 04 66 29 77 33
English spoken
A small, friendly hotel situated next to the train and bus stations in the town centre. The owner assures us you don't have to be royal to stay here!

23 bedrs, all ensuite, ♩ P 5 DB 240-280 B 35 No
restaurant CC MC Visa ॐ ▸ 2km 🖾 ♯ ✐ ♿
RAC 5 %

★★ Hôtel Nimotel
Parc Hôtelier Ville Active, 30900 Nîmes
☎ 04 66 38 13 84 Fax 04 66 38 14 06
English spoken

A 2-star hotel, with 3-star facilities, offering pleasant, well-equipped, air-conditioned rooms and an attractive restaurant specialising in fish and couscous. Meals can be served outside on the terrace in summer.

180 bedrs, all ensuite, ♩ P 250 DB 290-330 B 35 ✗ 83-175 (also buffet) CC MC Visa Amex ॐ ▸ 3km 🖾 ♯ ✐ ♿

★★ Hôtel Tuileries
22 rue Roussy, 30000 Nîmes
☎ 04 66 21 31 15 Fax 04 66 67 48 72
English spoken
A modern, air-conditioned, centrally situated hotel in a quiet street close to the arena and Roman monuments. Every room has a balcony.

10 bedrs, all ensuite, P DB 370-450 B 40 No
restaurant CC MC Visa Amex ▸ 2km 🖾 ✐

OLARGUES Hérault   5C

★★★ Domaine de Rieumégé
Parc Naturel du Haut Languedoc, Route de St-Pons,
34390 Olargues
☎ 04 67 97 73 99 Fax 04 67 97 78 52
English spoken
Closed 2 Nov-Apr

A charming 17th century residence, with a renowned restaurant, set in the quiet heart of a 14 hectare estate. The ideal location for lovers of exceptional countryside. From Béziers take D14 to Olargues and Rieumégé is 3 km along road to St-Pons.

14 bedrs, all ensuite, ♩ P 30 DB 490-545 B 65 ✗ 100-210 CC MC Visa Amex ॐ ▸ 18km 🔲 🔲 🖾 ♯
RAC 10 %

PORT-LA-NOUVELLE Aude   5C

★★★ Hôtel Méditerranée
BP 92, 11210 Port-la-Nouvelle
☎ 04 68 48 03 08 Fax 04 68 48 53 81
English spoken
Closed 5 Jan-5 Feb

A fine, modern building, centrally situated on the seafront, with a seafood- speciality restaurant overlooking the sea and the beach. A convenient location for tennis, water sports, horseriding, walking and boat trips by catamaran.

31 bedrs, all ensuite, **P** 20 **DB** 200-490 **B** 35-55 ✕ 60-190 **CC** MC Visa Amex ▸ 🖪 🗷 ▦
RAC

PRATS-DE-MOLLO-LA-PRESTE Pyrénées Orientales 5C

★★ Hostellerie Le Relais
3 place Josep de la Trinxeria, 66230 Prats-de-Mollo-la-Preste
📞 04 68 39 71 30 Fax 04 68 39 78 51
English spoken
A warm, welcoming country-inn, in the centre of a medieval walled village, with comfortable rooms and traditional French and Catalan-speciality cuisine. From Le Boulou take D115.

12 bedrs, 9 ensuite, ★ **P** **DB** 190-210 **B** 30-40 ✕ 78-150 **CC** MC Visa 🖪 🗷 𝌆
RAC 7 days incl breakfast for £140 pp.

★★ Hôtel Ribes
66230 Prats-de-Mollo-la-Preste
📞 04 68 39 71 04 Fax 04 68 39 78 02
English spoken
Closed 27 Oct-31 Mar
Situated at an altitude of 1130 m this hotel, 15 minutes from the medieval village, offers splendid views over the River Tech valley and easy access to the local nature reserve. Access: A9 to Le Boulou, D115 to Prats-de-Mollo, then D115A to La Preste.

24 bedrs, 17 ensuite, ★ **P** **DB** 165-295 **B** 33-50 ✕ 71-150 **CC** MC Visa ▸ 🗷 🗷 𝌆

★★★ Park Hôtel d'Estamarius
66230 Prats-de-Mollo-la-Preste
📞 04 68 39 70 04 Fax 04 68 39 75 68
English spoken
This hotel is situated on a large estate, formerly the Knights Templars headquarters, set between French and Spanish Catalonia, in an area known for its Roman art.

85 bedrs, 75 ensuite, ★ **P** 200 **DB** 185-350 **B** 35-45 ✕ 75-185 **CC** MC Visa 🚶 🖪 ▸ 🖪 🗷 🗷 𝌆 𝒜 ♿
RAC 10 %

ST-ALBAN-SUR-LIMAGNOLE Lozère 5A

★★★ Hôtel Relais St-Roch
Château de la Chastre, 48120 St-Alban-sur-Limagnole
📞 04 66 31 55 48 Fax 04 66 31 53 26
English spoken
Closed 3 Nov-31 Mar

This magnificent hotel, set in the heart of the Margeride area, with its own first class fishing course, will appeal to all fresh air lovers; restaurant has an excellent cellar stocked with 150 varieties of whisky. 5 minutes from A75 exit 34

9 bedrs, all ensuite, ★ **P** **DB** 540-720 **B** 58 ✕ 88-268 **CC** MC Visa Amex 🚶 ▸ 🗷 🗷 𝌆 𝒜

ST-CYPRIEN Pyrénées Orientales 5C

★★★ Hôtel Le Mas d'Huston
St-Cyprien-Plage, 66750 St-Cyprien
📞 04 68 37 63 63 Fax 04 68 37 64 64
English spoken

A very attractive, light and spacious, golf hotel with lovely gardens and a water-sports school in summer.

50 bedrs, all ensuite, ★ **P** 70 **DB** 550-770 **B** included ✕ 140-270 **CC** MC Visa Amex 🚶 🖪 ▸ 🖪 🗷 🗷 𝌆 𝒜 ♿
RAC 10 %

VALRAS-PLAGE Hérault   5C

★★ Hôtel Albizzia
12 bd du Chemin Creux, 34350 Valras-Plage
☎ 04 67 37 48 48 Fax 04 67 37 58 10
English spoken
*Recently built hotel located just 200 m from a fine
sandy beach. Via the A9 coming from Montpellier,
take the Béziers-Est exit. Coming from Narbonne, take
the Béziers-Ouest exit.*

28 bedrs, all ensuite, ⊨ P 30 DB 250-430 B 38 No
restaurant ₵ MC Visa Amex ⌐ ▸ 20km 🔲 🖾 🏊 ஃ

★★ Hôtel Méditerranée
32 rue Charles Thomas, 34350 Valras-Plage
☎ 04 67 32 38 60 Fax 04 67 32 30 91
English spoken
*The hotel is in a quiet pedestrian area in the centre
of Valras, just 100 m from a fine sandy beach.
Restaurant offers seafood specialities and regional
dishes: a delight for gourmets.*

9 bedrs, all ensuite, P DB 250-280 B 33 ✕ 90-270

VERGEZE Gard   5D

★★ Hôtel La Passiflore
1 rue Neuve, 30310 Vergèze
☎ 04 66 35 00 00 Fax 04 66 35 09 21
English spoken

*A lovely restored farmhouse with peaceful, air-
conditioned rooms and restaurant, in the village
famous for its Perrier spring, overlooking the central
courtyard. 5 km from the A9 Nimes to Montpellier
motorway, exit Gallangues.*

11 bedrs, all ensuite, ⊨ P 8 DB 225-325 B 38 ✕ 135
₵ MC Visa Amex ▸ 18km 🏊 ஃ

VERNET-LES-BAINS Pyrénées Orientales   5C

★★★ Hôtel Comte Guifred de Conflent
Avenue Thermes, 66820 Vernet-les-Bains
☎ 04 68 05 51 37 Fax 04 68 05 64 11
English spoken

*A very friendly hotel, with horse riding, tennis courts
and casino, located in a spa town in the heart of
Roman Art country: a good starting point for several
hiking paths. Meals can be served outdoors in
summer. 60 km from Mediterranean & ski resorts.*

10 bedrs, all ensuite, ⊨ P DB 360-460 B 40 ✕ 100-190
₵ MC Visa Amex 🔳 ⌐ ▸ 🖾 🔲 🖾

Provence,
Côte d'Azur
and Corsica

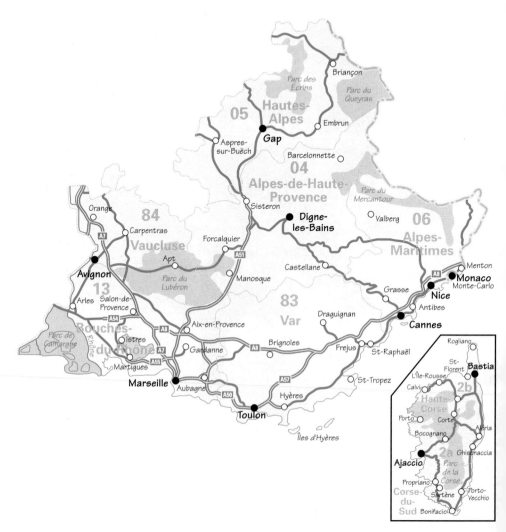

Provence

Provence has consistently been the most highly influential landscape on nineteenth and twentieth century art. It is easy to see why. There is something about the light here which lends the whole area a certain brightness and colour. It is an intangible property, but a striking one.

The appeal of Provence is its landscape rather than its towns; but there are three towns – the three 'A's – which should not be missed: Aix-en-Provence, Arles and Avignon.

Aix was once the capital of Provence, and the town still exerts a peculiarly powerful hold over the area's psychology.

Many visitors to Provence name Aix as their favourite destination. Indeed, it is an absorbing place which is rich in history and atmosphere.

Of the many diversions on offer, the Atelier Paul Cézanne is perhaps the most interesting.

The artist's studio has been restored to the state it was in when he died in 1906. Cézanne's Impressionist and Post-Impressionist paintings of Aix and its surroundings are intensely rich. Arguably, they come closer to capturing the light and mood of the region than any other artist's work. Strangely, then, Cézanne's studio is rather gloomy and even menacing. Still, it is a fascinating insight into his life and work.

Sadly, Aix has a serious traffic problem. To escape the fumes, head out to Croix de la Provence (past the Montagne Ste-Victoire, which was made famous by Cézanne). The climb up can be quite difficult, but the view from the top is outstanding.

Smaller, neater and more traditional than Aix, **Arles** is the centre of old Provençal culture. You are more likely to hear the native tongue here than anywhere else.

The town has several other claims to fame, including that Van Gogh lived here for 14 months of crazed fecundity.

He shared a house with Paul Gauguin – after a fight with whom Van Gogh famously chopped off his own ear. The tourist office will supply a map of Arles' Van Gogh trail. Arles also boasts a very old (46 BC) Roman arena.

The old city of **Avignon** was once one of the most powerful in Europe. Its history is extraordinary.

In 1309 the new Pope, Clément V, was persuaded to leave Rome (where life for the Papacy was made difficult by various power struggles and feuds) for Avignon. The entire Papal entourage moved to the town where, in 1334, Pope Benedict XII built the mighty Papal Palace, which still stands today. More a fort than a palace, the building was probably designed to prevent secrets getting out rather than to stop undesirables getting in.

In 1377, the Papacy returned to Rome, but some key figures refused to go. They were no doubt having too good a time in Avignon. The stragglers elected their own Pope and, for a while, the Catholic church was split. Avignon's 'anti-Pope' was eventually ejected from the city in 1403.

Avignon is an historically exciting and appealing place which should not be missed. The papal soap opera has long-since gone, but the city is still a powerful cultural centre.

Page 279: The lavender fields for which Provence is famed
Above: Aiguines Village and St Croix Lake in Provence

Côte d'Azur

Since Brigitte Bardot bared all in *And God Created Woman*, anyone who's anyone has been racing to the South of France for a slice of the action.

These days, however, whole stretches of this magnificent azure coast have been sunk under concrete. But love it or hate it, it's hard to deny that the Côte d'Azur still feels like the most glamorous stretch of coast on Earth.

This is a wonderful place to be, particularly if you can afford to stay in style, but be warned: over July and August the whole area becomes almost horribly overcrowded. The Côte d'Azur is not all giant motor cruisers and pampered lapdogs. After the exhilarating, but rather threatening, urban sprawl of Marseille, the autoroute slows to the far more leisurely pace of towns such as **Hyères** and **Cavalaire-sur-Mer**. Before leaving Marseille's orbit completely, try to find time to visit the exceptionally pretty resort of **Cassis**. French stars retire to Cassis, but, unlike St Tropez, the place still feels well within the reach of the less financially replete.

Hyères is an underrated, thus appealing, old town which is cheaper and less frantic than its easterly neighbours. Take a ferry to the **Île de Porquerolles** to find some lovely beaches.

Drivers will finally feel they have broken free of the grasp of Marseille and Toulon when they get onto the coastal road after Hyers. This beautiful route stays close to the sea and is a real treat.

Travellers often race towards the bright lights of Nice and Cannes too quickly. Don't rush; this westerly stretch of the Côte d'Azur is just as beautiful – probably more so. Cavalaire-sur-Mer is a great little town with gorgeous sandy beaches and some good value hotels and campsites (a rare thing in this part of the world). A short drive east from Cavalaire takes you to **St Tropez**.

This is where *And God Created Woman* was filmed; an event which was to lead to this former fishing village becoming the epicentre of sixties South of France-style chic. Owning a house in the hills behind the attractive village (and that's all it is) signifies extreme wealth.

The harbour is crammed with millionaires'

Above: Cassis is one of the most attractive of all Provençal bays. A sort of lagoon or miniature fjord (known locally as a calanque) makes an ideal natural swimming pool.

yachts and the restaurants are full of the 'beautiful people'.

St Tropez does enjoy an idyllic location and is an alluring place, but one would have to be an insensitive soul indeed not to feel a twinge of regret that the film was ever made. Clearly, St Tropez was once a beautiful and isolated fishing village – a gem of the Mediterranean coast.

Now, however, the tourists are too many and the prices too high. The place feels pretty inaccessible to most independent travellers. Of course, it would be a shame to miss St Tropez, but for longer stays head east towards the more practical St Raphaël and Frejus.

Both are pleasant coastal towns with excellent beaches never far away and a good choice of reasonably-priced accommodation. A semi-collapsed Roman amphitheatre provides an interesting distraction in **Frejus**, while **St Raphaël** has more bars, cafés and beaches.

Take time to dart inland to see La Garde-Freinet, which is one of the prettiest towns in the Massif de Maures hills.

From St Raphaël, the adrenaline-inducing Corniche de l'Esterel winds its way east. This tightly curled coastal road offers wonderful views across the Mediterranean. A James Bond Aston Martin is essential.

To most people, the next stop – **Cannes** – is a sudden and shocking splash of sophistication and extravagance.

The town is littered with thrusting glitterati and designer label-clad ladies (normally sporting an impossible amount of eye-shadow). It is a fascinating spectacle, all the more so when the famous Film Festival takes place in May. Pouting wannabes head for La Croisette, the main street, where they hope to be spotted by big Hollywood producers.

Even when you take away the palatial hotels and initial excitement, Cannes is an enjoyable mix of colour and elegance. The beach, though, is disappointing. Too many people and parasols are crammed onto this puny patch of sand.

The old town (Le Suquet) is perched on a hillside overlooking the Old Port. It is very attractive, particularly at night when the old Provençal-style restaurants and bars are floodlit to great effect. Climb to the top of Le Suquet for a fantastic view across the bay.

Above: The harbour at Antibes

Few people can legitimately claim to be unimpressed by Cannes. Despite its faults (expensive and too pretentious for some tastes) the town is exciting and will set your pulse racing.

After the rush of Cannes, the corniche begins to slow slightly for Antibes and Juan-les-Pins. **Antibes** is a charming town. Look for the forest of masts which marks the harbour or take a walk through the narrow streets of the medieval quarter.

Picasso spent six months working in Antibes as a guest of the mayor. He was given a studio in the town's castle (formerly home to the Grimaldi family), where he enjoyed a particularly prolific period in his life. Later, to thank Antibes, he gave his entire body of work from that period to the town's museum. That collection is now on show at the amazing Musée Picasso, which is housed in the castle.

Juan-les-Pins, a suburb of Antibes, is a stylish resort in its own right. Once a highly successful destination for the American jetset of the twenties and thirties, Juan-les-Pins attracts a rich and exclusive crowd. The town has lost some of its glamour since Fitzgerald described it as a 'constant carnival', but it is still an attractive retreat. Actually, Fitzgerald's description of Juan-les-Pins could more accurately be applied to **Nice**. This is a city of staggering contrasts. Glamour is flaunted alongside genuine poverty. Beautiful buildings stand a short walk from boarded-up squats.

The Niçoise are a lively bunch and their city (the capital of the Côte d'Azur) is very exciting. If you're looking for a peaceful holiday, Nice might prove too frenetic for your tastes. The most interesting part of Nice is undoubtedly the endearing old town, which is jammed between the castle and the Mediterranean. Italianate and labyrinthine, the Vieille Ville is well worth a detailed exploration.

Art lovers should waste no time in visiting two magnificent galleries: the Musée Marc Chagalle and the Musée Matisse. Both artists lived and worked in Nice for many years. If anywhere is likely to inspire the artist in you, it's **Eze**. Perched high above Cap-Ferrat, this fortified village occupies a dazzling position. The climb to the village proper is steep but well-rewarded.

Corsica

Looking as much to Italy as to France for cultural inspiration, Corsica is something of a hybrid of the two nations.

A rocky, but stunning, coast is punctuated by impressive beaches. Pretty, fortified towns are dotted across a forested and striking interior. This is a beautiful island, which has been protected by the deep contempt (and sometimes violence) with which the locals greet property developers. Corsica is split into two regions, each with its own capital.

Ajaccio, capital of the south, is a charming resort which rivals the Riviera. You could hardly fail to realise that Napoleon was born here – the place is peppered with Bonaparte memorabilia. There is not a great deal to do except relax, which, for most visitors, is fine. Atmospheric cafés line ancient streets and the pretty harbour front. To learn more about Corsica and its history, visit the Palais Fesch Museum.

The other capital on Corsica is **Bastia**, a busy place which is less geared up for tourism. However, it is, in some ways, more appealing than Ajaccio. The old town is wonderful and the working port is a joy to watch.

If you prefer to laze on the beach, set out for **Calvi**. Wedged between a great beach and the mountains, Calvi is the perfect resort town. It is popular, but remains friendly and endearing.

Above: Eze on the Côte d'Azur is almost impossibly quaint and the view is nothing short of breathtaking

Getting there

By road
Major road arteries:
* A6 and A7 (the 'Motorway to the Sun') links Paris, Lyon and Marseille
* A8 (the 'Provençale') Marseille to Nice (and Italy)
* A9 (the 'Languedocienne') Spain and Montpellier to Marseille
* A51 Aix to Sisteron

Motorway information 📞 4 91 78 78 78
Coach stations:
* Marseille 📞 4 91 50 57 68
* Nice 📞 4 93 85 61 81

By rail
By TGV:
* Paris Gare de Lyon to Avignon takes 3 hours 15 mins
* Paris Gare de Lyon to Cannes takes 5 hours 50 mins
* Paris Gare de Lyon to Nice takes 6 hours 20 mins
* Paris Gare de Lyon to Marseille takes 4 hours 15 mins
* Paris Gare de Lyon to Hyeres takes 5 hours 20 mins
* Paris Gare de Lyon to Antibes takes 6 hours 10 mins
* Cannes to Lyon takes 4 hours 30 mins
* Cannes to Lille takes 7 hours 40 mins

By air
Marseille Provence Airport (📞 4 42 14 14 14, Fax: 4 42 12 27 24) is 20 miles north-west of Marseille.
Get into Marseille by taxi (📞 4 91 02 20 20) or airport shuttle bus.
For car hire contact:
* Europcar 📞 4 42 78 24 75
* Hertz 📞 4 42 14 32 70

Nice Côte d'Azur Airport (📞 4 93 21 30 30, Fax: 4 93 21 30 29) is 4 miles west of Nice.
Get into Nice by taxi or bus (📞 4 93 13 78 78 or 4 93 16 52 10).
For car hire contact:
* Avis 📞 4 93 21 42 80
* Europcar 📞 4 93 21 42 80
* Hertz 📞 4 93 87 11 87

Bastia Poretta International Airport (Corsica) (📞 4 95 54 54 54, Fax: 4 95 54 54 56) is 15 miles south of Bastia.
Get into Bastia by taxi (📞 4 95 36 04 65) or bus (📞 4 95 31 06 65).
For car hire contact:
* Ada 📞 1 4 95 54 55 44
* Avis 📞 4 95 36 03 56
* Europcar 📞 4 95 30 09 50

Getting to Corsica by boat
Ferry companies:
SNCM:
* 61 Boulevard des Dames, 13002 Marseille 📞 4 91 56 32 00
* 49 avenue de L'Infanterie-de-Marine, 83000 Toulon 📞 4 94 16 66 60
* Quai du Commerce, 06359 Nice Cédex 04 📞 4 93 13 66 99

Southern Ferries Ltd, 179 Piccadilly, London W1V 9DB 📞 4 491 49 68

Departures from Marseille, Nice, Toulon to Ajaccio and Bastia to Calvi, Ile Rousse, Porto-Vecchio and Propiano only in high season.

Marseille–Ajaccio	8 hours 45mins
Marseille–Bastia	10 hours
Nice–Ajaccio	6 hours 45mins
Nice–Bastia	6 hours 15mins
Nice–Bastia by NGV	2 hours 30mins
Nice–Ajaccio by NGV	3 hours 45mins
Toulon–Ajaccio	7 hours
Toulon–Bastia	8 hours 30mins

NGV: Navires á Grand Vitesse (High Speed Boats)

TOURIST INFORMATION

* **Provence, Côte d'Azur Tourist Office**
  Espace Colbert, 14 rue Sainte-Barbe, 13231 Marseille Cedex
  📞 4 91 39 38 00
  Fax: 4 91 56 66 61
* **Bastia Tourist Office**
  Place St Nicolas BP 203, Bastia 20 200
  📞 4 95 31 00 89
  Fax: 4 95 55 96 00
* **Ajaccio Tourist Office**
  Place Foch, BP 21, Ajaccio 20 181
  📞 4 95 51 53 03
  Fax: 4 95 51 53 01

AIGUINES Var 6C

★★ Hôtel Grand Canyon du Verdon
Falaises des Cavaliers, 83630 Aiguines
04 94 76 91 31 Fax 04 94 76 92 29
English spoken
Closed 2 Nov-12 Apr

A real eagle's nest in the heart of the Verdon Gorges at an altitude of 800 m, 15 km from the village. In a picturesque setting enjoy the calm and comfort of the rooms, some with terraces. A8, junction Lemuy, then D71.

15 bedrs, all ensuite, **P** 50 **DB** 300-460 **B** 40-65 ✕ 100-180 **CC** MC Visa Amex
RAC 10 %

AIX-EN-PROVENCE Bouches du Rhône 5D

★★★ Arc Hôtel
3 Route de Nice, 13100 Aix-en-Provence
04 42 26 12 12 Fax 04 42 26 12 57
English spoken
Contemporary hotel. 40 air-conditioned rooms. Good prices for good quality. Easy to access; hospitable reception.

40 bedrs, all ensuite, **P** 17 **DB** 250-390 **B** 35-45 **CC** MC Visa Amex

★★★★ Domaine de Châteauneuf
au Logis de Nans, 83860 Nans-les-Pins
04 94 78 90 06 Fax 04 94 78 63 30
English spoken
Closed Dec-Feb

18th century provincial country house surrounded by a large wooded park, ideal for peace and relaxation. Located in the centre of an 18-hole international golf course.

30 bedrs, all ensuite, **P** 60 **DB** 675-1,200 **B** 75 ✕ 170-230 **CC** MC Visa Amex
RAC 8 % on room rate

★★★★ Grand Hôtel Roi René
24 bd du Roi René, 13100 Aix-en-Provence
04 42 37 61 00 Fax 04 42 37 61 11
English spoken

Recently built in Provençal style, the hotel is ideally situated in the heart of the city, close to the Mazarin quarter with its 17th century buildings and monuments. Very comfortable accommodation; warm, friendly atmosphere and pretty, tropical gardens.

134 bedrs, all ensuite, **P** 35 **DB** 650-1,075 **B** 80 ✕ 175 **CC** MC Visa Amex

★★★ Hôtel La Caravelle
29-31 bd Roi René, 13100 Aix-en-Provence
04 42 21 53 05 Fax 04 42 96 55 46
English spoken
Closed Nov
A town centre hotel 300 m from Cours-Mirabeau and 800 m from the railway station.

32 bedrs, all ensuite, **P** 10 **DB** 260-380 **B** 35 **CC** MC Visa Amex 4km 4km
RAC 8 %

★★★ Hôtel Le Mas des Ecureuils
Chemin de Castel Blanc, Petite route des Mille, 13090 Aix-en-Provence
04 42 24 40 48 Fax 04 42 39 24 57
English spoken
Closed 24-29 Dec
Set in woody, secluded site with swimming-pool, hammam and table tennis, the hotel has 23 rooms fully equipped with TV, minibar, desk, direct phone and private safe. Gourmet restaurant. Seminary and internationally renowned stable and riding nearby.

23 bedrs, all ensuite, **P** **DB** 480-760 **B** 50 ✕ 128-250 **CC** MC Visa Amex 2km
RAC 10 %

★★★ Hôtel Mas d'Entremont

Montée d'Avignon, 13090 Aix-en-Provence
☎ 04 42 17 42 42 Fax 04 42 21 15 83
English spoken
Closed 1 Nov-15 March
Set in lovely parkland, this is a comfortable, air-conditioned hotel with lots of antiques. 4 km north of Aix on the N7 towards Avignon.

17 bedrs, all ensuite, ♂ P DB 640-850 B 75 ✗ 200-240
CC MC Visa Amex ⅃ ▸ 10km 🔲 🔲 ⅲ ⅃

★★★ Hôtel Mercure Paul Cézanne

40 av Victor Hugo, 13100 Aix-en-Provence
☎ 04 42 26 34 73 Fax 04 42 27 20 95
English spoken

Rooms are individually and tastefully decorated in Provençal style. The hotel has all modern facilities including air-conditioning. Near the station in the town centre.

55 bedrs, all ensuite, ♂ P DB 490-955 B 55 No restaurant CC MC Visa Amex ▸ 🔲 ⅃

ANTIBES Alpes Maritime   6D

★★★ Hôtel Castel Garoupe

59 bd de la Garoupe, 06600 Cap d'Antibes
☎ 04 93 61 36 51 Fax 04 93 67 74 88
English spoken
Closed 9 Mar-3 Nov

A comfortable hotel, with a range of accommodation to suit all tastes, situated in the centre of Cap d'Antibes and having terraces and very pretty gardens. Take N98 11 km from Cannes towards Antibes.

27 bedrs, all ensuite, ♂ P 40 DB 670-820 B included ✗ 100-200 CC MC Visa Amex ⅃ ⅻ ▸ 5km 🔲 🔲 🔲 ⅃

★★ Hôtel Château Fleuri

15 bd du Cap, 06160 Cap d'Antibes
☎ 04 93 61 38 66 Fax 04 93 67 39 22
English spoken
Closed 2 Oct-31 Mar

A small hotel with pretty garden and parking; all the rooms have a terrace or balcony. 5 minutes from a sandy beach and 15 minutes from the old town towards Cap d'Antibes.

19 bedrs, all ensuite, P DB 250-400 B 30 CC MC Visa Amex ▸ 8km 🔲

APT Vaucluse   5D

★★★ Auberge du Lubéron

17 quai Léon Sagy, 84400 Apt
☎ 04 90 74 12 50 Fax 04 90 04 79 49
English spoken
Quiet hotel near town centre, with lovely views over Apt and the River Calavon. In the Lubéron Regional Park and 50 km from Avignon. The fine cuisine is based on fresh, quality products.

15 bedrs, all ensuite, ♂ P 4 DB 290-500 B 52 ✗ 155-395 CC MC Visa Amex 🔲 ⅲ

ARLES Bouches du Rhône   5D

★★★★ Hôtel Jules César
Restaurant Loumarques, 9 bd des Lices, BP 116,
13631 Arles
☎ 04 90 93 43 20 Fax 04 90 93 33 47
English spoken
Closed 3 Nov-23 Dec

*An old Carmelite convent, now an excellent hotel
belonging to the 'Relais et Châteaux' association. Air-
conditioned restaurant renowned for its Provençal
cuisine. In the heart of Provence, Arles is a town rich
in history, archaeology and culture.*

55 bedrs, all ensuite, ⊬ P DB 700-1,250 B 85 ✕ 195-
420 ℂℂ MC Visa Amex ⊰ ▸ 18km ▣ ▦ ⋒ ⓺
RAC On request

HÔTEL JULES-CÉSAR
Restaurant "LOU MARQUÈS"

The Jules-César is situated in the quiet and
elegant part of the town centre. Within a few
minutes you are in the middle of 2000 years
of history and in less than an hour you are in
the heart of the most touristical sites of
Provence. Entirely air-conditioned.
Cloister and Provençal gardens, outdoor
swimming pool for you to enjoy.

**BOULEVARD DES LICES, B.P. 116
13631 ARLES
(BOUCHES-DU-RHÔNE)
TEL: 04 90 93 43 20 TELEX: 400239 JULCÉSAR
FAX: 04 90 93 33 47**

★★★ Hôtel Les Cabanettes
RN 572, 13200 Saliers-par-Arles
☎ 04 66 87 31 53 Fax 04 66 87 35 39
English spoken
Closed 25 Jan-28 Feb
*Modern and quiet, an attractive hotel set around an
enclosed garden and pool area, with soundproofed
and air-conditioned rooms. Located 15 km from Arles
on N572 in St-Gilles.*

29 bedrs, all ensuite, ⊬ P 60 DB 435 B 50 ✕ 130-200
ℂℂ MC Visa Amex ⊰ ▸ 12km ▣ ▦ ⋒ ⓺

★★ Hôtel Mirador
3 rue Voltaire, 13200 Arles
☎ 04 90 96 28 05 Fax 04 90 96 59 89
English spoken
Closed 15 Jan-15 Feb
*A comfortable family hotel, close to the town centre,
buses and railway station.*

15 bedrs, all ensuite, ⊬ P DB 190-255 B 15-28 ℂℂ MC
Visa Amex ▸ 3km ▣
RAC low price breakfast

★★★ Hôtel d'Arlatan
26 rue Sauvage, 13200 Arles
☎ 04 90 93 56 66 Fax 04 90 49 68 45
English spoken
*A 15th century mansion with Roman relics,
courtyard and garden, situated on the east bank of
the Rhône. Leave N113 at Nouveau-Pont.*

40 bedrs, all ensuite, ⊬ P DB 465-795 B 62 No
restaurant ℂℂ MC Visa Amex ▸ 15km ▣ ▦ ⋒

AVIGNON Vaucluse   5D

★★★★ Hôtel Cloître St-Louis
20 rue Portail Boquier, 84000 Avignon
☎ 04 90 27 55 55 Fax 04 90 82 24 01
English spoken
Closed Feb

*An oasis of tranquillity, ideally located in the heart of
Avignon. The traditional and regional cuisine
includes croustillant de saumon à l'oseille and crème
brulée à l'orange et sa tuile.*

80 bedrs, all ensuite, ⊬ P 20 DB 520-680 B 65-70
✕ 99-180 ℂℂ MC Visa Amex ⊰ ▸ 5km ▣ 5km ▦ ⓺
RAC 10 %

★★ Hôtel Le Mas des Amandiers
Route d'Avignon, 13690 Graveson
☎ 04 90 95 81 76 Fax 04 90 95 85 18
English spoken
Closed 15 Oct-15 Mar

12 km south of Avignon, set in the heart of the countryside, this hotel has the warmth of a Provençal home. Quiet, with all modern comforts. Located south on the D570 towards Arles.

25 bedrs, all ensuite, ⌖ P 25 DB 300-320 B 40 ✕ 95-145 CC MC Visa Amex ⬚ ⬚ ▸ 12km 🔲 ⚌ ⌀ ♿

★★ Hôtel Les Cèdres
39 bd Pasteur, 30400 Villeneuve-lès-Avignon
☎ 04 90 25 43 92 Fax 04 90 25 14 66
English spoken
Closed 15 Nov-15 Mar
Not far from the gates of the city of Avignon, an 18th century building set in a flower-filled park and shaded by 100 year old cedar trees. The restaurant has a relaxed, family atmosphere with traditional and regional cuisine.

21 bedrs, all ensuite, ⌖ P DB 298-390 B 42 ✕ 108-168 CC MC Visa ⬚ ▸ 10km 🔲 ⚌

BANDOL Var   6C

★★ Golf Hôtel
Plage Renécros, 83150 Bandol
☎ 04 94 29 45 83 Fax 04 94 32 42 47
English spoken
Closed Nov-Apr

Set on a private beach with lovely sea views, the hotel is only 300 m from the town centre. Four apartments are also available. The beach restaurant specialises in fish and salads.

24 bedrs, 10 ensuite, P 24 DB 280-600 B 40 ✕ 95-140 CC MC Visa ▸ 3km 🔲 🔲

BARBENTANE Bouches du Rhône   5D

★★ Hôtel Castel Mouisson
quartier Castel Mouisson, 13570 Barbentane
☎ 04 90 95 51 17 Fax 04 90 95 67 63
English spoken
Closed 15 Oct-15 Mar
A Provençal farmhouse in a pretty setting. Leave A7 motorway at Avignon-Sud, follow directions towards Noves, Châteaurenard-Rognonas, then Barbentane. Reduced fees at local golf course to residents.

17 bedrs, all ensuite, ⌖ P 17 DB 280-350 B 40 No restaurant ⬚ ▸ 0.50km 🔲 🔲 🔲 ⌀ ♿
RᴄC 8 %

BEAULIEU-SUR-MER Alpes Maritime   6D

★★★★ Hôtel Métropole
15 bd Maréchal Leclerc, 06310 Beaulieu-sur-Mer
☎ 04 93 01 00 08 Fax 04 93 01 18 51
English spoken
Closed 20 Oct-20 Dec
Palatial hotel with garden, terraces and a gourmet restaurant overlooking the Mediterranean. Beaulieu is between Nice and Monte Carlo. Heated sea-water swimming pool (86 F).

46 bedrs, all ensuite, ⌖ P 30 DB 900-2,900 B 120 ✕ 300-500 CC MC Visa Amex ⬚ ▸ 15km 🔲 🔲

BREIL-SUR-ROYA Alpes Maritime   6C

★★ Hôtel Castel du Roy
route de Tende, 06540 Breil-sur-Roya
☎ 04 93 04 43 66 Fax 04 93 04 91 83
English spoken
Closed 2 Nov-28 Feb
Set in 2 hectares of parkland near the Vallée des Merveilles, the hotel has a lovely position beside the River Roya.

19 bedrs, all ensuite, P 30 DB 305-420 B 40 ✕ 110-210 CC MC Visa Amex ⬚ ▸ 20km 🔲 🔲 ⌀ ♿
RᴄC 5 % low Season

> When parking your car ensure you are not facing oncoming traffic. This will help you when you return to your car.

BRIANCON Hautes Alpes 6A

★★★ Hôtel Vauban

13 av Général de Gaulle, 05100 Briançon
☎ 04 92 21 12 11 Fax 04 92 20 58 20
English spoken
Closed 5 Nov-20 Dec
A family-run hotel with garden, close to the railway station in the town centre. The restaurant has a large dining room where you can appreciate regional specialities.

44 bedrs, 38 ensuite, ⚲ P DB 370-440 B 35 ✗ 110-170 ₵ MC Visa ▸ 12km ▣ ⋕
RAC 5 %

LA CADIERE-D'AZUR Var 6C

★★★ Hostellerie Bérard

rue Gabriel Peri, 83740 La Cadière-d'Azur
☎ 04 94 90 11 43 Fax 04 94 90 11 71
English spoken
L'Hostellerie Bérard is a group of houses with character surrounding a swimming pool. The dining room opens on to the vineyards of Bandol.

40 bedrs, all ensuite, ⚲ P DB 470-1,200 B 75 ✗ 170-450 ₵ MC Visa Amex ⌇ ▦ ▨ ▸ 7km ▣ ▧ ⋕ ♪

CAGNES-SUR-MER Alpes Maritime 6C

Country Club Cogagne

Route de Vence, 30 chemin du Pain de S, 06800 Cagnes-sur-Mer
☎ 04 92 13 57 77 Fax 04 92 13 57 89
English spoken
Closed Nov
A comfortable hotel with a choice of accommodation including suites. Situated on the top of a hill in the heart of the Côte d'Azur.

10 bedrs, all ensuite, ⚲ P 10 DB 450-850 B 40 ✗ 140-170 ₵ MC Visa ⌇ ▨ ▸ 4km ▧ ▧ ⋕

CANNES Alpes Maritime 6C

★★★ Hôtel Amarante

78 bd Carnot, 06400 Cannes
☎ 04 93 39 22 23 Fax 04 93 39 40 22
English spoken
Situated in the centre of Cannes, hotel has harmonious décor and air-conditioned rooms. 1 km from the beach.

71 bedrs, all ensuite, ⚲ P DB 480-950 B 60 ✗ 105-170 ₵ MC Visa Amex ⌇ ▸ 6km ▦ ▣ ▧ ⋕ ♿
RAC 15 %

★★★★ Hôtel Belle Plage

square Mistral, 06400 Cannes
☎ 04 93 39 86 25 Fax 04 93 99 61 06
English spoken
Closed 15 Nov-1 Feb

At the foot of the old town and set in shady parkland, the hotel is 50 m from the beach and 200 m from the port. Modern, air-conditioned and soundproofed hotel with some wonderful sea views.

48 bedrs, all ensuite, ⚲ P B 80 No restaurant ₵ MC Visa Amex ⌇ ▸ ♿
RAC 10 %

★★★ Hôtel Festival

3 rue Molière, 06400 Cannes
☎ 04 93 68 33 00 Fax 04 93 68 33 85
English spoken
A contemporary-style hotel with air-conditioning and with room-service meals available. From motorway A8, take the Cannes exit and the hotel is between La Croisette and rue d'Antibes.

14 bedrs, all ensuite, ⚲ P DB 480-690 B 45 ₵ MC Visa Amex ▨ ▸ 5km ▧ ♪
RAC 10 %

★★★★ Hôtel Savoy

5 rue François Einesy, 06400 Cannes
☎ 04 92 99 72 00 Fax 04 93 68 25 59
English spoken

Open all year with 101 bedrooms and 5 suites. The hotel offers an outdoor, panoramic swimming pool, golf 15 km and garage. Hôtel Savoy is a superb and charming establishment at the centre of La Croisette, 100 m from the sea and close to shops.

106 bedrs, all ensuite, ⚲ P 25 DB 730-1,455 B 98 ✗ 160 ₵ MC Visa Amex ⌇ ▸ 15km ▣ ⋕ ♪ ♿
RAC 10 %

181 rooms, including one suite, each with a private terrace. Air-conditioned, minibar, direct telephone, colour TV with cable channels. Free covered car park. Sports Club with 8 hard courts, of which 5 are floodlit, 2 clay courts, two swimming pools, one of which is covered and heated in winter. For a memorable stay.

25 AV BEAUSÉJOUR
6400 CANNES, FRANCE
TEL: 04 93 68 91 50
FAX: 04 93 38 37 08

★★★ Novotel Montfleury
25 av Beauséjour, 06400 Cannes
☎ 04 93 68 91 50 Fax 04 93 38 37 08
English spoken

The hotel is located in the peaceful setting of a beautiful park with comfortable rooms providing a restful atmosphere. Take motorway A8, exit 42, follow Cannes centre, Californie area.

181 bedrs, all ensuite, ⊬ P 300 DB 500-1,250 B 52-80 ⊀ 95 ℂℂ MC Visa Amex ⊠ ⅔ ⊦ ⊠ ⅲ

CARPENTRAS Vaucluse   5D

★★★ Hôtel Les Trois Colombes
48 av des Garrigues, 84210 St-Didier
☎ 04 90 66 07 01 Fax 04 90 66 11 54
English spoken
Closed Jan-Feb

A charming Provençal country residence with shady grounds covering 800 square metres. From the A7 take the Avignon-Nord exit and go through Carpentras towards St-Didier, following signposts to the hotel.

32 bedrs, all ensuite, ⊬ P DB 340-480 B 50 ✕ 120-230 ℂℂ MC Visa Amex ⅔ ⊠ ⊦ 6km ⊠ ⊡ ⊠ ⅲ ⋨ ⴵ
RAC 5 % with stay of 3 nights

CASSIS Bouches du Rhône   5D

★★★ Hôtel La Plage du Bestouan
Plage du Bestouan, 13260 Cassis
☎ 04 42 01 05 70 Fax 04 42 01 34 82
English spoken

A seaside hotel with a panoramic terrace and super location right beside the beach. Cassis is a lively fishing port off the D559.

29 bedrs, all ensuite, P DB 420-650 B 50 ℂℂ MC Visa Amex ⊠ ⅲ

CAVAILLON Vaucluse   5D

★★ Hôtel du Parc
183 place François Tourel, 84300 Cavaillon
☎ 04 90 71 57 78 Fax 04 90 76 10 35
English spoken
Located at the foot of 'Colline St-Jaques', 300 m from the town centre. Follow signs towards 'Arc Romain' and the hotel is opposite the arch.

40 bedrs, all ensuite, P 15 DB 240-260 B 32-36 No restaurant ℂℂ MC Visa ⋨

Roads that are marked with the Crafty Bison (*Bison Fute*) sign are shortcuts which avoid the busiest roads. Crafty Bison maps are available from Crafty Bison information centres, which are scattered along most major routes, or from tourist boards.

LA CHAPELLE-EN-VALGAUDEMAR
Hautes Alpes   6A

★★ Hôtel Mont-Olan
05800 St-Firmin
☎ 04 92 55 23 03
English spoken
Closed 15 Sep-Apr
*A quiet, comfortable chalet-style hotel in beautiful
countryside. The village is 90 km from Grenoble and
48 km from Gap. Restaurant specialities include
tourte de pommes de terre and raviolis au miel.*

30 bedrs, 26 ensuite, ⍧ P 25 DB 230-260 B 28 ✕ 70-
220 ℭℭ MC Visa ⌐ ▣ ▣ ⅲ
RAC 10 %

CHATEAUNEUF-DU-PAPE Vaucluse   5D

★★★ Hôtel La Sommellerie
84230 Chateauneuf-du-Pape
☎ 04 90 83 50 00 Fax 04 90 83 51 85
English spoken
Closed mid Feb-start Mar

*Former old sheep farm, renovated into a charming
Provençal residence and set in the heart of a
vineyard. Aromatic, traditional and creative cuisine
by P. Paumel, Maitre Cuisinier de France.*

14 bedrs, all ensuite, ⍧ P 40 DB 400-890 B 55 ✕ 170-
390 ℭℭ MC Visa Amex ⌐ ▣ 9km ⅲ ⌐
RAC 5 % on room rate except May-Sep & Easter

LA CIOTAT Bouches du Rhône   5D

★★★ Hôtel Miramar
3 bd Beaurivage, La Ciotat-Plage, 13600 La Ciotat
☎ 04 42 83 33 79 Fax 04 42 83 33 79
English spoken

*The hotel is situated opposite the main beach of La
Ciotat. Follow signs to 'Les Plages'. With a well-
regarded restaurant, specialities including mignon de
porc, civet de homard and filets de rouget.*

25 bedrs, all ensuite, ⍧ P 40 DB 465-900 B 55 ✕ 125-
395 ℭℭ MC Visa Amex ⌐ 7km ▣ ▣ ⅲ ⌐ ⌐
RAC 10 %

COMPS-SUR-ARTUBY Var   6C

★★ Grand Hôtel Bain
83840 Comps-sur-Artuby
☎ 04 94 76 90 06 Fax 04 94 76 92 24
English spoken
*Located on the road between Draguignan and
Castellane, the hotel has been handed down from
father to son since 1737. Currently being run by
Jean-Marie Bain, the 8th generation, with his son
Arnaud being the Chef de Cuisine.*

18 bedrs, all ensuite, ⍧ P 30 DB 250-270 B 38 ✕ 78-
190 ℭℭ MC Visa Amex ⌐ 17km ▣ ▣ ⅲ ⌐

CORSE (Corsica)

AJACCIO Corsica   6D

★★★ Hôtel Campo dell'Oro
Plage du Ricanto-BP582, 20189 Ajaccio Cedex
☎ 04 95 22 32 41 Fax 04 95 20 60 21
English spoken
Closed 1 Jan-15 Mar

*The hotel has modern, comfortable rooms with a
balcony, 60 of which are air-conditioned. The
restaurant 'Le Mediterranée', with its private beach, is
open all year long.*

140 bedrs, all ensuite, ⍧ P 60 DB 400-600 B 50 ✕ 110-
250 ℭℭ MC Visa Amex ⌐ ▣ ⌐ 10km ▣ ▣ ▣ ⅲ ⌐ ⌐
RAC 10 %

CORTE Corsica — 6D

★★ Hôtel de la Paix

Avenue du Gal de Gaulle, 20250 Corte, Corse
☎ 04 95 46 06 72 Fax 04 95 46 23 84
Closed 20 Dec-5 Jan
The hotel has 60 rooms with shower and WC ensuite. Located in the town centre, other facilities include lifts, bars and free indoor storage space for motorbikes and bicycles.

60 bedrs, all ensuite, ⊁ P DB 240-260 B 25-30 ✕ 80-120 ▨ ▧ ⾙ ✄
RAC 10 %

ERBALUNGA Corsica — 6D

★★★ Hôtel Castel Brando

Erbalunga, 20222 Brando, Corse
☎ 04 95 30 10 30 Fax 04 95 33 98 18
English spoken
Closed 15 Nov-1 Apr

A charming hotel with character, affiliated to the Châteaux and Hôtels Indépendants chain, in the small picturesque fishing port of the Cap Corse. 550 m from the sea.

20 bedrs, all ensuite, ⊁ P DB 380-580 B 35 No restaurant ⓒ MC Visa Amex ⟑ ▸ ▨ ▨ ▧ ৬
RAC 5 %

PORTICCIOLO Corsica — 6D

★★★ Hôtel Le Caribou

à la Marine de Porticciolo, 20228 Porticciolo, Corse
☎ 04 95 35 02 33 Fax 04 95 35 01 13
English spoken
Located 0.5 km from Porticciolo, the hotel has wonderful views of the sea and its own private mooring. Canoeing, windsurfing also available. Gourmet specialities include langouste flambée, loup grillé en fenouil and gigot en croûte.

40 bedrs, all ensuite, ⊁ P 40 DB 300-800 B 40 ✕ 200-350 ⓒ MC Visa Amex ⟑ ▨ ▨ ▨ ▨ ▧ ⾙ ✄ ৬
RAC 5 %

Le CARIBOU

The hotel is in a lush garden 20 metres from the shore. Traditional, renowned and aromatic cuisine. Private creek with deckchairs, canoes, windsurfing and motorboats.

CAP.CORSE, FAGNANO.20228
Tel: 04 95 35 02 33 Tel: 04 95 35 00 33
Fax: 04 95 35 01 13

PORTO-POLLO Corsica — 6D

★★ Hôtel Les Eucalyptus

20140 Petreto-Bicchisano, Corse
☎ 04 95 74 01 52 Fax 04 95 74 06 56
English spoken
Closed 1 Oct-1 May
A very comfortable, quiet hotel set back just 50 m from sandy beaches. Set in a green, pleasant position overlooking the Gulf of Valinco. Small dogs only. Cuisine includes fish and traditional dishes based on local produce.

27 bedrs, all ensuite, ⊁ P 30 DB 280-330 B 36 ✕ 100-140 ⓒ MC Visa Amex ▨ ▨ ▧
RAC 5 %

PROPRIANO Corsica — 6D

★★★ Hôtel Roc e Mare

20110 Propriano, Corse
☎ 04 95 76 04 85 Fax 04 95 76 17 55
English spoken
Closed 15 Oct-15 Apr
Located in the Gulf of Valinco, overlooking the sea and 1 km from Propriano. The hotel has a bar and lounge with panoramic views and a private beach with snack bar.

60 bedrs, all ensuite, P 60 DB 455-685 B 55 No restaurant ⓒ MC Visa Amex ▨ ▧ ⾙
RAC 10 %

QUENZA Corsica   6D

★★ Hôtel Sole e Monti
Quenza, 20122 Quenza, Corse
☎ 04 95 78 72 53 Fax 04 95 78 63 88
English spoken
Closed Oct-15 Mar
A hotel in a beautiful mountain village with superb views. The restaurant has an excellent reputation, specialities including game, trout and wild boar.

20 bedrs, all ensuite, ♔ P DB 350-400 B 50 ✗ 150-195 ℂℂ MC Visa Amex ▣ ♫

ST-FLORENT Corsica   6D

★★★ Hôtel Dolce Notte
20217 St-Florent, Corse
☎ 04 95 37 06 65 Fax 04 95 37 10 70
English spoken
Closed 20 Oct-20 Mar
A welcoming and quiet hotel, close to the beach. All rooms have a sea view. 300 m from the town centre, 25 km from Bastia.

20 bedrs, all ensuite, ♔ P DB 280-620 B 40 ℂℂ MC Visa Amex ▣ ▣ ♫
RAC 8 %

End of CORSE (Corsica) resorts

ENTRAIGUES Vaucluse   5D

★★ Hôtel du Parc
route de Carpentras, 84320 Entraigues
☎ 04 90 83 62 43 Fax 04 90 83 29 11
English spoken
The hotel is situated in parkland. Leave the motorway at Avignon-Nord, towards Carpentras.

30 bedrs, all ensuite, P 30 DB 250-350 B 32-36 ✗ 80-140 ℂℂ MC Visa ▤ ▣ ⧆ ♫ ♿

Bonjour '98 France welcomes the world
Since 1994, France has been encouraging its tourist industry to participate in the Bonjour scheme, which aims to improve the quality of French tourism services. That scheme has been enhanced for 1998 to include the Football World Cup. 'Bonjour 98 – France welcomes the world' is a nationwide effort to give a warm welcome and top quality service to visiting football fans and tourists alike. Any hotel or company displaying the 'Bonjour' logo has signed up to meet certain guidelines on the quality of their welcome and product. Look for the logo and expect a warm French welcome.

EZE Alpes Maritime   6D

Hôtel Hermitage
Grande Corniche, Eze Village, 06360 Eze
☎ 04 93 41 00 68 Fax 04 93 41 24 05
Closed 12 Nov-15 Feb
A Provençal-style hotel. From Nice, take the N98 coast road east to Eze.

14 bedrs, all ensuite, ♔ P DB 170-310 B 28 ✗ 95-190 ℂℂ MC Visa Amex ⚒ ▶ 5km ▣ ♫

GAP Hautes Alpes   6C

★★ Hôtel Le Pavillon Carina
rte de Veynes, 05000 Gap
☎ 04 92 52 02 73 Fax 04 92 53 34 72
English spoken
Closed 23 Dec-8 Jan
In a leafy setting, 800 m high in the southern Alps with woods nearby. Serving regional cuisine with Alsace specialities. 2 km from Gap town centre.

50 bedrs, all ensuite, ♔ P DB 190-320 B 37 ✗ 78-220 ℂℂ MC Visa Amex ▣ ▣ ▶ 7km ▣ ▣ 20km ▣ 3km ⧆ ♫ ♿
RAC 5 %

GRASSE Alpes Maritime   6D

★★★★ Auberge de la Vignette Haute
rte du Village, 06810 Auribeau-sur-Siagne
☎ 04 93 42 20 01 Fax 04 93 42 31 16
English spoken
Closed 12 Nov-12 Dec
A romantic 17th century inn, high above the city offering modern-day comfort in medieval surroundings. With a garden and terrace and farm beyond. From A8, exit Mandelieu-la-Napoule, towards Grasse.

12 bedrs, all ensuite, ♔ P 50 DB 700-1,400 B 80-110 ✗ 170-520 ℂℂ MC Visa Amex ⚒ ▶ 5km ▣ ⧆ ♿
RAC 8 %

★★ Hôtel Relais Impérial
06460 St-Vallier-de-Thiey
☎ 04 93 42 60 07 Fax 04 93 42 66 21
English spoken
A period hotel, completely refurbished and just 10 minutes from the centre of Grasse. It has a good atmosphere and rustic restaurant with a shady terrace.

30 bedrs, all ensuite, P DB 230-450 B 35 ✗ 95-200 ℂℂ MC Visa Amex ▶ 8km ▣ ▣ ⧆
RAC 10 %

GREOUX-LES-BAINS Alpes de Haute Provence6C

★★★ Hostellerie Villa Borghese
av des Thermes, 04800 Gréoux-les-Bains
📞 04 92 78 00 91 Fax 04 92 78 09 55
English spoken
Closed 25 Nov-20 Mar

Close to the Gorges du Verdon and facing the thermal park, a charming 'Silence' hotel with spacious accommodation and very pretty gardens. A51 motorway, Manosque exit.

67 bedrs, all ensuite, ⊬ P 40 DB 400-670 B 55 ✗ 155-250 ⒸⒸ MC Visa Amex ⊰ 🖼 ▸ 18km 🔄 🎿 🖼 ⸬ ♪
RAC 5 %

HYERES Var   6C

★★★ Hôtel Pins d'Argent
Port Saint-Pierre, bd de la Marine, 83400 Hyères-Plage
📞 04 94 57 63 60 Fax 04 94 38 33 65
English spoken
Closed 21 Dec-12 Jan
A 19th century residence elegantly converted into a hotel. Set in the middle of a pine wood but only 800 metres from the beach. From Hyéres, follow directions to the airport. The restaurant opens from 10 April to 30 Sept.

20 bedrs, all ensuite, ⊬ P DB 320-620 B 45 ✗ 100-150 ⒸⒸ MC Visa Amex ⊰ ▸ 15km 🖼 ⸬ ♪ ⸋
RAC 7 nights for 6 in July & August

JUAN-LES-PINS Alpes Maritime   6C

★★★ Beachôtel
av Alexandre III, 06160 Juan-les-Pins
📞 04 93 61 81 85 Fax 04 93 61 51 97
English spoken
A modern hotel, situated on the west side of Juan, a few metres from the beach. With a coffee shop/restaurant offering a wide choice of grills and seafood specialities.

43 bedrs, all ensuite, ⊬ P 20 DB 320-610 B 45 ✗ 95 ⒸⒸ MC Visa Amex ▸ 🎿 🖼 ⸬ ♪ ⸋
RAC 10 %

★★★★ Garden Beach Hôtel
15-17 bd Baudoin, 06160 Juan-les-Pins
📞 04 92 93 57 57 Fax 04 92 93 57 56
English spoken

Modern hotel with its own private sandy beach and casino. The restaurant has a good reputation for its fine Provençal cuisine. In the town centre next to the Cap d'Antibes. 25 km from Nice on N98 on the coast road south of Antibes.

172 bedrs, all ensuite, ⊬ P 300 DB 650-1,800 B 50-105 ✗ 180 ⒸⒸ MC Visa Amex ⊞ 🖼 ▸ 7km 🎿 🖼 ⸬ ⸋

LE LAVANDOU Var   6C

★★★ Hôtel Tamaris
plage de St-Clair, 83980 Le Lavandou
📞 04 94 71 79 19 Fax 04 94 71 88 64
English spoken
Closed 4 Nov-28 Mar
The hotel is set on St-Clair beach, 2 km from Le Lavadou. All the well-equipped rooms have sea views.

41 bedrs, all ensuite, ⊬ P 50 DB 350-500 B 40 No restaurant ⒸⒸ MC Visa Amex ▸ 5km 🎿 🖼 ♪ ⸋

LEVENS Alpes Maritime   6C

★★ Hôtel Cassini
06670 Plan-du-Var
📞 04 93 08 91 03 Fax 04 93 08 45 48
English spoken
A family run hotel, set between the sea and the mountains, with an award winning restaurant offering Provençal specialities. From Nice airport follow the N202 towards Digue for 25 km to Plan du Var; the hotel is in the middle of the village on the right.

14 bedrs, 10 ensuite, ⊬ P DB 120-200 B 30 ✗ 85-195 ⒸⒸ MC Visa Amex 🎿 ⸬ ♪

★★ Hôtel Malaussena
9 place de la République, 06670 Levens
☎ 04 93 79 70 06 Fax 04 93 79 85 89
English spoken
Closed 1 Nov-15 Dec
Hotel in the centre of Levens, offers horse riding,
mountain walks and a restaurant with a garden
view, specialising in regional cuisine. 22 km north of
Nice.

14 bedrs, 10 ensuite, **P DB** 180-200 **B** 35 ✕ 80-150 **CC**
MC Visa Amex ⌕ ► 🖾 🖳 🔄 ☷

LOURMARIN Vaucluse   **5D**

★★★ Hôtel Guilles
Route de Vaugines, 84160 Lourmarin
☎ 04 90 68 30 55 Fax 04 90 68 37 41
English spoken

Bouziés is a small village on the banks of the River
Lot, 27 km from historic Cahors.

28 bedrs, all ensuite, ⚡ **P DB** 400-620 **B** 65 ✕ 185-320
CC MC Visa Amex ⌕ ► 🖾 🖳 🔄 ☷ ⚲

MALAUCENE Vaucluse   **5D**

★★★★ Résidence Arts et Vie Malaucène
bd des Remparts, 84340 Malaucène
☎ 04 90 12 62 00 Fax 04 90 12 62 99
English spoken
Closed autumn
A recently built residential complex, set in 5 hectares
at the foot of Mont Ventoux, offers a choice of 2 to 4-
rooms, fully furnished and equipped apartments.
First class facilities for seminars and conferences.
Malaucène is just 200 m away.

94 bedrs, all ensuite, **P** 120 **DB** 1,000-4,200 (4 people
per week) **CC** MC Visa ⌕ 🖾 🖳 ► 🖾 🔄 ☷ ⚲ ⚹

MARSEILLE Bouches du Rhône   **5D**

★★★ Hôtel Mercure Centre
Rue Villeneuve St-Martin, 13001 Marseille
☎ 04 91 39 20 00 Fax 04 91 56 24 57
English spoken
A centrally located hotel, overlooking Notre Dame
Cathedral, with comfortable, Provençal-style, rooms
and 2 restaurants offering tasty local specialities. 200
m from the old harbour, conveniently situated for
exploring the city.

199 bedrs, all ensuite, ⚡ **P** 60 **DB** 555-1,475 **B** 65
✕ 140-250 **CC** MC Visa Amex ► 🔄 ☷ ⚲ ⚹
RAC 10 % on room rate

MAUSSANE-LES-ALPILLES Bouches du Rhône 5D

★★★ Hôtel Val Baussenc
122 av Vallée des Baux, 13520 Maussane-les-Alpilles
☎ 04 90 54 38 90 Fax 04 90 54 33 36
English spoken
Closed Jan-Feb
An attractive, spacious hotel offering a warm,
personal welcome and regional cuisine including
Provençal specialities. In Maussane, go towards
Mouries: the hotel is at the end of the village, on the
right hand side.

21 bedrs, all ensuite, ⚡ **P** 21 **DB** 540-650 **B** 60 ✕ 180-
240 **CC** MC Visa Amex ⌕ ► 4km 🔄 ☷ ⚹
RAC 10 %

MENTON Alpes Maritime   6D

★★★ Hôtel Méditerranée
5 rue République, 06500 Menton
☎ 04 93 28 25 25 Fax 04 93 57 88 38
English spoken
Closed 8 Nov-4 Dec

A quiet, comfortable, air-conditioned hotel centrally located, close to the sea and just a stone's throw from the old town and local market. 30 minutes from Nice airport. Full and half-board terms are available.

90 bedrs, all ensuite, ⊁ P 40 DB 360-485 B 40 ✕ 85-110 ℂℂ MC Visa Amex ▸ 18km ⊠ ⅲ ⅙
RᴀC 5 %

MONTE-CARLO Monaco   6D

★★★ Hôtel Abela
23 av des Papelins, 98000 Monaco
☎ +37792 05 90 00 Fax +377 92 05 93 06

Most of the rooms in this modern, luxury hotel have a balcony overlooking the Princess Grace Rose Gardens and the sea. Quietly located in the dynamic new Fontvieille district, 10 minutes drive from the station.

192 bedrs, all ensuite, P B 85-105 ▣ ⊠ ▥ ▶ ⊠ ⊠ ▢ ⊠

★★ Hôtel La Cigogne
rte de la Plage, Mala, 06320 Cap d'Ail
☎ 04 93 78 29 60 Fax 04 93 41 86 62
English spoken
Closed 5 Jan-15 Feb
A comfortable hotel, with a modern terrace restaurant, in a beautiful little town. An ideal choice for a quiet, enjoyable holiday and only minutes from Monaco. From Monte-Carlo, go west along the coast road to Cap d'Ail.

15 bedrs, all ensuite, ⊁ P 10 DB 430-450 B 35-40 ✕ 100-135 ℂℂ MC Visa ▸ ⌀
RᴀC 10 %

★★★★ Hôtel Mirabeau
1 av Princesse Grace, 98000 Monte-Carlo, Monaco
☎ +377 92 16 65 65 Fax +377 93 50 84 85
English spoken

A beautifully appointed hotel with large terraces, spacious rooms (most have a sea view) and 3 restaurants offering a range of dishes from gourmet to fixed price. Set in the heart of Monte-Carlo, easily accessible from Place du Casino and the seafront.

103 bedrs, all ensuite, ⊁ P DB 1,350-2,400 ✕ 260-450 ℂℂ MC Visa Amex ⅔ ⊠ ▥ ▸ ⊠ ⌀
RᴀC 10 %

MORNAS Vaucluse   5D

★★ Hôtel Le Manoir
av Jean Moulin, 84550 Mornas-en-Provence
☎ 04 90 37 00 79 Fax 04 90 37 10 34
English spoken
Closed 11 Nov-8 Dec &10 Jan-10 Feb
An 18th century manor house with stylish rooms,a beautiful terrace and a restaurant serving good, local cuisine in an elegant dining room. Exit A7 at Bollene then go south on N7 for 10 km or take exit from Orange and go north on N7.

25 bedrs, all ensuite, P DB 180-310 B 40 ✕ 100-180 (small buffet at 40 F) ℂℂ MC Visa Amex ▸ 10km ⊠ ⅲ ⅙
RᴀC 5 % on room with guide

MOUGINS Alpes Maritime	6D

★★★★ Hôtel Le Mas Candille
bd Rebuffel, 06250 Mougins
☎ 04 93 90 00 85 Fax 04 92 92 85 56
English spoken
Closed 10 Nov-31 Mar
An 18th century farmhouse, with a terrace restaurant, overlooking the Grasse valley. Set in a 5 hectare park of cypress and olive trees; five minutes walk from the old Provençal village of Mougins and ten minutes drive from Cannes and La Croisette.

23 bedrs, all ensuite, ⊭ P 40 DB 680-1,200 B 85
✗ 195-270 ₡ MC Visa Amex ⚓ ► 2km 🗫 🖾 ⚌ ♬
RAC 8 %

NICE Alpes Maritime	6D

★★★ Hôtel Agata
46 bd Carnot, 06300 Nice
☎ 04 93 55 97 13 Fax 04 93 55 67 38
English spoken
This elegant hotel, situated close to the port of Nice, offers air-conditioned rooms with sea views, reasonable prices and private parking.

45 bedrs, all ensuite, ⊭ P DB 280-400 B 30-40 No restaurant ₡ Visa Amex ▣ ♿
RAC 5 % on room rate

★★ Hôtel Excelsior
19 avenue Durante, 06000 Nice
☎ 04 93 88 18 05 Fax 04 93 88 38 69
English spoken

Situated in a calm, residential area in the centre of Nice, The Hôtel Excelsior provides excellent comfort, sitting rooms, garden terrace, a meeting room and the restaurant 'Le Romantica'.

45 bedrs, all ensuite, P DB 330-490 B included
✗ 110-165 ₡ MC Visa Amex ⚌
RAC 10 %

★★★ Hôtel Harvey
18 av de Suède, 06000 Nice
☎ 04 93 88 73 73 Fax 04 93 82 53 55
English spoken
Closed 1 Nov-1 Feb
A modern hotel, recently upgraded to three stars, with a classic façade. Situated in the centre of Nice, close to the beaches and casino, partly overlooking the pedestrian area.

62 bedrs, all ensuite, ⊭ P DB 320-420 B 30 No restaurant ₡ MC Visa Amex
RAC 5 % min 3 days

★★★★ Hôtel Splendid
50 bd Victor Hugo, 06048 Nice
☎ 04 93 16 41 00 Fax 04 93 87 02 46
English spoken
A family-run, air-conditioned hotel with a roof-top bar and terraces, in a quiet town centre position only 300 m from the beach. Restaurant offers traditional French cuisine.

128 bedrs, all ensuite, P 28 DB 695-950 B 80 ✗ 120-145 ₡ MC Visa Amex ⚓ ► 20km ⚌

★★★ Hôtel de Flore
2 rue Maccarani, 06000 Nice
☎ 04 92 14 40 20 Fax 04 92 14 40 21
English spoken

A centrally situated, recently renovated hotel, with comfortable rooms in refined Provençal surroundings, close to the pedestrian area, the beach and the famous Promenade des Anglais.

62 bedrs, all ensuite, ⋔ P DB 310-570 B 60 ⊄ MC Visa Amex ⁞⁞⁞ ♔ ⅃

RaC 5 %

★★★ Tulip Inn Brice Hôtel
44 rue Maréchal Joffre, 06000 Nice
☎ 04 93 88 14 44 Fax 04 93 87 38 54
English spoken

A centrally located, fully renovated hotel with air-conditioned rooms, flower garden, gym, solarium and a good restaurant. Just 200 m from the sea.

58 bedrs, all ensuite, ⋔ P DB 520-672 B 40 ✗ 125 ⊄ MC Visa Amex ⊠ ⊞ ▸ 15km ⊡ ⊠ ⁞⁞⁞
RaC 10%, 20% in restaurant with guide

ORANGE Vaucluse 5D

★★ Hôtel Cigaloun
4 rue Caristie, 84100 Orange
☎ 04 90 34 10 07 Fax 04 90 34 89 76
English spoken

A centrally situated, recently renovated hotel, offering very comfortable accommodation and a warm friendly welcome. Only 150 m from the famous Roman theatre. Managed by an Irish/French couple.

29 bedrs, all ensuite, ⋔ P DB 250-450 B 38 ⊄ MC Visa Amex ▸ 5km ⊠ ♔

★★★ Hôtel Louvre et Terminus
89 avenue F. Mistral, 84100 Orange
☎ 04 90 34 10 08 Fax 04 90 34 68 71
English spoken
A hotel of quality, charm and comfort with a friendly welcome and individualised rooms. There is a buffet breakfast service, a restaurant, indoor garage, lift, TV, pretty garden and swimming pool. Access close to SNCF station.

34 bedrs, all ensuite, ⋔ P 6 DB 280-390 B 38-45 ✗ 88-138 ⊄ MC Visa Amex ⊰ ▸ ⊡ ⊠ ⁞⁞⁞ ♔ ⅃
RaC 10 %

Hôtel Mas de Bouvau
Route de Cairanne, 84150 Violes
☎ 04 90 70 94 08 Fax 04 90 70 95 99
English spoken

A highly recommended hotel, with a good reputation for fine cuisine, set in the Mas Provençal, east of Orange. Take D975 north-east of Orange and after approx 13 km turn right on to D8. Hotel is 1 km ahead.

5 bedrs, all ensuite, P 40 DB 300-380 B 45 ✗ 130-250 ⊄ MC Visa Amex ▸ 5km ⊡ ⊠
RaC 10 % on room rate

Hôtel Mas des Aigras

Chemin des Aigras, Russamp-Est, 84100 Orange
☎ 04 90 34 81 01 Fax 04 90 34 05 66
English spoken
A typical Provençal hotel, in a garden setting, surrounded by vineyards and orchards. From Orange take the N7 north until you reach Chemin des Aigras crossroads and then turn left.

11 bedrs, all ensuite, ⌂ P 30 DB 380-460 B 50 No restaurant ⅭⅭ MC Visa ⋛ ▸ 4km ▦ ▣ ✍

RIANS Var   6C

★ **Hôtel L'Esplanade**
9 place du Colombier, 83560 Rians
☎ 04 94 80 31 12
English spoken
A peaceful, pleasant hotel in a typical Provençal village, 40 km from Aix-en-Provence.

9 bedrs, 6 ensuite, ⌂ P DB 150-220 B 30 ✗ 75-120 ⅭⅭ MC Visa Amex

---

ROGNAC Bouches du Rhône   5D

★★ **Hôtel Royal Provence**
N 113, 13340 Rognac
☎ 04 42 87 00 27 Fax 04 42 78 77 13
English spoken
Closed 28 Jul-20 Aug
Situated on the banks of the Etang de Berre, this hotel, with garden and terrace, is within easy reach of Aix-en-Provence, Marseille centre and the airport. The restaurant offers speciality cuisine.

10 bedrs, all ensuite, ⌂ P 50 DB 245 B 30-40 ✗ 105-245 ⅭⅭ MC Visa Amex ▸ 15km ▣ ▣ ⚌ ♿
RAC 5 %

ROQUEBRUNE-CAP-MARTIN Alpes Maritime   6D

★★ **Hôtel Westminster**
14 av L Laurent, 06190 Roquebrune-Cap-Martin
☎ 04 93 35 00 68 Fax 04 93 28 88 50
English spoken
Closed 25 Nov-15 Feb

Situated 800 m from Monaco, this quiet hotel has modern, balconied rooms overlooking the Bay of Cap-Martin and the exquisite Mediterranean gardens and terraces which drop down towards the sea. The restaurant offers traditional French home cooking.

27 bedrs, 24 ensuite, P 21 DB 280-440 B 25-40 ✗ 65-105 ⅭⅭ MC Visa Amex ▸ 10km ▣ ▣ ✍
RAC 5 %   ✓

ST-ANDRE-LES-ALPES Alpes de Haute Provence

★★ **Hôtel Le Clair Logis**
rte de Digne, 04170 St-André-les-Alpes
☎ 04 92 89 04 05 Fax 04 92 89 19 36
English spoken
Closed 1 Jan-28 Feb/1 Nov-31Dec
A chalet-style hotel, with a restaurant offering regional specialities and a choice of à la carte and set menus, situated 400 m out of town overlooking Lac de Castillon and the Verdon valley. Take N202 from Barrême to St-André-les-Alpes.

12 bedrs, all ensuite, ⌂ P 20 DB 230-270 B 35 ✗ 68-180 ⅭⅭ MC Visa Amex ▸ ▣ ⚌
RAC 5 %

ST-ANTONIN-DU-VAR Var   6C

★★ **Hôtel Lou Cigaloun**
83510 St-Antonin-du-Var
☎ 04 94 04 42 67 Fax 04 94 04 48 19
English spoken
Closed Feb-Oct

A haven of Provençal peace only one hour's journey from the Mediterranean. Come and enjoy fine regional cuisine, comfortable rooms and helpful bilingual service.

7 bedrs, all ensuite, ⌂ P DB 360 B included ✗ 80-140 ⅭⅭ MC Visa Amex ⋛ ▸ ▦ ▣ ▣
RAC 10 %

ST-PAUL Alpes Maritime 6D

★★★★ Hôtel Mas d'Artigny
Route de la Colle, 06570 St-Paul
📞 04 93 32 84 54 Fax 04 93 32 95 36
English spoken

Classic, traditional, family-run hotel next door to the casino and just 30 m from the sea and a fine sandy beach. Recently refurbished, the hotel has an English pub and all modern comforts including air-conditioning. Secure, chargeable parking. ✓

36 bedrs, 34 ensuite, ✝ **P DB** 620-900 **B** included
✗ 128-190 **CC** MC Visa Amex ▶ 3km 🖾 🖾 🖧

★★★ Hôtel Latitudes Valescure
Avenue du Golf, 83700 St-Raphaël
📞 04 94 82 42 42 Fax 04 94 44 61 37
English spoken

On the heights of St-Paul-de-Vence, in 20 acres of wooded parkland, the Mas d'Artigny overlooks the Côte d'Azur. From Nice or airport, take the motorway A8 or coast road to Cagnes-sur-Mer towards Grasse, turn right to Colle-sur-Loup and St-Paul-de-Vence.

85 bedrs, all ensuite, ✝ **P** 100 **DB** 640-1,850 **B** 100-140
✗ 290-400 **CC** MC Visa Amex ⚘ 🅿 ▶ 20km 🖾 🖾 ‖ 🖧

★★★ Hôtel Messugues
Domaine des Grandities, Imposse des Messugues, 06570 St-Paul
📞 04 93 32 53 32 Fax 04 93 32 94 15
English spoken
Closed 10 Jan-1 Apr
Quiet and peaceful with a lovely pool area. Set in unspoilt countryside just outside the village of St-Paul.

15 bedrs, all ensuite, **P** 40 **DB** 500-700 **B** 50 No
restaurant ⚘ 🖾 🖾 🅿 🖾
RƎC

ST-RAPHAEL Var 6D

★★ Hôtel Beau Site
Camp Long, 83530 Agay
📞 04 94 82 00 45 Fax 04 94 82 71 02
English spoken
The hotel restaurant Beau Site is situated opposite the sandy beach of Camp Long, in the Esterel in Agay/St Raphaël. On N98. 14 ensuite bedrooms, 3 suites, tropical garden, indoor car park.

19 bedrs, 17 ensuite, ✝ **P** 20 **DB** 240-490 **B** 37 ✗ 160
CC MC Visa Amex ▶ 1km 🖾 🖾 🖧
RƎC **15 % except July-August**

★★★ Hôtel Excelsior
Promenade du Président R Coty, 83700 St-Raphaël
📞 04 94 95 02 42 Fax 04 94 95 33 82
English spoken

The Hotel Latitudes Valescure is situated in the heart of an international golf course. An island of serenity between the red rocks of l'Esterel and the blue Mediterranean.

95 bedrs, all ensuite, ✝ **P** 100 **DB** 400-850 **B** 45 ✗ 150
CC MC Visa Amex ⚘ 🖾 🖾 🅿 ▶ 🖾 🖾 ‖ 🖧

Don't forget to mention the guide
When booking, please remember to tell the
hotel that you chose it from the
**RAC France for
the Independent Traveller**

★★ Hôtel Sol e Mar
rte Corniche d'Or, 83700 St-Raphaël
☎ 04 94 95 25 60 Fax 04 94 83 83 61 ✓
English spoken
Closed 6 Oct-9 Apr

Situated on the N98, between St-Raphaël and Cannes, this hotel is adjacent to the sea and the beach and has exceptional views.

46 bedrs, all ensuite, ⚊ **P** 50 **DB** 380-710 **B** 50 ✕ 140-200 **CC** MC Visa Amex ⌇ 🖾 🔍 🔳 ⌀

ST-REMY-DE-PROVENCE Bouches du Rhône   5D

★★★★ Hostellerie du Vallon de Valrugues
13210 St-Rémy-de-Provence
☎ 04 90 92 04 40 Fax 04 90 92 44 01
English spoken
Closed Feb

A luxurious hotel with a restful atmosphere, set in the enchanting landscape of the Alpilles. Apartments also available.

53 bedrs, all ensuite, ⚊ **P** 50 **DB** 870-1,480 **B** 95 ✕ 280-380 **CC** MC Visa Amex ⌇ 🖾 🔳 ⏵ ⏵ 8km 🔍 🔳 ⦙⦙⦙ ♿
ᖇᗩᑕ 5 %

★★ Hôtel Soleil
13 av Pasteur, 13210 St-Rémy-de-Provence
☎ 04 90 92 00 63 Fax 04 90 92 61 07
English spoken
Closed 15 Nov-15 Mar

A pleasant hotel with gardens and a terrace. From St-Rémy centre follow the signs for Les Baux. After the tourist office, turn left and back on yourself into the av Pasteur. The hotel is on the right.

21 bedrs, all ensuite, **P** 21 **DB** 297-375 **B** 38 No restaurant **CC** MC Visa Amex ⌇ ⏵ 12km 🔳 ⌀

ST-TROPEZ Var   6C

★★★★ Hôtel Byblos
av P Signac, 83991 St-Tropez
☎ 04 94 56 68 00 Fax 04 94 56 68 01
English spoken
Closed 13 Oct-4 Apr

Just a few steps away from the place des Lices, in the shadow of the Citadel. Hotel has excellent facilities including a beauty parlour. Each fully-equipped room has its own personal character and some have a jacuzzi.

102 bedrs, all ensuite, ⚊ **P** **DB** 1,500-2,670 **B** 125 ✕ 190-410 **CC** MC Visa Amex ⌇ 🖾 🔳 ⏵ 9km 🔳 ⦙⦙⦙ ⌀
ᖇᗩᑕ 5 %

★★★ Hôtel La Ferme d'Augustin
Plage de Tahiti, St-Tropez, 83350 Ramatuelle
☎ 04 94 55 97 00 Fax 04 94 97 40 30
English spoken
Closed 20 Oct-15 Mar
Just 5 minutes from St Tropez, a grand hotel in a garden. Traditionally furnished de luxe rooms overlooking the sea, countryside or park. Breakfast can be taken in your room, in the garden or on the terrace. Secure parking.

46 bedrs, all ensuite, ⚊ **P** 50 **B** 75 (plus à la carte) No restaurant **CC** MC Visa Amex 🔳 ⌇ 🔳 ⏵ 20km 🔳 🔳 ⦙⦙⦙ ⌀

★★★★ Hôtel Le Mas de Chastelas
Route de Gassin, 83990 St-Tropez
☎ 04 94 56 71 71 Fax 04 94 56 71 56
English spoken
An 18th century country house, lost in a mimosa and oak garden, the Mas de Chastelas is a quiet, tranquil place, in a unique location on the edge of St-Tropez.

The charm of the setting makes it a jewel of the St-Tropez peninsula.

18 bedrs, all ensuite, ⚓ **P** 60 **DB** 700-2,000 **B** 70 ✗ 210-265 **CC** MC Visa Amex ⤴ ▸ ▣ ▣ ⊞ ⅍
RAC 10%, 20% in low season

★★ Hôtel Châteaurenard
05350 St-Véran
📞 04 92 45 85 43 **Fax** 04 92 45 84 20
English spoken

Situated at 2080 m, the hotel overlooks historic St-Veran, the highest commune in Europe, in the Queyras regional nature park. The village is famous for its traditional architecture, sundials and wood sculptors. The Queyras is famous for its climate.

20 bedrs, all ensuite, ⚓ **P** 25 **DB** 315-365 **B** 40 ✗ 60-116 **CC** MC Visa ▣ ▣ ⊞ ⅍
RAC 5 %

★★ Hôtel Le Cognarel
Le Coin de Molines, 05350 Molines-En-Queyras
📞 04 92 45 81 03 **Fax** 04 92 45 81 17
English spoken
Closed 1 May-1 June & 1 Oct- 15 Dec
A Logis de France hotel offering all inclusive, winter or summer, sports packages for groups or individuals.

25 bedrs, all ensuite, ⚓ **P** 10 **DB** 313-384 **B** 38-45 ✗ 55-170 **CC** MC Visa Amex ▣ ▣ ⊞
RAC 5 %

Hôtel Villa Tricoli
Impasse du Temps Perdu, San-Peire, 83380 Les Issambres
📞 04 94 49 65 32 **Fax** 04 94 49 68 20
English spoken
Closed 20 Oct-5 Jan

A small, stylish and romantic, privately owned hotel set in a quiet street just 600 m from the beach. Along the coast from Ste-Maxime: look for the hotel signpost just after the port entrance in Les Issambres.

8 bedrs, all ensuite, ⚓ **P** 8 **DB** 390-540 **B** included **CC** MC Visa ▸ 6km ▣ ▣ ⅍ ⅍
RAC 10 %

★★★ Hôtel de la Poste
11 bd F Mistral, 83120 Ste-Maxime
📞 04 94 96 18 33 **Fax** 04 94 96 41 68
English spoken
Closed 5 Oct-5 May
The hotel is located in the middle of Ste-Maxime, opposite the Post Office, only 100 m from the fine sandy beach and the port. Breakfast is served on a terrace, surrounded by a garden, overlooking the swimming pool and solarium.

24 bedrs, all ensuite, ⚓ **P** 8 **DB** 300-620 **B** 45 No restaurant **CC** MC Visa Amex ⤴ ▸ 2km ▣ ▣

★★ Domaine de Roquerousse
rte d'Avignon, 13300 Salon-de-Provence
📞 04 90 59 50 11 **Fax** 04 90 59 53 75
English spoken
Closed 25 Dec

An attractive, stone-built, hotel with comfortable rooms and lovely gardens, peacefully set in 1000 acres in the heart of Provence. 4 km from Salon, towards Avignon.

30 bedrs, all ensuite, ⚓ **P** 100 **DB** 275-510 **B** 50 ✗ 78-175 **CC** MC Visa Amex ⤴ ▣ ▸ 7km ▣ ▣ ⊞ ⅍ ⅍
RAC 8 %

★★★★ Hôtel Le Mas du Soleil
38 chemin St-Come, 13300 Salon-de-Provence
📞 04 90 56 06 53 Fax 04 90 56 21 52
English spoken

Hotel with a patio and garden, set in a very quiet area 5 minutes from the centre of Salon-de-Provence with its castle and Nostradamus house. Near the hospital on the road to Avignon.

10 bedrs, all ensuite, ⊮ P DB 580-1,300 B 68 ✖ 170-650 ℂℂ MC Visa Amex ⊰ ℙ▸ 10km ⊠ ⫽ ♿

SANARY-SUR-MER Var   5D

★★ Hôtel de la Tour
Quai Général de Gaulle, 83110 Sanary-sur-Mer
📞 04 94 74 10 10 Fax 04 94 74 69 49
English spoken

Uniquely situated on the Sanary harbour, with a terrace on the sea shore and rooms overlooking the sea. Chef's specialities: fish and shellfish.

24 bedrs, all ensuite, ⊮ P DB 280-570 B 35-40 ✖ 120-235 ℂℂ MC Visa Amex ▸ ▣ ⫽
RAC 5 % low season

SERRE-CHEVALIER Hautes Alpes   6A

★★★ Hôtel Plein Sud
ChantMerle, 05330 Serre-Chevalier
📞 04 92 24 17 01 Fax 04 92 24 10 21
English spoken

Every modern comfort is offered in this resort-centre hotel, situated in the village of Chantmerle on N91, 5 km from Briançon.

42 bedrs, all ensuite, P DB 390-540 B 45 No restaurant ℂℂ MC Visa ⊠ ⊰ ⊞ ▦▸ 16km ⊠ ⫽

SISTERON Alpes de Haute Provence   6C

★★★ Grand Hôtel du Cours
Place de l'Eglise, 04200 Sisteron
📞 04 92 61 04 51 Fax 04 92 61 41 73
English spoken
Closed Dec-Feb

A beautifully presented, centrally situated, hotel offering comfortable rooms with modern facilities. Provençal styled restaurant faces city's ancient ramparts. Bar and tea room. The historic town of Sisteron, the gateway to Provence, is on A51.

50 bedrs, all ensuite, ⊮ P 30 DB 300-450 B 40-45 ✖ 120-150 ℂℂ MC Visa Amex ▣ ▣ ⊠ ⫽ ⫽ ♿

TARASCON Bouches du Rhône   5D

★★★ Hôtel Les Mazets des Roches
rte de Fontvieille, 13150 Tarascon
📞 04 90 91 34 89 Fax 04 90 43 53 29
English spoken
Closed 1 Nov-31 Mar

A comfortable, air-conditioned hotel, situated in quiet park in the heart of the famous sites of Provence. Restaurant offers refined, appealing cuisine. From junction Avignon-Nord take D35 towards Arles. Indoor car park.

38 bedrs, all ensuite, ⊭ P DB 350-800 B 50 ✗ 95-195 (plus à la carte) ((MC Visa Amex ⫶ ▸ 🔲 🔲 🔲 ⠿

Я∋⊂ except Jul & Aug

TENDE Alpes Maritime   6C

★★ Hôtel Le Mirval
06430 La Brigue
🔲 04 93 04 63 71 Fax 04 93 04 79 81
English spoken
Closed 2 Nov-1 Apr

This completely renovated, turn-of-the-century, hotel organises day trips to the archeological sites of the Vallées des Merveilles' in the national park of Mercantour. Restaurant offers many specialities including gambas au marsala and canard au whisky.

8 bedrs, all ensuite, ⊭ P 15 DB 250-350 B 35 ✗ 90-150 ((MC Visa Amex ▸ 🔲 🔲

★★ Hôtel Le Prieuré
rue Jean Médecin, St-Dalmas-de-Tende, 06430 Tende
🔲 04 93 04 75 70 Fax 04 93 04 71 58
English spoken

Le Prieuré hotel-restaurant offers for your comfort: 24 ensuite rooms with TV (Canal + channel) and telephone; horse riding, golf and swimming pool close by. Day trips by arrangement.

24 bedrs, all ensuite, ⊭ P DB 250-335 B 35 ✗ 80-150 ((MC Visa Amex ▸ 🔲 🔲 🔲 ⠿ ⅱ

THEOULE-SUR-MER Alpes Maritime   6D

★★ Hôtel Mas Provençal
9 av du Trayas, 06590 Théoule-sur-Mer
🔲 04 93 75 40 20 Fax 04 93 75 44 83
English spoken   ✓

Situated opposite the port and the sandy beaches, this hotel has a restaurant, swimming pool and tennis courts. The bedrooms are fully equipped with satellite TV, safe, telephone, baths/shower.

26 bedrs, all ensuite, P DB 270-480 B 45 ✗ 75-195 ((MC Visa Amex ⫶ ▸ 10km 🔲 🔲

Я∋⊂ 10 % on room rate

★★★★ Hôtel Miramar Beach
47 av de Miramar, Miramar, 06590 Théoule-sur-Mer
🔲 04 93 75 05 05 Fax 04 93 75 44 83
English spoken

The hotel offers breathtaking views of the Mediterranean. Facilities include a gourmet restaurant and bar overlooking the sea; a beach restaurant and bar (summer season only) plus a private beach and swimming pool (heated & covered in winter).

60 bedrs, all ensuite, ⊭ P 50 DB 600-1,700 B 90 ✗ 170-395 ((MC Visa Amex ⫶ 🔲 🔲 ▸ 7km 🔲 🔲 ⠿ ⅱ 🔲 ⅃

Я∋⊂ 10 % on room rate

Telephoning France
When telephoning France from the United Kingdom dial 00 33 and omit the initial 0 of the French code.
Telephoning the United Kingdom
When telephoning the United Kingdom from France dial 00 44 and omit the initial 0 of the United Kingdom code.

THORENC Alpes Maritime   6C

★★ Auberge Les Merisiers
Avenue du Belvédère, 06750 Thorenc
📞 04 93 60 00 23 Fax 04 93 60 00 17
English spoken
A charming country inn, renovated and run by a young Anglo-French couple, set in the heart of La Suisse Provençale - a good base for all outdoor activities. Refined regional cuisine. Take the N85 from Grasse, turn right after 12 km and follow signs.

12 bedrs, 9 ensuite, **P** 4 **DB** 230-250 **B** 30 ✕ 99-159 **CC** MC Visa Amex ⊩ 15km 🎱 ✈ ⌖

TOULON Var   6C

★★ Hôtel Flora
Sainte-Christine, 83210 Sollies-Pont
📞 04 94 28 83 64 Fax 04 94 33 63 77
English spoken
Set in a wooded estate, 15 minutes from the sea side, the Hotel Flora provides a relaxed atmosphere and very comfortable rooms at competitive rates. Large terrace next to the pool area.

120 bedrs, all ensuite, ⌁ **P** **DB** 150-305 **B** 30 ✕ 50-95 **CC** Visa ⊰ ⊩ ✈ ⌗ ⌖ ♿
RAC **10 % on room rate**

★★★ Hôtel La Corniche
17 Littoral Frédérick Mistral, 83000 Toulon
📞 04 94 41 35 12 Fax 04 94 41 24 58
English spoken

A recently renovated hotel with simple, stylish décor, air-conditioned rooms and 2 restaurants renowned for their good food. From Toulon, head for Le Mourillon and Les Plages, hotel overlooks the Port Saint-Louis.

23 bedrs, all ensuite, ⌁ **P** **DB** 350-650 **B** 50 ✕ 100-220 **CC** MC Visa Amex ⊩ ✈ ⌗ ⌖ ♿
RAC **10 %**

VAISON-LA-ROMAINE Vaucluse   5D

★★★ Hôtel Le Beffroi
rue de l'Evêché BP85, Ville Médiévale, 84110 Vaison-la-Romaine
📞 04 90 36 04 71 Fax 04 90 36 24 78
English spoken
Closed 15 Feb-16 Mar/15 Nov-16 Dec
A centrally situated hotel, with stunning views and terraced gardens, converted from two houses dating from the 16th and 17th centuries. Restaurant is renowned for its excellent food and fine wines.

22 bedrs, all ensuite, ⌁ **P** 11 **DB** 450-655 **B** 50 ✕ 98-195 **CC** MC Visa Amex ⊰ ⊩ 1km ✈ ⌗
RAC **Free breakfast with guide**

★★ Hôtel Les Aurics
rte d'Avignon, 84110 Vaison-la-Romaine
📞 04 90 36 03 15
English spoken
Closed 15 Oct-1 Apr
An old building, typical of Provence, with a beautiful view of vineyards. From Vaison-la-Romaine take D977 to Avignon, the hotel is about 2 km from Vaison-la-Romaine and Séguret.

14 bedrs, all ensuite, **P** 14 **DB** 240-300 **B** 30 **CC** MC Visa Amex ⊰ ⊩ 2km 🖼 🎱 ⌗

★★ Le Logis du Château
Les Hauts de Vaison, 84110 Vaison-la-Romaine
📞 04 90 36 09 98 Fax 04 90 36 10 95
English spoken
Closed 1 Nov-30 Apr
Get away from it all and enjoy the panoramic views, traditional cuisine, silence and tranquillity of Le Logis du Château. Follow the signs for Cité Médiévale.

43 bedrs, all ensuite, ⌁ **P** 25 **DB** 250-430 **B** 40 ✕ 95-165 **CC** MC Visa Amex ⊰ ⊩ 25km 🖼 ✈ ⌗ ♿

VENCE Alpes Maritime   6D

★★★ Hôtel Diana
Avenue des Poilus, 06140 Vence
📞 04 93 58 28 56 Fax 04 93 24 64 06
English spoken
A quiet hotel just 1 minutes walk from the town centre; indoor carpark available.

25 bedrs, all ensuite, ⌁ **P** 25 **DB** 410-430 **B** 40 No restaurant **CC** MC Visa Amex ⊩ 20km ✈ 5km ⌖ ♿
RAC

★★ Hôtel Le Provençal

4 av Maréchal Joffre, 06230 Villefranche-sur-Mer

☎ 04 93 01 71 42 Fax 04 93 76 96 00

English spoken

Closed 3 Nov-24 Dec

*A quiet, comfortable, centrally positioned hotel with
some rooms overlooking the sea. 150 m from the
harbour. Air-conditioned restaurant with Provençal
style dining room and a good reputation.*

45 bedrs, 43 ensuite, ★ P **DB** 210-420 **B** 42 ✕ 75-128
((MC Visa Amex ► 15km ⌗ ⌀

★★★ Hôtel Versailles

Avenue du Maréchal Foch, 06230 Villefranche-sur-
Mer

☎ 04 93 01 89 56 Fax 04 93 01 97 48

English spoken

Closed Oct-Dec

*A most attractive hotel, offering light, air-conditioned
rooms with balconies overlooking the sea. Restaurant
serves speciality cuisine including foie gras de canard
à l'Hennessy. Take the coast road eastwards from
Nice.*

50 bedrs, all ensuite, ★ P 30 **DB** 440-700 **B** 50-70
✕ 150-180 **((** MC Visa Amex ⌇ ► 15km ⌗ ⌀ &

★★★ Hôtel Welcome

1 quai Courbet, 06230 Villefranche-sur-Mer

☎ 04 93 76 76 93 Fax 04 93 01 88 81

English spoken

Closed 12 Nov-20 Dec

*A waterfront hotel in a former 17th century convent -
a favourite spot for the famous (Jean Cocteau,
Graham Sutherland and Somerset Maugham used to
stay here). Seafood specialities and haute cuisine. On
the coast road to the east of Nice.*

32 bedrs, all ensuite, P 2 **DB** 550-950 **B** 40 ✕ 140-260
((MC Visa Amex ► 15km ⌷ ⌗ &
RAC Complimentary breakfast

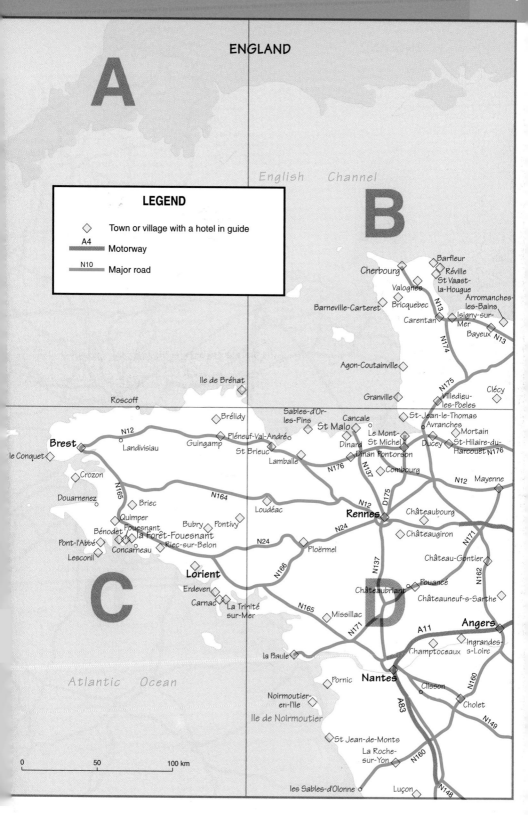

ENGLAND

English Channel

LEGEND

◇ Town or village with a hotel in guide
━━ A4 Motorway
━━ N10 Major road

B

Barfleur
Cherbourg ◇ Réville
St Vaast-
Valognes la-Hougue
Bricquebec Arromanches-
Barneville-Carteret ◇ les-Bains
Carentan Isigny-sur-
Mer
Bayeux N13
N174

Agon-Coutainville ◇

Ile de Bréhat ◇
Granville ◇ Villedieu- Clécy
les-Poeles
Roscoff St-Jean-le-Thomas
Brélidy Sables-d'Or- Cancale Avranches
les-Pins St Malo Le Mont- Mortain
N12 Pléneuf-Val-André Dinard St Michel Ducey St-Hilaire-du-
Brest Guingamp St Brieuc Dinan Pontorson Harcouët N176
Landivisiau Lamballe Combourg
le Conquet ◇ N176 N137 N12 Mayenne
Crozon N164 Loudéac N12 D175
Douarnenez N165 Briec Rennes Châteaubourg
Quimper Bubry Pontivy N24 Châteaugiron N171
Bénodet Fouesnant N24 Ploërmel
Pont-l'Abbé la Forêt-Fouesnant N166 Château-Gontier
Concarneau Riec-sur-Belon N137 N162
Lesconil
Lorient Châteaubriant Fouance
Erdeven Châteauneuf-s-Sarthe
Carnac La Trinité N165 Missillac
sur-Mer N171 A11 Angers
la Baule Ingrandes-
Champtoceaux s-Loire

Atlantic Ocean
Pornic Nantes Clisson
Noirmoutier- N160
en-l'Ile Cholet
Ile de Noirmoutier A83 N149

◇ St Jean-de-Monts
La Roche-
sur-Yon N160
0 50 100 km
les Sables-d'Olonne Luçon N148

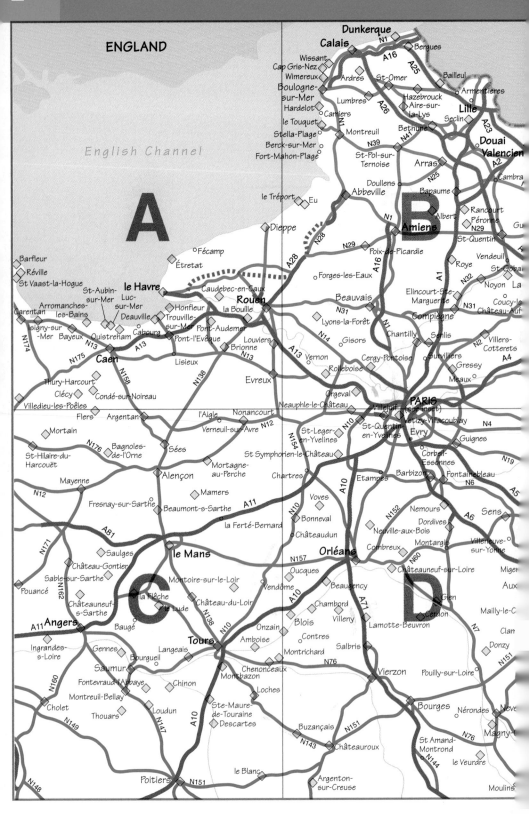

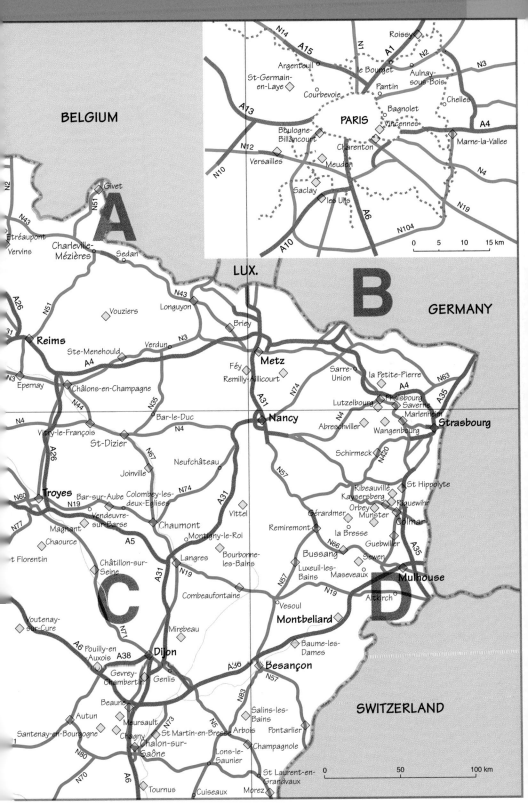

BELGIUM

PARIS

N14
N15
A15
Roissy
N1
A1
N2
Argenteuil
le Bourget
Aulnay-sous-Bois
N3
St-Germain-en-Laye
Pantin
Courbevoie
Chelles
A13
Bagnolet
Vincennes
A4
Boulogne-Billancourt
Marne-la-Vallee
N12
Charenton
Versailles
Meudon
N10
N4
Saclay
les Ulis
A6
N19
N104

0   5   10   15 km

A26
N51
31
Reims
N43
N51
A
Givet
Etréaupont
Vervins
N2
N43
Charleville-Mézières
Sedan
LUX.
B
GERMANY
Vouziers
Longuyon
N43
Briey
Ste-Menehould
A4
Verdun
N3
Féy
Metz
Sarre-Union
la Petite-Pierre
N63
N3
Epernay
Châlons-en-Champagne
Remilly-Aillicourt
N74
A4
Phalsbourg
Saverne
N35
Lutzelbourg
Marlenheim
A35
N44
Bar-le-Duc
N4
Nancy
Abreschviller
Wangenbourg
Strasbourg
N4
Vitry-le-François
St-Dizier
N4
N4
Schirmeck
N420
A26
Joinville
Neufchâteau
N57
St Hippolyte
N60
Troyes
Bar-sur-Aube
Colombey-les-deux-Eglises
N74
A31
Ribeauvillé
Kaysersberg
N19
Vittel
Orbey
Riquewihr
N77
Vendeuvre-sur-Barse
Gérardmer
Munster
Colmar
Chaource
Magnant
Chaumont
Remiremont
la Bresse
t Florentin
A5
Montigny-le-Roi
N66
Guebwiller
A35
Langres
Bourbonne-les-Bains
Bussang
Sewen
Châtillon-sur-Seine
N19
Luxeuil-les-Bains
Maseveaux
Mulhouse
Voutenay-sur-Cure
N31
C
Combeaufontaine
N57
N19
Altkirch
D
A6
Mirebeau
Vesoul
Pouilly-en-Auxois
A38
Dijon
Baume-les-Dames
Montbeliard
Gevrey-Chambertin
Genlis
A36
Besançon
N83
N57
Beaune
Salins-les-Bains
SWITZERLAND
Autun
Meursault
N73
Arbois
Pontarlier
Santenay-en-Bourgogne
Chagny
St Martin-en-Bresse
N5
Champagnole
Chalon-sur-Saône
Lons-le-Saunier
N80
N70
A6
Tournus
Cuiseaux
Morez
St Laurent-en-Grandvaux

0   50   100 km

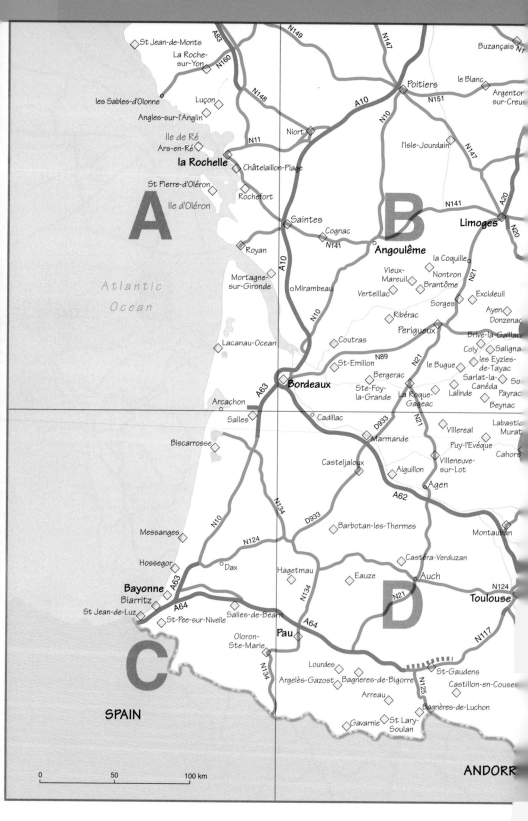

St Jean-de-Monts

La Roche-sur-Yon

A83

N160

N149

N147

Buzançais

le Blanc

Poitiers

N151

Argenton-sur-Creus

les Sables-d'Olonne

Luçon

N148

A10

N10

l'Isle-Jourdain

N147

Angles-sur-l'Anglin

Ile de Ré

Ars-en-Ré

N11

Niort

la Rochelle

Châtelaillon-Plage

St Pierre-d'Oléron

Rochefort

Ile d'Oléron

A

Saintes

Cognac

N141

Angoulême

N141

Limoges

N20

B

Royan

Mortagne-sur-Gironde

Mirambeau

Vieux-Mareuil

Verteillac

la Coquille

Nontron

Brantôme

Sorges

Excideuil

Ayen

Donzenac

Ribérac

Périgueux

Brive-la-Gaillarde

Coly

Saligna

N21

Atlantic Ocean

Lacanau-Ocean

Coutras

St-Emilion

N89

le Bugue

les Eyzies-de-Tayac

Bergerac

Ste-Foy-la-Grande

La Roque-Gageac

Sarlat-la-Canéda

Lalinde

So

Payrac

Beynac

A63

Bordeaux

N21

Arcachon

Salles

Cadillac

D933

Marmande

Villereal

Labastic

Murat

Puy-l'Evéque

Cahors

Biscarrosse

Casteljaloux

Aiguillon

Villeneuve-sur-Lot

Agen

A62

N134

D933

Barbotan-les-Thermes

Montauban

Messanges

N10

N124

Castéra-Verduzan

Hossegor

Dax

Hagetmau

Eauze

Auch

N124

A63

Bayonne

Biarritz

A64

Salies-de-Béarn

N134

A64

D

N21

Toulouse

St Jean-de-Luz

St-Pee-sur-Nivelle

Oloron-Ste-Marie

Pau

N117

C

N134

Lourdes

Argelès-Gazost

Bagnères-de-Bigorre

N125

St-Gaudens

Castillon-en-Couse

Arreau

Bagnères-de-Luchon

SPAIN

Gavarnie

St Lary-Soulan

0   50   100 km

ANDORR

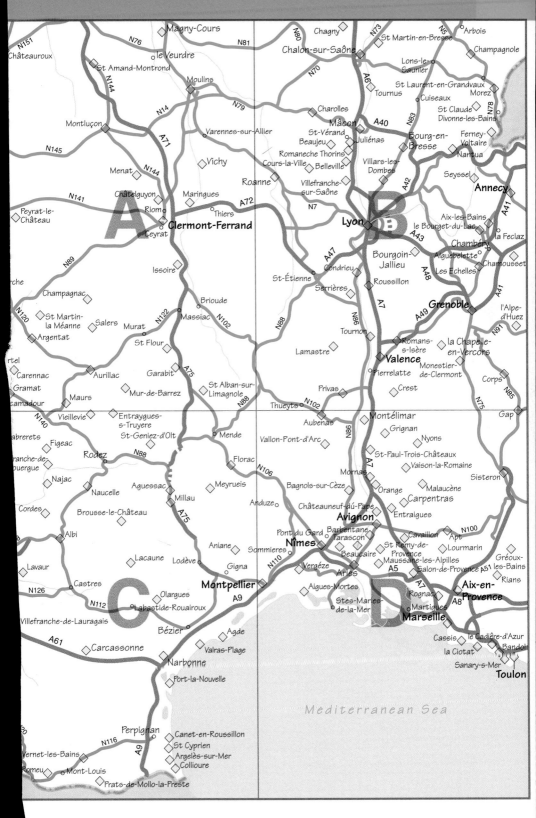

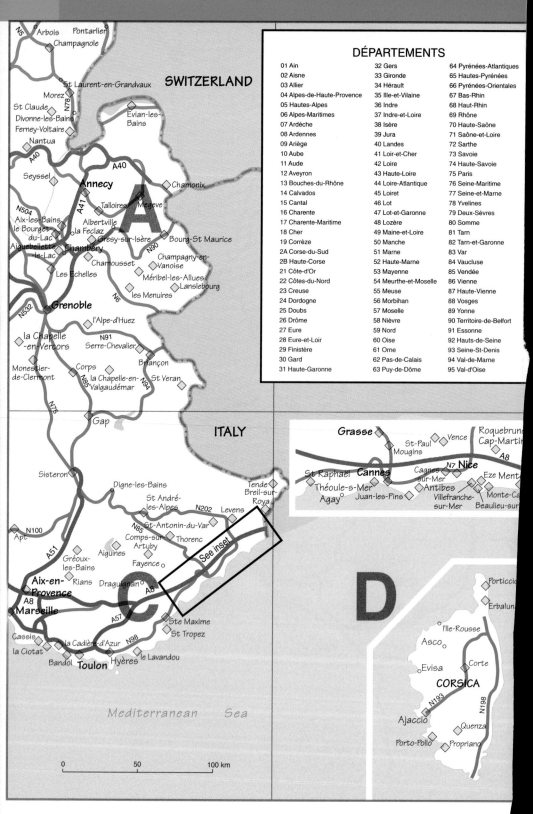

DÉPARTEMENTS

01 Ain	32 Gers	64 Pyrénées-Atlantiques
02 Aisne	33 Gironde	65 Hautes-Pyrénées
03 Allier	34 Hérault	66 Pyrénées-Orientales
04 Alpes-de-Haute-Provence	35 Ille-et-Vilaine	67 Bas-Rhin
05 Hautes-Alpes	36 Indre	68 Haut-Rhin
06 Alpes-Maritimes	37 Indre-et-Loire	69 Rhône
07 Ardèche	38 Isère	70 Haute-Saône
08 Ardennes	39 Jura	71 Saône-et-Loire
09 Ariège	40 Landes	72 Sarthe
10 Aube	41 Loir-et-Cher	73 Savoie
11 Aude	42 Loire	74 Haute-Savoie
12 Aveyron	43 Haute-Loire	75 Paris
13 Bouches-du-Rhône	44 Loire-Atlantique	76 Seine-Maritime
14 Calvados	45 Loiret	77 Seine-et-Marne
15 Cantal	46 Lot	78 Yvelines
16 Charente	47 Lot-et-Garonne	79 Deux-Sèvres
17 Charente-Maritime	48 Lozère	80 Somme
18 Cher	49 Maine-et-Loire	81 Tarn
19 Corrèze	50 Manche	82 Tarn-et-Garonne
2A Corse-du-Sud	51 Marne	83 Var
2B Haute-Corse	52 Haute-Marne	84 Vaucluse
21 Côte-d'Or	53 Mayenne	85 Vendée
22 Côtes-du-Nord	54 Meurthe-et-Moselle	86 Vienne
23 Creuse	55 Meuse	87 Haute-Vienne
24 Dordogne	56 Morbihan	88 Vosges
25 Doubs	57 Moselle	89 Yonne
26 Drôme	58 Nièvre	90 Territoire-de-Belfort
27 Eure	59 Nord	91 Essonne
28 Eure-et-Loir	60 Oise	92 Hauts-de-Seine
29 Finistère	61 Orne	93 Seine-St-Denis
30 Gard	62 Pas-de-Calais	94 Val-de-Marne
31 Haute-Garonne	63 Puy-de-Dôme	95 Val-d'Oise